I0715302

THE CHICAGO TRIBUNE'S
50 BEST
CHICAGO BEARS
OF ALL TIME

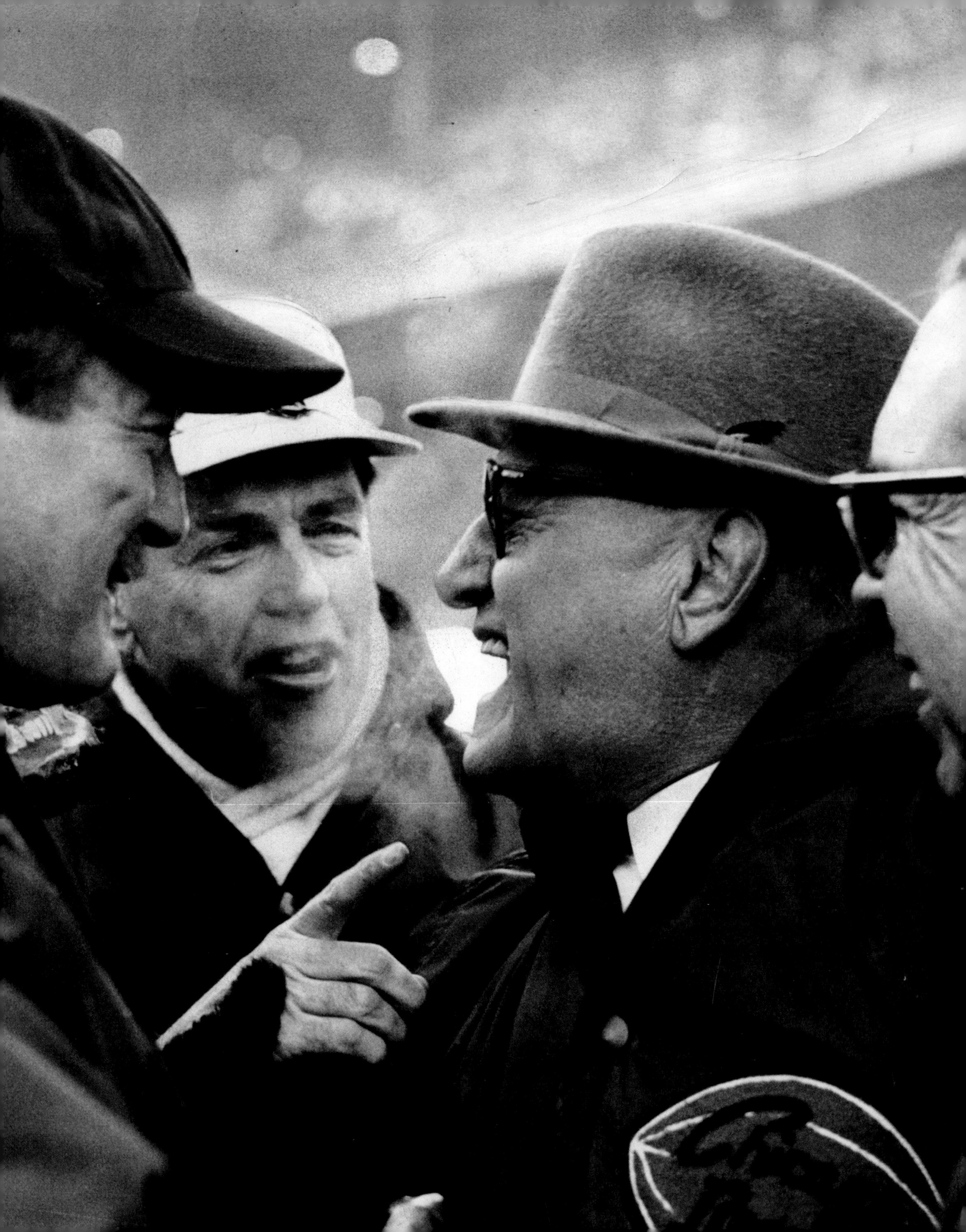

THE CHICAGO TRIBUNE'S

50 BEST
CHICAGO BEARS
OF ALL TIME

Chicago Tribune

A MIDWAY BOOK

AGATE

CHICAGO

Chicago Tribune
Colin McMahon, Editor-in-Chief; Christine W. Taylor, Managing Editor; Amanda Kaschube, Director of Content/Sports; Todd Panagopoulos, Director of Content/Visuals; Marianne Mather, Visual Editor; Kathleen B. O'Malley, Senior Content Editor; Amy Carr, former Director of Content/Life + Culture; Jennifer Day, former Books Editor

Printed in China

10 9 8 7 6 5 4 3 2 1   21 22 23 24 25

Library of Congress Cataloging-in-Publication Data

Names: Chicago Tribune
Title: The Chicago Tribune's 50 best Chicago Bears of all time / The
   Chicago Tribune.
Other titles: 50 best Chicago Bears of all time
Description: Chicago : Midway, [2021] | Summary: "An in-depth look at the
   fifty best Bears players in franchise history, featuring profiles and
   photography created by the Chicago Tribune"-- Provided by publisher.
Identifiers: LCCN 2021023865 (print) | LCCN 2021023866 (ebook) | ISBN
   9781572843059 (hardcover) | ISBN 9781572848559 (ebook)
Subjects: LCSH: Chicago Bears (Football team)--Biography. | Chicago Bears
   (Football team)--History. | Football
   players--Illinois--Chicago--Biography.
Classification: LCC GV956.C5 C56 2021 (print) | LCC GV956.C5 (ebook) |
   DDC 796.332/640977311--dc23
LC record available at https://lccn.loc.gov/2021023865
LC ebook record available at https://lccn.loc.gov/2021023866

Book design by Morgan Krehbiel

Midway Books is an imprint of Agate Publishing. Agate books are available in bulk at discount prices. For more information, visit agatepublishing.com.

Photo facing title page:
Head coach George Halas, second from right, celebrates the team's first division championship since 1956 with coaches Sid Luckman, from left, George Allen and Phil Handler on Dec. 15, 1963, at the end of the game at Wrigley Field.

Contents

Introduction

THE LONG AND STORIED HISTORY of the Chicago Bears begins with George Halas. But it hardly ends with him.

At 25, Halas in 1920 founded, coached and played for the Decatur Staleys, who competed in the newly formed American Professional Football Association. He moved the team to his hometown of Chicago a year later, and the Staleys won the APFL title. In 1922, the first season of the National Football League—of which he was a co-founder—Halas changed the team's nickname to Bears as a tribute to the Cubs, his favorite sports team.

"I noted football players are bigger than baseball players," he wrote in his 1979 autobiography, "Halas by Halas." "So, if baseball players are cubs, then certainly football players must be bears!"

The Bears won the NFL title in 1932 and have added seven more since then, including a 46-10 victory over the New England Patriots in Super Bowl XX, their last championship. From 1932-46, the Bears appeared in nine championship games, winning six.

In more than 100 seasons, more than 1,600 players have played for the Bears during a regular-season NFL game. With the election of left tackle Jimbo Covert and defensive end Ed Sprinkle in 2020, the Bears have 30 players,

coaches or administrators in the Pro Football Hall of Fame.

That's the most of any NFL team.

Among them are Halas, who was inducted in the inaugural Hall of Fame class in 1963, and old-time greats such as Sid Luckman and Bronko Nagurski, Red Grange and Dan Fortmann, Will Lyman and George Trafton. Luckman, who played all 12 of his seasons in Chicago from 1939-50, held the franchise record for passing yards until Jay Cutler surpassed him in 2013.

The Bears' Hall haul includes linebacker Dick Butkus and running back Gale Sayers, who were selected with the third and fourth overall picks, respectively, in the 1965 draft. Butkus was known as one of the nastiest players of his generation—and all time—and Sayers, aka the "Kansas Comet," set an NFL record by scoring 22 touchdowns in his rookie season, including a record-tying six in one game against the San Francisco 49ers.

"His way of running was like magic," Bears President Mike McCaskey told the Tribune in 1994. "In the mud against San Francisco, everybody else was slipping and trying to stay upright. He was running and cutting like there was magic in his shoes."

Tight end Mike Ditka, a five-time Pro Bowl

selection and two-time All-Pro during his six seasons with the Bears, was enshrined in 1988. He was a star on the 1963 championship team and then coached the Bears to their only Super Bowl title in the 1985 season.

Five players from that '85 team—running back Walter Payton, linebacker Mike Singletary, defensive lineman Dan Hampton, defensive end Richard Dent and Covert—are also Hall of Famers.

Many consider Payton among the top players in NFL history, a nine-time Pro Bowl selection and five-time All-Pro. With Covert leading the way, Payton broke Jim Brown's record for career rushing yards in 1984 with 16,726. (Emmitt Smith surpassed Payton in 2002 and finished with 18,355 yards.)

"Walter was the best runner, blocker, teammate and friend I've ever seen," said Ditka, the Bears coach for Payton's final six seasons, including the 1985 championship campaign. "Truly the best football player I've ever seen. Coach Halas is saying, 'Hey, I've finally got the greatest Bear of all.'"

Singletary, Hampton and Dent spearheaded a defense in 1985 that is renowned as one of the best in NFL history, leading the league in points allowed (198), yards allowed (4,135) and takeaways (54). The Bears finished 15-1, the lone loss a 38-24 "Monday Night Football" defeat to Dan Marino and the Miami Dolphins. They outscored their two playoff opponents 45-0, becoming the first team to record consecutive shutouts.

And linebacker Brian Urlacher, who starred on the Bears' Super Bowl XLI team that lost to the Indianapolis Colts, was inducted to the Hall in 2018. He ended his career after the 2012 season with unofficial Bears records of 1,353 career tackles and 153 in 2002. In 13 seasons, he made 180 starts, third-most in team history. He made eight Pro Bowls, was a four-time first-team All-Pro selection, the 2000 Defensive Rookie of the Year and the 2005 Defensive Player of the Year.

All are on the Chicago Tribune's 50 greatest players in Bears history list, a ranking compiled by Tribune writers and editors.

So take a walk with us down memory lane, from Luckman leading the Bears to four NFL titles to Charles Tillman's "Peanut Punch," from "The Galloping Ghost" to "Sweetness," from Johnny Morris to Bulldog Turner.

After all, the long and storied history of the Bears begins with Halas. But it hardly ends with him. ◼

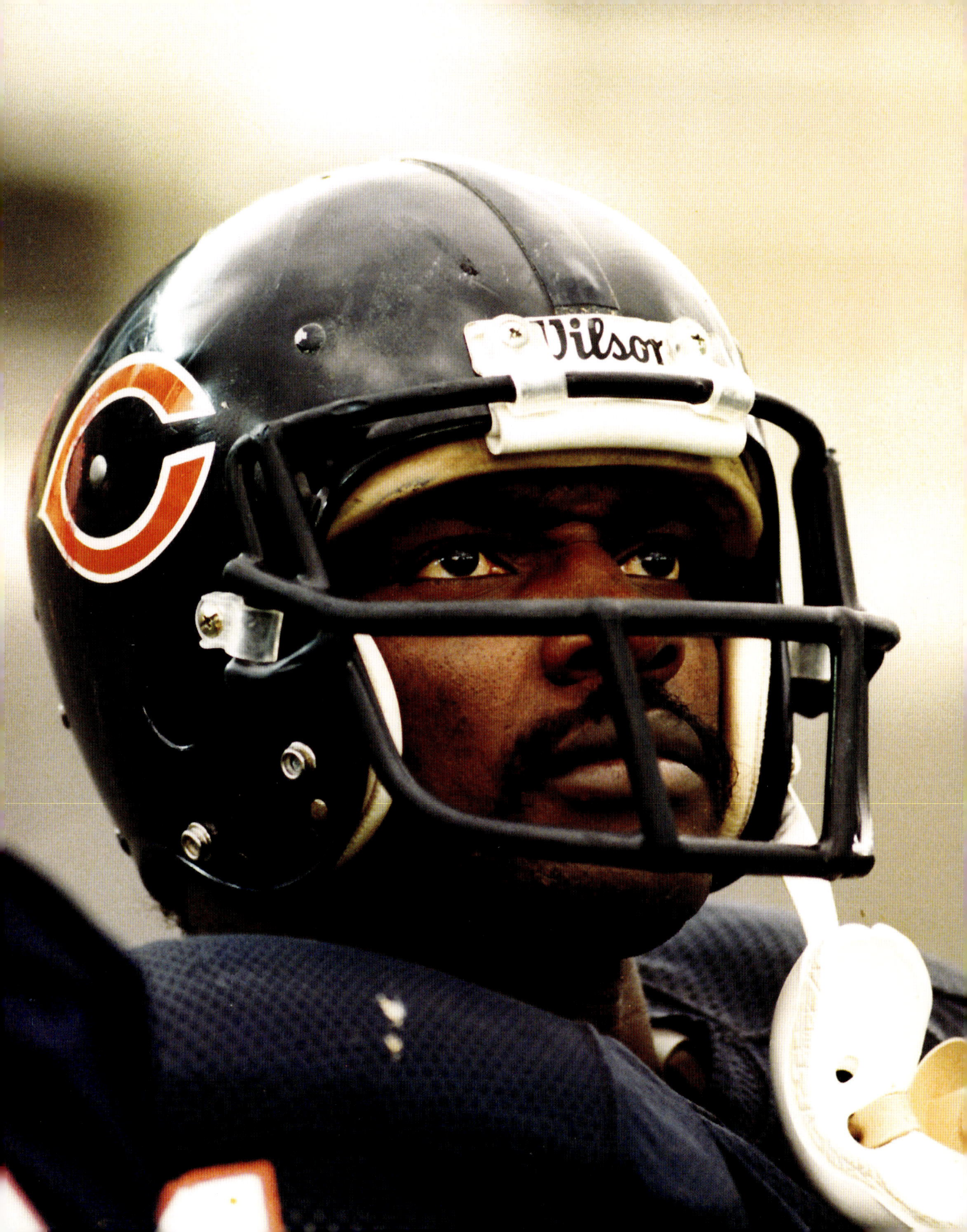
Wilson

Walter Payton

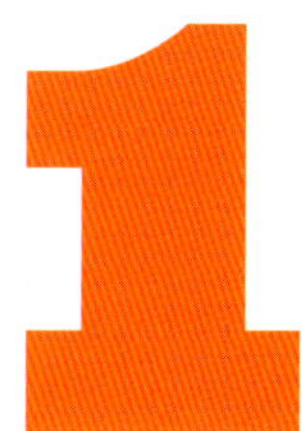

34 RUNNING BACK
1975-87

ONE THOUSAND, five hundred eighty-two players have played for the Bears during a regular-season NFL game, according to Pro Football Reference.

One hundred days ago the Tribune began counting down the best of them, the top 6.3% of the men who have suited up for the franchise since George Halas founded the Decatur Staleys in 1920.

The Bears' tradition of great players is unsurpassed; their 28 members of the Pro Football Hall of Fame are the most of any team. Hours went into deciding the rankings, with our Bears reporters and editors engaging in lively debate over the players' placement.

No discussion took place for the top spot; everybody felt the same. One player was an easy choice for No. 1 over the other 1,581.

Walter Payton is the best player in the history of the Chicago Bears.

When he died at 45 of bile duct cancer and liver failure on Nov. 1, 1999, the city mourned. His public memorial brought 20,000 people to Soldier Field, where speakers included NFL Commissioner Paul Tagliabue, Hall of Famers Dan Hampton and Mike Ditka and the Rev. Jesse Jackson.

Ditka imagined Halas, who coached the team for 40 years and died 16 years and one day earlier, getting a chance to greet his team's greatest player in the afterlife.

"Walter was the best runner, blocker, teammate and friend I've ever seen," said Ditka, the Bears coach for Payton's final six seasons, including the 1985 championship campaign. "Truly the best football player I've ever seen. Coach Halas is saying, 'Hey, I've finally got the greatest Bear of all.'"

John Madden has been a fixture in professional football for 50 years as coach of the Raiders, TV's most popular football analyst and namesake of the video-game franchise still going strong in its 32nd year. At Payton's funeral on Nov. 5, 1999, in South Barrington, Madden called Payton the greatest player any team ever has had.

"Walter Payton was the greatest," Madden said. "If you wanted yards, you'd want Walter Payton. Who do you want to block? Walter Payton. If you wanted someone to catch,

Walter Payton on Sept. 20, 1987, during a game against Tampa Bay.

Walter Payton. . . . How about if you want somebody to make a tackle after an interception? One year he had 18.”

The 5-foot-10, 200-pound Payton retired after the 1987 season as the NFL's all-time leading rusher with 16,726 yards, pushing well past Jim Brown's previous record of 12,312. It is the closest thing football has to baseball's hallowed home run mark, and Payton held it for 15 years before Emmitt Smith passed him in 2002 and ended up with 18,355.

Jim Finks, who made Payton his first draft pick as Bears general manager in 1975, believed Payton's chase of Brown's rushing record actually took attention away from how good he was as an all-around player.

“For instance,” Finks told the Tribune's Don Pierson in 1984, “there's no better blocker in the NFL. None. He flattens linebackers, he knocks down ends, he attacks nose guards.”

With his strong throwing arm, Payton tossed eight touchdown passes. He played single-wing quarterback late in one game in 1984, when Bears QBs Jim McMahon and Steve Fuller were injured and Rusty Lisch ineffective against the Packers. Some Bears coaches believed that if he practiced at it, Payton would have been a better punter in some seasons than the one the team employed.

“He did everything,” Ditka told Richard Whittingham in his 1991 book, “What Bears They Were.” “He could have played defense if we'd put him over there, and he'd have played it pretty darn good.”

Mike Singletary, the Bears' Hall of Fame linebacker from 1981-92, concurred, telling Pierson in 1985 that Payton was “the first running back I ever saw who I thought could play defense.”

Payton's rushing total still ranks second all time, his 125 total touchdowns rank 11th, and his 21,264 yards from scrimmage trail only Jerry Rice and Smith. Payton was voted to nine Pro Bowls in his 13 seasons, and his five first-team All-Pro selections were spread over 10 years, with his first in 1976 and last in 1985.

The Columbia, Miss., native was voted into the Hall of Fame in 1993, named to the NFL's 75th anniversary team the next year and to the All-Decade teams of the 1970s and '80s. In 2010, the NFL Network ranked the top 100 players of all time. Payton was fifth behind Rice, Brown, Lawrence Taylor and Joe Montana; Johnny Unitas, Reggie White, Peyton Manning, Don Hutson and Dick Butkus constituted the rest of the top 10.

Payton's place atop the Bears' rushing records might as well be written in indelible ink. Matt Forte ranks second in team history with 8,602 rushing yards; Neal Anderson is third with 6,166. Their combined total of 14,768 yards is 1,958 behind Payton. Similarly, Payton's 110 rushing touchdowns are more than Anderson's 51 and Rick Casares' 49 put together.

The eight best rushing seasons in Bears history belong to Payton, and he also ranks first in Bears history with 492 receptions and fourth with 4,538 receiving yards. On Nov. 20, 1977, Payton set the NFL single-game rushing record with 275 yards against the Vikings, a mark that now ranks fifth.

“The startling numbers in the record books only start to measure the greatness,” Pierson wrote in the epilogue of his 16-story special section published Nov. 7, 1999.

Payton played with a style all his own. Fans from the 1970s and '80s can close their eyes and see him running upright with high knees, holding the ball like a loaf of bread in his right hand.

From the bottom of the pile, he would stretch the ball forward a foot or 2 before the referee—most of the time—placed it back where he was downed. Payton liked to say he gained 100 extra yards in his career, inch by inch, with that trick.

On goal-line plays, Payton would leap over the pile and stretch the ball to the end zone, a move replicated by kids stretching a Nerf ball over a pile of couch cushions in living rooms across America.

On Oct. 7, 1979, Payton provided the points in a 7-0 win over the Bills with what Pierson called “a fourth-quarter leap into the end zone so high and so far it looked like an Olympic high dive.”

The Bills' Fred Smerlas knew what was coming, so he stood up and raised his arms

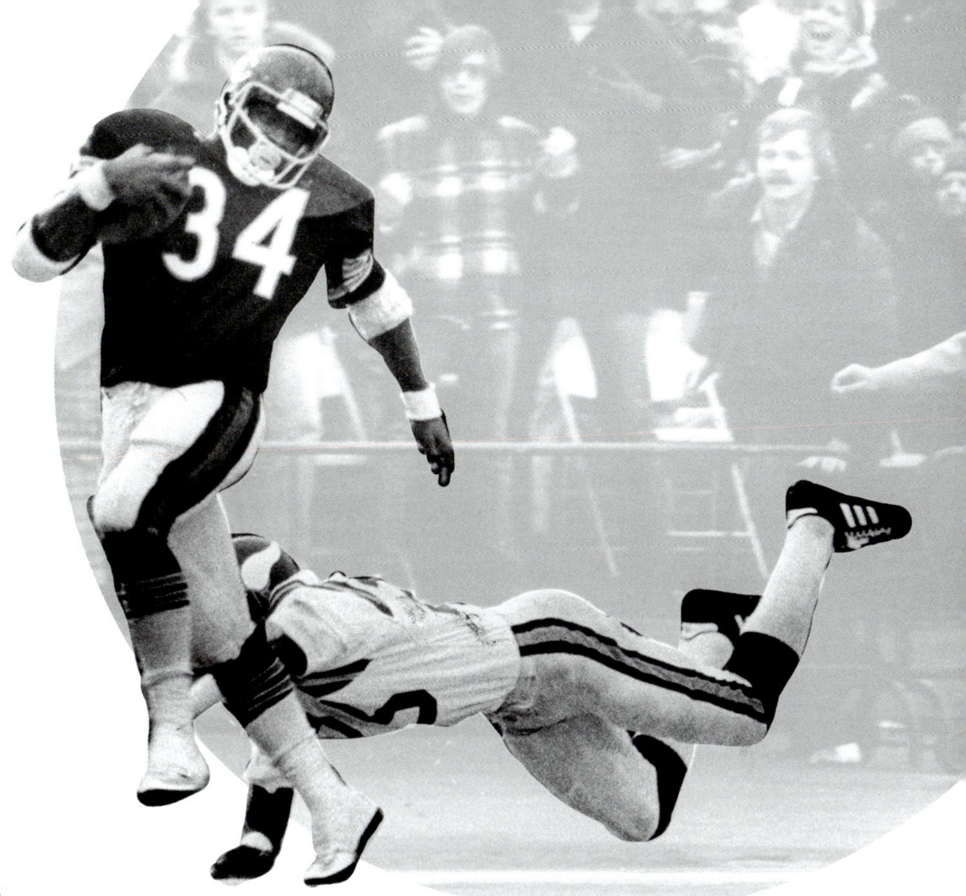

> ## He did everything. He could have played defense if we'd put him over there, and he'd have played it pretty darn good.
>
> —MIKE DITKA

Walter Payton (34) fights off a Minnesota Vikings defender on Nov. 20, 1977, the day he rushed for an NFL-record 275 yards.

during the play. Payton cleared the 6-foot-3 nose tackle with plenty of room to spare.

"The guy can leap so high he could stuff himself in the basket," Smerlas told Pierson. "He's like a fly."

His career highlight reel includes countless runs of him lowering his head as he neared would-be tacklers, bouncing off or plowing through them, his legs never stopping, and his stiff-arm was legendary.

Whenever Payton and a defender headed toward a sideline collision, Payton decided the other guy would take the bigger lick.

"Walter would explode into you at the moment of impact, bounce off, and continue running," Bears safety Gary Fencik told Whittingham. "A lot of runners, when they know they're going to get hit hard, will just kind of relax and go down. Not Walter."

When Payton became a superstar, he was just what Chicago needed. The city's sports scene was pitiful for most of the 1960s and '70s. After the Bears won the 1963 NFL championship, they suffered through nine losing seasons and no playoff appearances in the next 12 years.

The Blackhawks and Bulls were consistent playoff teams but regularly suffered heartbreaking series losses, including blown 3-2 leads for the Hawks against the Canadiens in the 1971 Stanley Cup Final and the Bulls to the Warriors in the 1975 Western Conference finals.

The less said about the baseball being played here at the time, the better. Between the White Sox's American League pennant in 1959 and their AL West title in 1983, they and the Cubs went without a playoff appearance in a combined 46 tries in 23 years.

Outside the arena things were even grimmer. Inflation was sky-high, and the proud class of workers who built the city were told their jobs were heading elsewhere.

"The city took to him and loved him," the

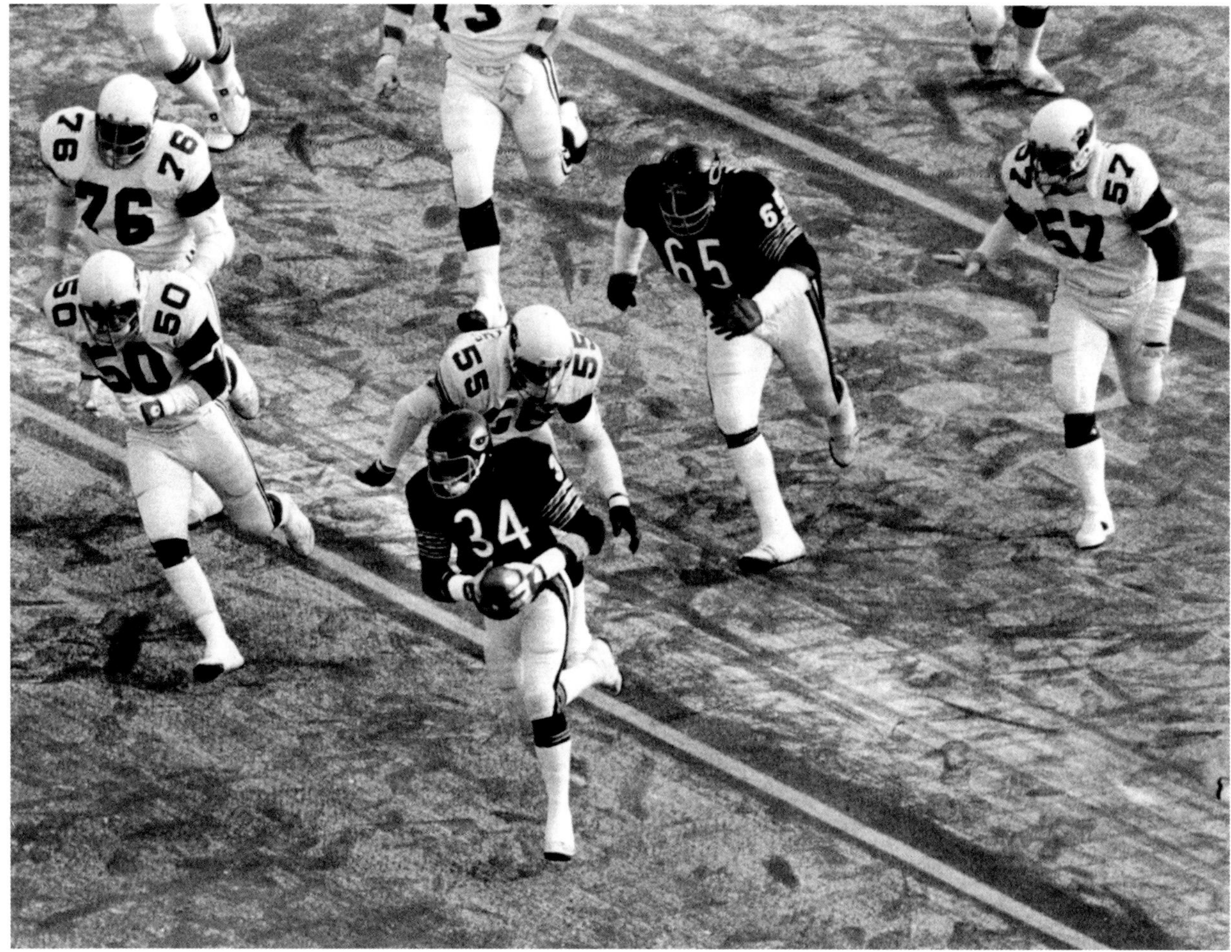

Walter Payton (34) picks up some of the 157 yards that enabled him to win the NFC rushing title on Dec. 16, 1979, at Soldier Field. Payton also scored three touchdowns.

Tribune's John Kass wrote on Nov. 2, 1999. "Not because of his excellence as a halfback but because he refused to run out of bounds and away from the pain. As people were being broken by the economy of the late '70s, Walter was the man who wouldn't be broken.

"Every team knew that the only player the Bears had was Walter, and they'd line up against him, and he would defy them, every Sunday, the way the rest of us wished we could defy the times."

In the first half of his career, Payton was a superstar on bad teams Bears fans still watched with pride. The Cowboys, Dolphins, Redskins and Raiders might have had championship trophies, but the Bears had Payton.

In the second half of his career, Payton became a key cog on championship-caliber teams. Bears fans became even prouder.

On Halloweens in the 1980s, it wouldn't be rare for half the boys in a Chicagoland or downstate grade-school class to dress as Walter Payton, seven or eight of them clad in identical polyester white pants, a blue No. 34 jersey and a plastic helmet.

Even his teammates were fans, sometimes to their detriment. When center Jay Hilgenberg got in on his first play as a rookie in 1981, he was thrown to the ground by a defensive tackle, and as he started to get back on his feet, his eyes wandered behind him.

"Remember watching as a kid the high step

Walter would do?" Hilgenberg asked the Tribune's Steve Rosenbloom on Nov. 7, 2005. "It was just like I was a little kid watching him high-step right at me. I tried to get out of his way, but I just catch his knee with my shoulder, and he goes down.

"I thought, 'Man, my first play in the NFL, and I tackle Walter Payton.' Walter goes, 'Next time, just lay on the ground.'"

Payton was a renowned prankster. The greatest player in Bears history also was the team's all-time practical joker.

He knew just when to break the monotony that could build during a long season. Once, when an NFL official led a morose meeting about drug use and its dangers, a few Bears noticed the never-punctual Payton missing. The mischievous superstar was at his locker, applying a layer of Sweet'N Low crystals to his mustache. As his teammates tried to stay awake and attentive through their apathy, Payton burst into the room: "Ain't no cocaine on this team!"

Teammate Dave Duerson was beaming as he made his way to Hawaii after the 1985 season for the first of his four Pro Bowl berths. Practice for the game became quite uncomfortable after Payton coated the safety's athletic supporter with unscented liquid heat.

"Let's just say it was a very hot afternoon in warm, sunny Hawaii," Duerson told John Mullin in his 2003 book, "Tales from the Chicago Bears Sidelines."

Pierson covered Payton for 25 years. He pointed out many times that Payton was more complicated than his fans wanted him to be, noting that while the public called him "Sweetness," Payton's CB radio handle was "Mississippi Maniac."

"He never pretended to be a perfect person or a perfect football player," Pierson wrote, "although he came as close to the latter as anybody who ever tried."

The Bears had fallen on hard times in the late 1960s and early '70s, with mostly barren drafts between when defensive coordinator and personnel director George Allen left to coach the Rams in 1966 and 1974, when Halas

hired Finks from the Vikings to become his general manager.

In Finks' first draft with the Bears in 1975, the Falcons took California quarterback Steve Bartkowski first, and three Hall of Famers went in the next five picks: Maryland defensive tackle Randy White to the Cowboys at No. 2, Payton to the Bears at No. 4 and Payton's Jackson State teammate Robert Brazile, a linebacker, to the Houston Oilers at No. 6.

Finks, fellow personnel man Jerry Vainisi and scouts Bill Tobin and Jim Parmer built around Payton year by year until the team was ready to compete for championships in the mid-1980s.

Payton came on slowly as a rookie, rushing for zero yards on eight carries in his debut on Sept. 21, 1975, a 35-7 loss against the Baltimore Colts at Soldier Field. He added efforts of 10 carries for zero yards against the Lions in Week 4 and four carries for 2 yards against the Rams in Week 9. He did go for 105 yards against the 49ers and 134 in the season finale against the Saints, but he finished his first year with a pedestrian 679 yards on 196 carries.

Still, his veteran teammates believed he was something special.

Fellow running back Mike Adamle later told Pierson of Payton's debut: "Zero yards, but it was like I'd just watched someone gain 150. He made a couple of moves in the backfield after he was trapped for losses just to get back to the line of scrimmage, and I said, 'This guy's great.'"

Safety Doug Plank had played with two-time Heisman Trophy winner Archie Griffin at Ohio State but said Payton's talent was on a different level.

"I realized very quickly after getting into training camp that Walter possessed skills and could do things Archie could never do," Plank told Whittingham. "He was the whole package, in terms of speed and power."

When Payton became a star in 1976, rushing for 1,390 yards, O.J. Simpson was his competition for the title of best running back in the NFL. Near the end of Payton's career, he vied with Eric Dickerson for the unofficial

The greatest player in the history of the game.

honor. In between, Payton was tracked by Earl Campbell, Tony Dorsett and Marcus Allen. Some had better years than Payton; none had a better career.

Payton won his only MVP award in his third season, 1977. In his 11th season, 1985, he finished second in the voting to Allen after gaining 1,551 yards for the Super Bowl XX champions.

"I hear people say he's lost a step. That's pure bull," fullback Matt Suhey told Pierson in 1985. "He's absolutely as good as he's ever been."

Payton played his final game, a crushing 21-17 loss to the Redskins in an NFC divisional-round playoff game on Jan. 10, 1988, at Soldier Field. After the other players left for the locker rooms, Payton sobbed by himself on the bench, looking down with his hands covering his helmeted head.

In retirement, Payton chased the thrills he experienced every day during his career as pro football's best player. Sometimes his pursuits were wholesome, such as his passion for auto racing and motivational speaking and business ventures that included restaurants, construction-equipment leasing and investments in forest land and nursing homes. Other times they were not, and when Jeff Pearlman detailed Payton's extramarital affairs, child born out of wedlock and prescription drug abuse in his 2011 biography "Sweetness: The Enigmatic Life of Walter Payton," Chicagoans—always protective toward Payton

and ready to shower him with unconditional love—reacted harshly.

When asked on WMAQ-TV how he would react if he were to see Pearlman, Ditka responded: "I'd spit on him."

In late 1998 and early '99, Payton had lost so much weight that people began to speculate that he was deathly ill, perhaps with AIDS. On Feb. 2, 1999, Payton held a news conference at a Rosemont restaurant to announce he had primary sclerosing cholangitis, a rare autoimmune disease that clogs bile ducts and causes liver failure unless a transplant can be performed.

"Am I scared?" Payton said. "Hell yeah, I'm scared."

Payton became emotional, obviously affected by the rumors that had spread.

"To the people who really care about me, just continue to pray," he said. "And for those who want to say what they want to say, may God be with you also."

Payton did not receive his liver transplant, and he died at his South Barrington home on Nov. 1, 1999. He was 45. The NFL Man of the Year Award, which he won along with his MVP in 1977, was renamed after Payton in 2000.

On Sept. 5, 2019, the Bears opened their 100th season. They played host to the Packers to begin the 99th year of professional football's oldest rivalry with its 199th meeting. Two days earlier, the team unveiled two statues at Soldier Field. One is of Halas, the team's founder.

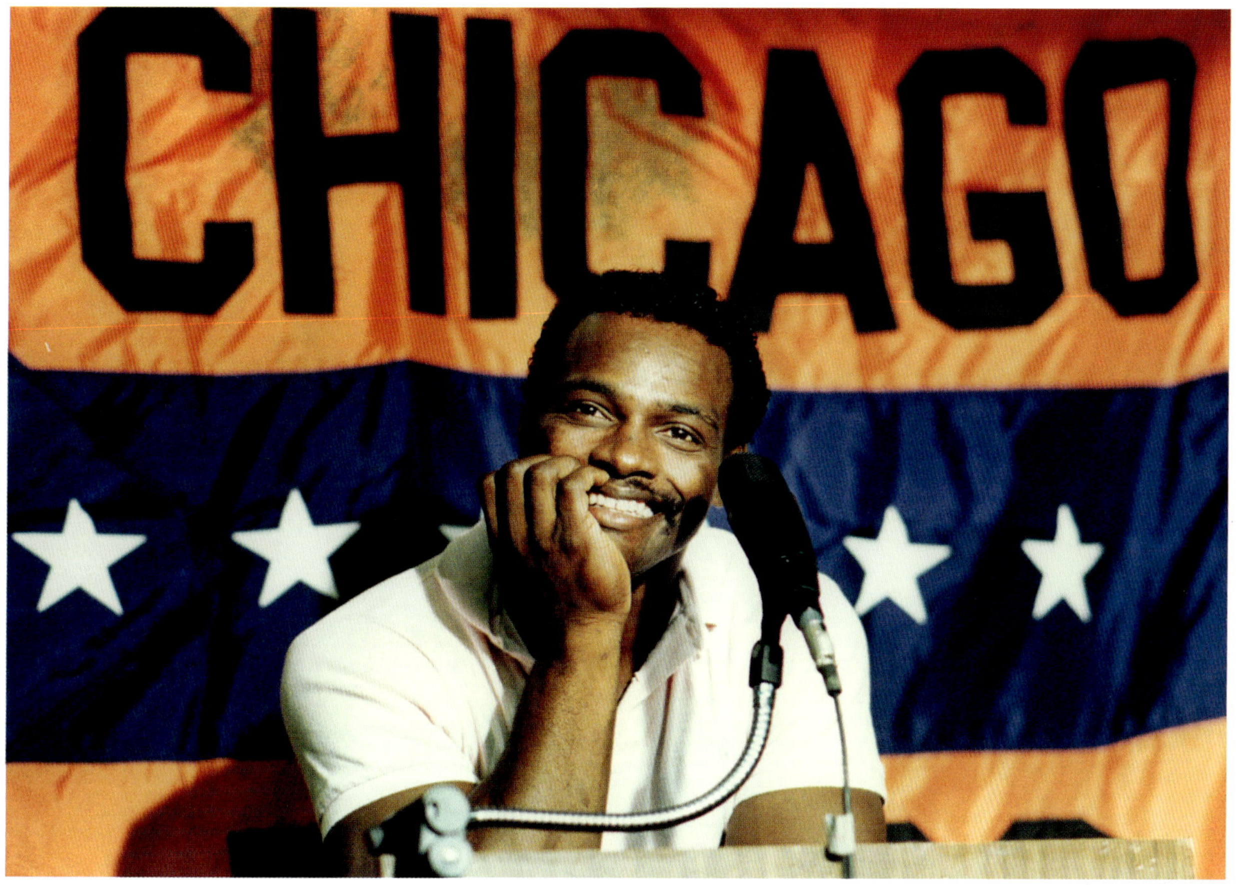

Walter Payton signs a one-year contract with the Chicago Bears on July 28, 1987, and announces that it will be his last year playing for the team.

The other depicts Payton, the greatest of all Bears players.

"Walter's legacy is secure," Bears President George McCaskey, Halas' grandson, said at the unveiling. "The greatest player in the history of the game."

At the same stadium nearly 20 years earlier, the Bears celebrated Payton's life, paying respect to the player who meant so much to them, the man who showed what a football player could be if he translated every ounce of his tremendous ability into a career that inspired his coaches, teammates, friends, family and fans and made them so proud.

When it was Hampton's turn to speak, the defensive lineman who played with Payton for nine years fought to control his emotions as he remembered what his greatest teammate meant to him.

"I have a little girl, 4 years old," Hampton said as tears filled his eyes. "Ten years from now, when she asks me about the Chicago Bears, I'll tell her about a championship and I'll tell her about great teams, great teammates and great coaches, and how great it was to be a part of it.

"But the first thing I'll tell her about is Walter Payton." ◾

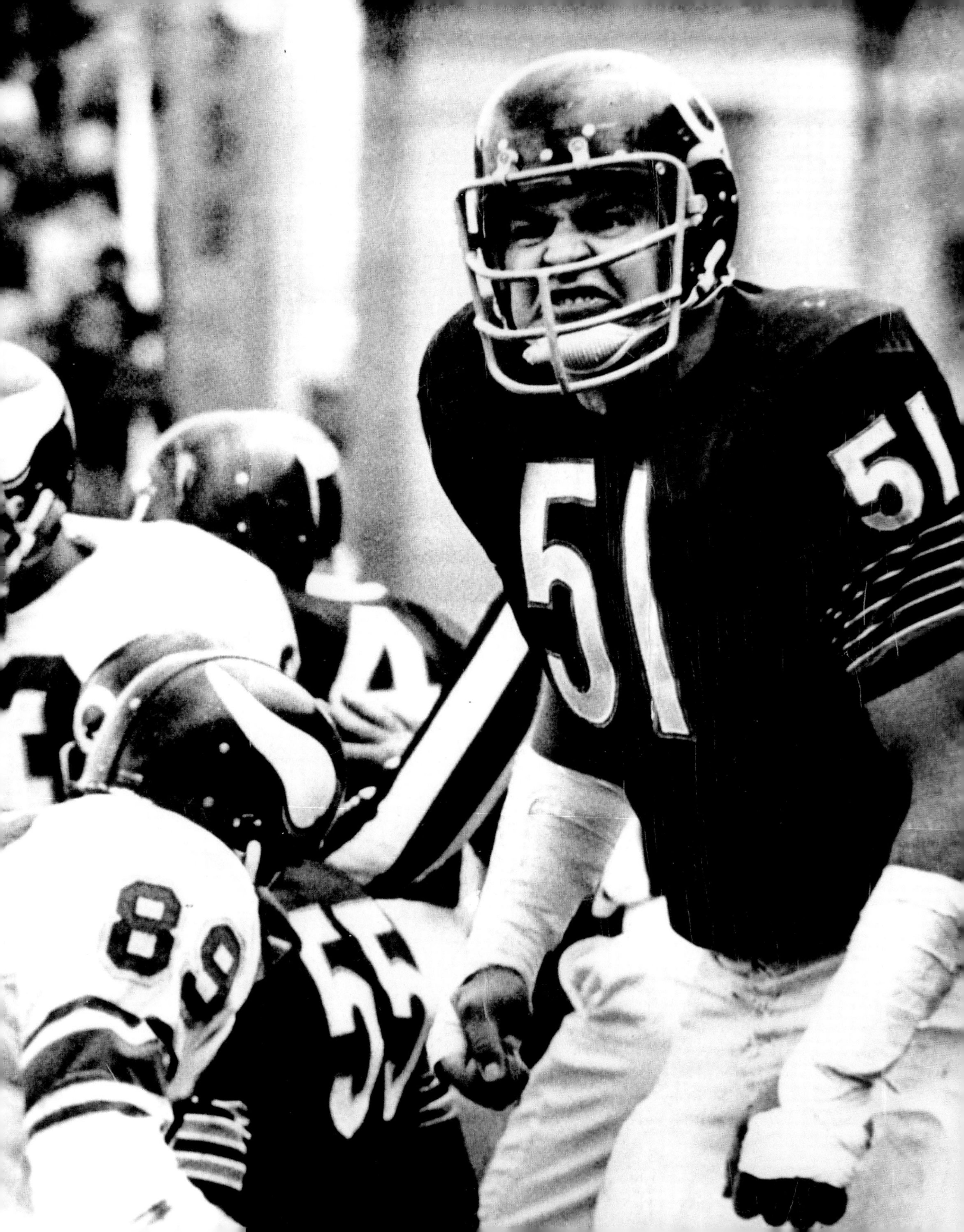

Dick Butkus

51 MIDDLE LINEBACKER
1965–73

Dʏ Jᴇɴᴋɪɴs ɪɴᴛʀᴏᴅᴜᴄᴇᴅ Dick Butkus to the nation with the first sentence of his cover story for the Oct. 12, 1964, issue of Sports Illustrated.

"If every college football team had a linebacker like Dick Butkus," Jenkins wrote, "all fullbacks would soon be 3 feet tall and sing soprano."

The city, the state and the rest of the Midwest already were familiar with Butkus. The Far South Side native was one of the best players Chicago ever produced, and after a dominant career at Vocational he became the Big Ten's best player at Illinois.

He was a year away from joining his hometown Bears, with whom he became a legend still spoken about in hushed tones 46 years after his final game—even though he never made the playoffs and enjoyed two winning seasons out of nine in the NFL.

Butkus was just that good.

What made the 6-foot-3, 245-pound middle linebacker different from every other player in the history of the Bears and the NFL was the ferocious way he played. His highlight reels still are shocking for their violence, as he was able to tap into a part of himself that even the most hardened professional football players find difficult to reach.

He simply had no regard for his opponents.

Rams defensive end Deacon Jones, a Hall of Famer and one of the most feared defensive players ever, once said: "I called him a maniac. A stone maniac. He was a well-conditioned animal, and every time he hit you, he tried to put you in the cemetery, not the hospital."

The films tell the story. In them, Butkus pushes back guards and centers with ease, slams quarterbacks to the ground and chases down and finishes off wide receivers.

The most striking moments occur when a running back hits a hole with a full head of steam, meets Butkus there and is propelled backward at an even higher rate of speed, like a four-wheeler suddenly thrown in reverse and giving its driver whiplash.

Dave Osborn, a tough 6-foot, 208-pound Viking who played halfback and fullback and made the 1970 Pro Bowl, told the Tribune's Don Pierson on Feb. 6, 1979: "With my running style, when I got hit by a linebacker, I usually

Dick Butkus (51) sneers at a ref during a game against the Vikings in 1969.

could drag him 2 yards. When Butkus hit me, I'd go backwards 2 yards."

Lions center Ed Flanagan, a longtime Butkus nemesis from his days at Purdue, added, "Our backs were half-scared to death of him. If their number was called in the huddle, their eyes would look like two big marbles."

In the NFL Films production "The Best Ever: Professionals," between jarring hits, Butkus says, "It was all the same objective. Not only to tackle and put the guy down, but also to maybe put it in his mind that it's not gonna be just a plain-old tackle, fall down and go boom and lift the guy up and go back. That wasn't the way I wanted to get the point across."

Home-video viewers were not the only ones who wore out the rewind button while watching Butkus highlights.

"Our own coaches used to run the film back and forth because they couldn't believe it," Bears center Rich Coady told Pierson.

Besides his violence, the next-most-striking aspect about Butkus' reel is his skill, especially in pass coverage. He finished his career with 22 interceptions, and he did it his way. After some of his picks, Butkus wagged the ball in the nearest receiver's face before embarking on his return, taunting his opponent as if he were a younger kid on the playground in his Roseland neighborhood.

"Most of the time it was like a man out there playing against children," Coady said.

Butkus' tactics were not limited to Bears opponents. In John Mullin's 2003 book, "Tales from the Chicago Bears Sideline," Baltimore Colts center Bill Curry said, "He even intimidated officials. He'd take the ball away from somebody after the play and shake it in the official's face, and the official pointed their way and gave them the ball."

Bill George, Mike Singletary or Brian Urlacher would be an easy choice for the best middle linebacker in most teams' histories. With the Bears they are, unquestionably, second-best at best.

As the voice-of-God narration in "Best Ever: Professionals" intoned: "No one has played middle linebacker better than Dick Butkus. And it's not likely that anyone ever will. He was the most dominant defensive player the game has ever known."

Pierson wrote on Feb. 4, 1979: "Some people are born to play football. Football was born for Dick Butkus."

His size, speed, instincts and ferocity made Butkus the perfect middle linebacker. Ross Brupbacher, who played next to Butkus as an outside linebacker for the Bears from 1970-72, said, "If you wanted to put one together like a Frankenstein, you couldn't have put a better one together."

"Uh-oh," outside linebacker Doug Buffone—a Bear for 14 years and a teammate of Butkus for eight—said upon hearing his teammate's description. "If Butkus hears Bru said that, he'll choke him."

Butkus was voted into the Pro Football Hall of Fame in 1979, his first year of eligibility. In 1994 he was named to the NFL's 75th anniversary team. The NFL Network named him the 10th-best player of all time in 2010, and a New York Daily News panel voted him No. 8 in 2014.

In 2001, Sports Illustrated's Paul Zimmerman ranked Butkus the best middle linebacker ever, leading a top five of Ray Lewis, Joe Schmidt, Willie Lanier and Ray Nitschke.

Butkus played nine seasons for the Bears, starting all 119 games he played. He was named first-team All-Pro five times and second-team once and he was voted to the Pro Bowl after his first eight seasons. He's the Bears' all-time leader with 27 fumble recoveries.

The Hall of Fame named Butkus to its All-Decade teams in both the 1960s and the '70s. The only other Bear to be named to two such teams was Walter Payton, in the 1970s and '80s.

Coady's man-against-boys analogy held true for Butkus from an early age. At Vocational, coach Bernie O'Brien sat Butkus during scrimmages so he wouldn't hurt teammates. Sports Illustrated's Robert F. Jones, in the Sept. 21, 1970, cover story on Butkus, described Vocational as "one of those technical schools where the corridors smell of sawed wood and burnt steel from the shops, where the lockers bear two-inch-deep dents from tough kids punching

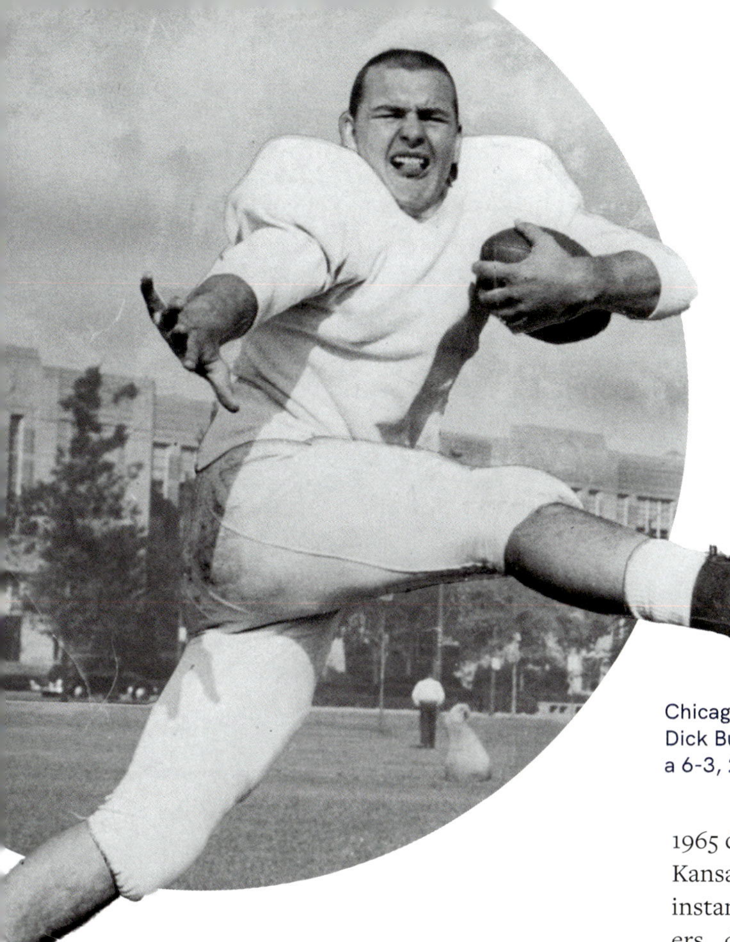

Chicago Vocational High School's
Dick Butkus, shown Oct. 19, 1960, is
a 6-3, 230-pound all-state fullback.

out their frustrations and where you can always find bloodstains from fistfights in the john."

Butkus was the toughest kid at the tough school.

In yet another SI profile, this time from Sept. 6, 1993, Butkus told Rick Telander of a time he excused himself from practice to deal with four boys in a car who were harassing his future wife, Helen Essenberg.

"Without hesitation," Telander wrote, "Butkus ran off the field, chased the car onto 87th Street, dived through the open front window on the passenger side and, in full uniform, thrashed each of the passengers. Then he climbed out of the car and walked back to the field."

At Illinois, he led the Illini to their most recent Rose Bowl win, 17-7 over Washington on Jan. 1, 1964. He won the Chicago Tribune Silver Football as the Big Ten's best player the next season and finished third in the 1964 Heisman Trophy balloting behind quarterbacks John Huarte of Notre Dame and Tulsa's Jerry Rhome.

The Bears selected Butkus third in the 1965 draft and paired him with the fourth pick, Kansas running back Gale Sayers. They almost instantly became two of the game's best players, demonstrating elite talent and skill as rookies. Sayers beat out Butkus for rookie of the year, Butkus was named defensive rookie of the year and both made first-team All-Pro.

George, the Bears' middle linebacker since he practically invented the position in 1954, knew his days were numbered after watching Butkus take part in one practice, he said in Richard Whittingham's 1991 book, "What Bears They Were."

"I've never seen anybody who was such a cinch," George said. "From the day Dick showed up in camp I knew I was out of a job."

Despite the presence of Butkus and Sayers, two of the best ever to play in the NFL, the Bears of their time were mostly terrible. After a 9-5 season in their rookie year of 1965 and a mediocre 7-6-1 mark in 1967, the Bears never had another winning season with their Class of 1965 superstars.

With wins scarce, Butkus competed with himself. His greatest enjoyment came from his personal rivalries with offensive linemen, particularly the NFC Central Division's great centers: Mick Tingelhoff of the Vikings, a

Hall of Famer; Flanagan, the Lions' four-time Pro Bowl selection; and Ken Bowman, who started for three championship teams with the Packers.

During the waning stages of a loss to the Lions, the Bears still had all three timeouts. As the Lions ran out the clock, Butkus called time after three consecutive plays so he could take three more runs at Flanagan.

Butkus looked to intimidate before games even started. During warmups he often went to the other team's side of the field to mark his territory.

"I was centering for punts in the pregame drill, and I took my warmup jacket off," Flanagan told Pierson. "I looked up and there was Butkus wiping his feet on it."

Tinglehoff added: "I was centering in warmups once, and I felt something wet on my hands. I couldn't figure out what it was because the sun was shining. I looked up and Butkus was standing there spitting on me. True story."

The way Butkus acted could be good or bad for his teammates, or sometimes both. Buffone and Brupbacher often were either bailed out of or put into tough situations by Butkus.

One one occasion, Buffone was, in his words, "getting worked over" by Lions tight end Charlie Sanders. Buffone told Butkus he needed some help.

"(Butkus) gave that little chuckle, like a little kid, and said, 'Give him a shove my way,'" Buffone said. "I did, and the collision was unbelievable."

On the other hand, Brubacher said, "It got disconcerting on some occasions. He had a violent temper, and he really worked himself up to play. . . . He did his best to make sure everybody on the field had blood in their eyes.

"Now that's a bad situation when you have Charlie Sanders out there with blood in his eyes. Dick would purposely try to make those people angry—call them names, give them a little shot when getting off the pile. That's what created a problem for you. You had to be ready."

Butkus started three fights during a game against the Lions in 1969, and in a 1970 preseason game against the St. Louis Cardinals he was flagged for four personal-foul penalties.

Was he a dirty player?

"Oh, yeah," said Flanagan, who like Butkus entered the NFL in 1965. "He'd kick, spit, grab my face mask, anything to get to the ball carrier. He bit me once in a pileup. In the leg. He was just nasty.

"He'd spit on the ball, insult me, my mother—we had a real resentment going. He used to love me on punts. He'd take three steps back and try to kill me."

Whether they liked or disliked Butkus— there was no in between—his opponents always respected him.

"Listen," Flanagan said. "We never liked each other. We sat two lockers away in some Pro Bowl games and never talked to each other. But I've played against the best—all of them— and he's right up there. You can't take that away from him."

Tingelhoff added: "He hammered me and I tried to hammer him. It's no picnic out there. I might have clipped him a few times. . . . He might have hit me with a forearm. That's the way the game is. He was rough and rugged, and you had to respect a guy like that."

The Vikings center said Butkus proved his intelligence by always being near the ball and seldom putting himself out of position: "He had an uncanny knack of knowing where the ball was going."

Butkus expanded on his instincts in great detail to Sports Illustrated's Jones.

"I can see it all about to happen," Butkus said. "At the key moment—the instant of the snap—I somehow know, most of the time, just how the flow pattern will develop. It's all there in the backdrop. I stare right through the center and the quarterback, right through their eyes. I watch for the keys, and they are very tiny keys, believe me. Tiny little twitches of their shoulders and their heads and their feet and eyes. There's just this split second, before it all starts to move, when you put those keys together and you know—you damned well know—how it's going."

Butkus liked to analyze. To a point. When

Brupbacher, a future lawyer, joined the team and began musing about defensive theories and philosophies, it didn't last long.

"Sometimes he'd go off on intellectual tangents in meetings," Buffone said, "and Butkus would grab him by the neck and push him down. Bru would be yelling for me to help him. I'd say, 'Hey, do I look stupid?'"

Like Sayers, knee injuries ended Butkus' career. Before the 1973 season Butkus and the Bears agreed to five one-year contracts of $115,000 apiece. He had played in constant pain for three years, and during the first season of his new deal, it became too much.

Butkus retired at 31, and in 1974 he sued the Bears and their team doctor, Ted Fox, for $1.6 million for mistreating his injuries and administering painkillers that Butkus and his attorney claimed hastened his knee's deterioration. The court battle lasted two years before the Bears and Butkus settled for $600,000.

Bears owner George Halas blacklisted Butkus during and immediately after the court case, but Papa Bear never could turn his back completely on a player that good. When the Bears owner published his autobiography, "Halas by Halas," in 1979, Butkus showed up to a book signing. Halas, according to Jeff Davis' 2005 biography, "Papa Bear: The Life and Legacy of George Halas," wrote an inscription above his signature.

"To Dick Butkus, the greatest player in the history of the Bears. You had that old zipperoo!"

While Halas and Butkus returned to speaking terms, forgiveness was not in the cards. Halas never got around to retiring Butkus' number even though the linebacker obviously deserved the honor. The stubborn decision meant that Sayers' number also remained unretired. Halas wished to honor Sayers, with whom he never had any trouble, but he knew Bears fans would react negatively to one of the paired greats being honored without the other, so he shelved the issue indefinitely.

Halas' feelings on the issue were known, however, to those paying attention. According to the Bears, replacement player Steve Trimble

in 1987 was the only Bear to wear No. 40 after Sayers retired. After Butkus left the Bears, his No. 51 was worn by six players: Mel Rogers, Doug Becker, Bruce Herron, Kelvin Atkins, Jim Morrissey and replacement player Mark Rodenhauser.

Butkus reentered the fold about 18 months after Halas died on Oct. 31, 1983. In 1985, Butkus, who had parlayed his humorous appearances in Miller Lite commercials into a full-time acting career, joined play-by-play man Wayne Larrivee and color commentator Jim Hart as a third man in the team's WGN radio booth.

Exactly 11 years after Papa Bear's death, on Halloween night 1994, his grandson, Bears President Michael McCaskey, finally retired Butkus' No. 51 and Sayers' No. 40. McCaskey figured the move would boost his flatlining popularity. Instead the ceremony symbolized both the dysfunction of the 1990s Bears and the sorry state of the team during the days of Butkus and Sayers.

It rained 2.26 inches that day in Chicago with 45-mph winds when the Bears played the Packers on "Monday Night Football." The rollicking Pack, led by superstars Brett Favre and Reggie White, frolicked in the downpour to the tune of a 33-6 win. At halftime, the soaked Butkus and Sayers were honored during the deluge in front of a sparse crowd due to the weather.

Butkus has stayed involved with football with his Butkus Awards for linebackers at the pro, college and prep levels and his "I Play Clean" anti-steroids program.

To this day, almost five decades after his career ended playing for Bears teams that went a combined 48-74-4, no NFL player has surpassed the standard Butkus set for ferocious football.

"You don't start early in life and become a Butkus," Brupbacher told Pierson in 1979. "You're just born, and through certain breaks you get that opportunity to realize all that ability. That's what happened to him.

"I don't think there will ever be another one. He has to be the toughest to ever play." ■

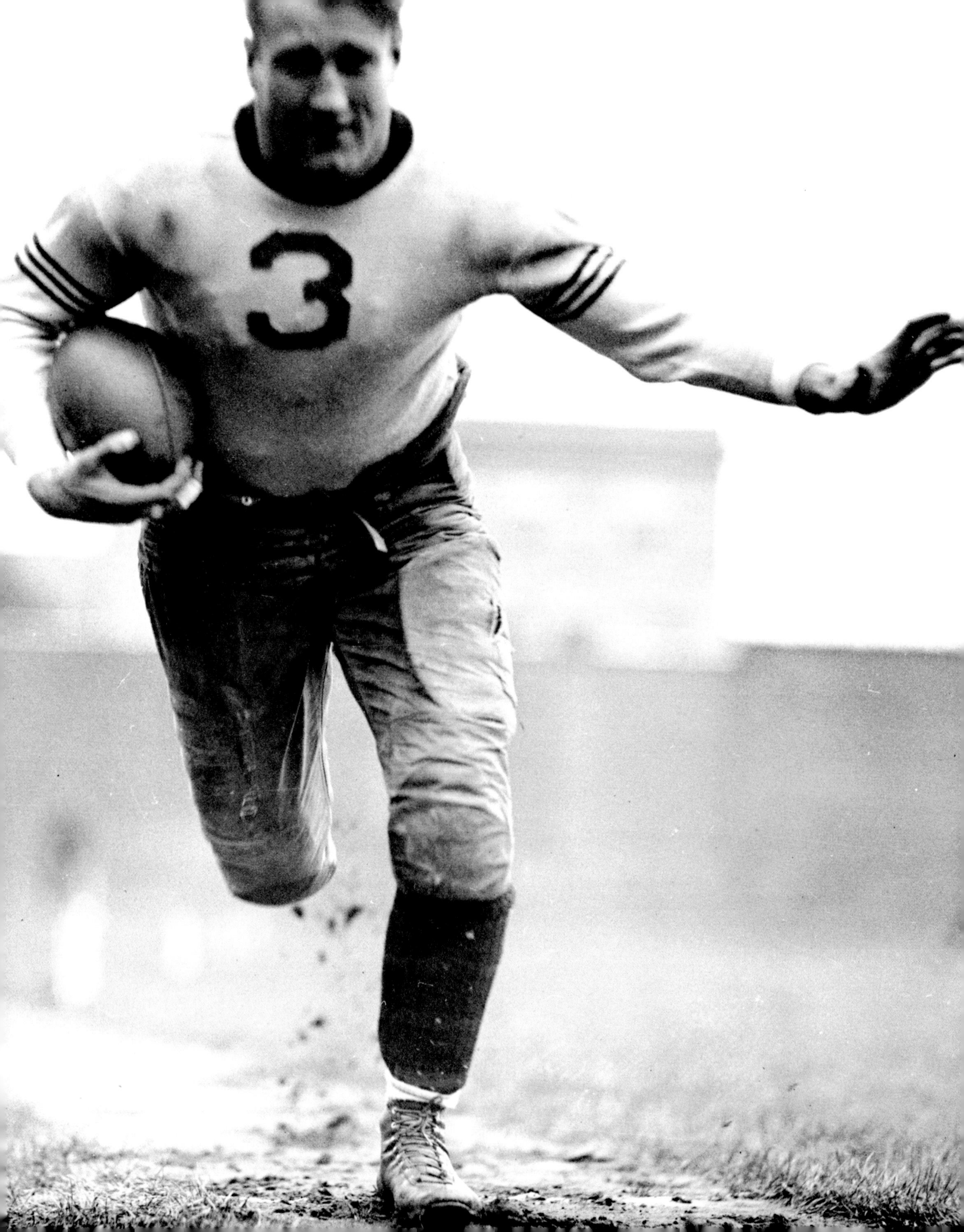

Bronko Nagurski

3, 16 FULLBACK, LINEBACKER, TACKLE
1930–37, 43

THE WORD "LEGEND" does not carry the weight it once did.

Taken literally, it applies only to figures who were larger than life. Paul Bunyan, for instance, created the Great Lakes so his blue ox, Babe, could have suitable watering holes. Or so the story goes.

John Henry won a hammering contest against a steam driver. The meek David slayed the mighty Goliath with a slingshot. As a baby, Hercules strangled a poisonous snake sent to kill him in his cradle.

Bronko Nagurski was a human who fit the description. It seemed the Bears' 6-foot-2, 226-pound fullback and defensive tackle had more in common with the giant lumberjack Bunyan, a fellow Minnesotan, than he did with Clarke Hinkle or Dutch Clark, his fellow standout running backs in the NFL of the 1930s.

Everyone who played or coached with or against Nagurski or watched him play from the stands had at least one story about him that defied belief. After his death at 81 of natural causes on Jan. 7, 1990, news outlets from all over the country asked players or reporters who were active in the '30s to share their memories of Nagurski.

Ray Didinger of the Philadelphia Daily News was on one such assignment for a story that ran Jan. 11. He sat for hours with Johnny "Blood" McNally, a halfback with the Packers and Steelers who, like Nagurski, entered the Pro Football Hall of Fame in its inaugural class in 1963.

Didinger wrote: "I thought a few of McNally's stories seemed a bit, well, exaggerated.

"I mentioned four or five. . . . Like the one about Nagurski carrying five Packers on his back 20 yards and not breaking stride until he reached the end zone. . . . Then there was the story about Nagurski trampling two Steelers en route to a score in 1937. One man suffered a broken shoulder, the other was knocked unconscious for 10 minutes. . . . I said that didn't seem possible."

McNally leaned close and looked into Didinger's eyes: "With Nagurski," he said, "believe everything you hear."

Nagurski's legend began at the Canadian border. He was born in Rainy River, Ontario, and grew up in International Falls, Minn. He

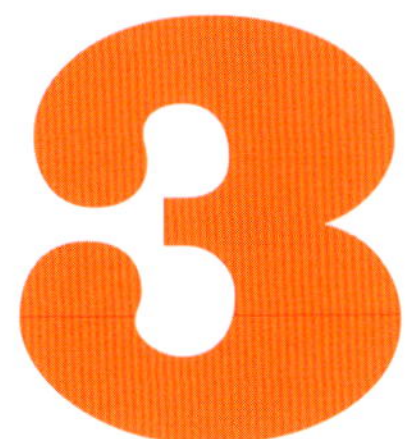

Bronko Nagurski (3), circa 1932.

chopped wood, pulled wagons and pushed plows, and he even ran two miles each way to school during winters that seldom saw temperatures reach positive digits. Nagurski grew to be the strongest person around by the time he was 15, and residents of the frigid border towns started calling him Bronko instead of Bronislau.

One day, Clarence "Doc" Spears, the football coach at the University of Minnesota, was on a summer recruiting trip 300 miles north of his Minneapolis campus. As he drove along the country roads, he stopped to ask a farm boy for directions.

Bronko, pushing a plow without a horse, showed Spears where he needed to go. He did so by picking up his implement with his right hand and using it as a pointer.

"Bronk does not tell the story himself," Bears owner and coach George Halas wrote in his 1979 autobiography "Halas by Halas." "But he does not deny it."

Spears forgot about the boy he was in town to see, and Nagurski was on his way to football stardom.

As a Golden Gopher he was among the best players in the nation. In 1929 he became the first to be named All-American at two positions, fullback and tackle, after injuries forced him into duty on the offensive line midway through the season.

"Doc finished with the Bronk in 1929," Halas wrote. "I made sure the Bears got him."

Halas signed Nagurski for $5,000, and when he started practicing his teammates could hardly believe what they were seeing. Or feeling. Red Grange, the sport's most famous player and one of its surest tacklers, changed his technique after the first time he tried to bring down Nagurski.

In Jeff Davis' 2005 biography, "Papa Bear: The Life and Legacy of George Halas," Grange is quoted as saying: "When you hit him at the ankles, it's like an electric shock. If you hit him above the ankles, you're likely to get killed!"

Of the 10 linemen who played for the Bears in 1930, Nagurski weighed more than five. Despite his bulk—which included a 22-inch neck that made buttoning shirts to the top an impossible task and a size 19½ ring that is the largest ever measured by the Hall of Fame— Nagurski was faster than every Bear except Grange. Nagurski ran a 10.2-second 100-yard dash at Minnesota.

Nagurski's first three seasons coincided with Ralph Jones' tenure as head coach of the Bears as Halas stepped down to concentrate full-time on his ownership duties during the Great Depression. With a talented cast that included Grange, Nagurski and linemen Link Lyman, Zuck Carlson and Luke Johnsos, the team became elite.

After a disastrous 4-9-2 season in 1929 that helped Halas decide to take a break from coaching, the Bears went 9-4-1 in 1930, 8-5 the next year and 6-1-6 in 1932. The Portsmouth Spartans also had an odd record that season, 6-1-4, so a tiebreaker game quickly was planned for the NFL championship.

A winter storm pushed the game to an 80-yard dirt field at Chicago Stadium. The Bears won 9-0, with the decisive play the result of some quick thinking by Nagurski.

The game was scoreless well into the fourth quarter when the Bears found themselves with first-and-goal from the Spartans' 1-yard line. Nagurski was stuffed three times, and on fourth down he again plowed toward the line. He kept his head up, though, and saw Grange by himself in the end zone. Nagurski leaped and tossed the ball to him for the only touchdown in the Bears' 9-0 win.

The Spartans protested that Nagurski was not 5 or more yards behind the line of scrimmage, as the rules of the time required of passers. The referees allowed the score, and in the offseason the rule was changed so that the ball could be passed from anywhere behind the line of scrimmage.

With his team now a championship team, Halas returned to the sideline in 1933. The Bears repeated as champs by winning a much more exciting title game, this time 23-21 over the Giants at Wrigley Field. Nagurski twice more threw trick passes that led to late scores. His 8-yard toss to Bill Karr put the Bears ahead

When you hit him at the ankles, it's like an electric shock. If you hit him above the ankles, you're likely to get killed! —RED GRANGE ON TACKLING NAGURSKI

16-14 late in the third quarter, and after the Giants took a 21-16 lead on a flea flicker, Nagurski led an even trickier play. He again rushed toward the line, leaped and threw, this time to Bill Hewitt, who lateraled to a wide-open Karr for the 19-yard touchdown that provided the winning points that held up when Grange made a game-saving tackle in the final seconds.

In 1934 the Bears lost the championship game 30-13 against the Giants, who scored 27 unanswered points in the fourth quarter after switching from cleats to sneakers on the iced-over field at the Polo Grounds. Until that game the Bears were unstoppable, outscoring their opponents 286-86 in a 13-0 regular season.

Beattie Feathers joined the Bears from Tennessee that season, sending Grange to the bench in what would be his final year. With Nagurski at fullback and the 5-foot-10, 185-pound Feathers at halfback, Halas ditched his beloved T formation to showcase their talents in the single wing. Following Nagurski's crushing blocks, Feathers became the NFL's first 1,000-yard rusher with 1,004 yards on 119 carries, an average of 8.4 yards per attempt.

"Bronko cleared the path, and all I had to do was run," said Feathers, who suffered a shoulder injury in the season's 10th game and never was the same. "He had the most incredible natural strength I've ever seen. One day he gave me a playful bop on the helmet and it knocked me down."

Nagurski told the Tribune's John Husar on Jan. 18, 1972: "Beattie would keep his hand on my tail and use me as a blocking post. It was a pleasure to have a smart back use you like that.

He'd just shove off and swing outside, and I'd cut 'em down."

That season also produced perhaps the most legendary of Nagurski tales. During a game at Wrigley Field, Bronko was called for holding. In the huddle, according to Halas, he said, "That was my fault. Give me the ball."

As the story goes, Nagurski put his head down and bowled through several tacklers for a touchdown. He hadn't noticed that he had reached the end zone, so he kept going until his helmet slammed into the brick wall beyond the end line. The blow knocked Nagurski out, and when he came to on the bench, he told a teammate, "Man, that last guy really hit me!"

Halas, neither confirming nor denying the story, wrote in 1979: "Some people will today show you a crack in the south wall at Wrigley Field they say was made by his helmeted head."

Nagurski was slowed by injuries in 1935, returned to form in 1936 and helped the Bears reach the title game in 1937. After the 28-21 loss to rookie sensation Sammy Baugh and the Redskins, Nagurski walked away from football.

Clarke Hinkle, who battled Nagurski head-to-head for years as the Packers' Hall of Fame fullback, said in 1990 after Nagurski's death: "My greatest thrill in football was the day Bronko Nagurski announced his retirement."

Halas faced cash-flow issues and had trouble paying his players for much of the 1930s. At season's end, in lieu of their paychecks, Grange and Nagurski sometimes received IOUs. Nagurski had moonlighted as a professional wrestler during his offseasons, and he knew he could make as much or more money

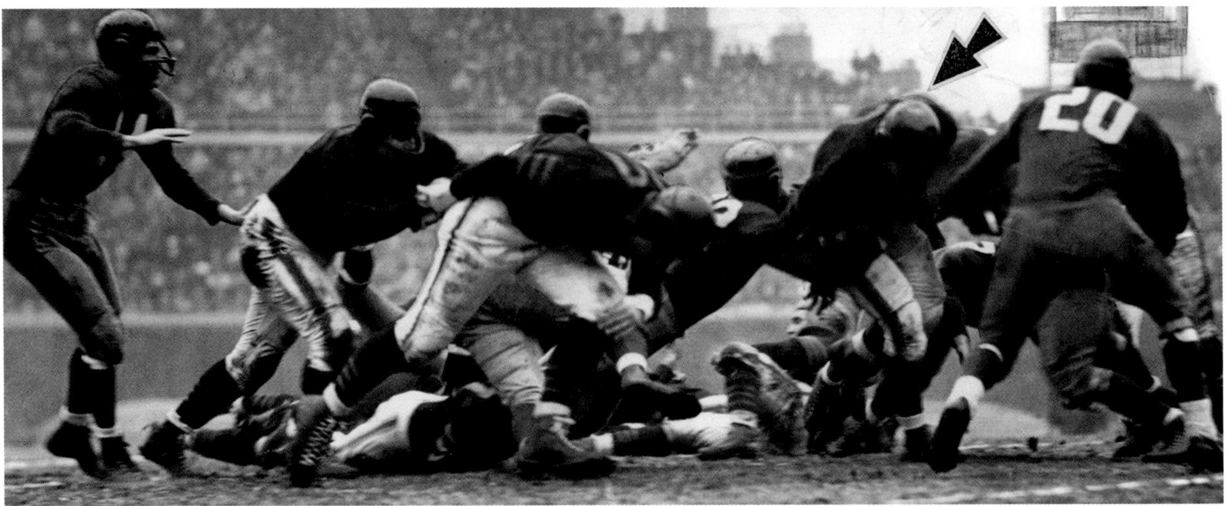

Bronko Nagurski (3) scores a touchdown Dec. 26, 1943, in the NFL title game at Wrigley Field against the Redskins.

in wrestling as he could in football. After all, despite his sterling play, Nagurski's salary had not gone up from the $5,000 he signed for as a rookie. Halas insisted the money just wasn't there for a raise, but after the 1937 season Nagurski demanded an increase to $6,000. Halas declined, and Nagurski, with a farm he was trying to pay off in Minnesota and a wife, Eileen, ready to start a family, made the leap to wrestling full time in 1938.

His successful run in the National Wrestling Alliance included high-profile matches against Lou Thesz, Ray Steele and Gorgeous George. Nagurski also bought a gas station in International Falls.

In 1943, six years after he left the Bears, he received calls from Johnsos and Hunk Anderson. With Halas gone to serve in World War II, his assistants served as co-head coaches. Many of the Bears' key players also were serving in the military, and Johnsos and Anderson wondered if Nagurski might be interested in returning to the football field.

Nagurski, 35, said he was far from football shape. Johnsos suggested he play tackle to keep running to a minimum. Nagurski agreed to rejoin the Bears.

By that time the locker room had changed. Only five players—Danny Fortmann, George Musso, Ray Nolting, Bob Snyder and George Wilson—remained from when Nagurski left.

Bronko felt apprehensive until his old friend Musso, the 6-foot-2, 262-pound "Moose," greeted him with a huge hug.

Seconds later, center Bulldog Turner, the brash new face—and mouth—of the Bears, also greeted Nagurski.

Jim Dent, author of the 2004 book, "Monster of the Midway: Bronko Nagurski, the 1943 Chicago Bears, and the Greatest Comeback Ever," described the first meeting between the taciturn 35-year-old Minnesota plowman and the ebullient 24-year-old from deep in the heart of central Texas.

"Gol' dog, Mr. Nagurski!" Turner said, extending his hand after wiping it on his pant leg. "I feel like I'm shaking the right hand of God. (Expletive), George Halas has been talking about you since the day I came to Chicago. I was wondering whether a superman like you really existed. It's a pleasure to see you with my own eyeballs."

Nagurski replied: "I've had my leg pulled, but never that hard."

The season went well, and the Bears were 7-1-1 going into the traditional final game of the regular season against the Chicago Cardinals at Comiskey Park. The Cardinals were 0-9 but led the Bears 24-14 after three quarters. Needing a win to hold off the Packers in the Western Division, Johnsos and Anderson called on Nagurski for a spark.

Playing with a metal brace on his back, Nagurski lined up at fullback for the first time in six years. Before his first play, he shared terse words with Turner. The reinvigorated back plowed up the middle time after time on runs of 4, 5 or 6 yards until he scored on a 1-yard plunge. Spark delivered, the Bears outscored the Cardinals 21-0 in the fourth quarter to win 35-21 and clinch the division title.

On each of his hard-driving runs, Nagurski followed Turner straight up the middle, the Bulldog and the Bronko barking and braying their way through the Cardinals.

After the game, Turner was asked what Nagurski said to him before the series. Halas relayed the answer 36 years later.

"Damnedest pep talk I ever heard in my life," Turner said. "He told me, 'If you don't want to block for me, all right, but just get out of my way or I'll break your back!'"

For once, someone had rendered Turner speechless.

Bears quarterback Sid Luckman, who had idolized Nagurski in the 1930s, felt like a fan giving the ball to the Bronko and watching him run wild.

"When I handed him the ball," Luckman told Richard Whittingham in his 1991 book, "What Bears They Were," "I could just sense the power. He would take it with such a great burst as he went into the line."

The Bears won the title, their third of the 1940s and Nagurski's third after his championships in 1932 and '33, with a 41-21 win over the Redskins at Wrigley Field. Nagurski walked away from the Bears for good this time, but not before scoring his final touchdown, a typical 3-yard blast that gave his team the lead for good at 14-7 in the second quarter.

Nagurski served as an assistant coach at UCLA for a year before retiring back to northern Minnesota and making wrestling appearances on and off until 1960. As the years passed, he looked for places to live farther away from the rest of the world. He settled on a log cabin on Lake Rainy, and he limited his travel mostly to his weekly trips to International Falls to check his mail.

In 1963 Nagurski was part of the charter class of the Pro Football Hall of Fame. Along with fellow Bears greats Halas and Grange, he was joined in the inaugural group by the best players of professional football's first 40 years: Baugh, Dutch Clark, Mel Hein, Pete Henry, Cal Hubbard, Don Hutson, McNally, Ernie Nevers and Jim Thorpe.

The original three Bears were joined in Canton, Ohio, in 1964 by Ed Healey, Lyman and George Trafton, in 1965 by Fortmann and Luckman, in 1966 by 1940 draftmates George McAfee and Turner and in 1967 by Joe Stydahar. Those 11 men formed the foundation of the Bears and helped Halas win seven championships in the NFL's first 27 years.

Nagurski had a TV in his cabin and kept up with the Bears. The 1985 team thrilled him, and the Tribune's Cooper Rollow caught up with the Bronk in the run-up to the Bears' most recent championship, one of two they have won in the 72 seasons since their 1946 title.

"They look like the Bears of old," Nagurski told Rollow. "I don't think I would have had any trouble making this team. I don't know whether I'd be playing fullback or defense, but I'd be playing someplace."

Grange died a year after Nagurski, in 1991. For the final 60 years of his life, he told anyone who would listen that Nagurski was the best player of all time.

In a 1978 radio interview with WGN's Wally Phillips, Grange said: "How good was he? . . . On defense, he was equal to Dick Butkus in Butkus' prime. On offense, he was faster and equal to Larry Csonka. Put the two together and you got Nagurski."

Nagurski, as was the nature of the quiet legend, didn't go quite that far. Like John Henry driving in a spike with one swing before spitting on the soil, he was just doing his job.

"I wasn't pretty, but I did all right," he said in 1984. "Our teams won most of the time, so that was good.

"I never enjoyed anything as much as I did playing football. It was something I was born to do." ◼

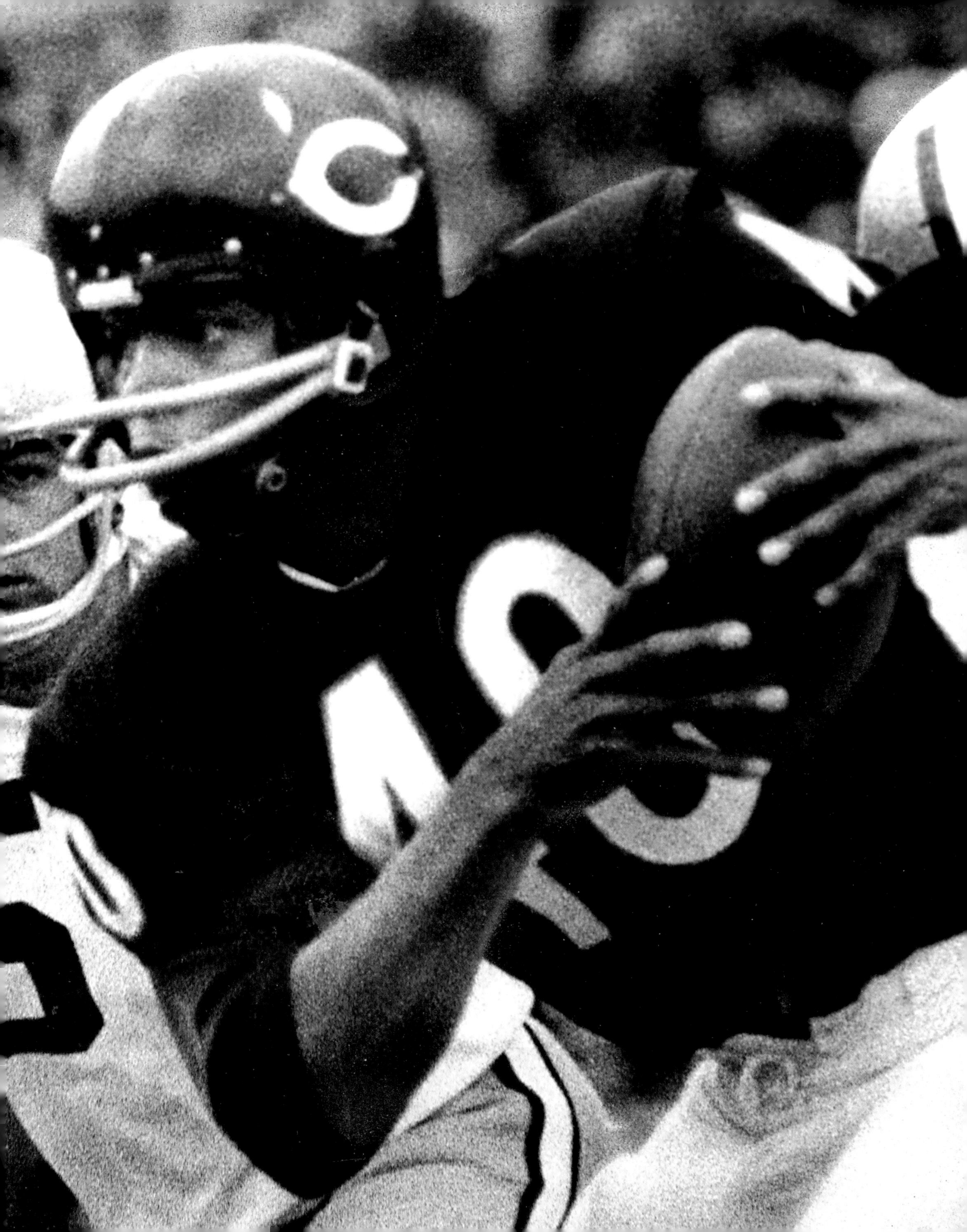

Gale Sayers

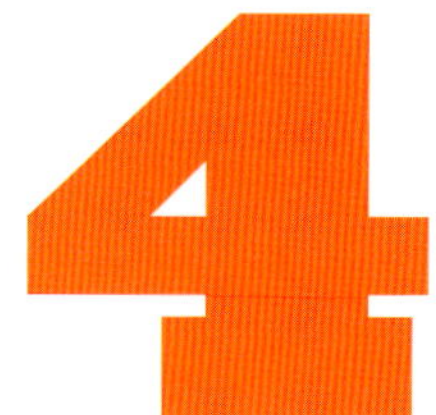

40 HALFBACK

1965–71

GALE SAYERS LOOKED OVER his right shoulder as if to say, "Where is every-body?"

Running up the left sideline with no Bears teammates or 49ers opponents within view of the TV camera at Wrigley Field, Sayers slowed down to enjoy the final 20 yards of his 85-yard punt return.

When he crossed the goal line for his sixth touchdown of the afternoon in a 61-20 win, Sayers tossed the ball above his head with both hands in the end zone at rain-soaked and sloppy Wrigley Field.

Sayers already was a rookie sensation before that game on Dec. 12, 1965. When he tied the NFL record with six touchdowns—an 80-yard reception, runs of 21, 7, 50 and 1 yard and his 85-yard punt return—people started wondering whether they ever had seen anything like "The Kansas Comet."

"His way of running was like magic," Bears President Mike McCaskey told the Tribune's Fred Mitchell on Oct. 25, 1994. "In the mud against San Francisco, everybody else was slipping and trying to stay upright. He was running and cutting like there was magic in his shoes."

Clark Miller, a 49ers defensive end on that record afternoon, told the Tribune's Sam Smith on Nov. 1, 1987: "The Bears really didn't even have a passing offense then. You knew what their strength on offense was. They were going to run, and by this game, you knew who was going to be running."

It didn't matter. Packers coach Vince Lombardi once said Sayers "would surprise you, even when you knew he was coming."

Sayers played a full season four times in a career that was cut short because of injuries to both his knees. Those four years were so incredible they put him at No. 4 on the Tribune's list of the 50 best Bears players ever.

He was voted first-team All-Pro five times, including in 1968, when he suffered a career-altering injury to his right knee in the ninth game, and in 1969, when he returned to lead the NFL with 1,032 rushing yards months later.

The 6-foot, 198-pound Sayers played his last game at 28 after injuring his left knee, then became the Pro Football Hall of Fame's youngest member at 34 in 1977. His 68 games were enough to put him among the all-time best. In

Gale Sayers (40), slashes through opponents Oct. 10, 1971, at Soldier Field.

1970 the Topeka, Kan., native who grew up in Omaha, Neb., was voted the best running back of the NFL's first 50 years.

The Bears have had spectacular runners before and after Sayers. Beattie Feathers was the NFL's first 1,000-yard rusher in 1934. George McAfee of the 1940s dynasty was nicknamed "One Play" for his ability to score from anywhere on the field. Willie Galimore, who was killed in a car accident mid-career in 1964, was so elusive he earned the moniker "The Wisp." Walter Payton retired in 1987 as the league's all-time rushing leader, and Devin Hester in the 21st century became the game's best special teams returner of all time.

None captured the imagination the way Sayers did. Tacklers had no clue where his runs would take him. Sometimes neither did he.

"I can't define my running style," Sayers told the Tribune's Cooper Rollow. "Really, I don't know where I'm going. I go where my feet take me. I like to think that if my blockers can get me 18 inches of clearance, I've got a shot at breaking a long one."

Sometimes an opponent's best move would be to simply stay where he was and hope one of Sayers' supernatural moves would lead him back to the tackler. In an NFL Films special on Sayers, former Eagles defensive tackle Floyd Peters recalled one such play.

"He gave me a fake, and my body went one way, my mind went the other way, and something happens to your motor when that happens," Peters said. "It's hard to explain. But my legs went limp and I had nothing left.

"The only problem was, Gale made one too many fakes and came back into me. I hit him and knocked him down and he said, 'Nice tackle, Floyd.' I told him, 'I didn't tackle you. You ran into me.'"

The special, part of NFL Films' "The Great Ones" series, said that Sayers' statistics, while impressive, didn't come close to measuring his impact.

"What we remember about Gale Sayers are not certain games or plays," the narrator intoned. "We remember the moves."

Those actions weren't easy to describe or explain and often needed video evidence to be believed. Bears center Mike Pyle, to the Tribune's Smith, said he regularly saw Sayers juke players who were chasing him from behind.

"I'm thinking, 'This guy must have eyes in the back of his head,'" Pyle said. "It was impossible to know that guy was coming up from behind. No one had that ability to elude tacklers."

Wide receiver Johnny Morris claimed to witness Sayers make cuts in midair.

"This sounds ridiculous, I know," Morris told Smith. "When you run downfield and cut, you've got to plant your foot and push off. But what Gale could do was turn his hip as he was in the air, turn his right foot over his left and he'd change direction."

Bears owner George Halas, also the team's coach for the first three of Sayers' seven seasons with the team, said one such play, made while Sayers was in college, prompted the Bears to take him with the No. 4 pick in the 1965 draft.

"I couldn't stand to let Gale go elsewhere after I saw him make a totally unique move in a Kansas game film," Halas told Rollow. "Gale started one way, left his feet and seemed to change direction in the air. When he landed, he was running the opposite direction. When I saw that move, I knew we had to get that young man."

Halas and personnel director George Allen hauled in Sayers and another all-time great, Dick Butkus, back-to-back in the 1965 draft. Butkus, the great Illinois linebacker, and Sayers went 3-4 after fullbacks Tucker Frederickson of Auburn and Ken Willard of North Carolina went 1-2 to the Giants and 49ers. Halas then held off aggressive offers from the AFL's Broncos for Butkus and Chiefs for Sayers.

Bears players were sure of what they were getting with the hard-charging Butkus, who immediately challenged 13-year starter Bill George at middle linebacker, the position George practically invented. They weren't as certain of Sayers, who had been accused of nursing injuries to protect his pro prospects at Kansas. Otto Graham, the Hall of Fame quarterback who coached the College All-Star Game

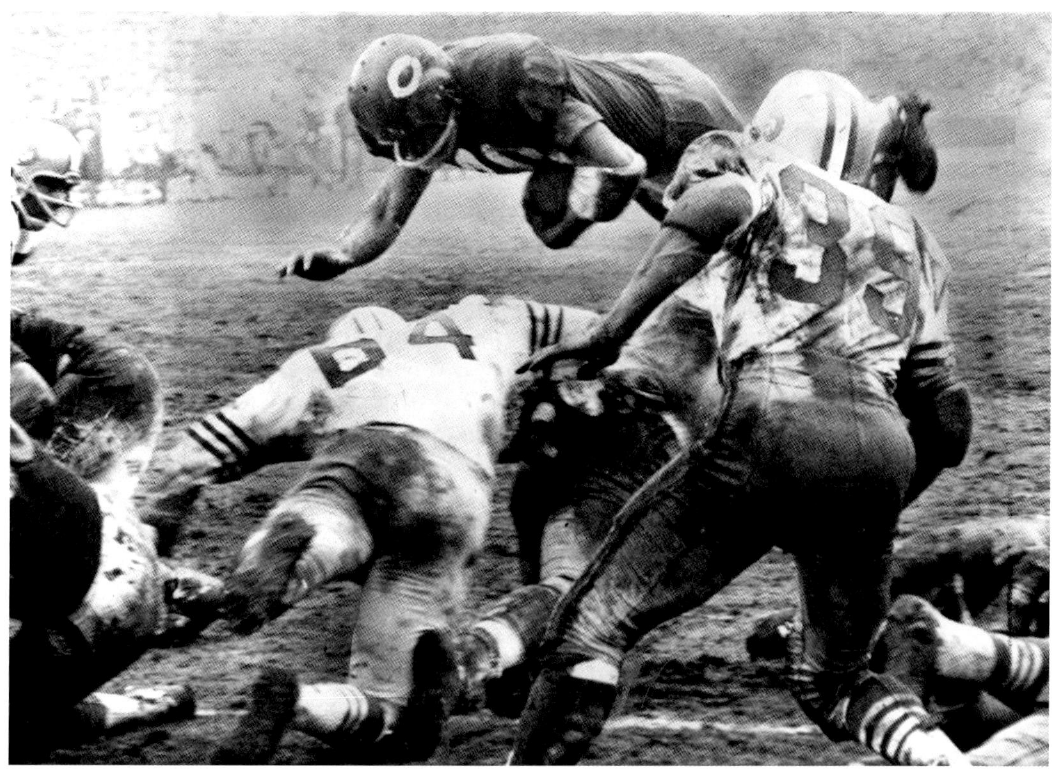

Gale Sayers (40) plunges over the line from a yard out for the fifth of his six touchdowns against the 49ers on Dec. 12, 1965, at Wrigley Field.

that year, said Sayers embellished an injury to get out of practice and sat him out of the game. Sayers also was viewed as a potential agitator after an arrest for protesting housing discrimination on the Kansas campus.

Sayers' personality was hard to read, and he often came off as aloof. Rollow wrote on Oct. 26, 1965, that "Sayers is a study in contradictions. He is quiet, yet garrulous; modest, yet confident; peaceful, yet intrepid. . . . He is not one for small talk, and he deplores the sports cliche."

Whatever doubts his teammates had about Sayers were answered with his play. Halas inserted him into the starting lineup at tailback in the third game of 1965, and Sayers scored two touchdowns in a 23-14 loss to the Packers. The defeat dropped the Bears to 0-3, but they proceeded to go on a rookie-led rampage, winning nine of their last 11 games.

Sayers almost single-handedly won a huge game against the Vikings, scoring four second-half touchdowns on two runs, a reception and a kickoff return in a 45-37 win in Bloomington, Minn.

The performance sent Bears players, coaches, fans and beat writers into orbit. Halas, very seldom one to praise a rookie, compared Sayers to the best ball carriers in team history just five games into his career.

In Robert Markus' game story in the Tribune, Halas gushed: "Red Grange, George McAfee and Gale Sayers. Not necessarily in that order. . . . Sayers rates with them all."

After his career, Sayers said he was prouder of the Vikings game than his performance against the 49ers because each of his touchdowns was necessary for the victory. After the game, though, he played it typically cool when former Bear George Connor asked him in a TV interview if the game was his biggest thrill in football.

"No," Sayers deadpanned. "I've had a lot of them."

It appeared the Bears were headed for another golden age, with a young all-time great on each side of the ball. Instead, the Bears somehow managed to make the Sayers-Butkus era one of the worst in franchise history. They had only one more winning season together, a 7-6-1 campaign in 1967, before knee injuries ended both their careers in the early 1970s.

The big blow came when Allen left to become coach of the Rams after Sayers' and Butkus' first season. Allen, who assumed he would succeed Halas as coach of the Bears, got tired of waiting for the Old Man's retirement. The Bears missed Allen's coaching skills but were devastated by the loss of his personnel expertise.

A nine-year stretch of poor drafting followed, ending only when the Bears in 1974 hired Jim Finks from the Vikings as general manager.

"One of the problems the Bears had when I got there was the age of a lot of the players," Sayers told Richard Whittingham in his 1991 book, "What Bears They Were." "There were some great ones—Doug Atkins, Bill George, Joe Fortunato, Stan Jones, Herm Lee—but they were about 35 years old then. You see, if you were loyal to the Old Man, he was loyal to you.

"Those guys had earned his respect by what they'd done in the past, which was quite a bit for the Bears. But it probably hurt the Bears in the middle '60s."

Sayers was one of the players Halas treated the best. While the coach viewed his rank-and-file players and even his second-tier standouts as replaceable cogs in the Bears machine, he spared no expense or compliment with true superstars such as Sayers.

"I never said a harsh word to Red Grange or Sid Luckman or Gale Sayers," the coach wrote in "Halas by Halas," his 1979 autobiography. "I spoke harshly to Bronko Nagurski just once, and regretted it ever after."

For Sayers, the respect was mutual.

"When I first saw Mr. Halas I was shocked," he told Whittingham. "You don't think of someone 73 out there coaching. But he was first on and last off. To see this 73-year-old man out there every day right through the season motivated me. He is the only person I could run for 100% on every play."

The big plays kept coming for Sayers until Nov. 10, 1968, when he tore the ACL, MCL and meniscus in his right knee during a game against the 49ers at Wrigley Field. On a toss play to the left, defensive back Kermit Alexander went low to avoid a blocker and slammed his helmet into Sayers' knee.

The Tribune covered the injury like a funeral for a head of state. Markus wrote: "The greatest running back in football history was carried off the field like a dying warrior being borne on his shield. Perhaps he heard the thunderous cheers of the mob, cheers that had so often sped him on his slippy-slidey way to a touchdown, cheers that now said only: 'Thank you, Gale, for the many memories. God be with you.'"

Most feared the end of Sayers' career, but after intense rehabilitation he was ready to resume play by the beginning of the 1969 season. Incredibly, he led the NFL in rushing for a second time, with 1,032 yards.

These yards were different than before, though. They were tougher. Sayers' longest run that season, for a 1-13 team that ranks as the Bears' worst ever, was 28 yards. In the preseason, Packers defensive back Herb Adderley noticed that Sayers was chased down on long runs by the Redskins' Rickie Harris and the Cardinals' Roger Wehrli.

Sayers became a star off the field in 1970, thanks to the TV movie "Brian's Song." The film, with breakout performances from James Caan and Billy Dee Williams, documented Sayers' friendship with fellow running back Brian Piccolo, who died of cancer on June 16, 1970.

Upon receiving the George Halas Courage Award for coming back from his serious knee injury, Sayers made a speech that honored Piccolo.

Sayers concluded by saying: "I love Brian Piccolo, and I'd like all of you to love him too. Tonight, when you hit your knees, please ask God to love him."

By the time Sayers finished, tears flowed from every eye in the banquet hall. A very emotional Lombardi told Sayers afterward, "Gale, you are a great American."

In the 1970 preseason, Sayers was injured again, suffering severe bone bruises to his left knee. He played two games that season and two more painful tries in 1971, totaling 90 yards on

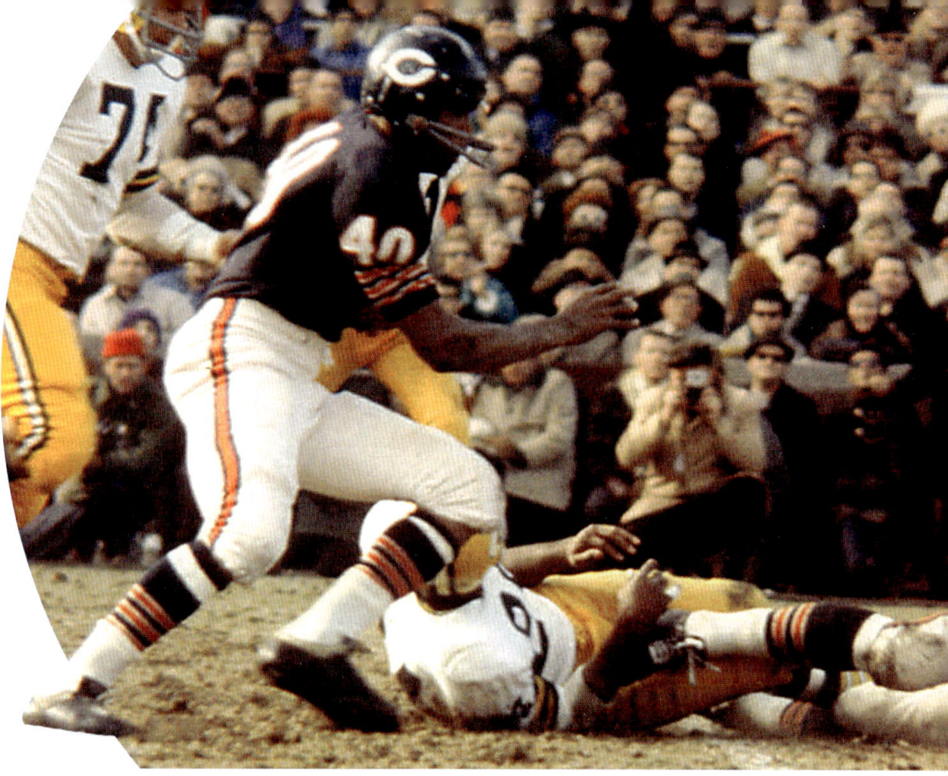

Gale Sayers (40) runs against the Packers in 1969 at Wrigley Field.

36 rushing attempts. He gave it another go in 1972, but after fumbling twice on three carries in an exhibition game against the Cardinals he decided to retire.

Again, the Tribune struck a somber tone. Jerry Shnay wrote: "Sunday, Sept. 10, 1972, was one of the blackest days in Bears history. In a mixture of sadness and broken dreams, the once-magnificent Gale Sayers called it quits after his comeback vision had turned into a nightmare."

Sayers, who worked at a stock brokerage during his career, was well-equipped for life after football. He went back to Kansas to become assistant athletic director in 1973, then served as AD at Southern Illinois from 1976-81. Spurred by his Piccolo speech, he became an in-demand motivational speaker, and he ran his own company, Sayers Computer Source in Mount Prospect, which distributed hardware and software to local businesses. Sayers died Sept. 23, 2020, after a yearslong decline in health that included dementia. He was 77.

Sayers was named to the 1960s All-Decade Team and the NFL's 1994 75th anniversary team, and in 2010 the NFL Network named him the 22nd-best player of all time. In 2014 the Tribune's Don Pierson ranked him the second-best running back in Bears history behind Payton, and in 2017 longtime Cowboys personnel director Gil Brandt, in a column for NFL.com, ranked Sayers the third-best running back ever behind Jim Brown and Payton.

Sayers still holds the NFL career record with 30.6 yards per kickoff return return, just ahead of former Bears returner Cordarrelle Patterson's 30.0. Sayers scored 56 touchdowns—39 rushing, nine receiving, six kick returns and two punt returns—and added a touchdown pass. He ranks fifth in Bears history with 4,956 rushing yards and 13th with 336 points.

When the Bears drafted Payton in 1975, he immediately was compared to Sayers by a fan base desperate for another star running back. The best rushing season by a Bear in the time between the two was quarterback Bobby Douglass' 968 yards in 1972. Other than that, Carl Garrett's 655 in 1973 was the most, and in 1970, '71 and '74 the Bears' leading rushers failed to reach 500 yards.

"It's an honor for me to be compared with Sayers, but there's really no comparison," Payton told the Tribune's Roy Damer on July 12, 1975. "He was my idol. He's the man and he'll always be the man. There will never be another Gale Sayers." ■

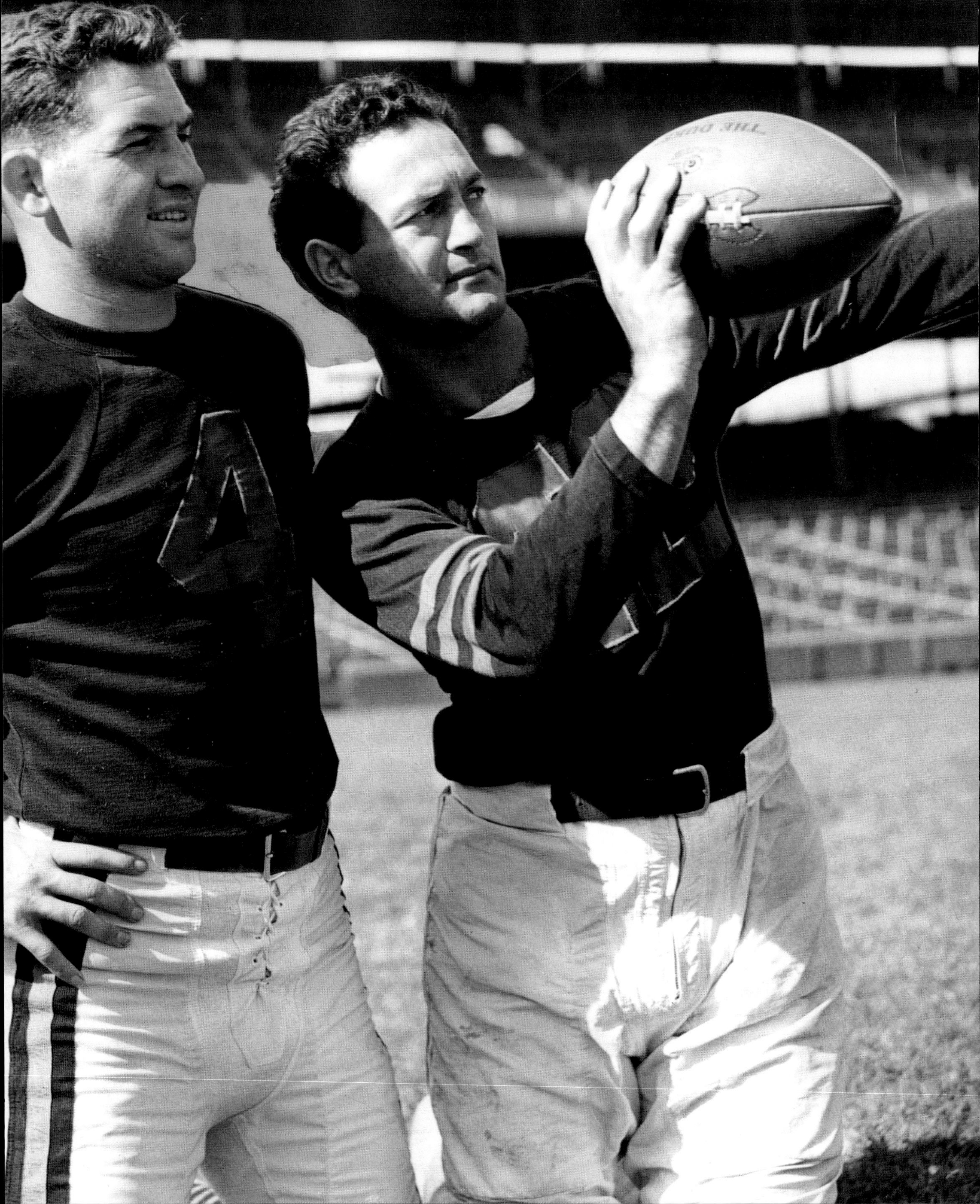

Sid Luckman

42 QUARTERBACK, HALFBACK, DEFENSIVE BACK
1939–50

THE BEARS HAD A rare afternoon off one training camp during their Monsters of the Midway heyday. Quarterback Sid Luckman asked a couple of his teammates, tackle George Connor and halfback Don Kindt, if they would like to take a top-down ride in his new Chrysler.

"Well, you know," Connor said, "when you're down in Rensselaer, Ind., riding in a new convertible was quite a thrill out of the ordinary."

Kindt drove, Connor rode shotgun and in the back seat sat an oiled-up Luckman.

"Sid loved to get tan; he tanned beautifully," Connor told Richard Whittingham in the 1991 book, "What Bears They Were."

Luckman instructed Kindt: "Slow down to 55½ mph. That's where I get my most even tan."

Even in the 1940s, it was good to be a superstar quarterback.

The Bears never have had a better one than Luckman, the only elite quarterback in franchise history. The 6-foot, 197-pound Brooklyn native was voted first-team All-Pro five times in the 1940s. The rest of the Bears quarterbacks have combined to earn that honor three times:

Joey Sternaman in 1924-25 and Johnny Lujack in 1950.

Luckman led the NFL in passing three times; Lujack was the only other Bear to do so, in 1949. Luckman had the league's top passer rating three times, a feat matched only by Ed Brown in 1956 and Bill Wade in 1961. Luckman had league highs in touchdown passes three times. So did Bernie Masterson in 1937 and Lujack in 1949.

When Luckman retired in 1950, he had amassed 14,686 passing yards and 137 touchdown passes, which stood as Bears records until Jay Cutler passed Luckman in yards in 2013 and TD passes in 2015, 65 years after Luckman threw his final pass.

The Bears have won nine championships in their history. Luckman was the quarterback for four of them, in 1940, '41, '43 and '46. In 1943 he won the Joe F. Carr Trophy as the NFL's most valuable player. He was elected to the Pro Football Hall of Fame in 1965.

"Luckman was Mr. Quarterback," Bears coach George Halas wrote in the Tribune on Feb. 3, 1967. "The finest in the history of the game, in my estimation."

Nick Sacrinty (4), left, is given pointers on accuracy by Sid Luckman (42) during a practice session Oct. 16, 1947.

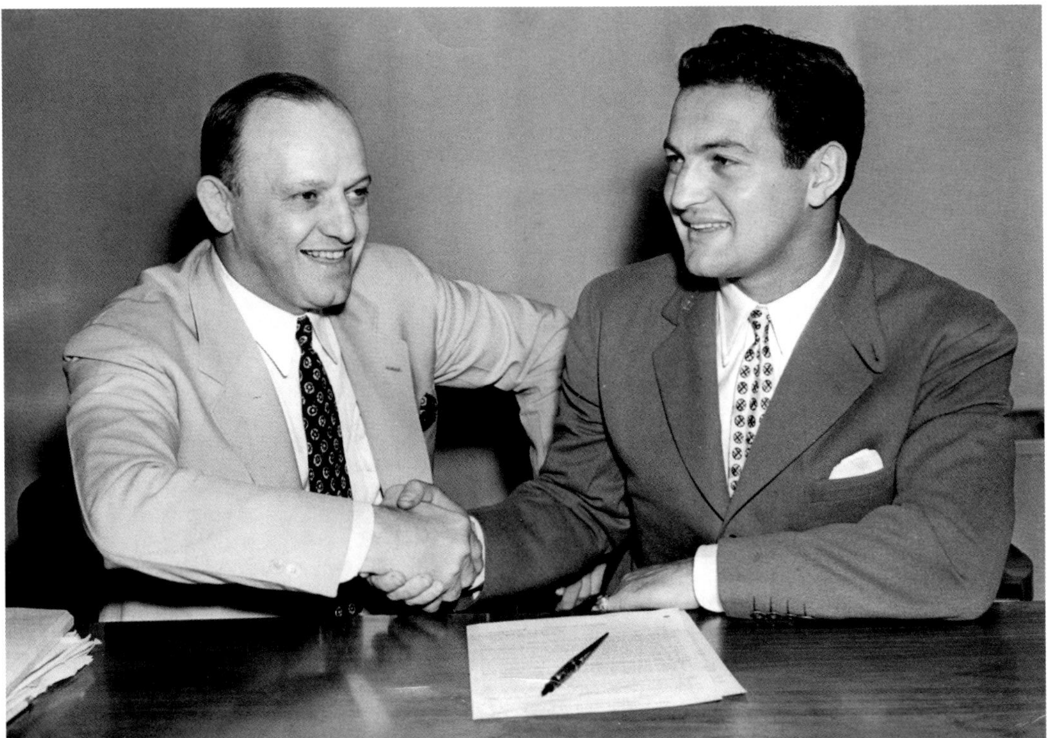

Sid Luckman, right, shakes the hand of team owner George Halas in July 1939 after signing a two-year contract.

Halas wanted to take the T formation to the next level in the 1940s. He needed a player with athleticism, intelligence and leadership ability to do so, and he identified a Columbia halfback as the key to his fortunes.

The T, with a seven-man line, a quarterback and fullback lined up behind center and two halfbacks next to the fullback, was one of the first formations used in football in the late 1800s. It fell out of style after the forward pass was legalized in 1906.

By the 1930s, the single wing was the dominant offense. In that formation, the center snapped the ball to the tailback, who had a fullback, a quarterback and wingback lined up to one side of him in a diagonal line toward the line of scrimmage. The quarterback lined up behind a tackle and usually served as a blocker

Halas brought back the T with help from Ralph Jones, who was Halas' freshman basketball coach at the University of Illinois before replacing him when Halas took three seasons off from coaching in 1930-32.

Meanwhile, University of Chicago coach Clark Shaughnessy, known as "The Father of the Modern T," was experimenting with variations of the offense.

The University of Chicago de-emphasized football in the 1930s, and unable to compete on Saturdays, Shaughnessy began attending Bears games on Sundays. He befriended Halas, and the two dreamed of ways to make the T formation a state-of-the-art scoring weapon.

When the University of Chicago dropped football after the 1939 season, Shaughnessy became head coach at Stanford. In the 1940 season, Stanford won the Rose Bowl 21-13 over Nebraska, and the Bears won the NFL championship with a record-setting 73-0 rout of the Redskins.

Halas and Shaughnessy—who would become the Bears defensive coordinator in the 1950s—had achieved their goal even quicker than they thought possible. The T formation's array of fakes, men in motion, traps, pulls, misdirection plays and play-action passes confused defenses for years.

In "Halas by Halas," the Bears coach's 1979

autobiography, he wrote: "Our astonishing victory and now the Stanford win made everyone in football aware of the benefits made available by the modern T formation with man in motion. . . . Before the decade ended, the (formation) was the basis for all offensive play in football."

As Jeff Davis wrote in "Papa Bear: The Life and Legacy of George Halas" in 2005: "The two coaches had retooled their improved model . . . into a 'boxing' type of offense. The quick openers were the left jabs. The man in motion and backfield faking were the feints. The fullback played to the real 'punch,' the hooks. The pass plays were the unexpected 'sock.'"

The system's ideal quarterback had to have great footwork to navigate the steps, spins and pivots it required to carry out the fakes and handoffs. He also had to be a quick thinker because players on the field still called all the plays. Luckman also was athletic enough not to hurt the team as a defensive back in the days before two-platoon football.

Luckman became Halas' coach on the field, thinking of which plays to call three or four steps ahead of the ones that were taking place on the field.

"He made it a point to find out everything that was going on on the field," halfback Hugh Gallarneau told Whittingham. "If I'd go in motion, he'd say, 'Hugh, who was covering you when you went out in motion?' Or if we spread Kenny Kavanaugh, our left end, out wide, he'd say, 'Kenny, when Hugh goes in motion and you're wide, who's covering you?'

"He would solicit information from all of the players. He wanted to know from (guard) Ray Bray which way he could take a guy, in or out."

Before he perfected the system or even became a quarterback, Luckman had doubts about a future in professional football. He had a good job lined up in Manhattan, and besides, as he told Whittingham: "I, as an Ivy League player, probably was not good enough or could possibly get good enough to play pro football."

Halas, who had traded up to the No. 2 spot in the 1939 draft to take Luckman, traveled to the newlywed's New York apartment to convince him to become a Bear.

Luckman agreed to a $6,000 contract. After typical negotiations with a hot-shot rookie, Halas often would declare that he hadn't spent that much money on a kid fresh out of college since Red Grange. After Luckman agreed to terms, Halas went even further. Papa Bear kissed Luckman's new bride, Estelle, on the cheek, raised a glass of wine and told Luckman: "You and Jesus Christ are the only two people I'd ever pay that much money to."

After the deal was done, Halas told his friend Irv Kupcinet to help Luckman acclimate to Chicago. At the time Kupcinet was a sports writer for the Chicago Daily Times and an NFL referee. After games he officiated, he would interview players and coaches and then hustle to file his game story. Bears opponents accused him of being in the bag for Halas, and it became a running joke that "Kup" got more excited than Halas would when a measurement resulted in a Bears first down.

"I've got a young kid coming from New York who's never been west of the Hudson River," Halas told Kupcinet, according to Whittingham. "He thinks we're all Indians out here."

Luckman soon was the toast of Chicago. He threw a 69-yard touchdown pass against the Giants in his first start, a 16-13 loss in the Bears' seventh game of 1939. Two weeks later, he shined against the powerhouse Packers, who would win the NFL championship that season. Trailing 27-24 late, Luckman led a winning drive that included an 18-yard pass to Eggs Manske, a 45-yard bomb to Bob MacLeod and Bill Osmanski's 10-yard touchdown run for the 30-27 win.

Trips to the NFL championship game followed in the first four years of the 1940s, with the Bears winning titles in 1940, '41, and '43. Luckman, like most of the Bears, served in the military during World War II. He joined the U.S. Merchant Marine, then returned to win a fourth title in 1946. Among the Bears standouts who lost years in their 20s to the war were Luckman, running backs George McAfee, Osmanski and Gallarneau, end Kavanaugh and linemen Bray, Bulldog Turner, Lee Artoe and Ed Kolman.

While Luckman's fame came thanks to his right arm, he made the biggest play of his career with his legs. With the score tied 14-14 in the fourth quarter of the 1946 championship game against the Giants, Luckman ran for a 19-yard touchdown on a play called "Bingo Keep It" that propelled the Bears to a 24-14 win.

"Halas didn't want me to run too much in the regular season," Luckman told Whittingham. "In the championship game, that was another matter. In the middle of the fourth period, I went over to talk to Coach Halas. I said, 'Now?' He knew the play I meant."

"I said 'Now!!'" Halas wrote in his autobiography.

He continued: "Sid called the play. It began exactly as the previous ones. Sid took the ball, pivoted as to hand the ball again to McAfee, who was already driving to the left behind a row of blockers. The Giants went for him. Sid put the ball on his hip, drifted around the right end and made a touchdown. Nobody touched him."

The win at the Polo Grounds was one of many fine performances by Luckman in his hometown. Halas let him have his first start there in 1939, and Luckman responded with his first touchdown pass. In 1943, the Giants held Sid Luckman Day for the hometown hero. Luckman threw a record seven touchdown passes in a 56-7 win.

It was one of the only times Luckman's mother watched him play football. Nervous her son would be injured, Ethel Luckman spent the game yelling at her son: "Please, Sid, please, Sid, give them the ball. Let them run the ball!"

Luckman was not the NFL's first passing star. That honor went to Sammy Baugh, who joined the Redskins in 1937 and made the forward pass a weapon. The brash Texan passed for a league-best 1,127 yards as a rookie and led his team to a 28-21 win over the Bears for the NFL title at Wrigley Field.

"Slingin' Sammy" set the NFL passing record with 1,367 yards in 1940. It was bested by the Packers' Cecil Isbell with 2,021 in 1942, and Luckman topped that total with 2,194 in 1943. Baugh put the mark out of reach with 2,938 in 1947. That record stood for 13 years until Johnny Unitas of the Colts passed for 3,099 yards in 1960.

Baugh was named first-team All-Pro by himself in 1937 and 1940, as was Luckman in 1941, '44 and '47. The two shared the honor in 1942 and '43.

In the 1940s, the superstar passers met three times for the NFL title, with the Bears blowing out the Redskins 73-0 at Griffith Stadium in 1940, the Redskins winning 14-6 at home in 1942 and the Bears bouncing back for a 41-21 win at Wrigley Field in 1943. The Bears also beat the Giants twice for titles in the 1940s, winning 37-9 in 1941 at Wrigley and 24-14 in 1946 at the Polo Grounds.

Through their battles Luckman and Baugh became friends, and after they retired they took turns calling each other the best quarterback of all time.

Halas wrote: "Sammy was the better passer, but Sid was the greatest all-around quarterback."

"Sammy Baugh was the most precise passer I ever played against," Bears end Ed Sprinkle told Davis. "But Sid got the job done. He could play."

After the 1940 season, which ended with Luckman leading the Bears to the largest victory margin in professional football history in the championship game, he asked for a $1,000 bonus. Halas said $250 was the best he could do. But Halas eventually found a way to grant the request. He asked Luckman to report early to 1941 training camp to learn new plays, offering a $750 bonus to do so.

"Sid got the $1,000 bonus he'd asked for," Kupcinet told Whittingham, "but in George's way."

Halas paid Luckman more than any player he had coached, other than Grange's special barnstorming contract. Kupcinet said Luckman's salary peaked at $20,000.

The reason? Halas heard that his rival, Redskins owner George Marshall, was paying Baugh $20,000 per season.

"I don't want any quarterback in this league to get more money than you," Halas told Luckman.

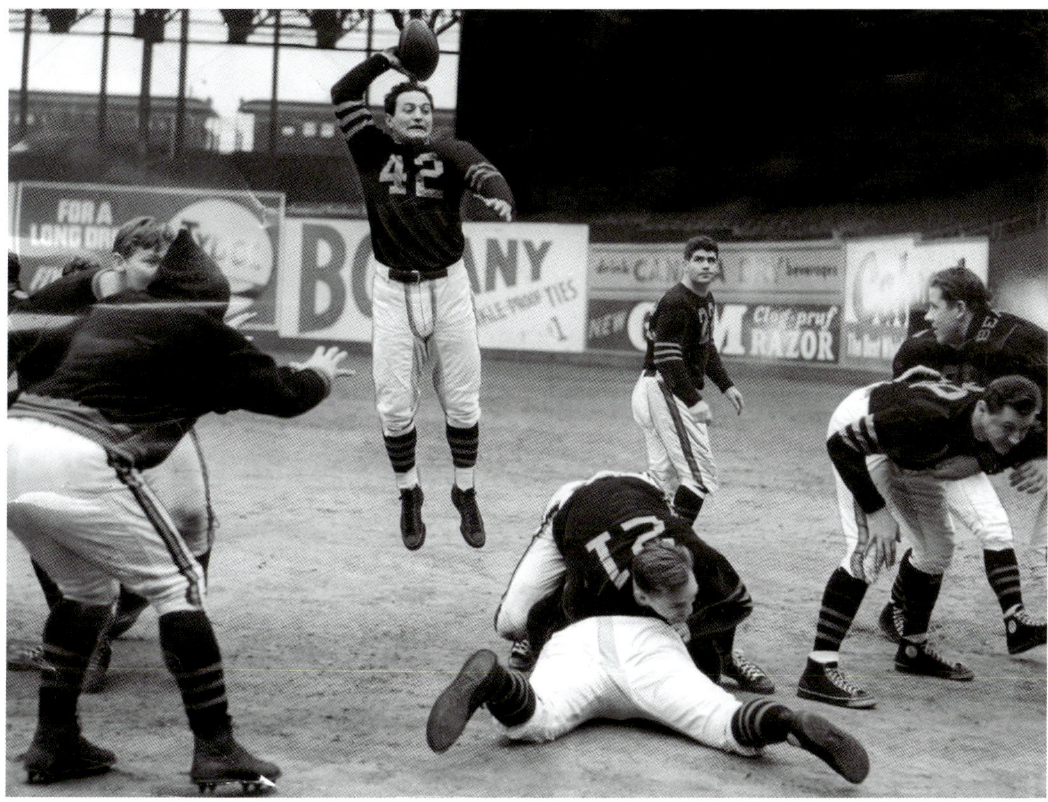

Sid Luckman (42), in his 12th season of professional football, works out with teammates in 1950.

Luckman remained Halas' golden boy for the rest of Papa Bear's life. He turned down a raise from the All-American Football League in 1947, telling Halas: "I was honored and flattered by the offer, but my life is destined to be spent in football with you."

When Halas' wife, Min, died in 1966, Luckman served as a pallbearer. Shortly before Halas' death on Oct. 31, 1983, Luckman, who was standing vigil, leaned over and kissed him on the forehead.

In a letter addressed to Luckman five months before the coach's death, Halas wrote: "'I love you with all my heart.' When I said this to you last night as I kissed you, I realized 44 wonderful years of knowing you were summed up by seven words. My boy, my pride in you has no words."

Luckman was a successful businessman during and after his career. He became wealthy while playing thanks to his dealerships for Chrysler cars and Dumont TVs. In 1946 he bought a half-interest in Cellucraft, a company that manufactured cellophane wrappers for Kraft Foods, Quaker Oats and Sara Lee, among other companies.

After his playing days he volunteered as a Bears assistant coach through 1970. Luckman and wealthy businessman Abram Nicholas Pritzker once offered to buy the Bears from Halas but were rebuffed. On July 5, 1988, Luckman died at 81 of a heart attack in Aventura, Fla.

On Feb. 14, 1951, Halas described Luckman's impact on the Bears and the NFL to the Tribune's Edward Prell.

"In Sid we created a new type of football player," Halas said. "Newspapers switched their attention from star runners to the quarterbacks. It marked a new era for the game. Colleges changed from the single and double wing to the T, using Luckman as their model in molding quarterbacks. In Sid's 12 years with the Bears, football was completely revolutionized." ■

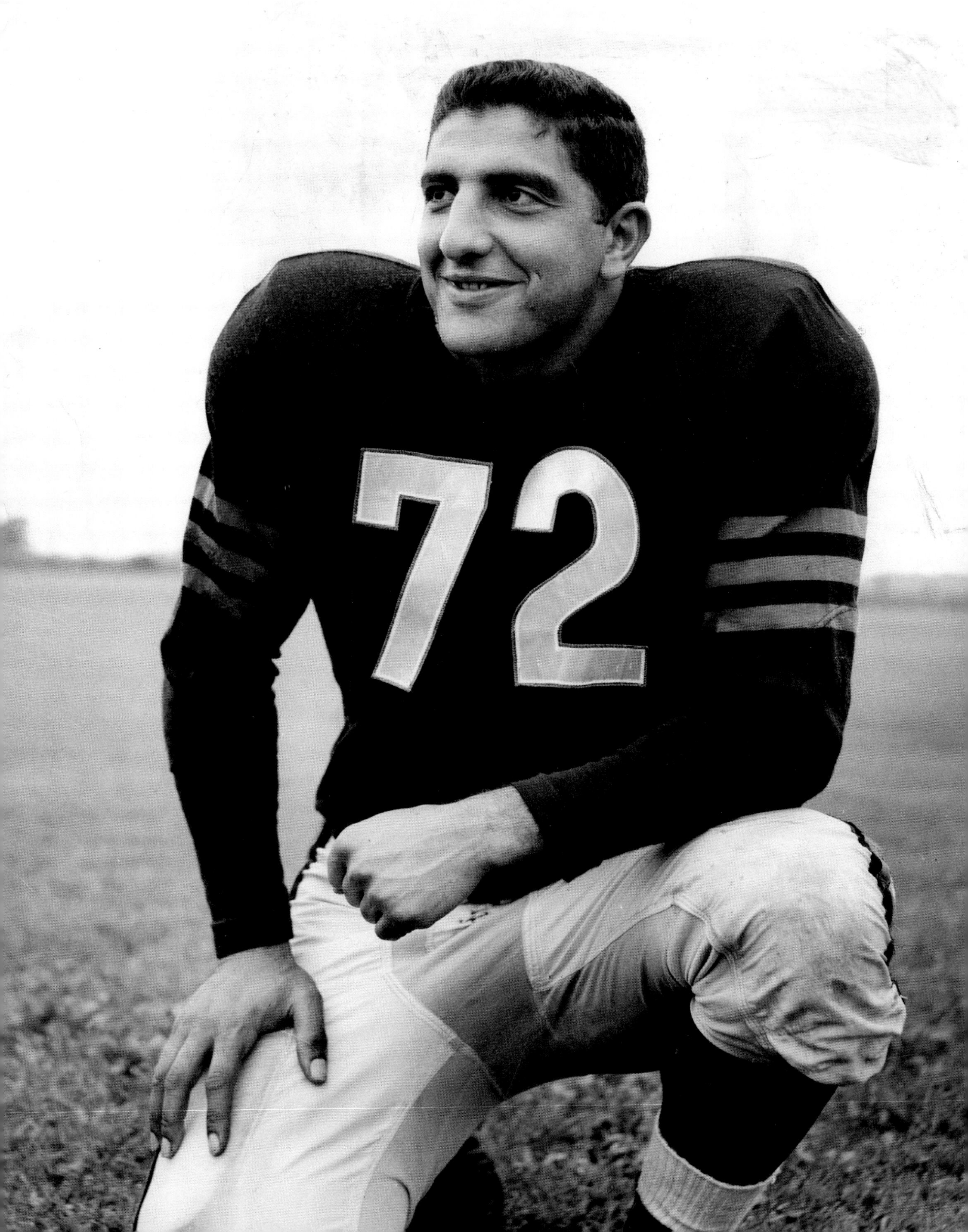

Bill George

72, 61 LINEBACKER, GUARD, DEFENSIVE TACKLE

1952–65

I N 1954 BILL GEORGE suffered the most fortuitous injury in Bears history.

During his first season as the first full-time middle linebacker in NFL history, George wasn't quite sure what to make of his new position. He had to guard against the run and pass equally, and even for the most intelligent player on the team, it sometimes got confusing.

George found himself chasing fakes, leaving his position in the middle of the field open for a fullback to run to or an end to settle in for a pass.

"You know how I finally overcame that weakness?" George told the Tribune's Cooper Rollow on Nov. 2, 1958. "I sprained my ankle. Had to stay where I belonged because I couldn't run fast enough to go anywhere else. And all at once people began telling me I was great."

George started his pro career in 1952 as a middle guard, lined up against the center in a five-man defensive line. His job was to gum up the middle of the line on running plays. On passing plays, he was to hit the center and retreat into coverage.

During a 1954 preseason game, George despaired as the Eagles dropped short pass after short pass into the middle of the field. He believed he could have broken up each one if he didn't have to engage with the center after the snap.

George Connor, George's teammate who five years earlier became the NFL's first outside linebacker, claimed credit for telling George to back away from the line before the snap. Bears coach George Halas and defensive coordinator Clark Shaughnessy also said the idea was theirs.

The way George told it to Rollow on Feb. 6, 1974, he said to Connor during the Eagles game: "Hell, I could break up that pass if I didn't have to hit that offensive center first."

"What are you hitting him for, then?" Connor responded. "Why don't you go for the ball?"

"So the next time the Eagles had a passing situation," George said, "I dropped back and knocked down a pass. The second time they tried it, I intercepted."

Before long, middle linebacker became the NFL's glamour position on defense, with Joe Schmidt of the Lions, Les Richter of the Rams, Sam Huff of the Giants and Ray Nitschke of the

Bill George (72), circa 1953.

"

Packers joining George before the end of the decade as players at the position who would be enshrined in the Pro Football Hall of Fame.

The Bears' legacy is stronger there than at any other position. Of the top 12 in the Tribune's ranking of the 100 best players in team history, four are middle linebackers: George, who played for the Bears from 1952 to '65, Dick Butkus (1965-73), Mike Singletary (1981-92) and Brian Urlacher (2000-12). All four are in the Hall of Fame, with Urlacher joining his three predecessors in Canton, Ohio, in 2018.

George's 14 seasons with the Bears are tied with linebacker Doug Buffone for second-most behind long snapper Patrick Mannelly's 16. George was voted to eight Pro Bowls, and his eight first-team All-Pro selections are the most in Bears history. The Hall of Fame named him to its 1950s All-Decade team. In 2014, the Tribune's Don Pierson ranked George the second-best linebacker in team history behind Butkus.

George Allen was a Bears assistant from 1958 to '65 before becoming head coach of the Rams (1966-70) and Redskins (1971-77). Like most of George's coaches, he was amazed at the linebacker's combination of ability and intelligence.

"Bill George was the smartest defensive player I ever coached," Allen told Rollow and Pierson on Oct. 1, 1982. "He called the defensive signals for the Bears when they were at their best defensively. He studied films, kept a notebook of his own, did his homework every week and always prepared to play his best.

"He practically invented the middle linebacker position and the 4-3 defense."

George served as a bridge between two other all-time great Bears. His first season, 1952, was Bulldog Turner's last. George's last season with the Bears, 1965, was Butkus' first.

The Bears drafted George, an All-American in football and wrestling at Wake Forest, in the second round as a future pick in 1951. From 1949 until the NFL-AFL merger in 1967, teams could pick players with a year of college eligibility remaining and keep their rights until they entered the NFL. Halas used the opportunity

wisely, gaining George, linebacker Joe Fortunato, fullback Rick Casares and quarterback Ed Brown under the rule before they played their senior seasons.

With George at middle guard, the Bears went 5-7 in 1952 and 3-8-1 in '53. After his move to middle linebacker, they went 8-4 in 1954 and '55, then 9-2-1 in '56, a season that ended with a 47-7 loss to the Giants in the NFL championship game at Yankee Stadium.

George returned to the title game in 1963, when the Bears defeated the Giants 14-10 at Wrigley Field as he won his only championship in his 12th season. After the game, George tossed the game ball to Allen, by that point the team's defensive coordinator. With George's old friend Connor conducting locker-room interviews for NBC, the Bears serenaded Allen with a song that created a bit of a stir among the national TV audience.

"Hooray for George! Hooray at last! Hooray for George! He's a horse's ass!"

Bill George—not to be confused with Georges Halas, Connor or Allen—was the first building block of the great 1963 defense that led the Bears to their only championship between 1946 and 1985.

Halas methodically added pieces year after year. He drafted Fortunato in 1952, traded for defensive end Doug Atkins in '55, drafted defensive tackle Earl Leggett in '57, drafted safety Richie Petitbon and traded for linebacker Larry Morris in '59, picked up safety Rosey Taylor as an undrafted free agent and cornerback Dave Whitsell off the Lions' scrap heap in '61 and drafted cornerback Bennie McRae and defensive end Ed O'Bradovich in '62.

In the final move to complete the championship unit, Allen switched 10-year veteran Stan Jones from offensive guard to defensive tackle before the 1963 season.

The Bears coaches—Halas and defensive coordinators Shaughnessy and Allen—always were comfortable adding wrinkles to their defense because they knew George could handle almost any responsibility. He also had a way of explaining complex schemes in a manner his teammates could understand.

"Shaughnessy was . . . a guru, a genius," Jones said in "Papa Bear: The Life and Legacy of George Halas," Jeff Davis' 2005 biography. "It was like having Albert Einstein work with first-year algebra students. . . . He'd be up there breaking chalk and writing up all those things. Bill George was the one who interpreted what he was doing."

Rollow wrote: "Shaughnessy has equipped the Bears with some 300 defenses—six basic alignments and approximately 50 variations of each. George is the only member of the squad who knows the assignment of every player on every variation."

O'Bradovich, 11 years younger than George, remembered in John Mullin's 2003 book, "Tales from the Chicago Bears Side-lines," that the linebacker's instincts and ability to read an offense regularly made his teammates look good.

"He could think right with (Colts quarterback) Johnny Unitas," O'Bradovich said. "Unitas would be calling an audible and George'd be yelling, 'OB, OB, jump inside, jump inside, they're coming inside!'

"Sure as (expletive), I'd jump inside the tackle or tight end and make the tackle and look great. He did that all the time."

George's intelligence made him the perfect prototype for a middle linebacker. His physical attributes also helped. His strength at 6-foot-2 and 237 pounds helped him shed blockers in the run game, and his long arms helped him bat down passes and reach for his 18 career interceptions.

In Richard Whittingham's 1991 book, "What Bears They Were," Jones said: "Somebody once said Bill George had the cross-build between a pelican and a gorilla. He had these enormous shoulders and long arms."

The way George played middle linebacker still provides the template for how it is played today. So do his interviews, in which he always was sure to thank the defensive linemen who played in front of him, which for his 1958 interview with Rollow included Fred Williams, Bill Bishop, Jack Hoffman and Atkins.

"Those guys make my assignment simple," George said. "They strip all interference away from the ball carrier, leaving me with the easy job: making the tackle."

Joe Marconi played against George from 1956 to '61 with the Rams and with him from 1962 to '65 with the Bears. The fullback called George one of the best players he competed against in his 11-year career.

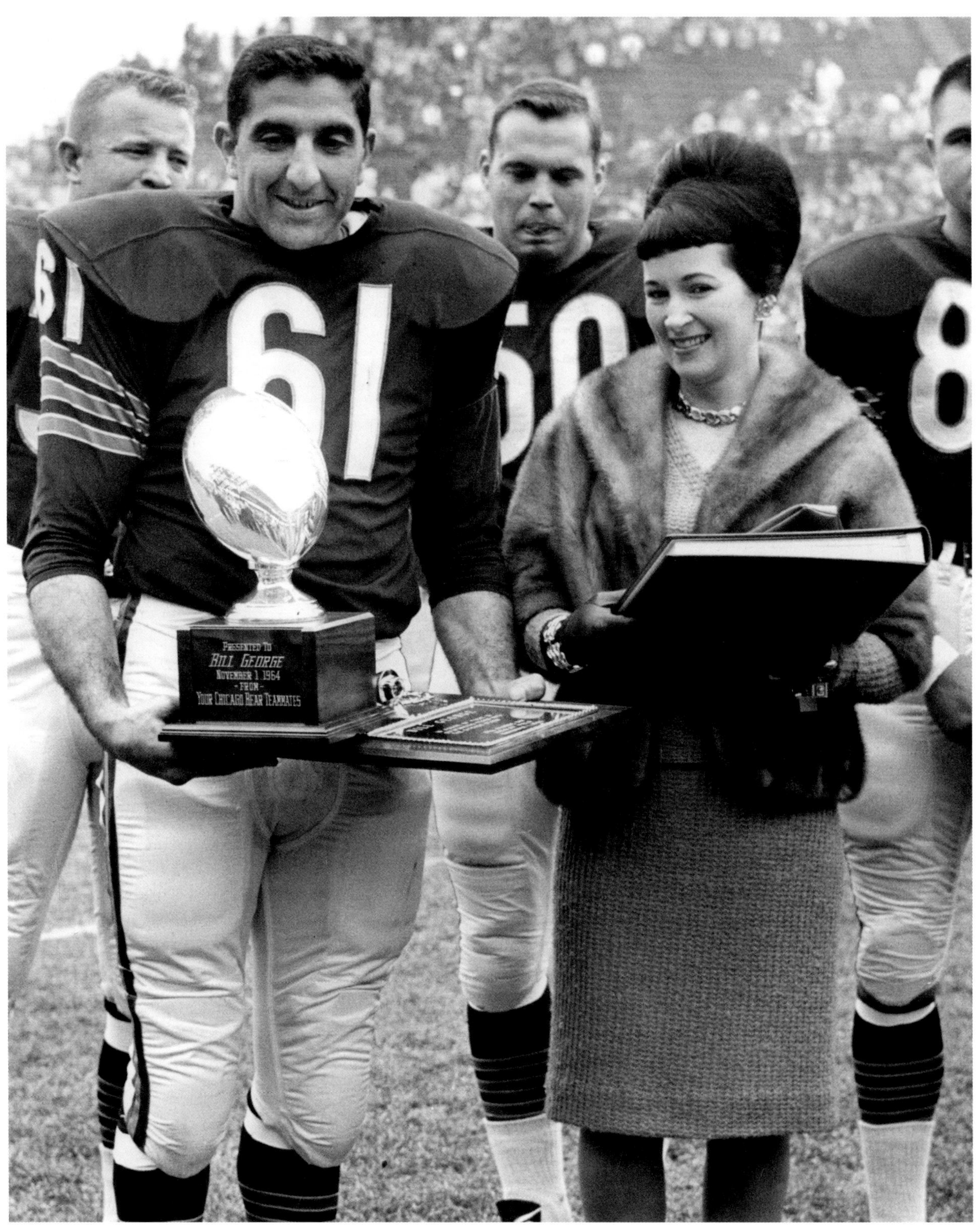

Bill George (61) is honored by friends and fans Nov. 1, 1964, before a game against Dallas at Wrigley Field.
George accepted a trophy from teammates as his wife beamed at his side.

"(Rams coach) Sid Gillman couldn't put in enough offensive plays to stay away from Mr. George," Marconi told Rollow and Pierson. "In fact, our pass protection was called George protection."

Marconi was one of many players from western Pennsylvania who went on to play in the NFL. He said George, a native of Waynesburg, Pa., was "everybody's hero."

George always liked to say: "All the good players don't come from Pennsylvania. Just all the great players."

While George and Connor were innovators on the field as pioneers of modern linebacker play, off the field they blazed a trail to just about every Greek restaurant located in an NFL city.

"We kidded George about being Greek, and he'd get furious," Connor told Davis. "'I'm no (expletive) Greek!' he'd scream."

After an exhibition game in Little Rock, Ark., Connor took George to "the best Greek restaurant in town" and told the owner George's nickname was "The Golden Greek."

"I said he was sort of shy, but he sure was one hell of a guy. The owner came out during dinner and poured us a glass of wine. 'Opaa! To my countryman, the Golden Greek!'

"Everyone in the restaurant stood up and cheered. Then the owner turned to Bill: 'This one is on me, my friends. You don't pay for a thing.'

"After that, when we went on the road, Bill and I always went to the best Greek place in town. Never paid a nickel for anything when I was with the Golden Greek."

George was ferocious on the field but mostly amiable off it. He did speak his mind, however, without regard to a listener's feelings. Two of his favorite targets were Huff, who he felt didn't measure up to the rest of the league's great middle linebackers, and players from Notre Dame, who he felt received preferential treatment from the press.

Huff became a national sensation when he was wired for sound during a game for a 1960 TV special titled, "The Violent World of Sam Huff." When asked by Sports Illustrated what he thought about the program, George said: "If they're really going to do it right, they ought to get Joe Schmidt to play the part of Huff."

In 1975, George was fired from WBBM-TV's Bears broadcasts, on which he served as color commentator to Brent Musburger's play-by-play. His offense was joking that defensive tackle Mike McCoy had to take a pay cut when he joined the Packers from Notre Dame.

The Bears honored George on Nov. 1, 1964, presenting him with a new car and a color TV before they played the Cowboys at Wrigley Field as Mayor Richard J. Daley proclaimed it "Bill George Day" in Chicago. George tore knee ligaments in the first quarter and missed the final eight games of that season. In 1965, he lost his starting position to Butkus.

George played a final season with the Rams in 1966, following Allen after he became a head coach for the first time. George coached the Bears linebackers for one season under coach Abe Gibron in 1972, then returned to his business as a manufacturer's representative.

George was elected to the Hall of Fame in 1974. He said he could not believe it when he received the news.

"When I got a call from Canton," he told Rollow on Feb. 6, 1974, "I figured Fred Williams was broke down and needed some money."

George died in a car accident just south of Rockford, when his vehicle collided with a tractor-trailer. The semi, trying to avoid George's car, crashed into another automobile, killing its driver as well.

Williams paid George a posthumous compliment that undoubtedly would have made "The Golden Greek" smile.

"He was the finest football player I've ever seen," the former Bears defensive tackle told Rollow and Pierson. "I played with Sam Huff two years at Washington after I left the Bears, and there just wasn't any comparison between the two." ■

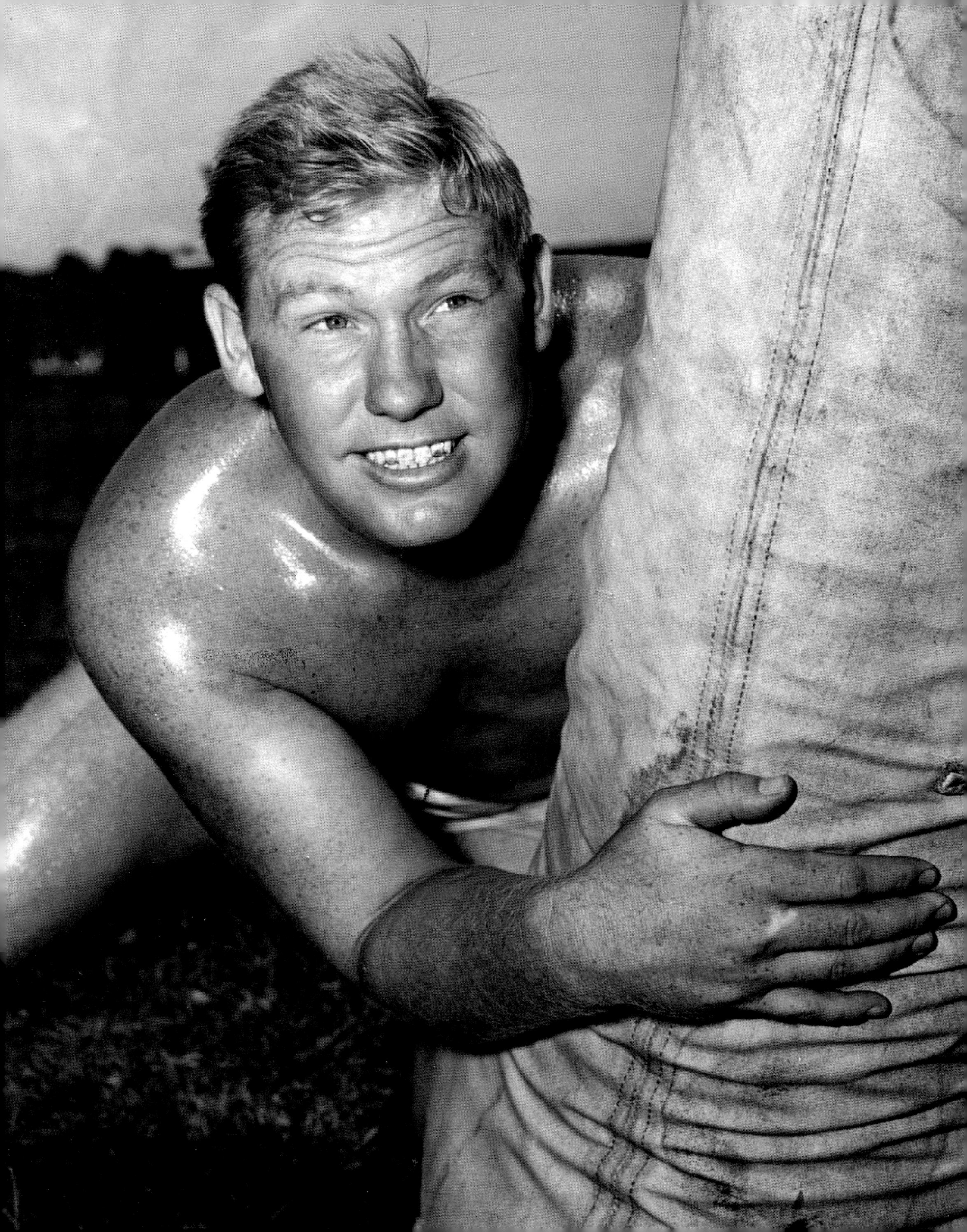

Bulldog Turner

66 CENTER, TACKLE, LINEBACKER, GUARD

1940–52

BULLDOG TURNER RETURNED an interception 24 yards for a touchdown for one of 11 trips the Bears took to the end zone in their record-setting 73-0 win against the Redskins in the 1940 NFL championship game.

It was one of four interceptions Turner made in five championship games as the Monsters of the Midway dynasty won titles in 1940, '41, '43 and '46 and lost in the championship game in '42.

None of those plays—or any of the other highlights of his sterling 13-year career—exemplified who Turner was as much as a botched extra point late in that 73-0 rout on Dec. 8, 1940, at Washington's Griffith Stadium.

In the days before netting behind the goal posts, extra points and field goals that were kicked into the stands were lost to the fans. As the Bears kept scoring that afternoon, they ran out of game balls and began using the beaten-up ones they used for practice. Coach George Halas instructed Turner, the team's All-Pro center and linebacker who handled long snaps, to intentionally misfire an extra-point snap so the Bears wouldn't lose another ball.

"I told Halas I wasn't going to make a bad snap, not in no championship game," Turner said in his Texas drawl 47 years later to the Tribune's Sam Smith on June 7, 1987. "Hell, I never made a bad pass in my life."

Rebuffed, Halas instead told his holder to mishandle the snap. After that, the Bears started passing for their extra points, going 1-for-2 on one-point conversions after their final two touchdowns.

Less than his best effort was unacceptable under any circumstances to Turner, one of the best players in football history. Turner was the kind of star who transcended time. Those who watched him play say he could have been a star during any era of the NFL, all the way to the 21st century.

At 6-foot-2 and 240 pounds, Turner was large for his era, when most players watched their weight so they could play a full 60 minutes. He was fast too. It is said that while at Hardin-Simmons University in Abilene, Texas, Turner once ran a 100-yard dash in 10.8 seconds—in full football gear.

Turner's intelligence set him apart. The son of a cattle rancher and a school teacher from tiny Dunn, Texas, Turner graduated from

Clyde "Bulldog" Turner (66), circa 1942.

Man, he'd run somebody down on the sideline and it sounded like a horse hitting a wall.

—DICK SCHWEIDLER, BEARS HALFBACK

Sweetwater High School at 16 and Hardin-Simmons with a journalism degree at 20. He not only memorized all the plays in Halas' playbook and all their variations, he knew what each player was supposed to do in each one, and he was more than willing to share his expertise.

Linebacker Bill George's eight first-team All-Pro selections are ahead of Turner and Mike Singletary's seven for the most in Bears history. George, whose first season, 1952, was Turner's last, told the Tribune's David Condon on Nov. 3, 1965: "I'm telling you, I learned more from Bulldog Turner in a short walk up to the line of scrimmage than I learned in four years of college football."

Halas, one of the hardest-driving coaches of that or any era, found himself constantly being pushed to improve by Turner.

"Let's use this instead of 43, George," Turner suggested to Halas at one practice. "That 43 is old stuff."

Turner's enthusiasm for learning new plays and systems rubbed off on his talented teammates and was one of the major reasons every other team played catch-up to the Bears in the 1940s.

The Tribune's William Fay wrote on Aug. 10, 1946: "Any play the Bears mastered was old stuff. They would urge Halas to modify or discard plays not yet used in a game.

"'Why don't you guys work crossword puzzles or learn gin rummy and leave my offense alone,' Halas would complain, but never seriously, because it was the Bears' enthusiasm for perfecting the T formation that made them champions."

Turner excelled at every aspect of football. He was regarded in his time as the best center in league history. As a linebacker, he led the league with eight interceptions in 1942, when the average team threw 20 passes per game. When the Bears were running low on running backs because of ejections during a typically nasty game against the crosstown Cardinals on Dec. 3, 1944, Bears coach Luke Johnsos switched Turner to halfback. On the only carry of his career, Turner burst through the line for a 48-yard touchdown, finishing off a 49-7 win at Comiskey Park.

His favorite play came on Oct. 26, 1947. Turner returned an interception 96 yards for a touchdown, showcasing his speed, agility and power as he weaved and plowed his way through the Redskins. For the last few yards he carried on his back Sammy Baugh, whom Turner had intercepted in the 1940 title game and who was a few years ahead of him at Sweetwater High.

Like many Texans of the era, including Baugh, Turner was brash and bold on and off the field. During Bobby Layne's one year as a backup quarterback for the Bears in 1948, before he became an All-Pro and title-winning quarterback with the Lions, Layne and Turner brought a little Texas flair to Chicago.

In Richard Whittingham's 1991 book, "What Bears They Were," teammate Don Kindt recalled: "Bobby got a party going. He got some gals, and he was up on the bar dancing and singing and raising all kinds of hell. He and Bulldog Turner were singing all these Texas songs. Finally Bobby and Bulldog decided they had to go take a leak, but the men's room was crowded, so they went outside. . . . The police caught them and took them over to the station house.

"The next day the Chicago Tribune ran a picture of them in jail. Bulldog had a roll of bills in his hands, which he was waving around. And don't think Halas didn't fine their fannies after he saw that."

Turner was one of Halas' all-time favorites, so the coach reacted with amusement rather than disappointment when a story of his Bulldog's misbehavior made it to his desk.

In his 1979 autobiography, "Halas by Halas," the coach wrote: "Bulldog Turner provided so much excitement on and off the field. There is a story that one night Bulldog fell from a third-story window of a hotel. An awning broke the fall. As Bulldog brushed himself off, a policeman ran up. 'What happened?' he asked. 'I don't know,' Bulldog is supposed to have replied. 'I just got here myself.'"

Turner employed the help of defensive end Ed Sprinkle, one of the toughest Bears ever and a fellow graduate of Hardin-Simmons, to keep him out of trouble after hours. In return, Turner taught Sprinkle how to carry himself as an NFL player.

"Bulldog influenced me more than anybody," Sprinkle told Whittingham. "He always tried to impress upon me that we were The World Champion Chicago Bears."

While Halas regretted trading Layne until the day he died, Turner joined his team thanks to some keen sleuthing by Papa Bear.

Even though Turner played at a small college, his talent was no secret by the time of the 1940 draft. In fact, Lions owner George A. Richards, who owned the No. 6 pick, paid Turner between $100 and $200 to tell other teams he wasn't planning to play pro football. When

Halas received a questionnaire from Turner that said as much, he became suspicious. Why would a player who wasn't interested in continuing his career even send back the form?

The Lions botched the situation all around. Their coach, "Gloomy Gus" Henderson, thinking no lineman would be picked in the 10-player first round, went against Richards' orders and selected USC quarterback Doyle Nave. Halas, picking next, shouted Turner's name before the Lions could reconsider their pick. Richards fired Henderson for the miscue, and Henderson responded by revealing Richards' pre-draft payment to Turner. The Lions were fined $5,000 for tampering, and Nave ended up skipping out on the NFL to become a cinematographer.

The Bears' 1965 first-round haul of Dick Butkus and Gale Sayers is well-known, but the team did almost as well in 1940. Besides Turner at No. 7, the Eagles picked halfback George McAfee for the Bears at No. 2 to complete an earlier trade. Turner and McAfee were inducted into the Pro Football Hall of Fame on the same day in 1966.

Turner was a revelation right away, and throughout his career. With all the great players the team had in the 1940s, he was the one they measured themselves against.

Joe Osmanski, a fullback like his brother, Bears standout Bill Osmanski, was trying to make the team in 1946. During a practice, Joe was waylaid by a brutal hit from Turner.

In his Sept. 19, 1947, Tribune column, Arch Ward wrote: "Joe started walking away from the huddle, which was the only tipoff that he was on Queer Street. When he returned to the group he asked the quarterback to give him the ball again on the same play."

"I wanted to find out right away if I could make it in the pro game," Joe Osmanski told Ward. "And I knew if I could stand two successive bumps from the Bulldog I'd get along."

"Sure enough," Ward wrote, "they barged into each other again and Joe survived."

Later that year, in a story relayed in his autobiography by Halas—who may or may not have remembered the younger Osmanski's first name—Turner stood up for his new teammate.

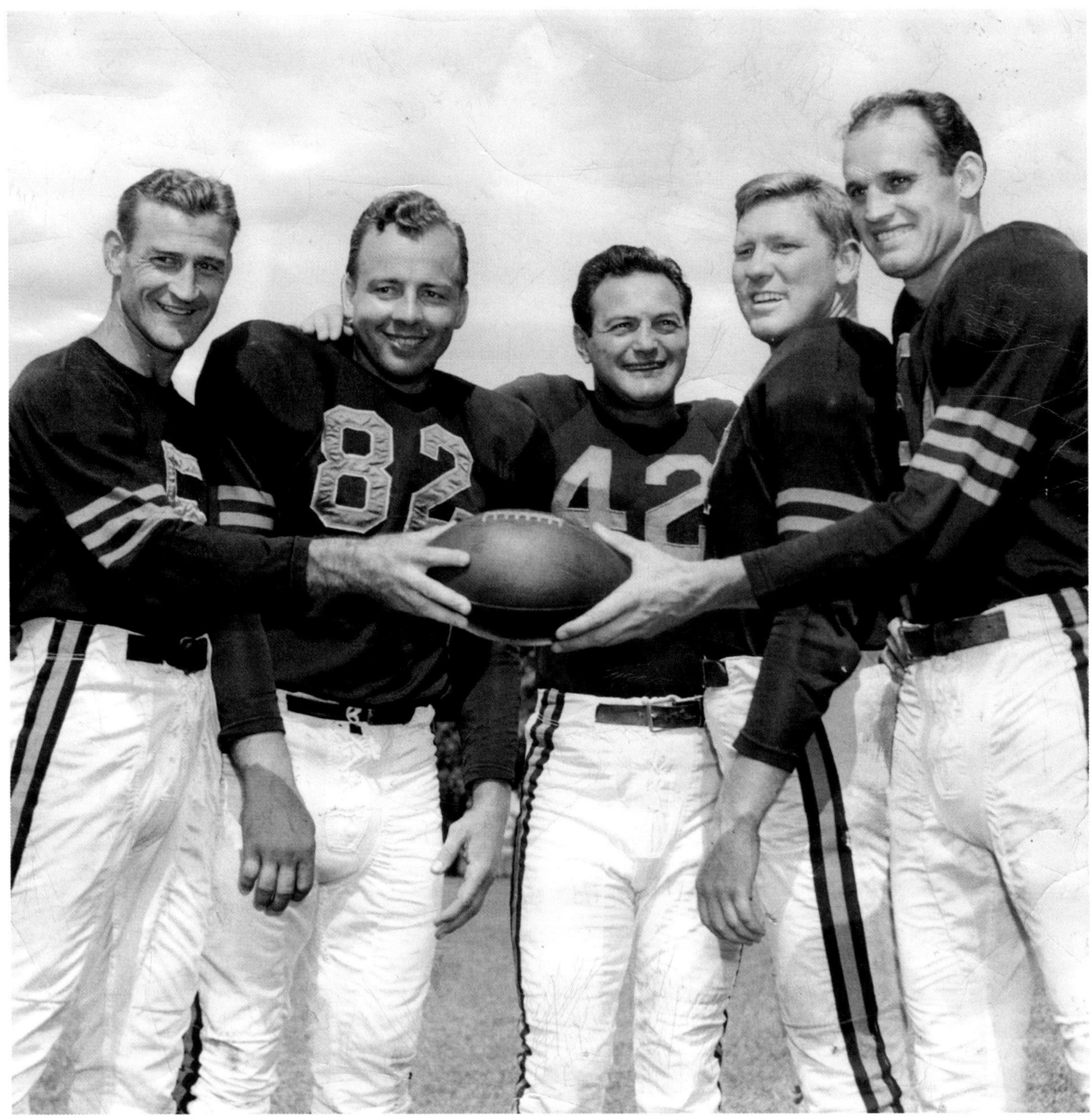

In 1949, five players remained from the 1940 championship squad: George McAfee (5), from left, Ray Bray (82), Sid Luckman (42), Bulldog Turner (66) and Ken Kavanaugh (51).

"One day a player jumped on Bill Osmanski's brother after he was down, breaking his back," Halas wrote. "Bill told the player he did it deliberately. He replied, 'That's part of football.' Bulldog Turner overheard. On the next punt Bulldog hit the guy so hard he was carried off."

Opponents respected Turner just as much as his teammates did. Gary D'Amato and Cliff Christl's 1997 book, "Mudbaths and Bloodbaths: The Inside Story of the Bears-Packers Rivalry," is filled with Packers and Bears paying homage to one of the best players either team has employed.

"I think I got hit the hardest in my life by Bulldog up in Green Bay," Packers fullback Don Perkins said. "It was just a dive play. . . . He hit me from the blind side; I did not see him. He put me in the nickel seats, I'll tell you."

Dick Schweidler, a Bears halfback in 1946, remembered: "Man, he'd run somebody down on the sideline and it sounded like a horse hitting a wall."

After helping lead the Bears to championships in three of his first four years in the league, Turner, like 19 of the 28 players on the 1943 roster, left for the military the next year during World War II. He joined the Air Force but did not see battle action, instead playing for the service football squad. Halas, who had enjoyed a similar situation during World War I, reenlisted in the Navy at age 48. Feeling like he wasn't really a part of the First World War, Halas requested and received an assignment in the Pacific theater.

When Halas and his full squad returned in 1946, it was the most relaxed environment Halas ever kept as a coach.

"Having been in the service 39 months, I knew my veterans would be fed up with petty regulations," the coach wrote. "When spring camp opened, I announced all rules were scrapped. Bears were men, responsible men, self-disciplined men, and would look after themselves."

Halas knew that, with his Bulldog back, he didn't have to be the one to push his players.

The Tribune's Fay wrote of a typical training camp practice on Aug. 10, 1946: "Along about 4:30, when the coaches retired to the beer room, Turner grabbed a football and yelled, 'Let's go.' . . . (Quarterback Sid) Luckman ran them through the T repertoire until 5 o'clock."

The reunited Bears won another NFL title, 24-14 against the Giants at the Polo Grounds.

Turner is one of six Bears players to win four championships. He, Luckman, Bill Osmanski, George Wilson and Ray McLean did it in 1940, '41, '43 and '46. Hall of Fame guard George Musso, whom some of the 1940s players mistook for a coach upon meeting him, won titles in 1933, '40, '41 and '43.

During those championship runs, Luckman told D'Amato and Christl, "Whenever we were in trouble and needed 1 yard, I'd give the ball to George McAfee or Hugh Gallarneau and they'd hit right off Bulldog's position, and I don't ever remember him failing."

Turner announced his retirement in 1952, but Halas convinced him to return as an assistant coach who would play only occasionally. That plan went by the wayside when the Bears needed a right tackle; Turner started all 12 games there.

He spent four more seasons with the Bears as an assistant. In 1962 Turner became head coach of the New York Titans of the American Football League. The team was sold the next year, changed its name to the Jets, fired Turner after one season, and replaced him with Weeb Ewbank.

Turner retired to his farm in Texas, where he raised racehorses and Hereford cattle. Health problems for Turner and his wife, Gladys, drained their savings, and in the 1980s his condition became a rallying point for players who were active before the NFL pension system was implemented in 1959.

While trying to make a living farming, he told the Tribune's Smith in 1987: "At 68, what else is there to do? Its kind of like riding a tiger. It's not great, but it's a hell of a lot worse if you try to get off."

In 1993, the pre-1959 players finally received their first pension checks from the league. Clyde Douglas Turner, who helped the league grow for 13 years as one of the best players ever to buckle a chinstrap, died of lung cancer at 79 in 1998 in Gatesville, Texas.

"Bulldog Turner is one of the greatest athletes who ever played in the National Football League," Luckman told D'Amato and Christl. "In my honest-to-God opinion, I don't think there ever was a greater football player." ■

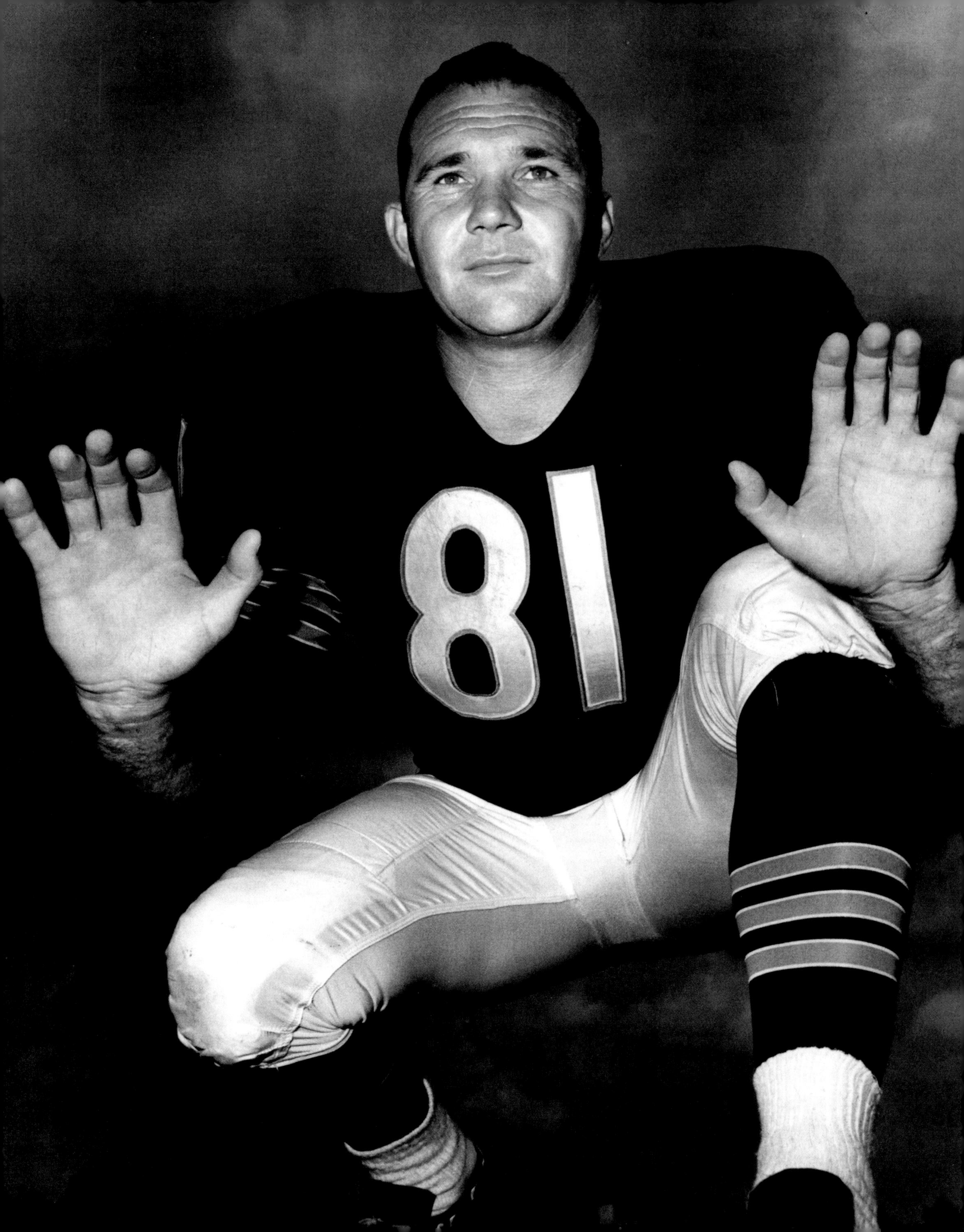

Doug Atkins

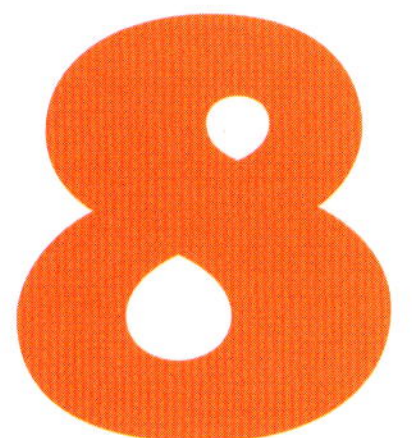

83, 81 DEFENSIVE END
1955–66

FOR 17 YEARS, NFL players lived by one rule concerning Doug Atkins, the 6-foot-8, 257-pound freak of nature who played with the Bears for 12 of those seasons.

Don't make him mad.

"We used to hope somebody would hold him," Rick Casares, a fullback for the Bears from 1955-64, once said. "The next play you would see guys flying around like King Kong had gotten a hold of them."

The Tribune's Don Pierson pointed out that Atkins was roughly the same size as LeBron James, and that the defensive end he replaced with the Bears, Ed Sprinkle, was 6-1 and 206 pounds.

Like James, Atkins possessed freakish athleticism. He led his high school basketball team to the 1949 Tennessee state championship, played football and basketball at Tennessee and finished second place at the 1952 SEC track and field meet with a high jump of 6-foot-6. Atkins was perhaps the strongest man in the NFL. He certainly was the only defensive lineman able to leap over an offensive lineman or fullback to get to the quarterback, a move he made several times per season.

While Atkins resembled James as an athlete, thankfully for the rest of the NFL he didn't quite have the motor of the man he replaced.

"If he'd had the temperament of Ed Sprinkle, they would have had to bar him from football," Bears tackle Bill Bishop said in Richard Whittingham's 1991 book, "What Bears They Were."

Pierson also pointed out that Atkins was the one superstar who left the league's other legends in awe. In 2002, when Pierson helped elect Bears defensive lineman Dan Hampton into the Pro Football Hall of Fame, the writer, Hampton and his presenter, Ed O'Bradovich, another former Bears defensive lineman and a teammate of Atkins, attended the luncheon for Hall of Famers, presenters and electors. Their table included some of pro football's toughest all-time players: Merlin Olsen, Bob St. Clair, Jack Youngblood and Dante Lavelli.

"All they did for most of the meal was tell stories about Doug Atkins, literally a legend among legends," Pierson wrote on Jan. 3, 2016.

The tales about Atkins, who played for the Bears from 1955 to 1966, have taken a life of their own through the years. It is hard to tell

Doug Atkins (81) played on eight Pro Bowl teams and was elected to the Hall of Fame in 1982.

the facts from the embellishments and exaggerations as his improbable actions seem to have become more outlandish with each telling.

A few of the most repeated:

— Atkins, always trying to figure out new ways to skip practice, once bewildered his teammates and coaches by running around the practice field in shorts, a T-shirt and a new helmet with no face mask or chin strap, running in crazy patterns, sometimes with his long arms spread wide like an airplane's wings. Bears coach George Halas, Atkins' constant foil, asked him what in the hell he was doing. Atkins replied: "Breaking in my helmet."

— An assistant coach noticed Atkins missing from practice one day at training camp in Rensselaer, Ind., and finally located him in the coaches' crow's nest, shooting pigeons with a rifle.

— Atkins used that same rifle to stifle a teammate's loud music on the floor above him in the dorms at St. Joseph's College. In one version of the story, Atkins shouted from below to turn it down, then when the player failed to comply he fired a shot through the ceiling. In another version, Atkins walked upstairs, knocked on the door, walked into the teammate's room and shot the radio.

— Safety Richie Petitbon was one of the teammates Atkins invited to the parties he held in his dorm room. The coaches would not conduct bed checks on Atkins because of the pit bull named Rebel he brought to camp and, according to Petitbon, trained to kill.

"He'd get himself three or four guys in there and you'd drink until he let you go," Petitbon told Pierson on July 28, 1978. The other players would become captives in the room of Atkins, who often did not have to practice in the morning because of injury, and sometimes he would keep his teammates there until 3 a.m. If a player tried to leave Atkins' room before he declared the party over, Rebel would stand at attention and start growling. Petitbon thought he could escape by saying he had to go to the restroom. Atkins instructed him to use the dorm-room window.

"So I go out the window, sit down, and listen to some more hillbilly music," Petitbon said.

— Halas and Atkins argued over a bottle of Coca-Cola at halftime of a game that the Bears won with an improbable second-half comeback. The ruckus in the locker room caused reporters to credit Halas with a rousing pep talk that led to the victory. Instead, the septuagenarian Halas and the 6-8 Atkins were playing tug of war over a glass bottle of Coke.

In one version of the story, Atkins grabbed one of the Cokes that Halas had specially prepared for him with whiskey. In another, Halas was upset because Atkins grabbed the beverage from the cooler that was intended for after the game, not halftime.

— One night O'Bradovich went into Atkins' dorm room and found him playing darts. O'Bradovich grabbed a dart from Atkins' hand, but before he could toss it, Atkins tossed him. He lifted his 6-foot-3, 255-pound teammate over his head and "threw him down on the floor like a sack of potatoes," John Mullin wrote in his 2003 book, "Tales from the Chicago Bears Sidelines."

"That was it for the darts," O'Bradovich told Mullin. "I learned damn quick right there. Don't interrupt the Big Fella when he's playing darts."

— Atkins once ran into an Eagles player at a bar after an exhibition game. An argument ensued, and Atkins supposedly picked up the player and pressed him against the ceiling with one hand while drinking his beer with the other.

— Upon learning that beer is fattening, Atkins switched to martinis. An unnamed New Orleans sports writer told Mike Downey of the Los Angeles Times on Jan. 24, 1986, that he once witnessed Atkins consume a meal of 45 pieces of fried chicken and two pitchers of martinis.

— During one training camp, a few of the Bears' wallets went missing, and the players started referring to the thief as "The Phantom." Before Rebel's time in Rensselaer, coaches still made bed checks on Atkins, and when Halas stepped into Atkins' room with his flashlight, Atkins

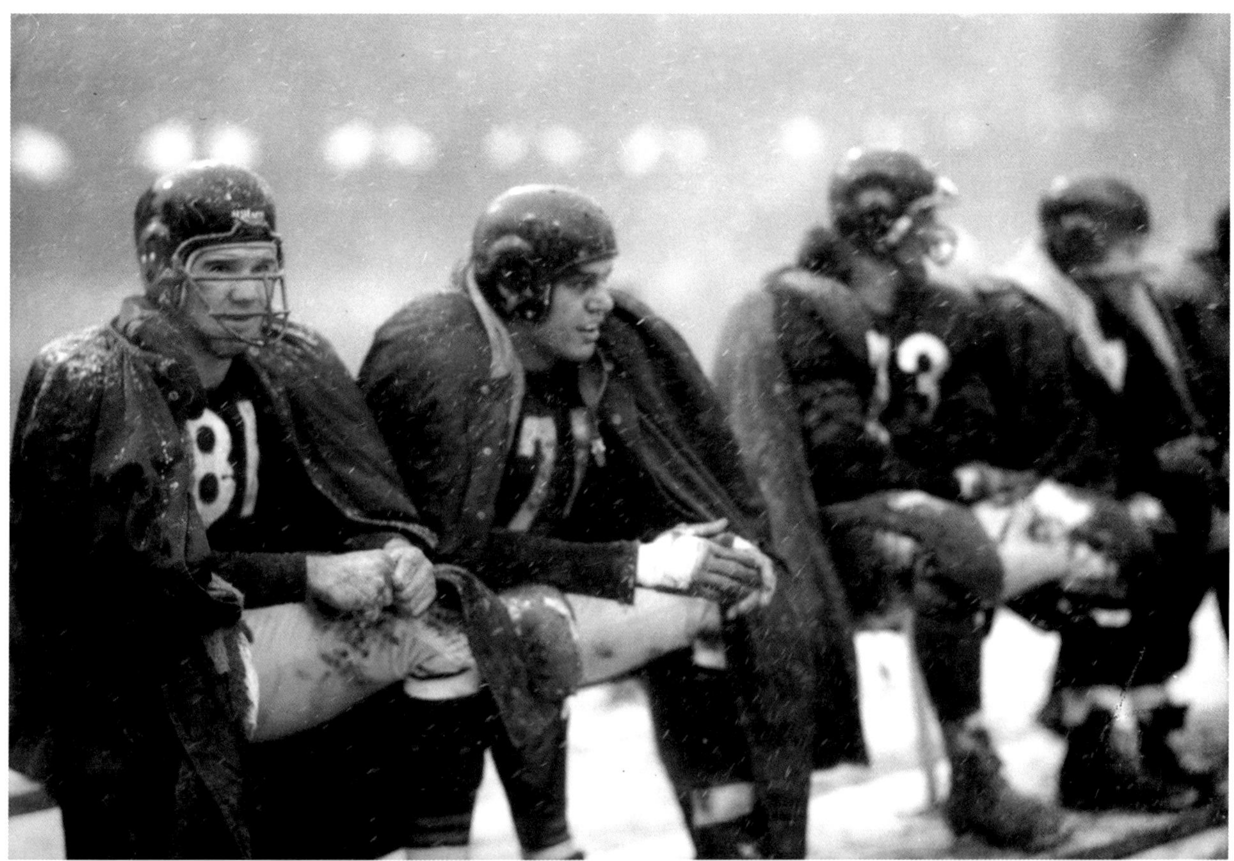

pounced on Papa Bear from behind his door and covered the coach with a blanket.

"I got the Phantom! I got the Phantom!" Atkins shouted.

Atkins' bouts with Halas got the biggest rise out of his teammates, most of whom were terrified of the Bears' coach and founder.

"How Doug got away with it, I'll never know," teammate Stan Jones told Whittingham. "He always had these things going with Coach Halas. . . . Halas, of course, always won out, but Doug gave everybody a lot of laughs along the way."

Halas took pride in the way he handled his assortment of "wild horses" and "night crawlers," rebellious players such as Atkins, Casares, Mike Ditka and Harlon Hill. Halas felt he struck the perfect balance between letting these players be themselves off the field and getting peak performances on it while maintaining a semblance of team harmony.

He did hire a detective agency to keep tabs on them, though, and would share the files come contract time. Halas was, however, much more progressive with such players than his contemporary Paul Brown, the NFL's other owner/personnel director/coach.

Brown had a zero-tolerance policy for malcontents with his namesake franchise, and as his Browns won seven championships in 10 years in the All-American Football League and the NFL between 1946 and 1955, his word was golden. The Browns had selected Atkins with the No. 11 pick in the 1953 draft but quickly tired of his antics. The last straw, according to reports, came when Atkins belched loudly in the middle of a Brown-led meeting.

In 1955, Halas acquired Atkins and safety Ken Gorgal from the Browns for third- and sixth-round draft picks. Halas called the trade his best ever, and he always thought the way he prodded Atkins to produce gave him an

Doug Atkins (81) sits with teammates on the bench Nov. 27, 1955, during a game against the Cardinals at Comiskey Park.

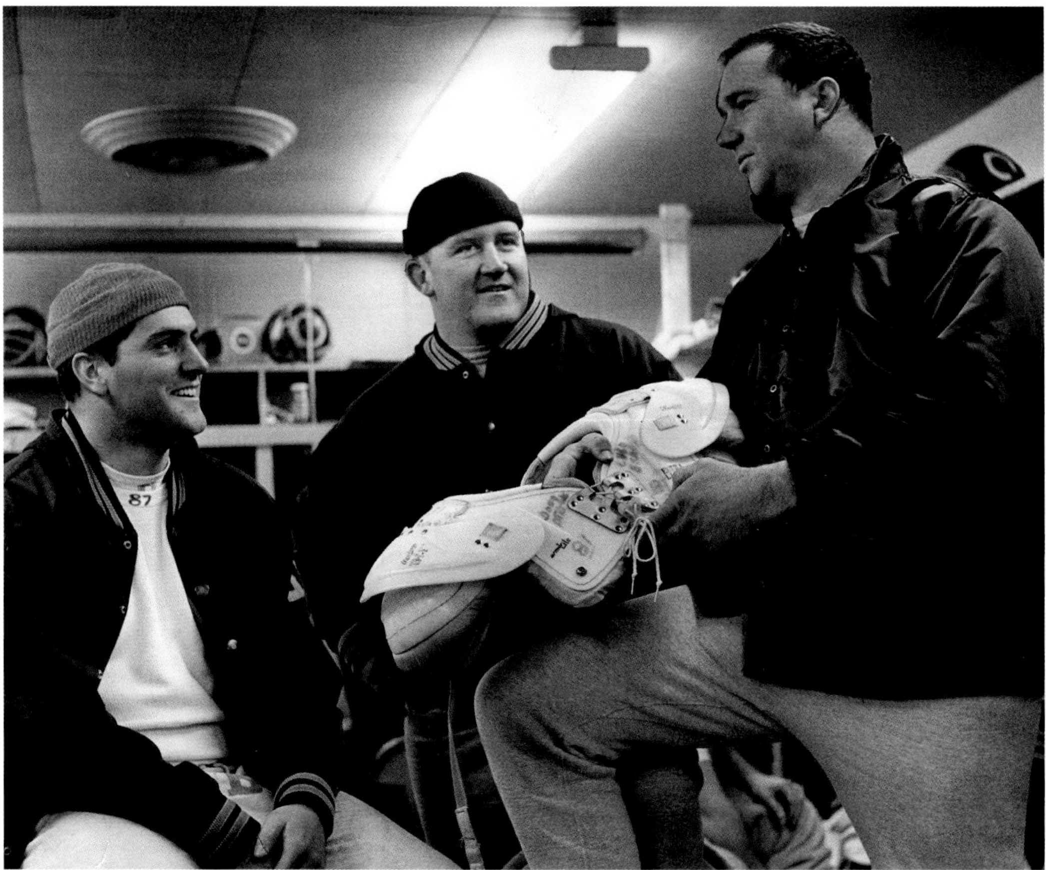

Ed O'Bradovich, from left, Bob Kilcullen and Doug Atkins, three of the team's sturdiest linemen, discuss the king-size shoulder pads they plan to wear in the closing game against the Detroit Lions in 1962 at Wrigley Field. The three men weigh a total of 763 pounds. O'Bradovich is the smallest at 240, with Kilcullen at 253 and Atkins tipping the scales at 270.

edge over Brown when it came to dealing with players.

Halas took his share of abuse—and hazy 3 a.m. phone calls from Atkins, who would share his opinions of his contract or Halas' play calling—but he gave as good as he got.

In his 1979 autobiography, "Halas by Halas," the Bears coach said: "One night a fan phoned that Doug was cutting up drunk at a bar. I drove over. Doug saw me enter and shouted a tumultuous river of profanities. I walked up to him and countered with a barrage that for volume and variety made his assault a peaceful brook compared to my Niagara.

"Doug put down his glass and came to camp. At 10 minutes before 9 in the morning, he was out there on the field with no trace of foggy-headedness or wobbly limbs. Doug became a powerful Bear. We became good friends."

Atkins, from the Tennessee hill town of Humboldt, disliked the constant drills and studying that came with football; he became despondent upon learning that Brown gave his players regularly scheduled written tests. He always preferred his first love, basketball. He hated practice but terrorized the league on Sundays.

Therefore, Halas reluctantly put up with Atkins' poor practice habits. It is said that the Bears coach didn't fully endorse Atkins for the Hall of Fame because of his inconsistent effort, but after Atkins was elected in 1982, Halas, late in his life, called him the best defensive end he'd ever seen.

Atkins, who never could figure why he wasn't enshrined until 13 years after he retired, felt he had a good reason for disdaining practice.

"I used to hurt all the time," Atkins told the Tribune's Cooper Rollow on Jan. 31, 1982. "One time Halas asked me to play against Green Bay even though I had two bad ankles after a hard week of practice. I couldn't even walk. Well, somebody blocked me once, and I heard (Bears assistant coach) Luke Johnsos say, 'Atkins, All-Pro? Bull!'

"I decided right then that practice isn't important."

Besides Halas and Brown, Atkins butted heads with another all-time great coach, Gen. Robert Neyland, at Tennessee. It wasn't until George Allen became Bears defensive coordinator in 1963 that Atkins found a coach with whom he connected. Allen replaced the overly technical Clark Shaughnessy, whose complex schemes and terms confused not only Atkins but the entire defense.

"Shaughnessy had one scheme where I lined up at defensive end; then I had five places to go," Atkins said in "Papa Bear: The Life and Legacy of George Halas," Jeff Davis' 2005 biography. "It was slam, slide, slue, smooch and all that. . . . You just can't do that. We were struggling all the time."

Under Allen in 1963, "We knew exactly what we were going to do," Atkins told Davis. "We'd line up and just tee off and play football."

Atkins responded with his only first-team All-Pro season in Allen's first year as defensive coordinator, and the Bears won the 1963 championship. Atkins was named second-team All-Pro five times with the Bears, and his eight Pro Bowl appearances rank second in team history behind Mike Singletary's 10. In 2014, Pierson named Atkins the best Bears defensive lineman ever. Three years later, longtime Cowboys personnel director Gil Brandt, now an NFL Network analyst, ranked Atkins the fifth-best defensive end ever behind Reggie White, Deacon Jones, Bruce Smith and Gino Marchetti.

While Atkins' practice habits ranked near the bottom of the league, not many players ever played better during games. His coaches put up with him not only because he was talented, but also because he was a winner. He led his high school basketball team to a 44-0 record, helped Tennessee win the 1951 national championship and won NFL titles with the Browns (in 1954) and Bears.

In 1967 the Bears traded Atkins to the Saints. He was 37 at the time but played well enough in three seasons in New Orleans that the Saints retired his No. 81. He is the highest-ranked player on the Tribune's list of the top 100 Bears players not to receive that honor in Chicago.

When he was elected to the Hall of Fame, Atkins took a moment to defend himself and his reputation.

"Sure I'm outspoken," Atkins told Rollow. "But I'm going to tell you something. I don't lie. I don't cheat. I don't steal. And if I'm at your house, you can trust me with your wife, your money and your kids.

"Yet all I hear is stuff about my character: 'You done this. You done that.' I may have gone out and gotten drunk as a player, but I'll put my moral character against anyone in the Hall of Fame."

In retirement, Atkins performed various jobs including pipefitter, shipyard worker, exterminator and, at separate times, selling eyeglasses and caskets. In his later years, he used a wheelchair because of the effects of the injuries accumulated during his 17-year NFL career. Atkins died at 85 on Dec. 30, 2015, in Knoxville, Tenn.

Ditka, another rough-and-tumble player whom Atkins awed, calls "The Big Fella" the best defensive end he ever saw.

"Doug Atkins would demand $10 million today as a football player," Ditka said to the Tribune's Fred Mitchell on April 17, 1994. "He would be the best defensive lineman in football."

Linebacker Larry Morris, Atkins' road roommate for eight years, took it one step further, telling Mitchell: "These people who are playing now, pardon the expression, couldn't carry his jock. . . . Doug is the best player at his position who ever lived." ■

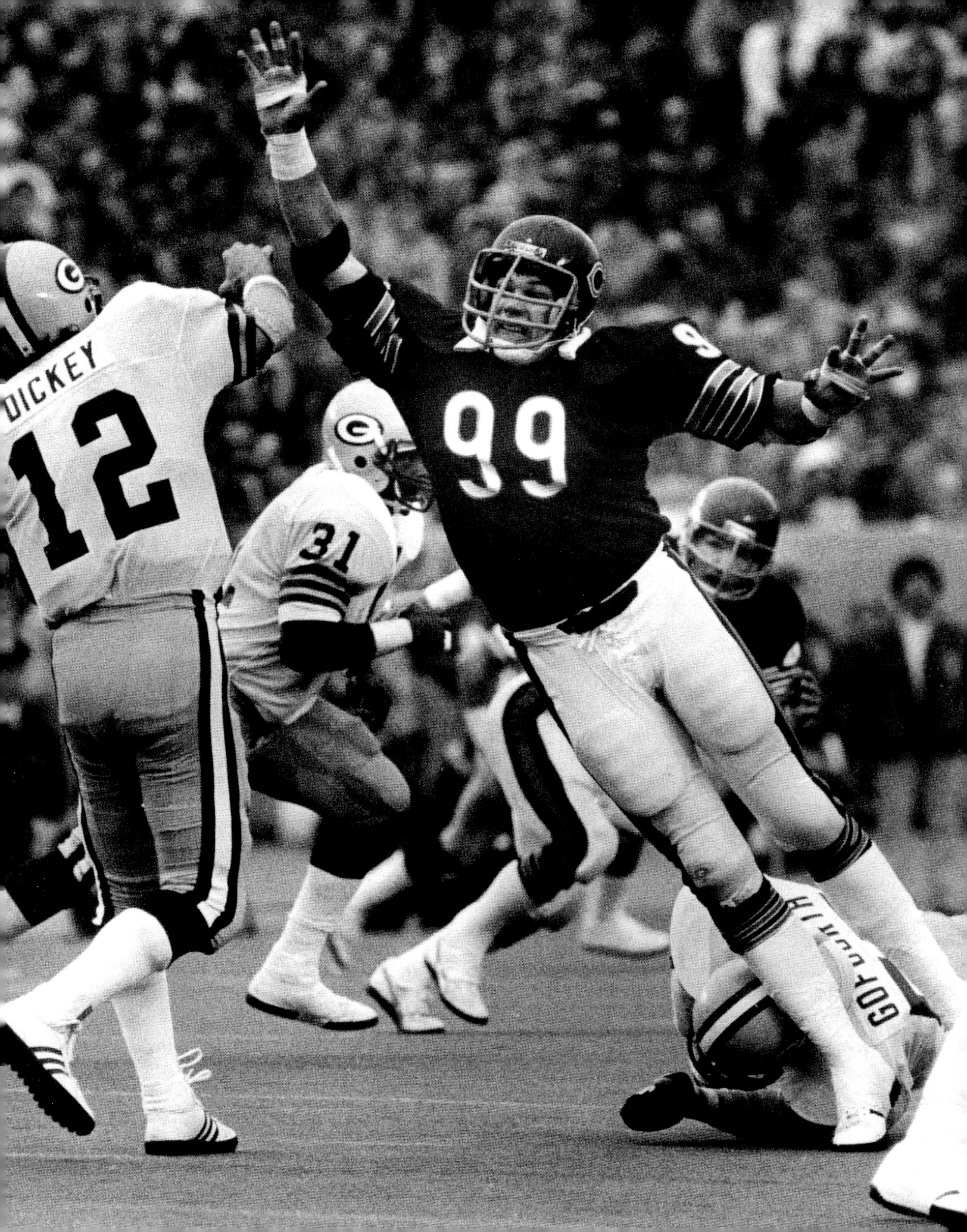

DICKEY
12
31
99

Dan Hampton

9

99 DEFENSIVE TACKLE, DEFENSIVE END
1979-90

DAN AND MATT HAMPTON were playing in the yard of their family's farm one 1960s afternoon in Cabot, Ark.

Shooting bottle rockets at each other was among the rambunctious brothers' favorite pastimes, so that day's activity was not out of the ordinary.

Dan climbed above the boys' treehouse and began to cut with a knife a rope tied to one of the branches. Matt was swinging back and forth on the rope about 45 feet below, shooting up at Dan with a BB gun.

Dan grabbed a rotted branch for support. It snapped, and he broke both legs and an arm in the fall.

He said his injuries would have been much worse had he not drank so much fresh milk from his family's dairy cows. "None of that pasteurized stuff."

That was the first of Dan Hampton's many injuries. He came back from that sixth-grade setback and many more to become one of the greatest NFL players of the 1980s, a Super Bowl champion with the Bears and a member of the Pro Football Hall of Fame.

In the Oct. 9, 1989, issue of Sports Illustrated, former Bears defensive coordinator Buddy Ryan, then head coach of the Eagles, told Jill Lieber: "Nobody has played (defensive) tackle better than Hampton. And surely no one has played it with more heart. Dan's my hero."

After his fall from the tree, Hampton's doctor advised him to give up sports. He did and became immersed in the world of music. He learned to play six instruments—the bass guitar, classical guitar, drums, saxophone, piano and organ—and in high school played bass for a rock band and saxophone in the marching band.

In his 2013 book, "Monsters: The 1985 Chicago Bears and the Wild Heart of Football," Rich Cohen said the 6-foot-5, 264-pound Hampton was the Bears' "thumping bass that made everything rock." Years earlier Hampton was known for his long hair, thick glasses and distinction as by far the largest member of the horn section.

"Until the 11th grade, I was walking around with a saxophone," Hampton told the Tribune's

Packers quarterback Lynn Dickey (12) manages to get off a pass against a furious rush by Dan Hampton (99) on Dec. 7, 1980.

Fred Mitchell on Feb. 3, 2002. "The football coaches were looking at me like I was from Mars."

Bill Reed, his coach in Jacksonville, Ark., convinced Hampton to join the football team, and as Hampton dominated, Reed ensured his new star's next stop would be the University of Arkansas. A huge Razorbacks fan, Reed threw recruiting letters to Hampton from Texas and Oklahoma in the trash.

As the Bears scouted Hampton before the 1979 draft, they flew him to Chicago for interviews with the staff. The highlight for him was a film session with Ryan.

In Richard Whittingham's 1991 book, "What Bears They Were," Hampton remembered: "They brought me to this room, which was dark, and film was running. Buddy never turned the light on or anything. He just said, 'Sit down, big boy.' So I sat down by the desk, and he didn't say another thing for about 10 minutes.

"Finally he said, 'See that guy, No. 82? That's Alan Page. He's one of the greatest who ever played the game. Boy, I'd sure like to have you. I betcha I could get you to play like that someday.'"

The Bears took Hampton with the No. 4 overall pick, and he got to learn from Page every day for three years as the former Viking finished his Hall of Fame career with the Bears. Hampton supplemented the lessons by watching film of Buccaneers defensive end Lee Roy Selmon, studying how he used balance and leverage just as much as speed and power to disrupt blockers.

Most defensive players had a rough time for a few years under Ryan, who despised rookies and in most cases put them on the field only in an emergency. Not so with Hampton, who started all 16 games his first season and was one of the few players Ryan consistently singled out for praise.

Hampton was named to his first Pro Bowl in 1980 after his second season, an honor he would gain three more times. Individual accolades proved hard to come by for Hampton, mostly because of his willingness to switch between defensive end and tackle as needed and the roster full of stars the Bears assembled by the mid-1980s.

In his 11 full seasons, Hampton played seven mostly at end and four mostly at tackle. He started out at left end with tackle occupied by Page and Jim Osborne, moved inside after Page retired in 1982, went back outside when William Perry joined the starting lineup in the middle of the 1985 championship season, returned inside when Perry was demoted from the starting lineup in 1988 and stayed there after the Bears drafted defensive end Trace Armstrong in 1989.

It's hard to say which position suited Hampton better. His strength and quickness made him an ideal defensive tackle, while his speed, ability to keep outside containment and array of pass-rush techniques allowed him to excel at end.

Jim Hanifan, the St. Louis Cardinals' head coach from 1980-85 who was an offensive line coach in the NFL for 23 years, rejoiced when Hampton moved from end to tackle.

"I thought he was such a great end that the move would take away his playing skills," Hanifan told the Tribune's Don Pierson on July 30, 2002. "Well, it didn't. He was even more dominating inside."

John Michels, Vikings offensive line coach from 1985-93, offered the opposite opinion.

"We felt he was more dangerous at end because we had a tougher time doubling him out there," Michels told Pierson. "We felt we could never single him constantly or he'd beat us."

Larry McCarren, the Packers' center from 1973-84 and a two-time Pro Bowl selection, said Hampton presented unique problems at both positions because of his well-rounded skill set.

"Hampton made the 46 defense because he was such a unique player," McCarren told Pierson. "They would line him up on the nose, and here was a guy with defensive end-type dimensions who would present totally different blocking problems. . . . He collapsed the pocket, and that's where the best defense of all time started."

No matter where he played, Hampton was awesome. So were the Bears, as long as he was

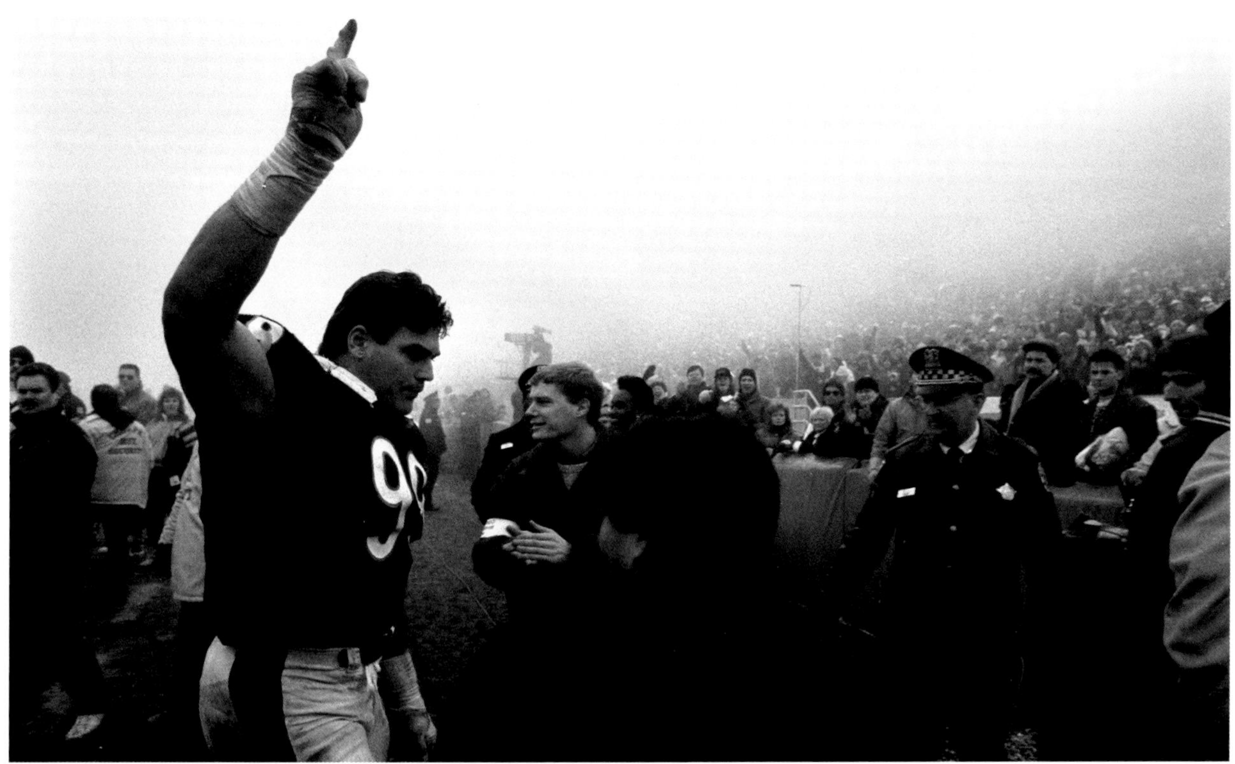

Dan Hampton (99) celebrates the team's win over the Philadelphia Eagles on Dec. 31, 1988, in a game that became known as Fog Bowl. The Bears won 20-12.

on the field. In the 27 games he missed while recovering from 10 knee surgeries and an assortment of broken bones, the Bears went 10-17. In the 157 games he played, the Bears went 103-54.

In the seven years Hampton spent on the Hall of Fame ballot before he was elected, Pierson, a member of the selection committee, collected stats that proved Hampton's worth. Many were sent to him by John Turney, an amateur statistician and gift-shop owner from New Mexico.

The Bears allowed 23.1 points without Hampton and 14.7 with him. Without Hampton, the Bears averaged 4.02 yards allowed per rush while sacking the quarterback 2.3 times. With "Danimal," those numbers were 3.7 and 3.6. During Hampton's career, from 1979-90, the Bears allowed the fewest points, total yards, rushing yards and rushing touchdowns while totaling the most sacks in the NFL.

As Pierson pointed out: "Second in rushing yards over those years were the Steelers with Jack Lambert and Mel Blount. Second in rushing touchdowns and points were the 49ers with Ronnie Lott. Second in sacks were the Raiders with Howie Long. Second in total yards were the Giants with Lawrence Taylor. But in each category, the Bears were first."

Lieber, in Sports Illustrated, wrote: "Hampton is the one Chicago player on whom opposing offensive coordinators focus their game plans. No offensive lineman can block him alone. He has tremendous reflexes and quickness and the unusual ability to move with equal effectiveness to the right or left. Most pass rushers have a favorite move to get to the quarterback, but Hampton's package of tricks includes almost every technique—among them the rip, the swim and the slap."

Hampton finally was elected to the Hall of Fame in 2002. He was first-team All-Pro once, in 1984, and second-team four times. In 2014, Pierson ranked him the second-best defensive lineman in Bears history behind only Doug

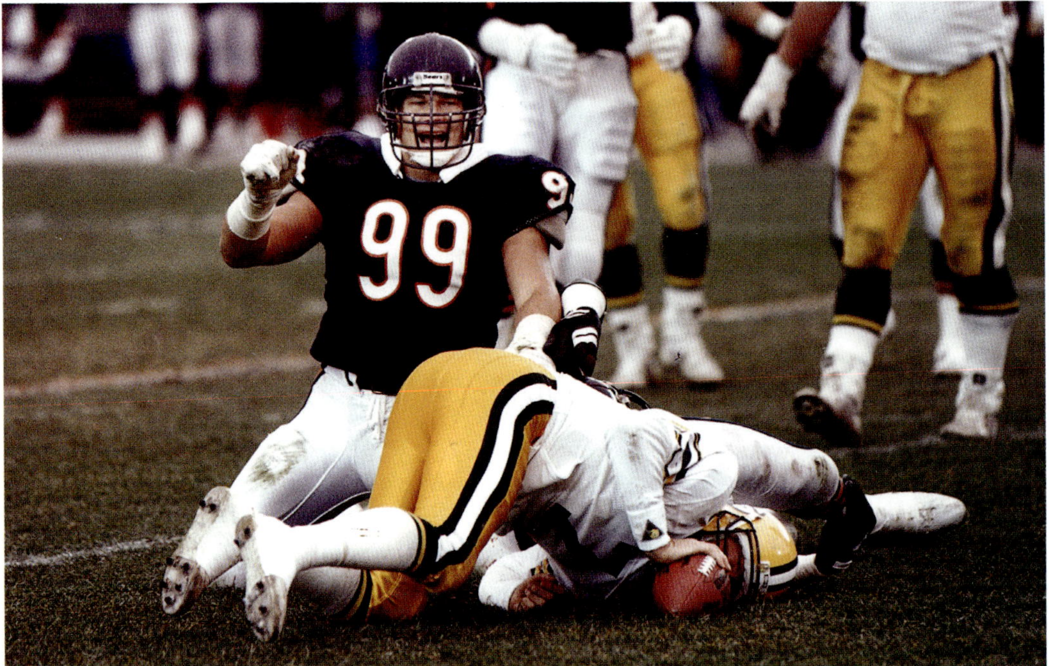

Dan Hampton (99) celebrates after sacking Packers quarterback Don Majkowski (7) on Nov. 27, 1988, at Soldier Field.

Atkins. Four defensive linemen were named to the 1980s All-Decade first team: Reggie White, Randy White, Long and Hampton.

"Dan is a definite Hall of Famer," Ditka told Lieber in 1989, when the Bears started 4-0 before Hampton missed the rest of the season with another knee injury and won two of their final 12 games. "He rates up there with the very best. Dan reminds me a lot of Bob Lilly, although he'll never get the recognition Bob got."

Hampton was the second piece the Bears added while constructing what would become by acclimation the best defense in NFL history. Gary Fencik was the first, in 1976. Personnel men Jim Finks, Jerry Vainisi and Bill Tobin added Otis Wilson in 1980, Mike Singletary, Steve McMichael and Leslie Frazier in 1981, Richard Dent, Dave Duerson and Mike Richardson in 1983, Wilber Marshall in 1984 and Perry in 1985.

"In the beginning," Ditka told the Tribune's Fred Mitchell on Jan. 25, 2001, "when people look at our defense, they said, 'We have to handle (Hampton) on the line. Then we have to handle that linebacker (Singletary), No. 50.' Then we started putting Otis next to him and Wilber, then they had to handle a lot of people

they couldn't handle. That's what made us really good."

The debate in Chicago was whether Hampton or Singletary was the indispensable member of the defense. With Hampton, McMichael and Perry clogging the paths of opposing centers and guards, Singletary was free to make plays all over the field. He was named the league's Defensive Player of the Year in 1985 and 1988; in the latter year, Hampton gained the highest grades from the Bears coaching staff.

The two butted heads often as both tried to be the vocal leader of the unit. Singletary especially would become annoyed when Hampton would interrupt the linebacker's signal calls to yell instructions at McMichael or Dent.

"Dan and I argued most of the time," Singletary told Pierson. "I was so focused on Dan running his mouth. . . . Every one of us thought at the time, 'I'm the reason this thing is working.'"

When Hampton joined Singletary, who was voted into the Hall of Fame in 1998, in Canton, Ohio, Singletary called to congratulate him and "let him know how much I appreciated what he did for our defense and for me."

Many of the Bears of that era despised the media—almost as many as would become members of it themselves after retirement. Hampton, though, was a hit with the press from his first day in Chicago. At his introductory news conference after he was drafted, Hampton began spinning homespun wisdom that continued for 12 years.

"Dale Haupt, our defensive line coach then, picked me up at the airport and brought me downtown for the press conference," Hampton told Whittingham. "It went pretty well. I ran off a bunch of one-liners. And I got along with the media right off."

Longtime Bears beat writer Cooper Rollow compared Hampton to Will Rogers on May 5, 1979, after hearing quips such as, "Fayetteville is just a little bitty town. You don't really buy tickets on the local airline. You buy chances."

Hampton reversed course in 1986, announcing a press boycott in response to what he felt was his teammates' unhealthy preoccupation with the growing spotlight.

"Everybody on the team was too busy with their own selves, who they were, how much airtime they got, rather than worrying about the team," Hampton told Lieber. "They were driven by money and star power, what they could become. It's not important to me to show up at all the restaurant openings or have a different BMW or Mercedes in my driveway for every day of the week."

While Hampton preached humility, he was not above a little trash talking, especially after wins such as the 44-0 pasting of the Cowboys on Nov. 17, 1985, in Irving, Texas. Before the game, Cowboys defensive back Everson Walls said he wasn't impressed with the 10-0 Bears because of their soft schedule.

Hampton told Whittingham: "All week, Walls is saying crap like, 'The Bears haven't played anybody.' After we finish up with them . . . a bunch of writers are around the locker, and I said, 'I have to give Everson Walls credit. He was right. We're 11-0 and still haven't played anybody.'"

Hampton finished with one last productive season as a situational player in 1990. He said he knew the end was near, though, when Raiders guard Steve Wisniewski rendered him ineffective.

"They kept pitching the ball and going left, and I'd never been hooked in my entire life," Hampton told Whittingham. "He got to the shoulder about four times and drove me off the ball 2 or 3 yards, which I'd seen other people have happen, but I'd never had that before. That was like sticking a knife in me. I thought, I'm done."

Hampton's final game was the 31-3 loss to the eventual champion Giants in the NFC divisional round on Jan. 13, 1991, in East Rutherford, N.J. He has been a fixture on local media ever since, and he hosts a postgame show after Bears games on WGN-AM 720. Hampton scratched his musical itch by playing bass with the Chicago 6, which included McMichael, Wilson and professional musicians John McFarland, Matt Kammerer and Ed Kammerer. He likes to joke that if he never quit the high school band he might have become president like fellow sax-playing Arkansan Bill Clinton.

Hampton's knees have deteriorated to the point that, as he said to the Tribune's Steve Rosenbloom on Dec. 5, 2005, "I couldn't run out of the house if it was on fire, but at the end of the day, I'm glad I was able to do what I was supposed to do."

"Every time the surgeons go in that joint, they change it and it gets worse," Hampton told Whittingham. "And every rehab you have gets harder and harder. It was no big deal; don't pin a Purple Heart on me. All I knew was that I had no choice in the matter—it was either fish or cut bait. And I decided to fish as long as I could."

As far as Hampton's role on the great Bears defenses of the 1980s, the Tribune's Bernie Lincicome wrote on Jan. 30, 1998, that "Singletary would not have been the great linebacker he was without Hampton in front of him. Richard Dent would not have been the pass rusher he was without Hampton inside of him. William Perry would not have become rich and celebrated if Hampton had not moved to end."

"Hampton was the focus of all defensive game plans, not Singletary, not Otis Wilson, not Wilber Marshall. First, teams figured out how to handle Hampton. Then they figured out the rest." ■

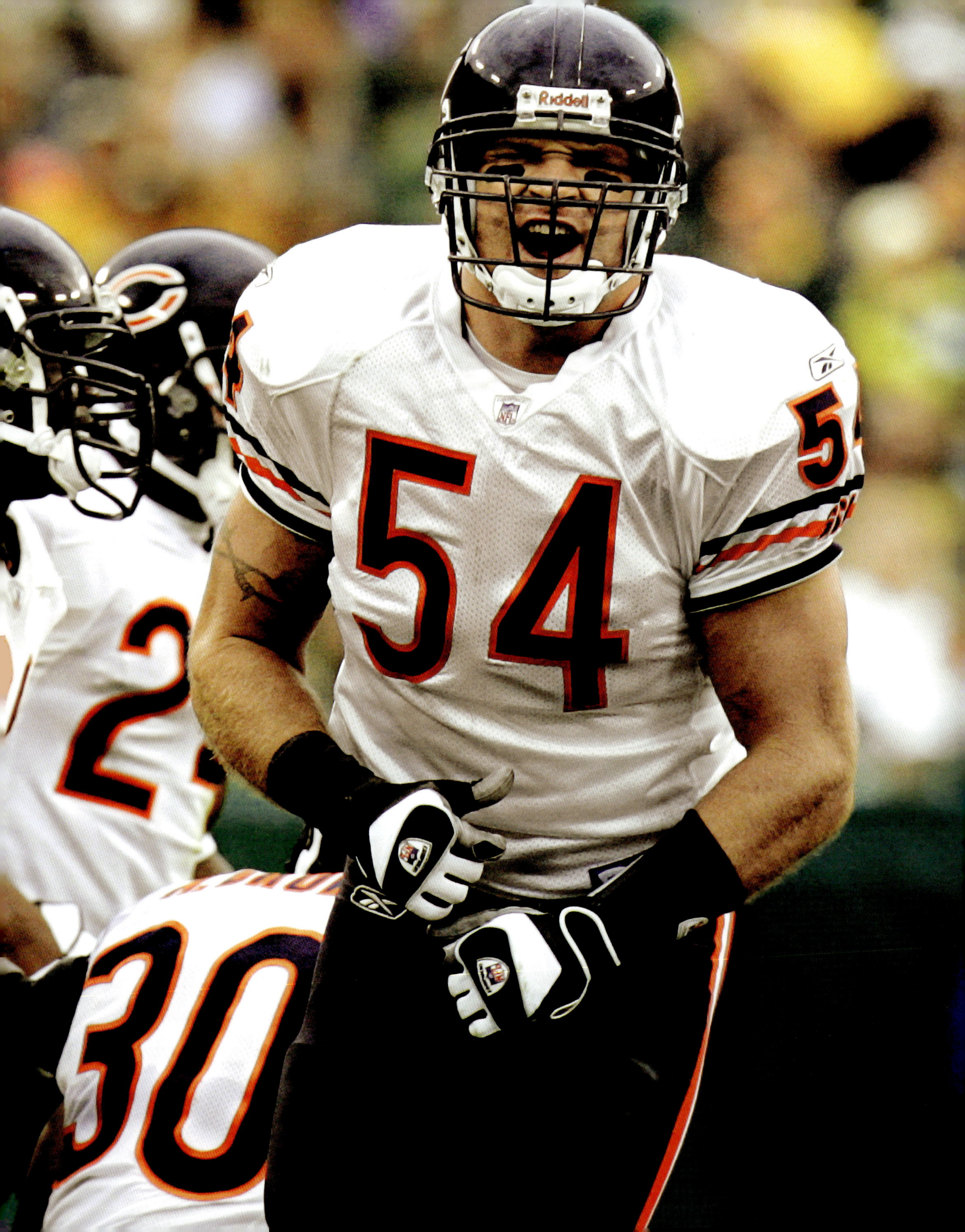

10

Brian Urlacher

54 LINEBACKER
2000–12

O LIN KREUTZ DID a double take.

For the Bears center, blocking linebackers on outside zone runs was "easy. . . . I cut them off in a second." So on one of the first days of training camp in Platteville, Wis., in 2000, Kreutz thought something must have been off when a rookie linebacker sprinted past him as if he weren't there.

"This is my block. I'm going to kill this guy," Kreutz remembered thinking in a Tribune story on July 30, 2018. "He just flew by me big and strong and fast, and I don't know if I've ever seen anything like that."

Offensive players around the NFL soon shared the feeling. Competing against Brian Urlacher sometimes defied belief. How in the world could a 6-foot-4, 258-pound middle linebacker be so fast?

"I came back to the huddle and was like, '(Wow!) That guy is fast!,'" Kreutz said. "I don't even think 'Lach' knew how fast he was at that time. . . . There wasn't a linebacker I played against—Pro Bowl, All-Pro—that I wasn't cutting off with ease, and Lach's speed was on a whole other level."

The Bears drafted Urlacher with the ninth pick of the first round in 2000. He played strong-side linebacker for most of training camp and for his first two games as a Bear. When defensive coordinator Greg Blache and linebackers coach Dale Lindsey shifted Urlacher to the middle, he became a revelation. His combination of size, speed, athleticism, football intelligence and instincts had never been seen at the position.

"The versatility and his athleticism was incredible," former Bears safety Tony Parrish told the Tribune's Dan Wiederer on Aug. 2, 2018. "This was a guy who played safety and returned punts at New Mexico. And now he's at middle linebacker in the NFL."

Like Kreutz, Bears coach Dick Jauron, who played safety in the NFL for eight years, had trouble believing his eyes. The Tribune's Don Pierson wrote on Feb. 2, 2018, that Jauron, who was 4 inches shorter and about 70 pounds lighter than Urlacher, "marveled at being able to witness evolution before his very eyes." Pierson also noted that Urlacher's 40-yard dash time of 4.59 seconds at the scouting combine was comparable to Bears running back Walter Payton's time 25 years earlier.

Brian Urlacher (54) reacts during a 26-0 victory over the Packers on Sept. 10, 2006, at Lambeau Field.

and linemen. Always around the ball. Always making plays."

At New Mexico, Urlacher played a hybrid safety/linebacker position. He also returned punts, averaging 15.8 yards per return, and he was a red-zone receiving threat, catching seven passes, a team-leading six for touchdowns. Dave Bliss, then the Lobos' basketball coach, wanted him to try out for his team. Urlacher had considered playing junior-college basketball after his preferred football program, Texas Tech, didn't offer him a scholarship.

Going into the draft, Falcons scout Mike Hagen told the Tribune's Skip Bayless on April 13, 2000: "Urlacher's combination of size, speed, strength, smarts, character, maturity, throwback toughness, athletic ability, cover skills and hands just doesn't come around very often. You could put him at middle linebacker and know he'd never have to come off the field. These days you need more than just a run stuffer in the middle. This guy can blitz and intercept passes. He could really become the leader of a defense."

The Bears were hoping one of Jones, wide receiver Plaxico Burress or Urlacher would fall to them at No. 9. The Cardinals selected Jones at No. 7, the Steelers took Burress next, and the Bears were happy to take Urlacher. They drafted safety Mike Brown in the second round, and the two picks infused the Bears defense with the talent, intelligence and instincts the unit would come to be known for in the next decade.

Urlacher moved into the starting lineup in the third game of 2000 after Barry Minter suffered a back injury. After his rookie-of-the-year season, Urlacher took off in 2001 after the Bears signed huge defensive tackles Ted Washington and Keith Traylor to make it difficult for centers and guards to reach him. Fans across the country took notice of Urlacher's athleticism on Oct. 7 against the Falcons, when he hounded quarterback Michael Vick in a 31-3 win that included an interception and a 90-yard fumble return for a touchdown for Urlacher.

Dan Pompei, a former Tribune reporter who successfully presented Urlacher's case to the Hall of Fame committee, said that game made him realize he was covering a player who had a chance to become an all-time great.

"Michael Vick came into the league in 2001, and he could not be stopped," Pompei told the Tribune on July 30, 2018. "It looked like he was playing a different game from everyone else in terms of his speed. . . . And then the Bears played him, and Urlacher just chased him all over the field, ran him down, kept hitting him the whole game.

"It really was an eye-opener about the kind of athleticism this guy had. Playing at over 250 pounds, he could chase this incredible, one-of-a-kind quarterback all over the field and not only match his speed or exceed his speed but beat him up physically to the point where he basically defeated him."

Jauron was fired after the 2003 season and replaced with Lovie Smith, whose defense showcased Urlacher's special talents. The linebacker's speed, size and coverage ability allowed Smith to tweak his Cover-2 zone, with Urlacher covering the deep middle on pass plays and allowing the safeties to help the cornerbacks outside if needed.

The result was Urlacher's Defensive Player of the Year honor in 2005, one year after the Sporting News named him the league's most overrated player.

"That pissed me off," Urlacher told the Tribune's David Haugh on Feb. 4, 2018. "And the next year what happened? . . . I think I was vindicated."

Lance Briggs, the outside linebacker who played beside Urlacher for 10 years and was named to seven Pro Bowls, told the Tribune: "I remember the first game in 2005 against the Redskins. Brian was flying around. . . . I remember saying to myself, 'Man, he's going to win defensive player of the year this year.' And sure enough, he did!"

Urlacher led the Bears to Super Bowl XLI after they went 13-3 in the 2006 regular season with a defense that ranked third in scoring, fifth overall, sixth against the run and 11th against the pass. That season is remembered mostly for rookie Devin Hester's amazing kick and punt returns, Rex Grossman's inconsistency at quarterback and the time Urlacher simply willed his team to a win on "Monday Night Football."

Down 23-3 late in the third quarter against the Cardinals on Oct. 16 in Glendale, Ariz., Urlacher led the charge to a 24-23 win. He was credited by the Bears with 25 tackles, and when he yanked the ball from Edgerrin James' hands for a 40-yard touchdown return by Charles Tillman, the Bears suddenly were within 6 points with 5 minutes to play. Hester's 83-yard punt return and a Neil Rackers missed field goal clinched the victory.

Smith said he gave a special pep talk to Urlacher between the third and fourth quarters and that Urlacher responded beyond what even his coach thought was possible.

"I said, 'You're freaking Brian Urlacher,'" Smith remembered on July 30, 2018. "'You need to make something happen right now.' And Brian did."

Urlacher did not make the Pro Bowl after the 2007-09 seasons but returned to form for his final two selections in 2010-11. He suffered a hamstring injury chasing down Seahawks rookie quarterback Russell Wilson in a 23-17 overtime loss on Dec. 2, 2012, and missed the final four games of the season. The Bears finished 10-6 after a 7-1 start, missed the playoffs, and Smith was fired. General manager Phil Emery did not come close to reaching a contract agreement with Urlacher, who was a free agent and ended up retiring after the awkward exit.

While his teammates loved Urlacher, he had a sometimes-shaky relationship with the media. He took slights against his teammates and coaches personally, so when, for instance, Smith's conservative game plans or Briggs' holdouts came under fire, Urlacher would become surly and offer one-word answers during interviews.

He feared that gruffness might negatively affect his Hall of Fame candidacy, so when he was up for election in 2018 he started lauding his career for the first time.

"I hate talking about myself," he told Haugh, "but just look at the way I changed my position. I changed what was asked of middle

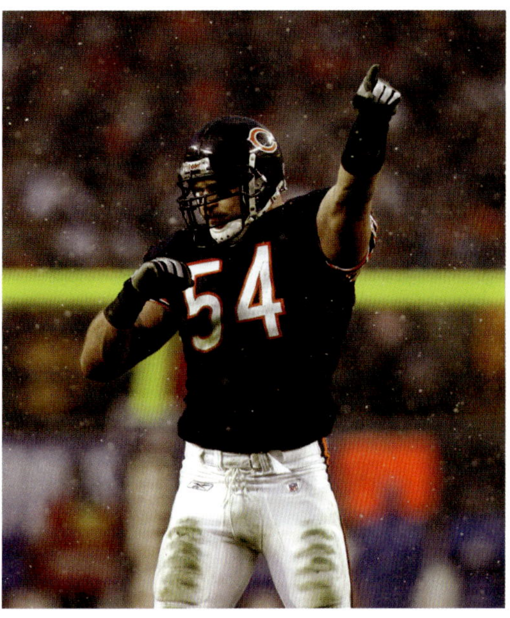

Brian Urlacher (54) celebrates Jan. 21, 2007, after the Chicago Bears stopped the New Orleans Saints during the NFC championship game at Soldier Field.

linebackers, to do what a lot of guys can't do: cover 40 yards down the middle and still play the run.

"There were no glaring weaknesses in my game. Of course I didn't get off blocks great; not a lot of guys did."

Urlacher, whom Haugh called the best Bear since Payton, had nothing to worry about. He was voted in on the first ballot, and on Aug. 4, 2018, he took his place among the game's greats. In his speech, he said he had only one goal as a football player.

"I just want to be remembered as a great teammate," Urlacher said. "That's it."

Smith said Urlacher will go down as much more than that.

"Brian was everything you want a linebacker to be," Smith said. "First off, that leader. That voice. The guy who's out in front. He's an imposing figure. Every play they see a 6-4, 260-pound, 6% body-fat guy in front of you. And Brian was a guy who knew what he was supposed to do. You expect that guy, in big games, to come through. If we needed him to make a big hit, he did that time after time. . . . You expected that out of a first-ballot Hall of Famer.

"The Chicago Bears should have a player like that. And they did." ■

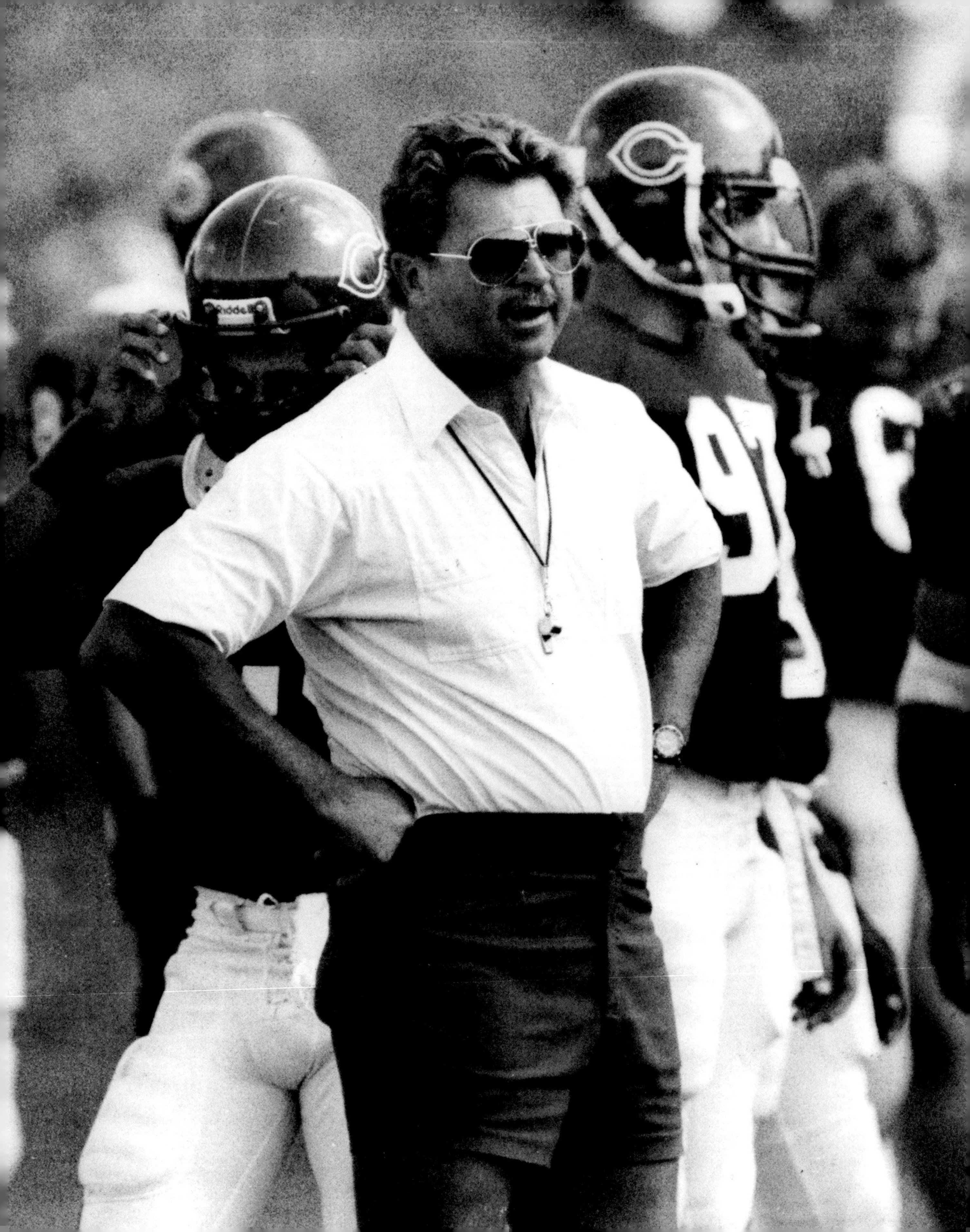

11

Mike Ditka

89 TIGHT END, HEAD COACH
1961-66, 1982-92

G EORGE HALAS WAS conducting film study after his Bears were embarrassed by the 49ers 52-24 in the opening game of the 1965 season.

With the entire team watching, Halas dissected play after disastrous play, harshly pointing out who was at fault for each one and why.

Halas told his players they were terrible blockers. He said they were awful tacklers. He said he wished he had another player like 1940s two-way standout George McAfee: "He didn't weigh 160 pounds wringing wet, and he could cut those guys down like they were nothing!"

From the back of the dark room, a brash voice startled everyone.

"(Expletive) George McAfee!"

After a few seconds of shock, Halas shouted: "Who said that?"

Mike Ditka stood.

"I said it," the All-Pro tight end announced. "This is 1965. This isn't 1940. Who cares about George McAfee?"

Wide receiver Johnny Morris, telling the story in Richard Whittingham's 1991 book, "What Bears They Were," said: "Well, it was the first time I ever saw George Halas flustered. He just said, 'I'll see you after the meeting.'"

Ditka, like mob boss Frank Costello in "The Departed," was not a product of his environment; his environment was a product of him. Besides Halas, no person has done more to shape the Chicago Bears than Ditka. While Halas oversaw the franchise for 64 years, Ditka made his everlasting impact in 17: six as a player, 11 as head coach.

At Soldier Field during Bears games, fans still dress like the 1985 championship-winning version of "Da Coach": navy blue sweater vest with "BEARS" emblazoned in white between two orange stripes across the chest, slicked-back hair, shades, thick mustache and a chomped-upon cigar.

Before he was the coach who returned the Bears to glory and connected with fans by extolling the virtues of the blue-collar "Grabowski" lifestyle over the flashiness of New York and Los Angeles, "Iron Mike" Ditka was the NFL's first great tight end.

Halas and George Allen, the Bears defensive coordinator and personnel director, selected

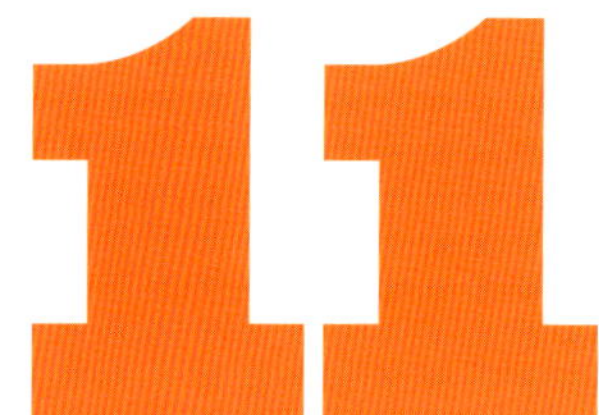

Coach Mike Ditka surrounded by players on Aug. 14, 1985.

Ditka with the fifth pick in the 1961 draft. Even though Ditka was mostly a blocker at Pittsburgh, Halas and offensive coordinator Luke Johnsos had an audacious plan. Ditka would become the first tight end to affect the receiving and rushing games equally.

They enlisted Bill Wade, the quarterback the Bears acquired from the Rams that offseason, and Sid Luckman, an offensive assistant and the greatest passer in team history, to turn Ditka into a receiver.

"I had to learn. I led Pitt with 12 catches in 1960," Ditka told Jeff Davis in his 2005 book, "Papa Bear: The Life and Legacy of George Halas."

Wade, Ditka and young teammates Bill Brown and Richie Petitbon showed up for extra workouts each day for four weeks that summer at vacant Soldier Field. Luckman taught Ditka to catch with his hands, to reach up to grab the ball at the highest point he could. To help Ditka learn to watch the ball all the way in, Luckman drew a number on each one and told Ditka to yell the number of the ball he caught before he ran with it.

"Sid took the time to work with me," Ditka told Whittingham. "Sid guided me, and Bill Wade worked with me, throwing the ball to me; we just did it over and over."

The drills paid off in a huge way. The 6-foot-3, 228-pound Ditka blindsided the NFL with 56 receptions for 1,076 yards and 12 touchdowns and was a runaway winner as the UPI's rookie of the year. He nearly dragged the Bears to an upset of the Packers—who won the first of their five championships in seven years that season—catching nine passes for 190 yards and three touchdowns in a game the Bears lost 31-28 at Wrigley Field after trailing 31-7.

Two years later, John Mackey joined the Colts and became the NFL's second great tight end. By the end of the decade, the position was an offensive staple, with Ditka and Mackey the models until Kellen Winslow re-revolutionized the position with the San Diego Chargers in the 1980s. Ditka finished his career with 427 receptions, 5,812 yards and 43 touchdowns, and in 1988 he was the first tight end voted to the Pro Football Hall of Fame. In 1994, he and Winslow were the two tight ends named to the NFL's 75th anniversary team.

"Halas revolutionized the position," Ditka told Davis.

"There were no tight ends catching a lot of passes until he and Luke started flexing the tight end out, dropping him off the line," Ditka told the Tribune's Cooper Rollow on July 29, 1988. "It gave me a chance to get off the line of scrimmage and release."

Halas' first impression of Ditka stayed with him always. The Bears, as was their custom, scrimmaged against the College All-Stars before their exhibition against the defending NFL champions, who in 1961 were the Eagles.

"I caught a couple of passes and ran over a guy or something," Ditka remembered to Davis.

"Who the hell is that guy?" Halas yelled. One of his assistants informed him it was the Bears' first-round pick.

Halas smiled. He always was looking for players who possessed, in his words, "the old zipperoo." Ditka displayed more of it than perhaps any other player Halas coached.

Upon joining the Bears, Ditka walked into a locker room that included 10 veterans in their 30s: Doug Atkins, Ed Brown, Rick Casares, Jim Dooley, Joe Fortunato, Bill George, Stan Jones, Herman Lee, Fred Williams and Wade.

Before long, it was Ditka's team.

"His practice habits were incredible, and he earned instant respect," defensive lineman Ed O'Bradovich told Rollow. "After Mike arrived on the Bears, every day of practice might as well have been a game day."

In the 1961 opener, the Bears were destroyed by the Vikings 37-13 in Minneapolis. Ditka couldn't stand it, and throughout the game he berated his teammates.

Center Mike Pyle, a fellow rookie, told Davis: "Ditka came into the huddle and screamed at everybody, 'Get your head and heart into this game! We aren't going to let this happen!'

"Every veteran in the huddle looked up as if to say, 'Who is this guy?' No one had seen this behavior. . . . They stared at this guy and said, 'Uh-oh.'"

The Bears improved from 5-6-1 in 1960 to 8-6 in 1961 and 9-5 in '62. In 1963, Ditka, by then a captain with Pyle and Fortunato, told Halas the Bears were ready to win it all.

They did, with a lot of help from Ditka.

The Bears swept the two-time defending champion Packers, with the second win putting them in first place at 9-1. The next week, two days after the assassination of President John F. Kennedy, the Bears found themselves in danger of falling back into second place.

They trailed the Steelers 17-14 late in the fourth quarter in Pittsburgh. They faced third-and-35 from their own 22. Wade asked Ditka if he could run a deep pattern.

"I don't have any gas left," said Ditka, who had drained himself playing in front of fans from his hometown of Aliquippa, Pa., for the first time since college. "I'll go down 12 or 13 yards and turn away from the linebacker. Try to hit me in the hole and I'll try to get us moving. We don't have to do it all in one play."

Rollow wrote: "But, as it turned out, Ditka did do it all in one play. He cradled Wade's short pass and headed upfield. Steeler after Steeler climbed on the back of the big man, but Ditka kept running until he collapsed on the Pittsburgh 15 with half the team on top of him."

Ditka lay on the field before staggering off. "I kind of passed out," he said. "I thought I was dead."

Roger LeClerc's 18-yard field goal preserved a 17-17 tie, which kept the Bears in first place, a position they held on to with an 11-1-2 record. They beat the Giants 14-10 for the NFL title at Wrigley Field, with Ditka making another huge catch late in the game to set up Wade's winning 1-yard sneak.

"If Mike doesn't make that run in Pittsburgh," O'Bradovich said, "we're not wearing rings."

Morris told Whittingham: "I was on the field at the time, blocking somebody, but I saw him going down the field, and it was incredible. . . . He knocked over everybody in sight."

Like Ditka's Bears of the 1980s, the championship never was repeated. The team sputtered with two losing seasons in the next three.

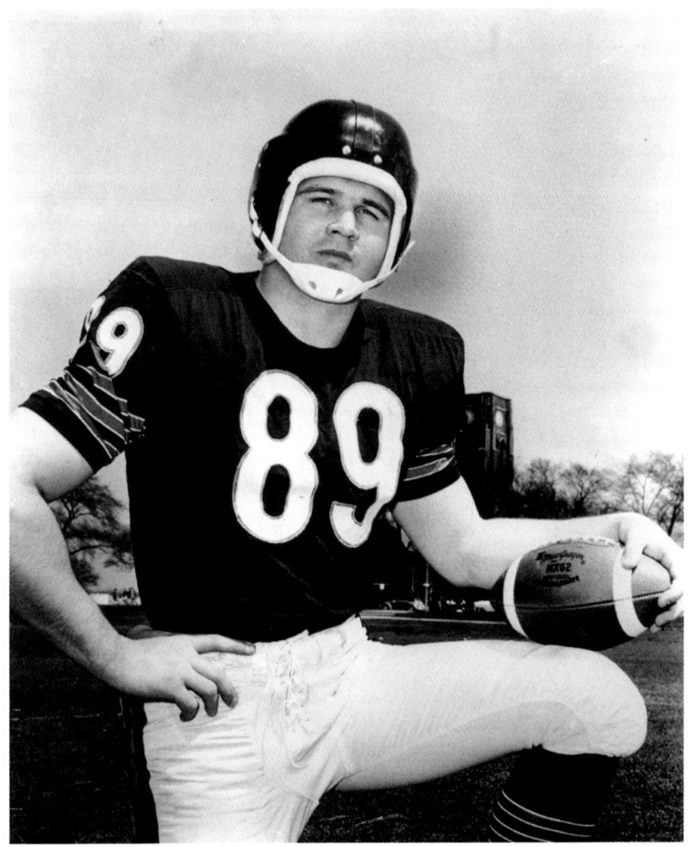

Mike Ditka (89), circa 1963.

Ditka and Morris, meanwhile, became one of the league's best receiving tandems. They set a record for most catches by a receiver and tight end in a season in 1964, when Morris had an NFL-record 93 and Ditka added 75.

Ditka's feuds with Halas worsened as the winning decreased. They always were at odds over money, and in 1964, the Chicago Daily News' Ray Sons reported that Ditka and Morris had let slip at a banquet that they thought Rudy Bukich should take over at starting quarterback for Wade.

Halas demanded they apologize in front of the team. Morris did so; Ditka refused.

"I don't have any apology," Ditka said in front of the gathered players and coaches. "Forget it."

"He was a guy who really defied Halas," Morris told Whittingham. "He kind of stood up and talked back to him, and people just didn't ordinarily do that to George Halas in those days.

"I think in the long run, however, that Halas actually respected Mike for doing that."

In 1966, Al Davis became commissioner of the American Football League and suggested its teams try to raid the NFL for as much talent as they could buy. The Houston Oilers, who had picked Ditka in the AFL draft five years earlier but lost him to the Bears, offered him a $50,000 bonus to sign with them. Ditka's salary at the time was in the $20,000 range.

Ditka agreed to the deal, but it was voided, as were the AFL's other signings, when NFL Commissioner Pete Rozelle announced a merger between the leagues on June 8. Ditka kept the bonus money. Halas was furious when he found out and gave Ditka a 10% pay cut.

"It wasn't that I was greedy about the money," Ditka told Jeff Davis. "Money was money. What the hell—we didn't make enough in those days to worry about it."

Still, the fuming Ditka sealed his fate with Halas with a quote that still stings 53 years later: "He throws nickels around like manhole covers."

On Sept. 16 in Los Angeles, Ditka punched a drunken fan who ran onto the field during a 31-17 Bears loss to the Rams. On April 26, 1967, after six seasons, five Pro Bowls and two first-team All-Pro selections, Halas traded the 27-year-old Ditka to the Eagles for quarterback Jack Concannon and a draft pick.

Ditka spent two years foundering with the Eagles before becoming a contributor again with Tom Landry's Cowboys. When he arrived in Dallas in 1969, he made the same kind of impression he did in Chicago, as halfback Dan Reeves, like Ditka a future Super Bowl coach, told Whittingham.

"We were playing gin rummy one night, and after Ditka lost a couple of hands he picked up a chair and threw it across the room," Reeves said. "All four legs stuck in the wall. All I could say was 'God, this guy hates to lose.'"

After the 1971 season, Ditka helped the Cowboys win Super Bowl VI with a touchdown reception in the 24-3 victory against the Dolphins. Ditka retired after the 1972 season, and Landry hired him as an assistant. The Cowboys won Super Bowl XII 27-10 over the Broncos after the '77 season.

Halas hired Ditka as Bears head coach in 1982, and he coached the team to a 46-10 win over the Patriots in Super Bowl XX after the 1985 season. He was named NFL Coach of the Year that year and for a second time in 1988, but the Bears have yet to win another championship. Halas' grandson Mike McCaskey fired Ditka in 1992, and "Da Coach" went 15-33 in three disastrous seasons with the Saints in 1997-99.

Ditka embarked upon a long broadcasting career, and he remains in the public eye more than any former Bear. He's still in demand for endorsements after shilling for countless products since he first put his name on a Willowbrook bowling alley during his playing days. He has co-written three autobiographies; one with Rick Telander is titled "In Life, First You Kick Ass."

He has appeared in TV shows including "Cheers," "L.A. Law" and "Saturday Night Live," and in 2005 he played himself in the comedy "Kicking & Screaming." He was the film's third-billed star after Will Ferrell and Robert Duvall.

A vocal conservative, Ditka considered running in 2004 for Illinois' vacant U.S. Senate seat after Republican nominee Jack Ryan withdrew from the race. Ditka decided against it, and Alan Keyes ended up losing that election to Barack Obama.

Ditka and Obama met in 2011, when the president invited the 1985 Bears to finally celebrate at the White House. Their planned trip to visit President Ronald Reagan in 1986 was canceled after the space shuttle Challenger exploded two days after Super Bowl XX. Ditka presented the president with a Bears No. 85 jersey with "Obama" on the back.

With his Gridiron Greats Assistance Fund, Ditka has raised awareness for the health problems of players from his era. In 1988 Ditka suffered a heart attack. In 2012 he suffered a stroke, and he had a second heart attack Nov. 23, 2018.

In many ways the story of the Bears can be

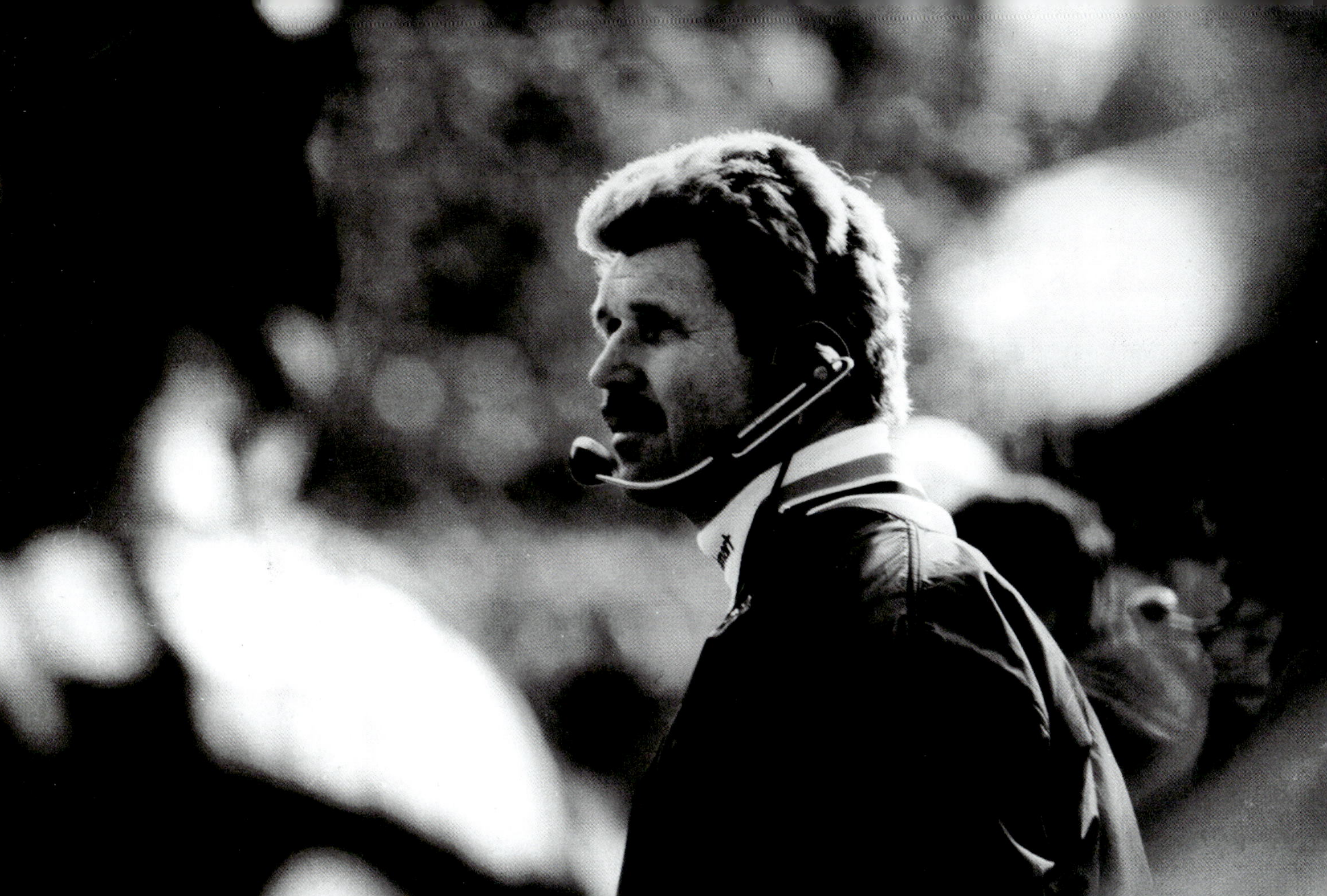

Coach Mike Ditka during a game, circa 1982.

told through Halas and Ditka. In many ways the man Ditka rebelled against so thoroughly is responsible for who Mike Ditka became.

On Dec. 28, 1960, Halas drafted Ditka. On Jan. 4, 1982, Halas took control of the team's operations from general manager Jim Finks. Halas quickly made three moves: He fired Neill Amstrong as head coach, retained Buddy Ryan as defensive coordinator and hired Mike Ditka as head coach.

Stan Jones, Ditka's old teammate, quipped: "It was like Orville Wright coming back to run United Airlines." The Tribune's Bill Jauss questioned whether the 86-year-old Halas had all of his faculties. "There's not a senile bone in this body!" Halas snapped at the Jan. 20 news conference introducing Ditka.

Halas' plan, which would see the Bears through until the 1990s, was in place. He presented Ditka with a bottle of Dom Perignon, not to be opened until the night the Bears won the Super Bowl. On Oct. 31, 1983, Halas died. On Jan. 26, 1986, Ditka opened his bottle.

"He gave me that opportunity, and I'm forever grateful," Ditka told Whittingham. "It's just a shame that he couldn't have stayed around to see all the good things that happened. . . . But I think he knows they happened. I think he had an inkling they were going to happen. I really do.

"The only job I ever wanted was the Bears job. I was committed to the Bears type of football—the kind that George Halas fostered. Anybody can think what they want to think or write what they want to write.

"It was just meant to be."

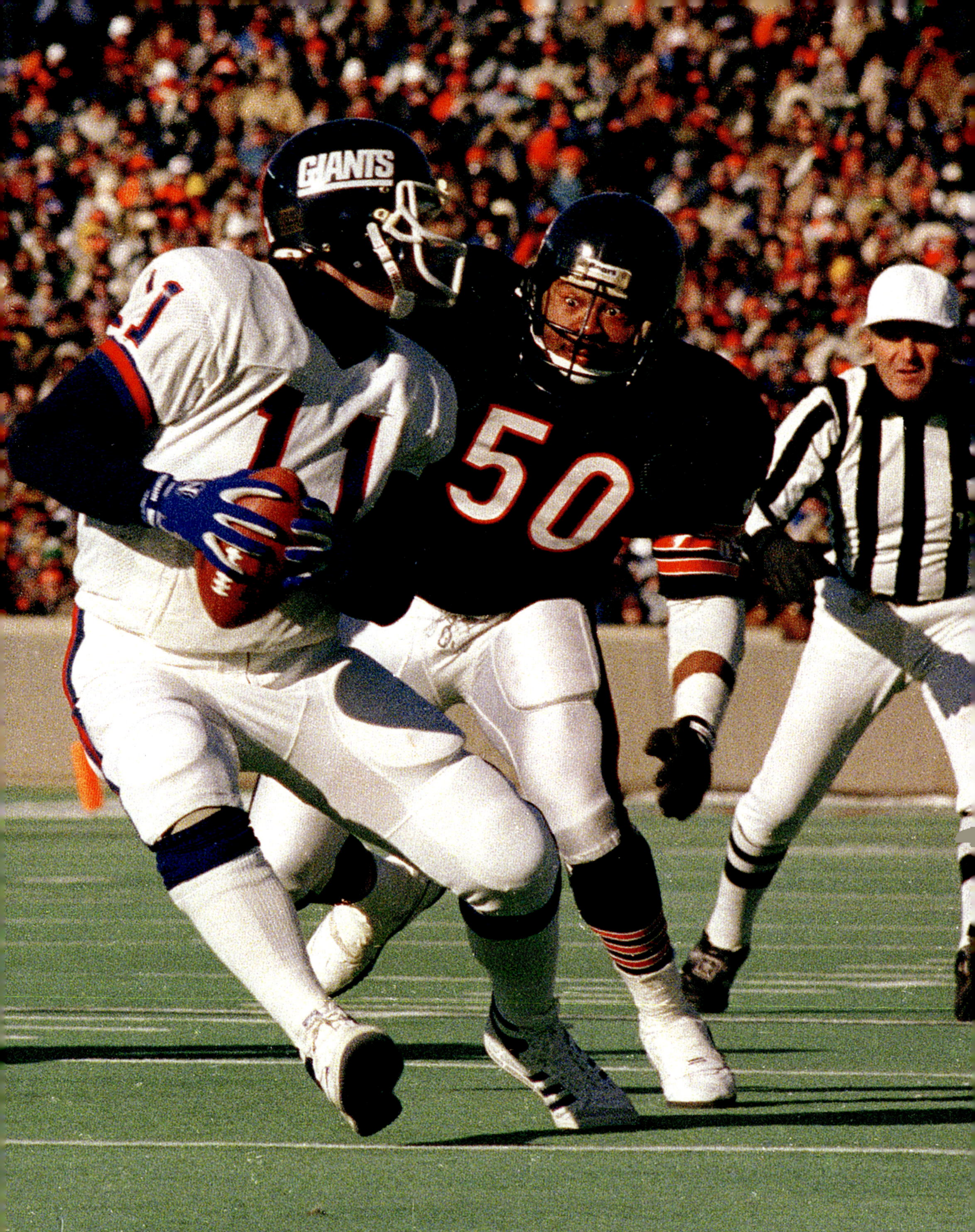
GIANTS
50

12

Mike Singletary

50 LINEBACKER
1981-92

MIKE SINGLETARY set a goal to become a starting middle linebacker in the NFL. He accomplished it in his seventh game with the Bears as a rookie in 1981.

Then Singletary wanted to become a three-down player who was good enough in pass coverage to stay on the field in nickel packages. After losing 20 pounds, he accomplished that in 1983.

When he was named to the Pro Bowl after that season for the first of 10 consecutive times, Singletary declared he would become the Defensive Player of the Year.

He was voted the winner of the Associated Press award in 1985 and again in '88.

"I don't look how things might be. I look at how things will be," Singletary told the Tribune's Philip Hersh on Sept. 7, 1986. "I don't just dream, I go to work."

After winning the award for the second time, Singletary set one last goal: to retire after the 1990 season, his 10th in the NFL.

Singletary finally made a promise to himself he couldn't keep. He didn't leave the Bears until 1992, playing two more Pro Bowl seasons after his planned exit date.

"What amazes me is to find out how much I love the game," Singletary explained to the Tribune's Don Pierson on Aug. 28, 1991. "I thought by this time, I'd get tired of looking at film, get tired of the politics, get tired of the cuts. I'm not.

"I still want to know more about the game, more about my job."

Singletary was the youngest of 10 children in a poor Houston home and was in and out of hospitals with various ailments until he was 7. He grew to a generously listed 6 feet and 230 pounds and became an All-America linebacker at Baylor. Singletary became known for hitting like a sledgehammer, and the count of the gold helmets he broke by smashing them into opponents is between 16 and 25 depending on the source.

Jim Parmer, an NFL scout for 35 years, traveled to Waco, Texas, to get a look at Singletary for the Bears.

"His attitude was so different than 99 out of 100 college kids I see," Parmer told Hersh. "He was dead serious, very businesslike. He looked right at me and said, 'Mr. Parmer, if you draft me, I'm going to be the best linebacker in the National Football League.'"

Mike Singletary (50) closes in on New York's Phil Simms (11) on Jan. 5, 1986, during the NFC semifinals at Soldier Field.

General manager Jim Finks selected Singletary in the second round of the 1981 draft with the 38th pick. Two years before the 1983 draft brought so much quarterback talent into the NFL, the '81 class made a similar impact on defense. The draft produced six defensive players—Singletary, Lawrence Taylor, Ronnie Lott, Howie Long, Rickey Jackson and Kenny Easley—who would be elected to the Pro Football Hall of Fame, plus six-time Pro Bowl selection Dennis Smith. Singletary was the first of the group enshrined in Canton, Ohio, in 1998.

That was a long way off when Singletary arrived to Bears camp in Lake Forest. Defensive coordinator Buddy Ryan was there to greet him with the contempt he gave all rookies. Ryan was particularly hard on Singletary, whose teammates nicknamed him "Samurai" for the shrieks he made on the field. Ryan called Singletary fat—a common Ryan epithet—and a slur for Japanese people after misidentifying the Cherokee features Singletary inherited from his mother.

Defensive tackle Jim Osborne somehow could tell Ryan liked Singletary and advised the rookie linebacker to stay the course instead of blowing up at his demanding and demeaning coach.

Osborne was right. Singletary entered the starting lineup—a rarity for a rookie under Ryan—in the Bears' seventh game and stayed there for 12 seasons. As he became one of the league's best middle linebackers, fans rushed to compare him to Bears middle linebackers Bill George and especially Dick Butkus.

Singletary resisted the comparison, but Osborne, the only player to play with him and Butkus, saw similarities.

"The intensity level was the same between Dick and Mike," Osborne told Pierson on Aug. 2, 1998. "But while Dick would be on the bottom of the pile trying to bite someone or twist an ankle, Mike would help you up. Dick was instinctive . . . Mike watched more film than some of the coaches.

"He would knock your head off, and then kneel beside you and lead you in prayer."

As Singletary achieved his goal of staying on the field for passing downs, the Bears defense rose to the top of the league. They finished eighth in yards and fifth in points allowed in 1983, then began a five-year run of ranking first or second in total defense.

The Bears linebacker unit of Singletary and outside backers Wilber Marshall and Otis Wilson—the "Bermuda Triangle"—became the best in the league. Defensive tackles Dan Hampton and Steve McMichael gave Singletary plenty of time to diagnose plays and strike.

The 1985 Bears ranked first in total, scoring and rushing defense and third in passing yards allowed. After shutout wins against the Giants and Rams in the NFC playoffs, the Bears won Super Bowl XX 46-10 over the Patriots.

At the Superdome in New Orleans, Singletary recovered two of the Patriots' four fumbles. He rated the Bears' defensive effort a "9.999 out of 10" before lamenting a miscommunication that led to the Patriots' first first down 4 minutes, 14 seconds before halftime.

Throughout that season, Ryan sang a new tune about his now-prized middle linebacker. Late in the year he called for Singletary to be named not only Defensive Player of the Year but MVP of the NFL.

"No question he's the best linebacker in the NFL," Ryan told Pierson on Nov. 15, 1985. "Look at the things he can do. Cover people, run with people, tackle, run the defense."

Like most of the Bears, Singletary's profile grew after the championship win. Closeups of his wide eyes became a favorite of TV producers, as did the audio of his on-field exhortation, "I like this kind of party!"

The 49ers' Roger Craig told Pierson on Jan. 5, 1989: "When I look into his face mask, it's like he's hungry. He's like a wolf, trying to get some raw meat."

The Bears seemed primed for a dynasty, but that honor went to Craig's 49ers. After each missed opportunity the Bears core shrank, but Singletary kept up his excellent play no matter who was on the field with him.

Perhaps his finest effort came in 1988. With Marshall gone to the Redskins and Wilson out for the season with a knee injury, the Bears still finished first in scoring and rushing defense and second in yards allowed. Ron Rivera and Jim Morrissey moved into the starting lineup and, thanks in large part to Singletary's guidance, performed admirably as the team finished 12-4 and won its fifth consecutive NFC Central Division title.

"Mike Singletary was kind of the glue that kept us together," Rivera told the Tribune's Fred Mitchell on Dec. 29, 1988. "A lot of what he does rubs off on you. You learn to be a more complete football player."

Coach Mike Ditka added: "He's a great credit to the game of football, and I appreciate the fact we have the good fortune to have him on our team."

As captain of the defense, Singletary handled the complicated play-calling for Ryan's system and its multiple formation, blitzing and coverage audibles.

"It could be two or three pre-snap changes," safety Gary Fencik told Pierson on Aug. 2, 1998. "To be able to slap those guys around up front and communicate to the rest of us while you're trying to do your job, I don't think we really quite appreciated how difficult that was."

In 1988, the Tribune's Bob Sakamoto asked 20 members of the Bears whom they considered the leader of the team. Singletary earned 15 votes.

"He is the most dedicated athlete I've ever seen in my life," guard Tom Thayer said. "It's an honor to be on the same team as him. If you're looking for one person who epitomizes a leader, a captain, a professional football player, there's no doubt it's Mike Singletary."

What Singletary said, his teammates generally did. During the difficult 1987 players' strike, 15% of the league's players—including Taylor, Long, Craig, Joe Montana, Tony Dorsett and Steve Largent—crossed the picket line. The Bears were one of four teams, with the Vikings, Eagles and Redskins, that had no veterans play in replacement games.

"A lot of guys around the league live from check to check, and a lot of guys just don't care," Singletary told Pierson on Oct. 30, 1987, after the strike ended. "On the Bears, I was very fortunate to have guys who really cared. . . . It wasn't me holding them together; it was us holding each other together."

Off the field, Singletary's simple life stood in contrast to the wild ways of many of his teammates. He liked to read the Bible and Norman Vincent Peale's "The Amazing Results of Positive Thinking," watch reruns of "The Andy Griffith Show" or "Leave It to Beaver" and think about how nice it would be if the rest of the world adopted the Amish way of life.

His only vice was his on-field swearing, for which he immediately would ask the Lord's forgiveness. Singletary set a goal and got better at that, too, according to Rivera.

"He's got a modified 'Damn,' " Rivera said. "He says, 'Amn.' "

Singletary was heavily involved in charity work and was named the NFL's Man of the Year in 1990. He has written four books, and after a decade away from the game he joined the Ravens as linebackers coach in 2003. He took a job with the 49ers in '05, became their interim coach in '08 and head coach the following year. In 2½ seasons as an NFL head coach, Singletary went 18-22. He was fired before the last game in 2010 with a 5-10 record.

In 2014, Pierson ranked Singletary the fourth-best linebacker in Bears history behind fellow middlemen Butkus, George and Brian Urlacher. Singletary's seven first-team All-Pro selections rank second in team history, tied with Bulldog Turner and one behind George.

On Dec. 13, 1992, as Singletary's career with the Bears drew to a close, the Tribune's Bernie Lincicome wrote: "Singletary's tenure passed through the bad, the great, the good, the current of the Bears, and it gives the frame to how this all will be recalled in the leaner times ahead.

"When we think back to these days, when time exaggerates those Bears, it will be impossible even then to overpraise Mike Singletary. He was simply the best of them all." ■

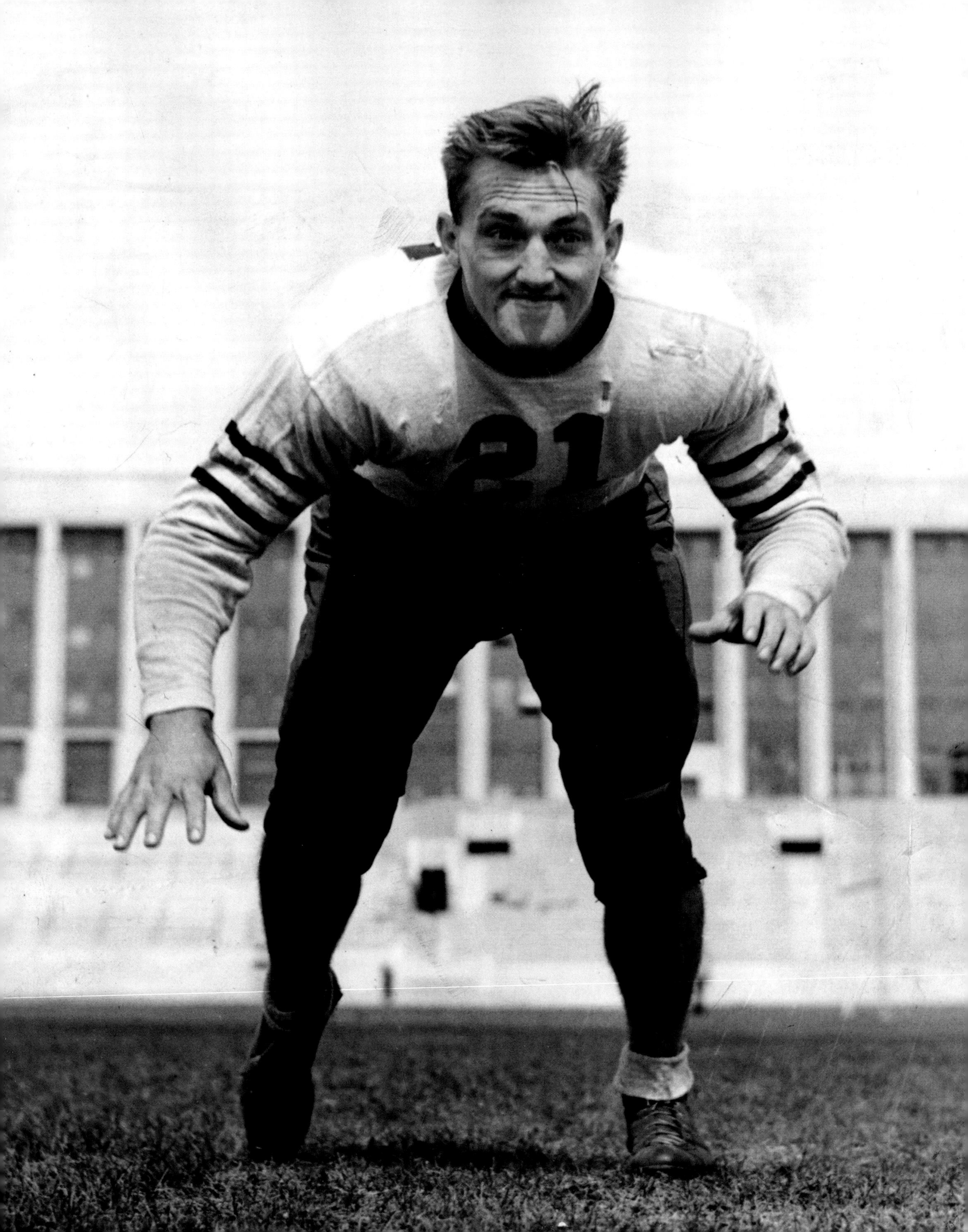

13

Danny Fortmann

21 GUARD
1936–43

T HE BEARS WENT INTO the 1936 draft, the first in NFL history, woefully unprepared.

The team employed one man, Frank Korch, as its public relations director and talent scout. As the nine-round, 81-player draft began, he and owner/coach George Halas had scouting reports on 14 players.

When the Bears' final turn came around at No. 78, any prospect familiar at all to Halas and Korch had been off the board for hours.

Halas looked at the list of remaining players.

"I saw a name I liked: Danny Fortmann," the coach wrote in "Halas by Halas," his 1979 autobiography. "It had a good sound. I said, 'I'll take this Danny Fortmann.'"

Four future members of the Pro Football Hall of Fame were selected in that first draft. The Bears took two: Joe Stydahar from West Virginia, their first-round pick at No. 6, and Fortmann, a 19-year-old pre-med graduate from Colgate.

The two would play next to each other, Stydahar at left tackle and Fortmann at left guard, for five years, and Fortmann anchored the lines that served as the foundation of the greatest era in Bears history.

Fortmann was one of the smallest linemen of his era at 6 feet and 210 pounds. There were not many who ever were better. He played eight seasons, all with the Bears, and was named All-Pro each year, including six first-team nods. The Bears went 69-17-2 in those seasons, finishing first in the Western Division five times, second twice and third once.

Bears quarterback Sid Luckman was inducted into the Hall of Fame with Fortmann—a 60-minute player at offensive and defensive guard—in its third class in 1965.

"You'd look at Danny and wonder how he'd ever compete," Luckman told the Tribune's David Condon on Sept. 16, 1965. "Check old movies and you'll see Fortmann all over the field. I'll bet he made 40% of the tackles in some games. I honestly never remember him missing a tackle."

The Bears won three NFL championships in four years in 1940, '41 and '43. The 1942 team was perhaps the best of the bunch. The Bears finished 11-0 that year with a point differential of 376-84 but lost the title game 14-6 to the Redskins at Griffith Stadium.

In four years from 1940 to '43, the Bears

Danny Fortmann (21), circa 1940.

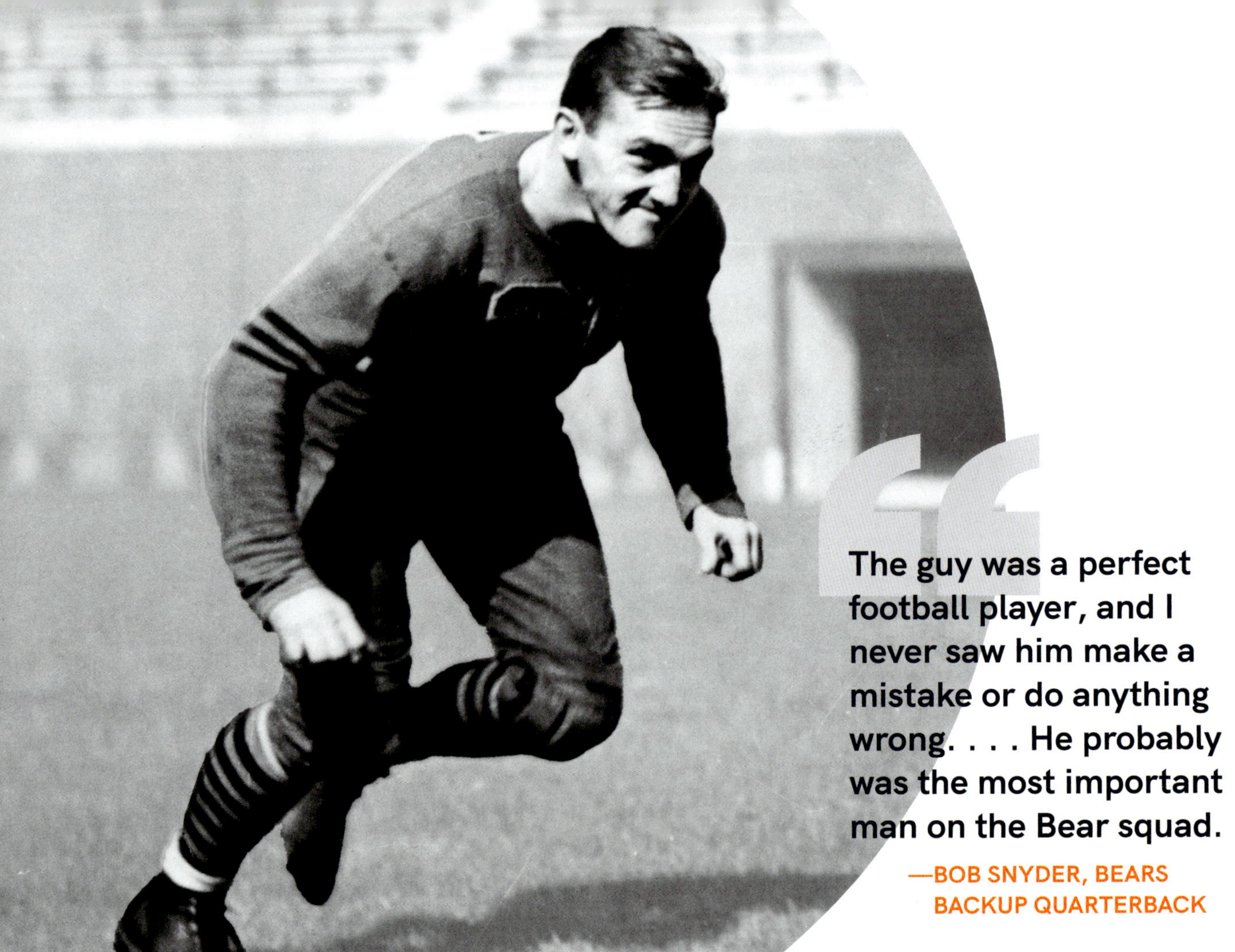

Danny Fortmann (21), in his third year with the Bears in 1938.

went 37-5-1 and outscored their opponents 1,313-540, an average game score of 31-13. In their four championship games, their point differential was 157-44, including the 73-0 victory over the Redskins on Dec. 8, 1940, in Washington.

Bob Snyder, Luckman's backup at quarterback, told the Tribune's Edward Prell on Aug. 25, 1942, that Fortmann was the most valuable player of the Monsters of the Midway dynasty.

"Dan was always at his best when the chips were down. 'As Danny goes, so go the Bears' is what we used to say," Snyder said. "The guy was a perfect football player, and I never saw him make a mistake or do anything wrong. . . . He probably was the most important man on the Bear squad."

The Bears lines of the era were some of the best in NFL history. The 1940 edition featured four Hall of Famers side by side by side by side: Stydahar, Fortmann, center Bulldog Turner and right guard George Musso. In 1942, four Bears linemen were voted first-team All-Pro: Fortmann, Turner, right tackle Lee Artoe and right end George Wilson.

In Richard Whittingham's 1991 book, "What Bears They Were," halfback George McAfee credited them with making many of his runs easy.

"Most of the time people give too much credit to the guy with the ball," McAfee said. "They don't give near enough credit to the guys up front who make all those runs possible. Look at who I had up front blocking for me then. . . . It was a pleasure to run behind them."

As Fortmann led the Bears to their greatest heights on Sundays, he studied to become a surgeon during the week. Halas convinced Dr.

B.C.H. Harvey, dean at the University of Chicago's Rush Medical College, to allow Fortmann to play for the Bears as he earned his medical degree.

Fortmann, in an article by Jim Campbell from the June 1985 issue of Legends magazine, said: "Normally, Halas didn't give anyone permission to miss practice. But he believed medical school was a tremendous ambition. It was almost as important to him as it was to me. Without Mr. Halas, I could never have prepared for my future."

After Fortmann earned his degree, he served as the resident physician at hospitals in Detroit and Pittsburgh. Halas kept the same lenient schedule with him as when Fortmann was in medical school; often Fortmann would show up in Chicago the day before the Bears played at home or were scheduled to travel to a road game.

"We marveled because Danny could do all this and keep up his medical studies," Luckman said. "He worked so hard studying medicine.... To him, the pro season was a vacation."

Fortmann's intelligence and steadiness, traits that served him well on and off the field, made him a natural leader, and Halas named him co-captain with Musso in 1940. The two guards were as different as could be: the trim, cautious Fortmann from a genteel New York suburb, where he was valedictorian of his high school class, and Musso, the loud, large "Collinsville Cowboy" who came to the Bears from Millikin University.

Early in their careers, the guards collided behind the line during practice when each thought it was his turn to pull. Fortmann, of course, was correct.

"What's the matter, Danny, haven't you learned the signals yet?" Musso shouted sarcastically, a story he told to Bob Braunwart and Bob Carroll of the Pro Football Researchers Association in 1981.

Fortmann had to laugh at his teammate's sense of humor, and the two became great friends. When Musso suffered a near-fatal car crash in 1962, Fortmann flew overnight from Los Angeles to St. Louis to sit at his bedside.

Unlike most linemen of the 1930s and '40s, Fortmann was respectful to his opponents during an era when cheap shots happened on almost every play.

In their 1997 book, "Mudbaths and Bloodbaths: The Inside Story of the Bears-Packers Rivalry," Gary D'Amato and Cliff Christl wrote: "Fortmann was undersized but a master of the submarine block. He also was one of the few Bears that the Packers never squawked about."

"Now there was a gentleman," Packers halfback Hal Van Every told D'Amato and Christl. "Everyone liked him."

Fortmann retired after the 1942 season, but Bears co-coaches Luke Johnsos and Hunk Anderson—filling in while Halas served in World War II—persuaded Fortmann to return for one more year. After winning his third title, Fortmann walked away for good to join the Navy and work on a hospital ship in the Pacific Ocean. He was one of 19 players the Bears lost to the service from their 28-man roster between the 1943 and '44 seasons.

After returning from the war, Fortmann set up his practice in Southern California, where he would work until 1984. From 1947 to '63 he served as the team physician for the Los Angeles Rams, whom his old friend Stydahar coached in 1950-52. Fortmann was diagnosed with Alzheimer's disease late in life and died at 79 in 1995 in Pasadena, Calif.

When Stydahar compared one of his Rams players, guard Duane Putnam, to Fortmann, Prell was taken aback. In the Aug. 1, 1952, Tribune, Prell wrote that "comparing a freshman guard to the great Bear of a decade ago is something like calling a baseball rookie a new Cobb. Fortmann was that good."

In his Hall of Fame speech, Fortmann said the lessons he learned playing football served him well in his true calling.

"The experiences you gain on the football field can be carried over in many other aspects of life," he said. "Teamwork is something that's important in both professions. A surgical team must work together. I learned a lot about teamwork playing football with the Bears." ■

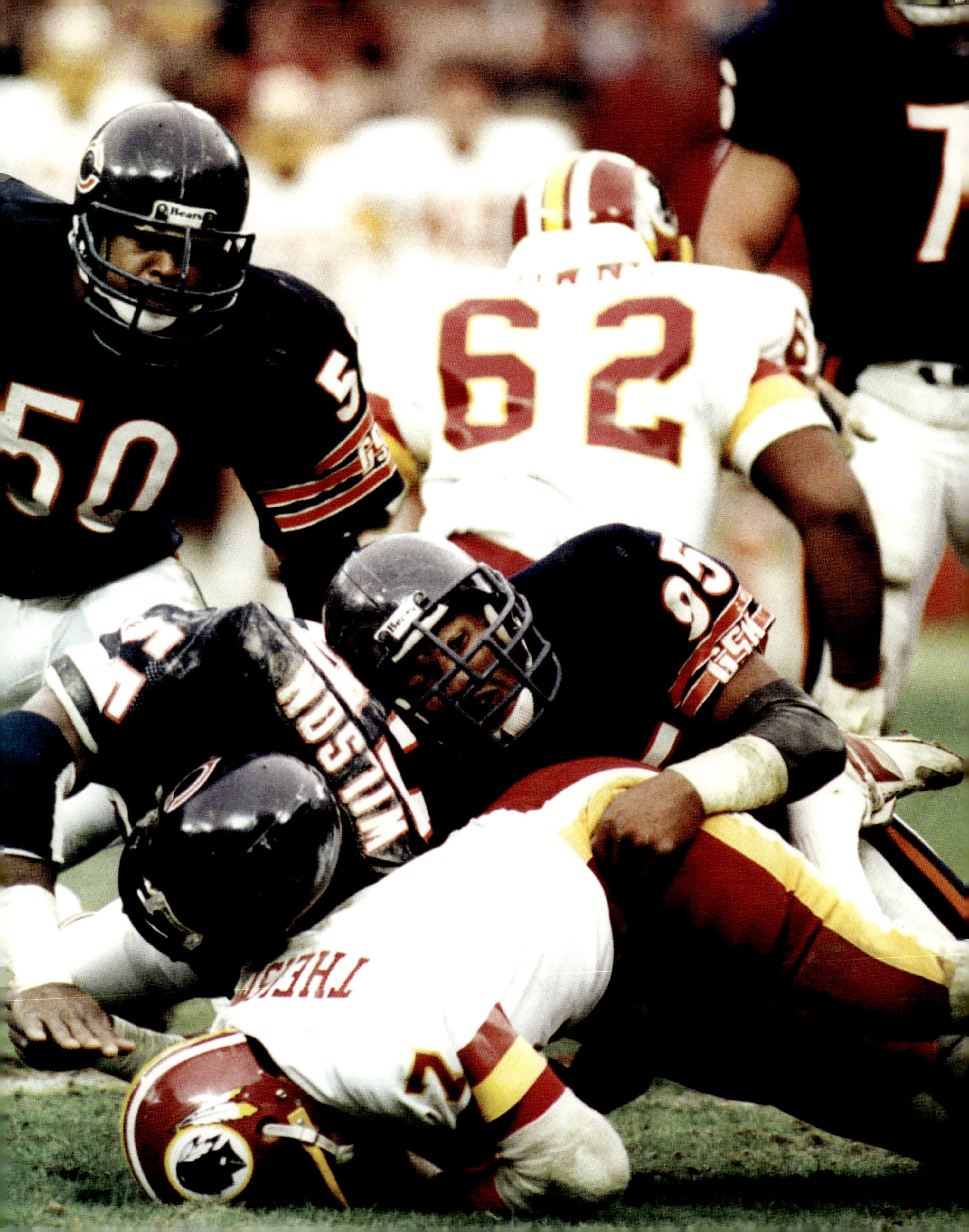

14

Richard Dent

95 DEFENSIVE END
1983–93, 1995

O N THE FIRST PLAY of Super Bowl XX, Richard Dent ended up on his back, looking at the Superdome ceiling.

The Bears defensive end had spent a moment trying to figure out what type of play the Patriots were running. It was one moment too long, and tackle Brian Holloway made Dent pay.

"He caught me watching," Dent told Ed Sherman for the Jan. 27, 1986, Tribune. "He put me down good. I had never been hit like that before. The first lick is all you need. It gets you going."

Dent laid waste to Holloway, Hall of Fame guard John Hannah and the rest of the Patriots the rest of the game. On the Patriots' second possession, Dent and Wilber Marshall sacked Tony Eason for a 10-yard loss. After the Bears tied the score 3-3 on their next possession, Dent and Steve McMichael sacked Eason again, forcing a fumble Dan Hampton recovered at the Patriots 13-yard line.

The Bears took a 6-3 lead on Kevin Butler's second field goal, and Dent gave his team the ball back at the same spot on the Patriots' next play when he stripped running back Craig James. Mike Singletary recovered, the Bears took a 13-3 lead on Matt Suhey's 11-yard touchdown run, and with about a minute to play in the opening quarter, the game—which the Bears won 46-10—essentially was decided.

"Dent single-handedly set the tone for the game," Sherman wrote. "He had to go up against two of the best offensive linemen in the league in Holloway and Hannah. But they couldn't stop the Sackman."

Dent was named the game's most valuable player, the fifth defensive player to earn the honor. In 53 Super Bowls through the 2018 season, 10 defensive players have been named the game's MVP.

"Holloway and Hannah give a lot of people trouble," Dent told Sherman. "But as I said earlier in the week, you can put anyone on me, and nothing is going to stop me. I plan on playing right through those guys."

The Super Bowl capped Dent's spectacular playoff run. He had six sacks in the Bears' three postseason games: 3½ in the 21-0 win against the Giants in the divisional round, one against the Rams in the NFC championship game and 1½ against the Patriots.

Richard Dent (95) and Otis Wilson (55) take down Washington's Joe Theismann (7) on Dec. 31, 1984.

Dent was at his best in the Bears' biggest games. In their seven playoff games after the 1984-87 seasons, Dent collected 10½ sacks.

After the win against the Giants, in which Dent added six tackles, a forced fumble, a pass deflection and three tackles for a loss, Bears coach Mike Ditka told Don Pierson for the Jan. 7, 1986, Tribune: "You can go back the 20 years I've been around and be hard-pressed to find a defensive end play any better in a big game than Richard Dent."

Dent's breakout performance came on Nov. 4, 1984, in a 17-6 win against the defending champion Los Angeles Raiders at Soldier Field. Dent had 4½ sacks in the victory, which placed the Bears among the NFL's elite for the first time in 20 years. It also gave Dent the first of his six career NFC defensive player of the week honors.

After the game, Hampton told the Tribune's Bob Verdi: "Richard lately has been super. He's learning technique all the time, but the big thing he's got going for him is his quickness. He just bursts off the ball. He bowls over the offensive lineman. Makes him tough to stop."

Dent led the NFL with a Bears-record 17½ sacks that season. He also holds the team mark for career sacks with 124½, and he matched his single-game mark of 4½, again against the Raiders, in 1987.

In 2014, Pierson ranked Dent the third-best defensive lineman in Bears history behind Doug Atkins and Hampton. Dent's 137½ career sacks rank ninth all time, and his eight years with double-digit sacks rank behind only Bruce Smith's 13, Reggie White's 12, Kevin Greene's and Julius Peppers' 10 and John Randle's nine.

Dent produced more turnovers than the average defensive end, too, forcing 37 fumbles, recovering 13 and grabbing eight interceptions.

Hampton said Dent had the best second step he ever saw. "The first step is important," Pierson wrote on Oct. 27, 1995, "but Dent beat tackles with the second step."

Dent did not play football—or any organized sport—until his junior year at Atlanta's Murphy High School. His coach there, the late William Lester, arranged for Dent to play at Tennessee State as a walk-on.

He was an undersized offensive tackle as a redshirt freshman, then was moved to defense. Tennessee State's defensive coordinator at the time, Joe Gilliam, told the Tribune's Dan Pompei on July 31, 2001: "He was put on me by the offensive coaches. He was 215 pounds, too small for an offensive tackle, so I took him. But I told the coaches I have cornerbacks bigger than Dent."

Dent became a three-time Division I-AA All-American but was not much of a pro prospect. Bears scout Bill Tobin saw potential in him and argued for the team to take him as early as the third round in the 1983 draft. General manager Jim Finks wasn't high on Dent but allowed Tobin to have him in the eighth round.

The Bears noticed Dent's bad teeth and paid to straighten them. It always had hurt him to eat, and once his teeth were fixed, he quickly gained 30 pounds and became a different player. The Bears struck twice in the eighth round that year with Dent and guard Mark Bortz, who like Dent would become a stalwart for more than a decade.

Dent and Bortz were two of seven starters the Bears drafted in 1983, along with Jimbo Covert, Willie Gault, Mike Richardson, Dave Duerson and Tom Thayer. In addition to undrafted free agent Dennis McKinnon, the group helped turn the Bears into Super Bowl champions by their third year in the NFL.

In practice, Covert and Dent gave each other pointers during pass-rush drills. Dent told the Tribune's David Haugh on Feb. 6, 2011, that going against Covert every day in practice "made the games seem easy." Covert told Pompei that Dent's "repertoire of pass rushes really increased over the years. He could do pretty much anything he wanted."

Dent learned some defensive tricks from veteran linemen Hampton, McMichael, Jim Osborne and Mike Hartenstine. Dent tried to repay the favor to young Bears through the years.

Outside linebacker John Roper told the

Tribune's Bob Sakamoto on Oct. 3, 1989, that "Richard helps me every day in practice. . . . He shows me things like technique and how to keep the blocker off balance so you can move right by him."

Dent kept helping Bears defenders even in retirement. He told Alex Brown to watch the play clock when the offense breaks the huddle. If it is in the last 10 seconds, Brown told the Tribune's John Mullin on Nov. 28, 2005, "you know it's going to be on the first or second sound, so that gives you that little edge."

As a young player Dent displayed one elite skill, which was explained by his nicknames. In addition to "Sackman," Dent was called "The Colonel" because like Kentucky Fried Chicken's founder, he did one thing and did it very well. As he gained experience, Dent became solid at all aspects of defensive line play.

"Dent wasn't only the best pass rusher in team history," Pierson wrote on Dec. 26, 2014, "he learned to play the run as well or better than any of the great pass rushers."

Dent became the highest-paid Bear ever in 1989 when he signed a five-year, $6 million contract extension. It was the culmination of years of Dent pointing out he was underpaid compared with the league's best pass rushers. He contemplated sitting out Super Bowl XX in protest of his $90,000 salary.

As Dent's paycheck grew, so did a feud between him and Ditka. After a slow start in 1987, the Bears coach took to calling Dent "Robert" instead of Richard. Dent was furious, and whether it was out of motivation or spite, he closed the season in a fury and finished second in the NFL with 12½ sacks in the strike-shortened year.

"Always, when things don't go well, the finger's pointed at me," Dent told Pierson on Nov. 19, 1987. "I guess I'm the finger guy. . . . When we lose, I'm the target. When we win, nothing is said about what I did."

Dent didn't go all out every play, which annoyed Ditka but was part of a strategy, according to Dent, to feel out opposing linemen for their weaknesses like a heavyweight boxer.

"In your eyes, you think I'm taking a play off," Dent told the Tribune's Steve Rosenbloom on Oct. 17, 2005. "But you don't understand the game, so you wouldn't know what I'm doing."

Dent won his second Super Bowl ring with the 49ers after the 1994 season, but in contrast to his MVP performance nine years earlier, he was inactive for the loaded team. He returned to the Bears in 1995 as coach Dave Wannstedt thought Dent might be able to give his dormant defense a spark, but that experiment lasted only three games before the Bears released Dent. He played his final two seasons as a situational pass rusher for the Colts and Eagles, combining for 11 sacks in 1996 and '97 before retiring.

In 2011, Dent was elected to the Pro Football Hall of Fame in his ninth year of eligibility, joining 1985 teammates Walter Payton, Singletary and Hampton—as well as Ditka—in the Hall.

"I didn't really know what the hang-up was," Dent told the Tribune's Fred Mitchell on Feb. 10, 2011. "I felt I was one who made a change in the game in pass rushing and taking the ball from the quarterback. . . . I was patient, didn't care to call anybody out. My day has come."

Dent focused on homelessness awareness during his career and remains active with his Make A Dent charity foundation. He is president and CEO of RLD Enterprises, an energy products and services company. He still offers Bears players advice on how to get to the quarterback quicker.

At the Bears100 Celebration Weekend in June 2019, Dent took All-Pro outside linebacker Khalil Mack aside for a half-hour chat.

"You can tell he loves the game, and he wanted to teach everything he knew in one little sitting," Mack told the Tribune's Rich Campbell on June 12, 2019. "He kept telling me about how you check somebody in basketball. The same way he put his elbow on somebody is the same thing I saw on film."

Did Mack plan on using Dent's advice in 2019?

"Hell, yeah." ▪

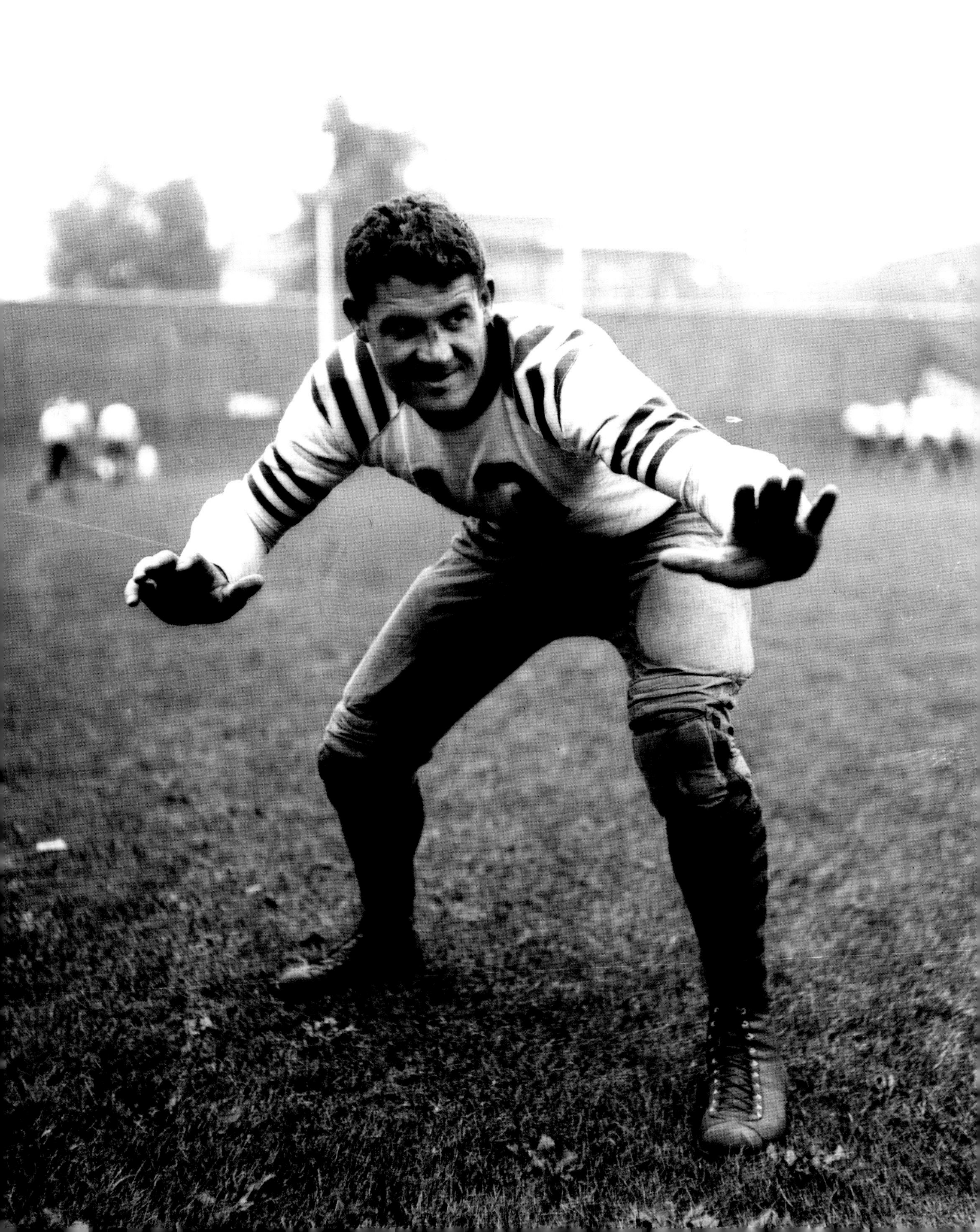

Joe Stydahar

15

THE BEARS OF THE 1940S were the most successful group in franchise history. By all accounts they were the closest too.

Each player had a specific role before, during and after a play. Joe Stydahar, the 6-foot-4, 233-pound tackle from coal country in West Virginia, performed his duties with gusto.

"Jumbo Joe" was the first draft pick in Bears history in 1936, and the first lineman ever taken, at No. 6. Before a play, Stydahar, usually the largest player on the field, often would crawl along on his hands and knees, "apparently sizing up the opposing players from all angles," Bears coach George Halas wrote in the Feb. 9, 1967, Tribune.

"Nobody suspected that Joe really was trying to get an unobstructed view of the quarterback's face," Halas continued, "because Joe never bothered to tell anybody that he could read lips."

During the play, Stydahar was one of the NFL's best two-way tackles. After it, any Bear would report to him when an opponent got away with a cheap shot, and Stydahar would make sure it didn't happen again.

Halfback Hugh Gallarneau, in Richard Whittingham's 1991 book, "What Bears They Were," remembered Eagles lineman Bucko Kilroy giving him a particularly hard time.

"Every time I'd go through the line, he'd elbow me at my mouth," Gallarneau said. "I remember coming back to the huddle one time bleeding like mad.

"Joe Stydahar . . . took a look at me . . . then told (quarterback Sid) Luckman which play to call, one that was kind of away from Kilroy. After the play I turned around and Kilroy was on the ground, out like a light. There was a definite camaraderie on that team."

Stydahar became one of the league's best linemen very quickly. In his second season, he led all players in voting for the All-Pro team, leading an AP report on Dec. 15, 1937, to gush: "The standout player of the 1937 national pro football league season wasn't Slingin' Sammy Baugh of the Washington Redskins, as the headlines and his game-winning tosses might have led the fans to believe, but Joe Stydahar, veteran tackle of the Chicago Bears.

"That was the way the coaches of the 10 league clubs figured, at least, when it came to casting their ballots for the all-league

Joe Stydahar (13), circa 1936.

team. . . . Stydahar received 43 points out of a possible 50."

In 1939, only Packers receiver Don Hutson and Bears guard Danny Fortmann—a ninth-round pick in 1936—finished ahead of Stydahar in the voting.

Stydahar was named second-team All-Pro as a rookie in 1936, then first-team after the next four seasons. He helped the Bears win NFL championships in 1940 and '41, served in the Navy in 1943-44, returned for the final three games of the 1945 season, and in his final year helped the Bears win another title in 1946.

The Bears went 72-52-2 (.737) in his nine seasons. In 1999, the Tribune's Bernie Lincicome picked his all-time Bears team with Stydahar and Jim Covert as tackles: "A Jimbo and a Jumbo."

Before each of his games with the Bears, Stydahar would vomit in a locker-room toilet. It got to be a familiar ritual for his teammates, many of whom didn't feel comfortable taking the field until "Old Faithful" erupted.

Stydahar was thankful to play for a team that was so good and with players who were so friendly with each other.

"We had something special," he told the Tribune's David Condon on April 21, 1967. "No other team I've ever known has ever had the same spirit. There were great men who had more than the ability to play championship football. They had spirit and loyalty."

Stydahar felt fortunate most of all to be playing a game for a living after watching his father, an immigrant from Yugoslavia, toil in the mines.

"One little kneecap isn't too much to pay," Stydahar once said, "for a kid who might be shoveling coal."

After Stydahar excelled at football and basketball in high school, a recruiting war erupted between Pittsburgh and West Virginia for his services. Stydahar originally chose Pitt and enrolled there, only to change his mind and switch to West Virginia before his freshman season. The Pitt coaches went to Morgantown, W. Va., to look for their star recruit, but Mountaineers coach Greasy Neale, who would coach the Eagles to the NFL title in 1949, hid him in a fraternity house until the Panthers coaches gave up their search.

The whole experience was bewildering to Stydahar, who went on to star in both sports at West Virginia and was the best basketball player to wear No. 44 there until Jerry West came along.

"I was strictly an honest kid," Stydahar told Condon, "accustomed to chewing tobacco and saying hello to anyone I met along the road. I didn't know that if you said hello to a stranger in a big city you were apt to wind up in the hoosegow."

After Stydahar left the Bears in 1947 he went into coaching, catching on with the Rams as an assistant and becoming their head coach in 1950. He led them to consecutive title games against the Browns, falling in 1950 and winning in '51.

In 1952, Stydahar got into a power struggle with assistant Hampton Pool, a former Bears teammate. Rams owner Dan Reeves chose Pool's side and fired Stydahar one game into the season. Stydahar joined the Packers as an assistant for the rest of the season, then became head coach of the Chicago Cardinals in 1953.

Stydahar's two years on the South Side were terrible, and he was fired in 1955. In two-plus seasons with the Rams, Stydahar went 17-8; he was 3-20-1 with the Cardinals.

His motivational techniques were talked about by his players for decades. Stydahar once chastised his Rams for being poor tacklers and said their lack of missing teeth proved his point.

"By way of illustration," Halas wrote, "he extracted from his own mouth a sparkling denture containing five uppers which had been provided by his former employers, the Chicago Bears. Then, waving his upper plate like a battle flag, Stydahar exhorted the Rams to get in there with their chins up, regardless of consequences."

Halas claimed Stydahar, in an espionage tactic similar to his lip-reading as a player, would rent a hotel room adjacent to the visiting coach and put a stethoscope up to the wall to try to hear the opponent's game plan.

When Stydahar was with the Cardinals, he

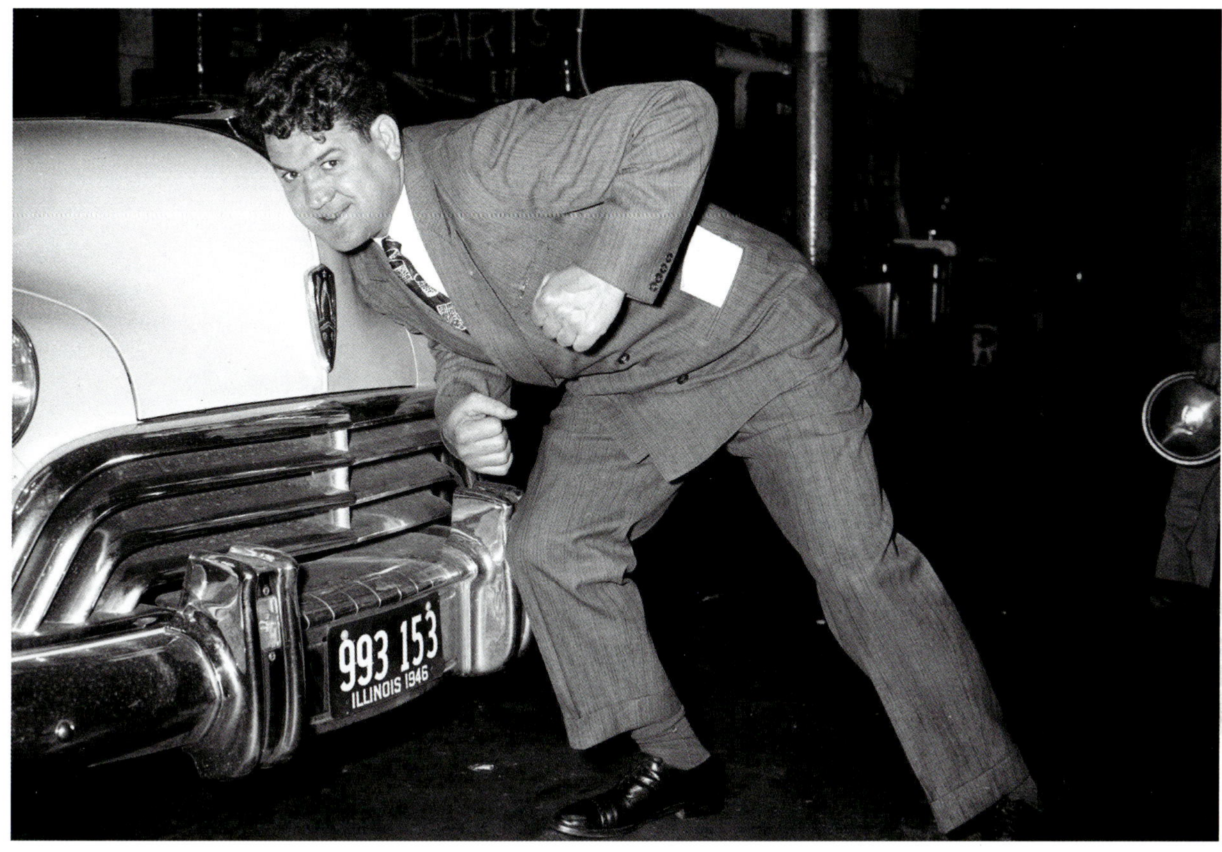

Joe Stydahar, circa 1946.

once took his players' paychecks for an upcoming game against the Bears and threw the rubber-banded bundle across the locker room at Comiskey Park.

In Jeff Davis' 2005 book, "Papa Bear: The Life and Legacy of George Halas," Cardinals end Pat Summerall remembered: "Joe said, 'All right, you gutless sons of bitches, if you don't beat the Bears, you don't get paid.' That's about as severe a fine as you can get. . . . We beat the Bears anyway."

Summerall couldn't help but be impressed, though, by one of his coach's talents. "He was the only person I knew who could smoke a cigar, chew tobacco and drink whiskey all at the same time."

Halas hired Stydahar as an assistant coach for the Bears defensive line in 1963, saying to the Tribune's George Strickler on Feb. 15: "We are confident Stydahar can help us. Nobody ever ran very far against Joe."

The 1963 team won the NFL championship, but Stydahar lasted only one more season as a coach before retiring to tend to his container company. He died of heart failure at 65 in 1977 on a business trip in Beckley, W.Va.

In 1967, Stydahar was elected to the Pro Football Hall of Fame. Condon wrote: "Joe was one of pro football's first ogres, and he was one of the best. They have recently ushered Joe into the Professional Hall of Fame, which is a select sport shrine and probably the only one not controlled by a group of ninnies. . . . Very few ever have deserved a testimonial as much as this giant."

After Stydahar's death, Halas said: "Joe was something special for me. Football fans know him as the first lineman drafted in the first round in 1936, as a true All-Pro, as a great football player. . . . But more important to any football accomplishments, Joe Stydahar was a man of outstanding character and loyalty." ■

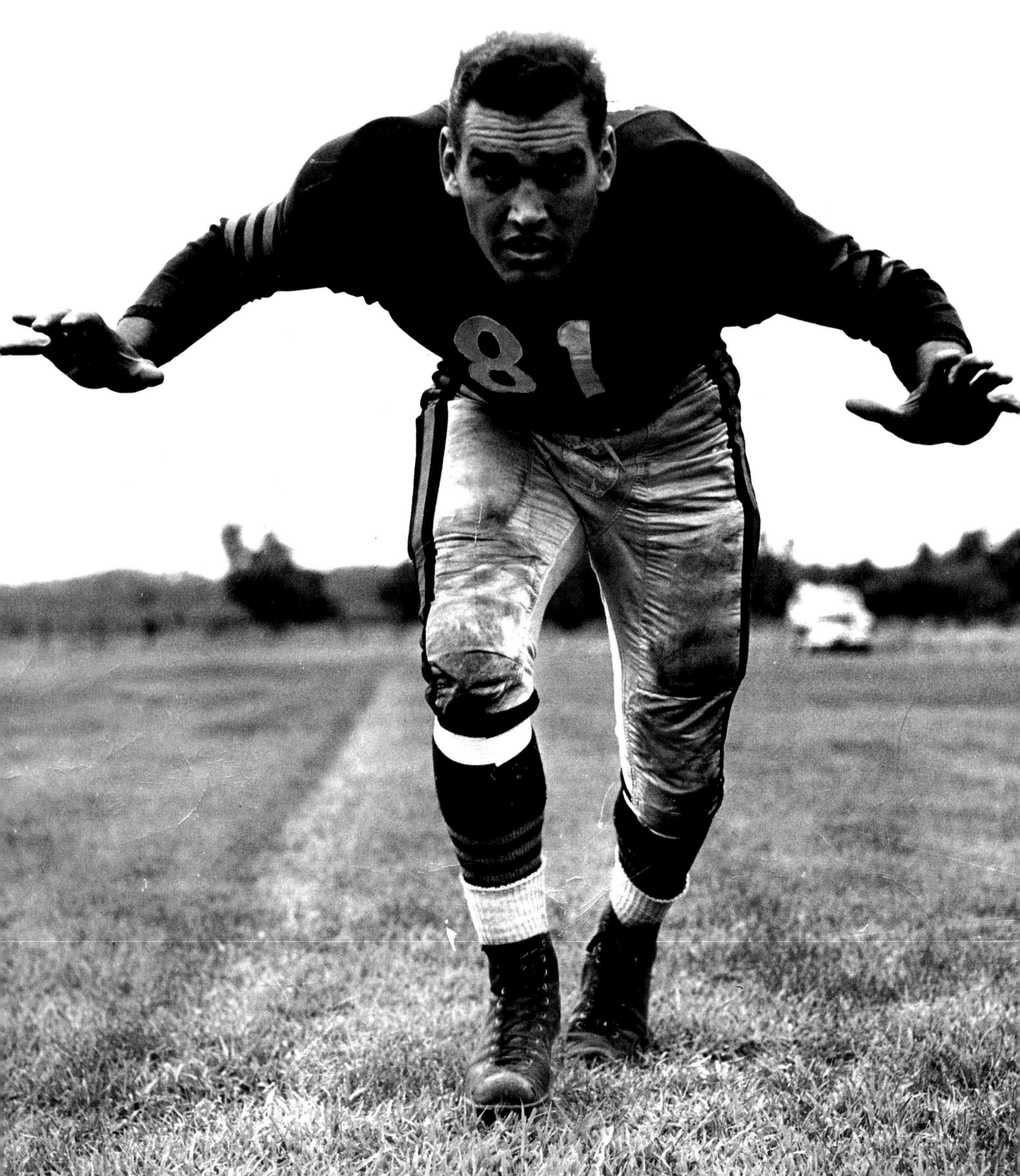

George Connor

GEORGE CONNOR KNEW he was playing against the Packers for the final time on Nov. 6, 1955, at Wrigley Field.

Not only that, the Bears' two-way star's parents, Esther and Dr. Charles Connor, were in the stands at Wrigley Field, as was his brother Jack, on leave from the Marines.

"I wanted to show them something," Connor told Jeff Davis in his 2005 book, "Papa Bear: The Life and Legacy of George Halas."

In the second quarter, with the Bears already up 21-3 on the way to a 52-31 win, Connor made what still is acknowledged as the biggest hit in the history of the series.

"Some 40 years later, players still spoke of Connor's hit with a mixture of awe and amazement," former Milwaukee Journal Sentinel reporters Gary D'Amato and Cliff Christl wrote in their book "Mudbaths and Bloodbaths: The Inside Story of the Bears-Packers Rivalry" in 1997. It was "a collision so violent, many players on the field involuntarily shuddered in horror."

The Bears' George Blanda kicked off the ball to the Packers' Veryl Switzer. Connor, the wedge buster on kickoffs who was tasked with breaking up the three- or four-man wall in front of the returner, sprinted down the field with a full head of steam.

The Packers' wedge fell apart, either confused about which way the return was going or wanting no part of the 6-foot-3, 240-pound Connor, whom Grantland Rice once described as "the closest thing to a Greek god since Apollo."

Connor ran untouched to Switzer, lowered his shoulder and exploded. The ball, Switzer and his helmet went in different directions.

Bill George recovered the fumble. Bill Bishop was one of the next Bears on the scene.

"I was right next to Switzer," Bishop told D'Amato and Christl. "I picked up his headgear. I thought he had lost his head."

"A lot of people in the stands thought I had decapitated him," Connor said in Richard Whittingham's 1991 book "What Bears They Were."

Switzer had been an excellent returner. The Packers drafted him fourth overall out of Kansas State in 1954, and as a rookie he led the NFL with a 12.8-yard punt-return average, including a 93-yard touchdown against the

George Connor (81) ushered in the era of the large but quick linebacker.

Bears. After the hit from Connor, he played sparingly the rest of the season and did not return in 1956.

Gary Knafelc, an end for the Packers at the time and their public-address announcer from 1964 to 2004, called it "the worst hit I've ever seen in my life."

"I mean, the whole stadium, there wasn't a sound," Knafelc told D'Amato and Christl. "They thought Switzer was dead."

Connor's combination of size and speed made him perhaps the most feared hitter of his era. He once delivered a knockout blow on 49ers fullback Joe Perry that was so fierce it broke the tape Connor used to hold up his high socks.

Cardinals quarterback Paul Christman told the Tribune's Jack Rosenberg on Nov. 11, 1956, that Connor's hits were fierce but clean. "He used to hit me in the face, then apologize."

"I wasn't mean," Connor told Rosenberg, "but I wasn't meek."

Connor made his first mark on the NFL as one of its first outside linebackers in a package the Bears introduced for a game against the Eagles in 1949. Until then, NFL linebackers generally were centers and fullbacks who stood a few steps behind the linemen. Bears coach George Halas and defensive coordinator Hunk Anderson had Connor, a tackle on offense, stand up outside an end about 2 yards behind the line.

Anderson concocted the scheme to slow down the Eagles' powerful running game. Steve Van Buren would lead the NFL in rushing that season for the fourth time in five years. In 1947 he was the second NFL player to rush for more than 1,000 yards, breaking Beattie Feathers' 1934 record of 1,004 yards by 4 yards. In 1949 Van Buren was on his way to a new mark of 1,146 that would stand until Jim Brown rushed for 1,527 in 1958.

The 1949 Eagles went 11-1, then defeated the Rams 14-0 for the championship. The Bears handed them their only loss on Oct. 16, outgaining them 457-255. The Eagles rushed for 42 yards, 175 fewer than their league-leading average of 217 per game. The Bears stuck with their new formation and allowed the fewest rushing yards in the NFL, an average of 100 per game.

A new position was born. Connor was the first of the big, mobile outside linebackers who still disrupt offenses today. The Bears' great players who followed Connor at the position include Joe Fortunato, Larry Morris, Doug Buffone, Otis Wilson, Wilber Marshall, Lance Briggs and Khalil Mack.

"It was a lot of fun playing the position back then," Connor told The Associated Press on Nov. 9, 1984. "Most teams had never seen it before. Blockers didn't really know how to handle me out there off the line of scrimmage. And all the fans were looking at me because the newspapers made such a big thing about it with diagrams and all."

Connor found a play could be diagnosed more easily from his new vantage point.

"If you tried to follow the ball," he told the AP, "a slick quarterback could fool you every time. So I just started picking out one or two players on the offensive line and moved with their first moves."

Connor was equally adept on both sides of the ball. He was named first- or second-team All-Pro six times, and three of those times he earned the honor as both a tackle and a linebacker. He was elected to the Pro Football Hall of Fame in 1975, and the institution named him to its All-Decade team of the 1940s, even though his best years came in the '50s. In 1994, the Tribune's Don Pierson and Fred Mitchell named Connor and Jimbo Covert the starting tackles on their all-time Bears team.

Introducing Connor at his Hall of Fame induction, Halas said: "He just simply was great all the way—born to heroics and completely at ease and efficient in the role."

Connor, a Chicago native, was born two months premature. Weighing 3 pounds, he was given a grave prognosis. His doctor advised he be fed boiled cabbage juice with an eyedropper in addition to his mother's milk. Connor's mother, a nurse, and his father, a general practitioner, took turns caring for him by his bedside for a year until he improbably gained full health.

"Boiled cabbage juice and faith are a strange mixture," Connor told Rosenberg, "but they saved my life."

Connor entered De La Salle High School on the South Side still on the small side at 5-foot-3 and 135 pounds, but by the time he graduated he was 6-1, 215. His coach, Joe Gleason, kept him out of contact drills so he wouldn't hurt his teammates.

An all-out recruiting battle followed, and while Connor wanted to attend Notre Dame, he followed his family's wishes and went to Holy Cross, where his uncle and namesake, Monsignor George Connor, was president of the alumni association. As a freshman in 1942, Connor dominated, and he led the Crusaders to a 55-12 shocker against No. 1 Boston College at Fenway Park.

Connor joined the Navy in 1944 and was stationed in the Pacific during World War II with Notre Dame coach Frank Leahy, who re-recruited Connor with the promise that he would become an All-American and the Irish would win a national title. Both came true when Connor's tour ended as he became the first Outland Trophy winner as the nation's best lineman in 1946 and Notre Dame was voted national champion in 1947.

The Giants drafted Connor with the fifth overall pick in 1946, but Connor informed them he wouldn't play anywhere but Chicago and went back to Notre Dame. After the 1947 season the South Sider hoped to join the Chicago Cardinals, who had won the NFL title that year, but coach Jimmy Conzelman said the team was full at tackle.

So, Connor went to Halas, who told him, "Stick to your guns, kid, and I'll get you."

By that time, the Boston Yanks had acquired Connor's rights from the Giants, and eventually Halas sent them tackle Mike Jarmoluk for those rights. Halas wanted Connor so badly that he broke his rule of not acquiring a player who employed an agent for one of only three times in the Bears' first 45 years;

the others were Red Grange in 1925 and Dick Butkus in 1965.

Before the 1948 season Connor signed for an unheard-of $13,000 per year for three years with a $6,000 signing bonus. When his new teammates learned Connor made more than established stars such as Bulldog Turner and Ray Bray, they took it out on the rookie.

"When I went to my first training camp, I found out just how poorly that sat with the other players," Connor told Whittingham. "They really gave me a bad time. Most of the scars I have on my face today are from my teammates that year."

Connor took the abuse in stride, and his talent and toughness became apparent. At the end of camp Turner said: "Kid, you're all right. You took everything we gave you. Welcome to the team."

A knee injury in 1954 limited Connor's effectiveness, and he retired after a bounce-back season in '55, saying he wanted to leave to cheers rather than boos. He served as an assistant coach for the Bears in 1956 and '57 under new coach Paddy Driscoll, a stretch Connor called the worst two years of his life.

He stayed with the team as a broadcaster, teaming for years with Grange, and he was a salesman for a corrugated box company. One of Connor's greatest skills was public speaking, and he was a regular emcee at local charity events for much of the rest of his life. Connor died of a variety of ailments at 78 on March 31, 2003, in Evanston.

Connor's sons, George Jr. and Al, never saw him play football but were in awe of their father's other talent, the Tribune's Don Pierson wrote on April 1, 2003.

"He was probably just as accomplished as a public speaker," George Jr. said. "We used to marvel at how little preparation he did. He'd show up at the Notre Dame Club or wherever he was speaking, talk to a few people, jot down some notes and just talk. And he'd be great at it." ■

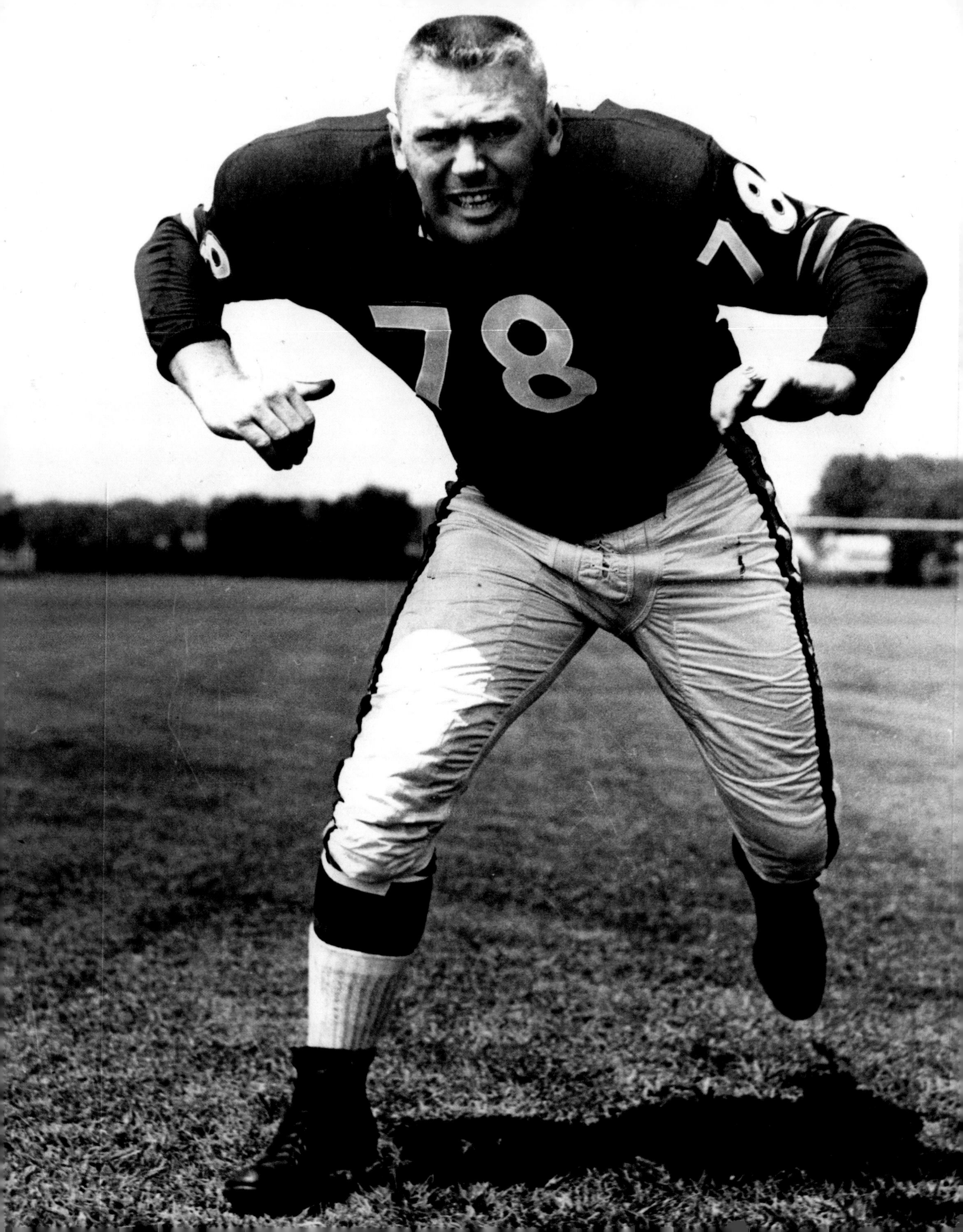

17

Stan Jones

73, 78 GUARD, TACKLE

1954–65

STAN JONES ALWAYS sat next to his telephone on cutdown day.

As the Bears' strongest player and one of their top performers, he never had a reason to worry, but Jones was so humble he never took anything for granted.

One year, the phone rang.

"This is it," he thought.

On the other line was, in fact, George Halas, the Bears' gruff owner and coach.

"Stan," Halas said, "would you mind moving from left guard to right guard?"

"Jeez!" Jones replied. "I think that's a great idea!"

Jones told the story to the Tribune's Cooper Rollow on July 26, 1991, as Jones prepared to enter the Pro Football Hall of Fame. Jones was one of the NFL's best offensive linemen from 1954 to '61, earning first-team All-Pro honors three times, second-team once and seven consecutive trips to the Pro Bowl.

When he lost some speed and no longer was able to make it to the hole before Bears backs on pulling plays, coaches thought he still could be useful. They moved him to defensive tackle, and he played both ways as a reserve in 1962. The next year he moved into the starting lineup at defensive tackle. He, Earl Leggett and Fred Williams held down the middle for one of the best defenses ever, and the Bears won the 1963 NFL championship.

Defensive coordinator George Allen and line coach Joe Stydahar, a two-way Hall of Famer for the Bears in the 1930s and '40s, were not surprised to see Jones excel on their side of the ball.

"The first time I saw him in training camp, I knew Stan would fill the position easily," Stydahar told Rollow on Dec. 23, 1963. "He can catch plays going away from either direction. . . . I rate Jones and Earl Leggett as the outstanding tackles in the league this year."

Allen believed Jones would be an asset to the defense but was taken aback at how quickly he "picked up all the little tricks" needed to succeed as a defensive lineman.

"You don't expect a person coming over from offense to pick up the traps, the screens, the suckers so quickly," Allen told Rollow on Jan. 27, 1991. "He learned the job almost instantly."

Jones thought he was closer to being out of the league than playing a key role for the NFL champs.

Stan Jones (78), circa 1957.

"I didn't know what to expect when I went down to training camp this year," he told Rollow. "I never went to camp with such a feeling before. Looking back, I can see that the coaches had a lot more confidence in me than I did in myself."

Jones fit right in on a unit that included linemen Leggett, Williams, Doug Atkins and Ed O'Bradovich and linebackers Bill George, Joe Fortunato and Larry Morris. His best friend on the defense was backup end Bob Kilcullen, who played major minutes in 1963 while O'Bradovich was in and out of the lineup because of injuries.

Kilcullen and Jones played next to each other, leading the Chicago American's Bill Gleason to predict other teams might exploit the two as the weak links in an otherwise excellent defense. After all, Gleason reasoned, in the offseason Jones was a public-school teacher and Kilcullen an artist.

In Richard Whittingham's 1991 book, "What Bears They Were," Jones said the two friends went out to dinner the night before the opening game against the Packers and saw Gleason. Kilcullen loudly told the writer that the Bears had nothing to worry about with their two new defensive linemen.

Jones, still humble at times to a fault in his 10th NFL season and "not knowing how this whole transition was going to turn out," told Kilcullen, "Hey, don't call any more attention to us."

The Bears beat the Packers 10-3 with plenty of plays going toward Jones and Kilcullen. The defense dominated that game and the rest of the season, leading the NFL in scoring, total defense, passing and rushing defense and takeaways. When the Bears beat the high-scoring Giants 14-10 for the NFL championship, Jones called it the greatest thrill of his career.

While Jones was one of the NFL's last two-way linemen, he was one of the league's first players to take weight training seriously. He started lifting in high school, and he claims to have gained 20 pounds per year for eight consecutive years from his freshman year in high school in LeMoyne, Pa., to his senior year at Maryland. In his first 12 NFL seasons, the 6-foot-1, 252-pound Jones missed two games.

"I developed my own form of conditioning," Jones told Whittingham. "No one was lifting weights with the Bears when I got there. In fact I was warned that I might be risking my career working with weights. They thought I'd become muscle-bound and lose my speed and agility. . . . Just the opposite. It made me stronger and more durable."

As an All-America two-way lineman, Jones helped the Terrapins become the 1953 national champions. In his first appearance in the Tribune, while training for the 1954 College All-Star Game at Soldier Field against the defending NFL champion Lions, Jones was pictured doing a pushup with smiling Maryland teammate Bobby Morgan on his back. "The training maneuver," the caption read, "is popular only with Jones."

Halas saw Jones play once in college, against Georgia in 1953. Almost nothing made Halas happier than when one of his players would annihilate an opposing quarterback on an interception return. Jones did just that with Halas in the stands, plowing over Zeke Bratkowski, who would become Jones' road roommate for a few years with the Bears.

"Halas kind of liked that," Jones told Whittingham.

The Bears selected Jones as a fifth-round future pick in the 1953 draft. After college, Jones tried to become a pilot in the Air Force but was too big to pass the physical. He decided to join the Bears. So began Jones' relationship with Halas, which featured all sorts of interesting interactions. Jones, one of the best storytellers the Bears have employed, relished sharing them.

Halas stripped Jones and Bill George of their longtime captaincies in 1962 when the team voted to join the players' association.

After the players voted to unionize, almost unanimously, Jones was charged with telling Halas, whose team had been the last union holdout. In Jeff Davis' 2005 book, "Papa Bear: The Life and Legacy of George Halas," Jones told the story of Halas hearing the unwanted news.

"I came and that jaw went out," Jones said, "He took me into the bathroom section of the clubhouse."

"What was the result of your (expletive) vote?" Halas asked.

"It wasn't my (expletive vote)! It was the team's vote!"

"You're fired!" Halas screamed. "That reflects on the leadership of this team!"

Jones didn't have the heart to ask if he was fired as captain or released from the team altogether. Jones and George were replaced as captains by Fortunato and center Mike Pyle, who would become the team's first union representative.

"In time it passed and he never held that against me," Jones said. "I know he liked me, but he never would say anything like that, you know?

"It might have been the most courageous thing I ever did in my life to face that man. I was shaking; I guarantee that."

Jones never made more than $14,000 playing for Halas. In 1966 Papa Bear did Jones a favor by trading him to the Redskins so he could play near his home in Landover, Md. In his only year in Washington, Jones made $20,000. Every time Jones would ask for more money, Halas said there was no way he could present a raise like that to the board of directors.

"There was no board of directors," Jones told Davis. "Halas was the board of directors."

When Jones left the Bears, he thought for a great while of just the right words to convey how much he appreciated the chance to play for Halas and his team.

"Well, Coach, this has been a great opportunity, and I certainly appreciate it," Jones said. "It's been a great experience."

Halas briefly looked up from the newspaper he was reading and told Jones, "Well, kid, keep in touch."

After Jones retired he mentioned to Halas that he planned to open a restaurant. Halas mailed Jones a signed blank check and told him to cash it for however much he needed to get started.

Jones changed his mind and went into coaching. He served as an assistant with the Broncos for 17 of the next 21 years for four head coaches as well as stints with the Bills, Browns, Patriots and the Scottish Claymores of NFL Europe before he retired in 1998.

All the while, Jones kept Halas' blank check as a memento of the man's complicated nature.

Jones was voted into the Pro Football Hall of Fame by the old-timers committee in 1991 at age 59. He was known as a friend to all, and Rollow once described him as "one of our city's more innocuous and gentle citizens." Still, Jones saved some classic back-in-my-day vitriol for his induction speech. After Kilcullen introduced Jones and the requisite mention of those who helped him along the way, Jones spoke until the flashing red lights behind the audience indicated his time was up.

Jones blew through the stop sign and delivered a screed against the modern game, decrying artificial turf, indoor games and what really made him "half sick": "Second-and-long, everybody comes off the bench, everybody goes back to the bench. . . . All the trick football, get rid of it.

"For the 'What It's Worth' department, my suggestion for the future of the NFL is bring back the sledgehammer offense. Put back the drive blocks, the traps and trench warfare. Bring back the seven-man sled and quit popping and recoiling all over the place.

"Thank you very much," he concluded to a standing ovation.

In 1985, the Tribune's Don Pierson named Jones and Danny Fortmann the Bears' all-time guards. In 1994, Pierson and Fred Mitchell chose Jones and Ray Bray. In 1999, Bernie Lincicome selected Jones and Mark Bortz. Jones' seven Pro Bowl selections are tied with Jay Hilgenberg for the most by a Bears offensive lineman, and only Mike Singletary with 10 and Atkins with eight have made more consecutive Pro Bowls as a Bear.

While guards are well-represented with 11 players in the Tribune's list of the Bears' top 100 players ever, Jones was only the sixth guard selected for the Hall of Fame.

He remained a regular at Bears alumni events, often telling stories until well after midnight, for most of the rest of his life. Jones died at 78 on May 21, 2010, in Broomfield, Colo. ■

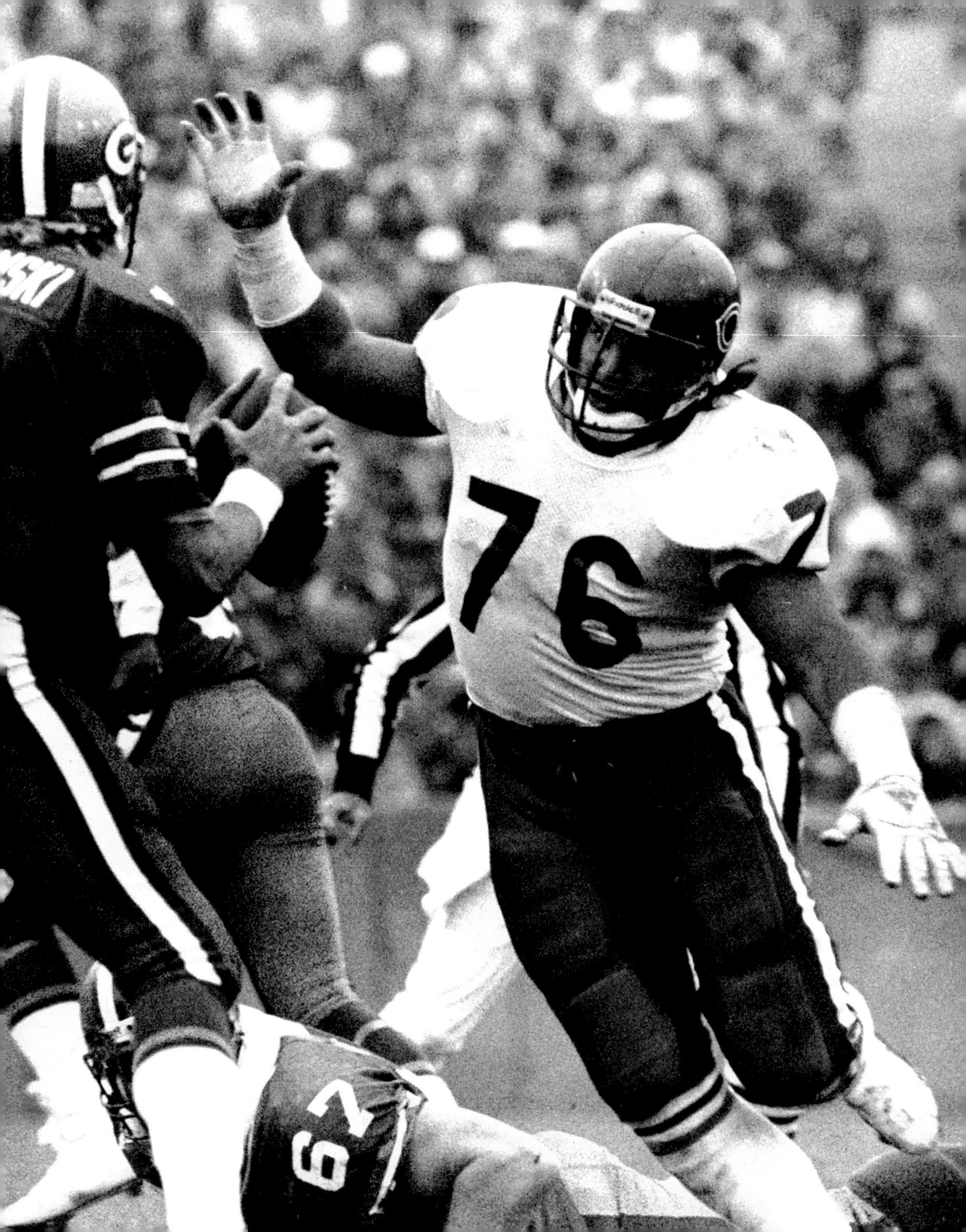

18

Steve McMichael

76 DEFENSIVE TACKLE
1981–93

W**HEN THE PATRIOTS RELEASED** Steve McMichael in 1981, giving up on their 1980 third-round pick after only one year, coach Ron Erhardt added an insult on the defensive tackle's way out the door.

According to McMichael, Erhardt told him: "We believe you're part of the criminal element in the league."

The Patriots didn't like the hours McMichael kept or the places he kept them. They hated how he would go all out during workouts against guard John Hannah, who just had been christened "The Best Offensive Lineman of All Time" by Sports Illustrated on its Aug. 3, 1981, cover.

"I'd go 'live' against him to see how I could do against the very best," McMichael told the Tribune's Bill Jauss on Dec. 14, 1983. "John didn't mind, but the coaches complained."

McMichael returned to his hometown of Freer, Texas, "to start the rest of my life," he said. The Bears called midway through the 1981 season and brought him on as a special teams player. He didn't get much action on defense that season or in '82, but he felt more at home than he had in New England.

That was thanks to three men in Chicago. Coach Mike Ditka encouraged his players to be themselves and didn't keep tabs on them too closely as long as they practiced hard and produced on Sundays. Dan Hampton, one of the best defensive linemen in the league and equally adept as a tackle or an end, served as McMichael's role model on and off the field. Defensive coordinator Buddy Ryan told his players to get after it on every snap—the way McMichael liked to practice and play.

Ditka and McMichael hit it off immediately as kindred spirits. Ditka pushed Ryan to insert McMichael into the starting lineup, and he advocated for him during and after his career.

"Steve transcended every era," Dikta told the Tribune's Rick Kogan on Aug. 28, 2005. "He could have played in the '40s, '50s, '60s, '70s. What he had, he gave to me, all of it. There was never a down where he didn't go all out."

Hampton and McMichael, born one month apart in 1957, might as well have been brothers. The big, brash linemen—Hampton from Arkansas, McMichael from Texas—raised hell at all hours on and off the field and became the best tackle tandem in the league.

Steve McMichael (76) on Nov. 5, 1989, during a game against the Packers in Wisconsin.

In McMichael and Phil Arvia's 2004 book, "Steve McMichael's Tales from the Chicago Bears Sideline," he wrote: "I guess we got along because we were both country boys, small-towners, and had a lot in common. Thank God he was on the team at the time. He became my big brother, my guide through chaos, really.

"It especially motivated me in practice to dominate and kick ass. Impressing him was a big factor. I wanted to show him that I . . . fit in with what he considered important about playing football. Every guy who plays that smash-mouth brand of football is impressing other guys who do."

Ryan was not as easy to win over. When McMichael joined the Bears, Ryan—who called players by their uniform number or a derogatory nickname until they proved they deserved better—asked him before his first practice whether he was in shape. McMichael responded that he regularly went jogging with his Great Dane.

"They worked my ass off," McMichael wrote. "I was taking every rep. . . . So I was gassed after practice."

As Ryan walked off the field, he remarked to McMichael: "(Expletive), 76, we shoulda hired the dog."

Eventually, Ryan called McMichael "Tex," a big upgrade. Hampton nicknamed McMichael "Mongo" after the dimwitted and violent yet lovable "Blazing Saddles" character played by Alex Karras. Eventually, Hampton changed McMichael's moniker to "Ming the Merciless" after the "Flash Gordon" villain.

"'Mongo' was something Dan thought was funny," McMichael wrote. "'Ming' was a sign of respect."

McMichael moved into the starting lineup alongside Hampton in 1983 and produced immediately. Off the field he generally behaved like a professional wrestler, which he would become a dozen years later, even peppering his pronouncements by calling the person he was addressing "baby" or "brother."

Trace Armstrong, McMichael's teammate from 1989 to '93, told John Mullin in his 2003 book, "Tales from the Chicago Bears Sideline,"

that McMichael "had this Hollywood style. He bought a Rolls-Royce convertible, red with white interior and a white top. . . . Here comes this red convertible, big guy driving with long hair flapping in the breeze, and this little chihuahua he's holding as he's driving. And the chihuahua's got some kind of outfit on. That was vintage Ming."

Mullin wrote: "Ming was a really intelligent guy. When he got on camera he understood that for notoriety, he had to push the envelope a little bit and he did. So he really developed a shtick and a persona that was his signature."

McMichael gained revenge on the Patriots by helping the Bears beat them 46-10 in Super Bowl XX after the 1985 season, and his profile grew. Those who paid attention only to McMichael's outlandish behavior missed the fact that he had become one of the game's best defensive tackles. He was named first-team All-Pro in 1985 and '87, second-team in 1986 and '91, and to the Pro Bowl in 1986-87.

At 6-foot-2, 270 pounds, McMichael was smaller than the average tackle, but he thrived in Ryan's system because of his strength and quickness. He was able to stuff the run, and he was one of the best pass rushers from the inside in NFL history.

McMichael recorded 10 or more sacks in 1984, '88 and '92. Since sacks became an official statistic in 1982, his career total of 95 ranks third among defensive tackles behind only John Randle's 137½ and Warren Sapp's 96½. McMichael's 92½ sacks with the Bears rank second since the team began tracking the stat in 1970 behind only teammate Richard Dent's 124½.

Armstrong played 15 NFL seasons as a defensive end with teammates who included Dent, Hampton and Mike Singletary with the Bears, Zach Thomas and Jason Taylor with the Dolphins and Charles Woodson and Rod Woodson with the Raiders. Those seven players combined for 51 Pro Bowl berths, 26 first-team All-Pro selections and five spots in the Pro Football Hall of Fame.

"Steve was the best football player I ever played with," Amstrong told Mullin. "He didn't have dominant ability, yet he was a dominant player for a long time. He did it by working at it. I played with Steve for five years and he never missed a practice."

McMichael played 191 games for the Bears— consecutive if the 1987 strike games are dismissed—to pass Walter Payton's team record of 190. He still ranks second, tied with Olin Kreutz behind long snapper Patrick Mannelly's 245.

On Aug. 4, 1994, the Tribune's Don Pierson wrote: "To play the perilous inside position for such a long time at such a consistently high level puts McMichael in the company of Merlin Olsen and not many others."

McMichael never came out of the lineup despite a collection of battered body parts, including knees that required eight operations. It was hard to get McMichael to even miss practice.

"Practice was a joy, baby," McMichael wrote. "I loved every aspect of the game. Preparing for it and playing it are the same. When they say I even loved wind sprints, it's kind of the truth. . . . Pushing through the limits, that's what makes the games easy."

McMichael's athleticism was underrated to start, and his tireless workouts ensured he didn't lose much of it as he aged. In high school he lettered in six sports: football, basketball, baseball, track, tennis and golf.

"Every athletic event they had, I did," McMichael told the Tribune's Robert Markus on Dec. 12, 1991. "I think it's very important for a young kid to play all of them. The skills you learn will lead you into the one you like."

Vince Tobin, who replaced Ryan as the Bears defensive coordinator in 1986, called McMichael one of the most intelligent players he ever coached.

"He's extremely smart," Tobin told Markus. "He studies film; he reads offensive players. He has the ability to know if a guy is pulling, whether he's going to block him left or right, whether it will be a pass or run, before the ball is snapped."

McMichael added: "Quickness is deciphering the play and going instead of standing there waiting for it to happen. . . . You're not born with that. Nobody knows the nuances of the game until he takes the time to learn."

In 2014, Pierson ranked McMichael the fourth-best defensive lineman in Bears history, behind Doug Atkins, Hampton and Dent. At No. 18, McMichael is the highest-ranked player on the Tribune's list of the top 100 Bears who is not in the Hall of Fame, just ahead of No. 19 Devin Hester, No. 21 Jimbo Covert and No. 23 Jay Hilgenberg.

McMichael played his last season for the Packers in 1994, starting all 16 games after the Bears released him rather than pay his $1 million salary.

He joined World Championship Wrestling as a broadcaster in 1995 and became a wrestler a few months later. In 2001 McMichael was ejected from Wrigley Field when he followed his rendition of "Take Me Out to the Ball Game" by criticizing umpire Angel Hernandez.

In 2013 he ran for mayor of Romeoville and earned 39% of the vote in a loss to incumbent John Noak.

In April 2021, the 63-year-old revealed he has amyotrophic lateral sclerosis (ALS), often known as Lou Gehrig's disease, the progressive nervous system disease that is disrupting his brain's ability to communicate with his muscles.

If McMichael's personality and antics overshadowed his fine play for 13 seasons with the Bears and the years since, he figures it's all part of the same package, and it could not have happened any place else.

"Thank God New England got rid of me," McMichael told the Tribune's Bob Verdi on Oct. 14, 1984. "Some teams, they want you to have a certain image. Other teams, like this one, they just want you to get down and dirty. . . . I'm really proud to be a Bear.

"The Patriots, yeah, they thought I was a little weird. And I guess I am. But here they don't care, long as you play hard. . . . The town, the coach, the team—it's Steve McMichael. I wouldn't want to be anywhere else." ■

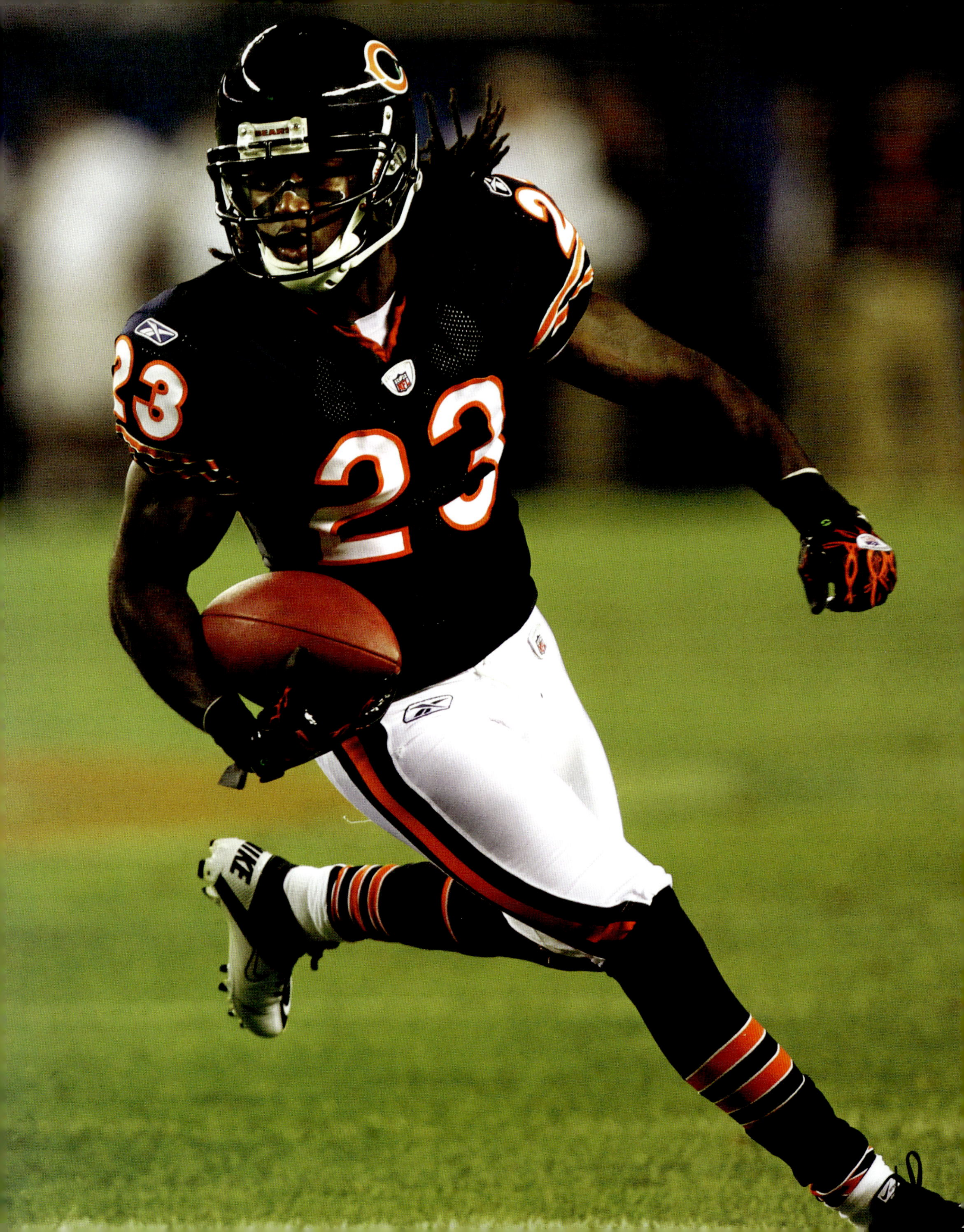

19

Devin Hester

DEVIN HESTER FIELDED THE PUNT just outside the right hash mark at his 16-yard line at Lambeau Field.

He caught the ball, took two steps forward, planted his left foot, took four strides to his right and turned upfield.

No one touched him as he zoomed through the Packers' punt team. Big blocks by Ian Scott, Todd Johnson and few others sprung him, and Muhsin Muhammad and Charles Tillman took care of the last two Packers who had any shot at Hester.

In a flash, the Bears had increased their lead to 26-0, which held up as the final score on Sept. 10, 2006. Just as quickly, the rest of the NFL was in serious trouble.

"Right then and there, you knew he had a special and different talent," teammate Chris Harris told the Tribune's Dan Wiederer on Sept. 22, 2013.

Hester's first touchdown return came on his fourth try in his first game. Most of the rest of his NFL-record 20 return touchdowns—21 including his score on the opening kickoff of Super Bowl XLI—followed the same script: one or two changes of direction, an explosion through a hole and helpless tacklers chasing No. 23 from behind.

His returns usually did not feature the spin moves of Dante Hall or broken tackles of Josh Cribbs. Hester's main weapon was his uncanny ability to change direction almost at full speed. By the time opposing special teams players adjusted to one quick cut, it often was too late to prevent a big gain or a score.

"Full speed one way," Dante Rosario, who blocked for Hester with the Bears and tried to tackle him with the Panthers and Chargers, told Wiederer. "Then a foot in the ground, one cut and gone."

It was evident very quickly that the Bears had something special in Hester. He scored his second return touchdown to cap the crazy Monday night win against the Cardinals in the Bears' sixth game. Three games later he returned a short field goal 108 yards for a touchdown against the Giants on "Sunday Night Football." Against the Vikings on Dec. 3 he returned another punt for a score, and in a Monday night game the next week he ran back two kickoffs for touchdowns against the Rams.

"Hester already is better than good," the

Devin Hester (23) looks upfield after making a reception Aug. 21, 2010, in a preseason game against the Oakland Raiders at Soldier Field.

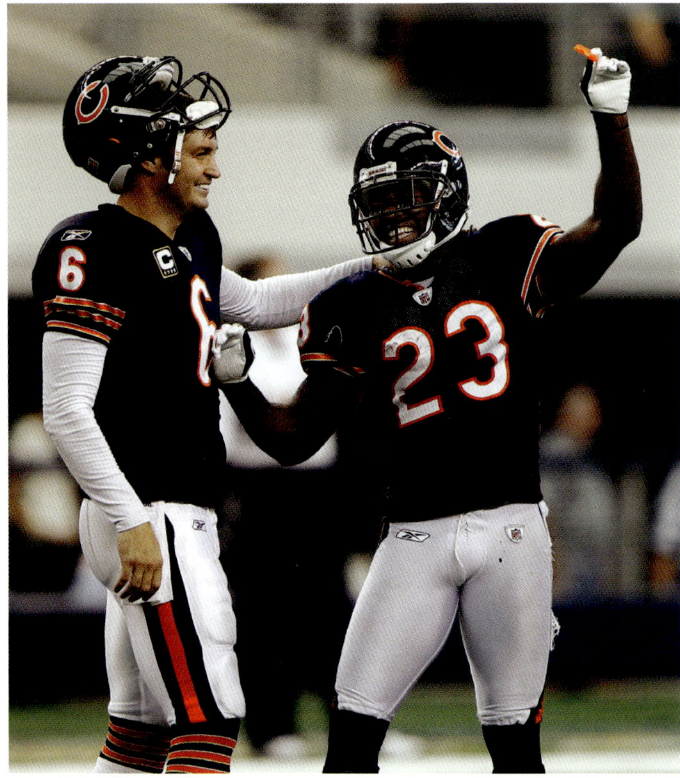

Jay Cutler (6) celebrates with Devin Hester (23) on Sept. 19, 2010, during a game against the Cowboys.

Tribune's Don Pierson wrote on Dec. 15, 2006. "Great may be overused in sports, but nobody has ever seen the likes of Devin Hester."

Pierson noted that in 2000, the NFL named its all-time team with Gale Sayers at kick returner and Deion Sanders as punt returner. Pierson, never one for hyperbole during his 38 years covering the Bears, said Hester was better than both as a return man.

Sanders mentored Hester at Miami, where he returned six kicks for touchdowns before the Bears selected him in the second round of the 2006 draft. "Prime Time" agreed with Pierson's assessment.

"I never accomplished the feats he has accomplished," Sanders told the Tribune's David Haugh on Dec. 13, 2006. "It's sort of like you can believe it but can't fathom the idea that he's doing what he knows he could do."

Hester's 92-yard kickoff return against the Colts to begin Super Bowl XLI in Miami is the best Bears memory for most fans 35 or younger, even though the Bears lost 29-17 on Feb. 4, 2007.

After setting the NFL single-season record with six return touchdowns in 2006, Hester was just as good in 2007. He returned six more kicks for touchdowns and added two receiving scores as the Bears tried to find more ways to get him the ball.

Hester seemed to get even better in crucial moments. Of his 14 touchdowns in 2006-07, eight either tied the score or gave the Bears the lead.

Perhaps his best game came on Nov. 25, 2007, at Soldier Field against Jay Cutler, Brandon Marshall and the Broncos. With the Bears trailing 13-6 in the third quarter, Hester returned a punt 75 yards for a touchdown, leaping over former Bears punter Todd Sauerbrun in the process. Immediately after the Broncos took a 20-13 lead later in the quarter, Hester returned the kickoff 88 yards to tie the score again. The Bears won 37-34 in overtime.

Broncos cornerback Dre Bly told the Denver Post's Bill Williamson: "Devin Hester single-handedly won the game for them."

Marshall added: "If it wasn't for Devin Hester, we would have blown them out."

Hester could affect games even when he didn't touch the ball. Opposing special teams coaches, kickers and punters spent their weeks scheming how to best limit Hester and sometimes concluded they would rather kick the ball out of bounds, giving the Bears great field position, rather than give Hester a chance to make a game-changing return.

Lions coach Rod Marinelli said he'd rather have his punter kick the ball in Lake Michigan than to Hester. The Redskins' Joe Gibbs, in his 28th and final season as an NFL head or assistant coach, said Hester changed the game unlike any player.

"I've never seen this before in the NFL, just kicking out of bounds," Gibbs told the Tribune's Fred Mitchell on Dec. 7, 2007. "Just saying, 'Hey, we're kicking off out of bounds. We're going to give them the ball at the 40.' . . . What an unusual guy. I don't think anybody has the (right) game plan yet, it's obvious."

The Bears drafted Hester as a cornerback but switched him to receiver in 2007, with coach Lovie Smith suggesting the move more and more forcefully before the season to Hester, who wanted to follow in Sanders' footsteps as a lockdown corner.

"It went from once a month to once a week to every day," Hester told the Tribune's John Mullin on May 20, 2007. "If the head coach thinks it's going to be better for the team . . . I have 100% trust in Lovie Smith and the decisions he's making. I'm just hoping I can live up to it and contribute."

Hester never became more than an average receiver, and his return game suffered as most of his mental energy was spent learning a new position with late receivers coach Darryl Drake. Hester had career highs of 57 receptions and 757 yards in 2009, and he never caught more than his four touchdown passes of 2010.

In a 2013 appearance on ESPN, Smith explained moving Hester to offense.

"Whenever you can get the ball in Devin Hester's hands, it's a good thing," Smith said. "What I tried to do . . . was give him a little bit more. It hasn't turned out that way. But I just think you need him on the football field in some kind of way."

In 2010, Hester broke a 30-game drought between punt returns for a touchdown with a 62-yarder on Sept. 28 against the Packers. In 2010 and '11 he returned to his status as an elite returner as his receiving responsibilities lessened. On Dec. 20, 2010, he set the NFL record with his 14th return of a punt, kickoff or missed field goal for a touchdown. Brian Mitchell, the previous record holder, scored 13 touchdowns on 1,070 returns. Hester scored his 14th on his 286th.

Hester left the Bears as a free agent after the 2013 season. He spent two years with the Falcons, earning his fourth and final Pro Bowl berth in 2014, and finished his career in 2016 with the Ravens and Seahawks. He finished with 14 punt-return touchdowns, four more than second-place Eric Metcalf on the all-time list. Hester's 20 all-time total return touchdowns (14 punts, five kickoffs and a missed field goal) beat Sanders' record of 19 (nine interceptions, six punts, three kickoffs and a fumble).

Hester spread anxiety evenly throughout the league, returning kicks for scores against 14 teams and 16 kickers and punters. He often was asked to explain his gift.

"For some reason, I kind of see things in slow motion," he told the Tribune's K.C. Johnson on Sept. 2, 2006, before he had played a game in the NFL. "That gives me time to react. I don't concentrate on one guy. I concentrate on surroundings and jersey colors. That way, I can pick up a little more and try to make more than one defender miss."

And when he was on his way to the end zone?

"It looks like the gates of heaven opening up for me," Hester told the Tribune's Rick Morrissey on Dec. 13, 2006.

Hester has an interesting case for the Pro Football Hall of Fame when he becomes eligible in 2022. Of the 346 players enshrined in Canton, Ohio, three are special-teamers: kickers Jan Stenerud and Morten Andersen and punter Ray Guy.

Steve Rosenbloom stated Hester's case in the Dec. 13, 2017, Tribune.

"There never will be anyone like Hester," Rosenbloom wrote. "He was the best. He will always be that. Hester changed the game. . . . Look at the list of players in the Hall of Fame and circle the names who brought such game-changing dynamism. Go ahead. I'll wait."

Whether Hester makes it to Canton, for eight years Bears fans saw the best at what he did in NFL history.

"Just coming out of college, coaches told me I wasn't going to be anything but a kickoff and punt returner," Hester said to the Tribune's Vaughn McClure on Dec. 21, 2010. "I'm here today to say I am a kickoff and punt returner, but at the same time, I'm the best to ever do it." ■

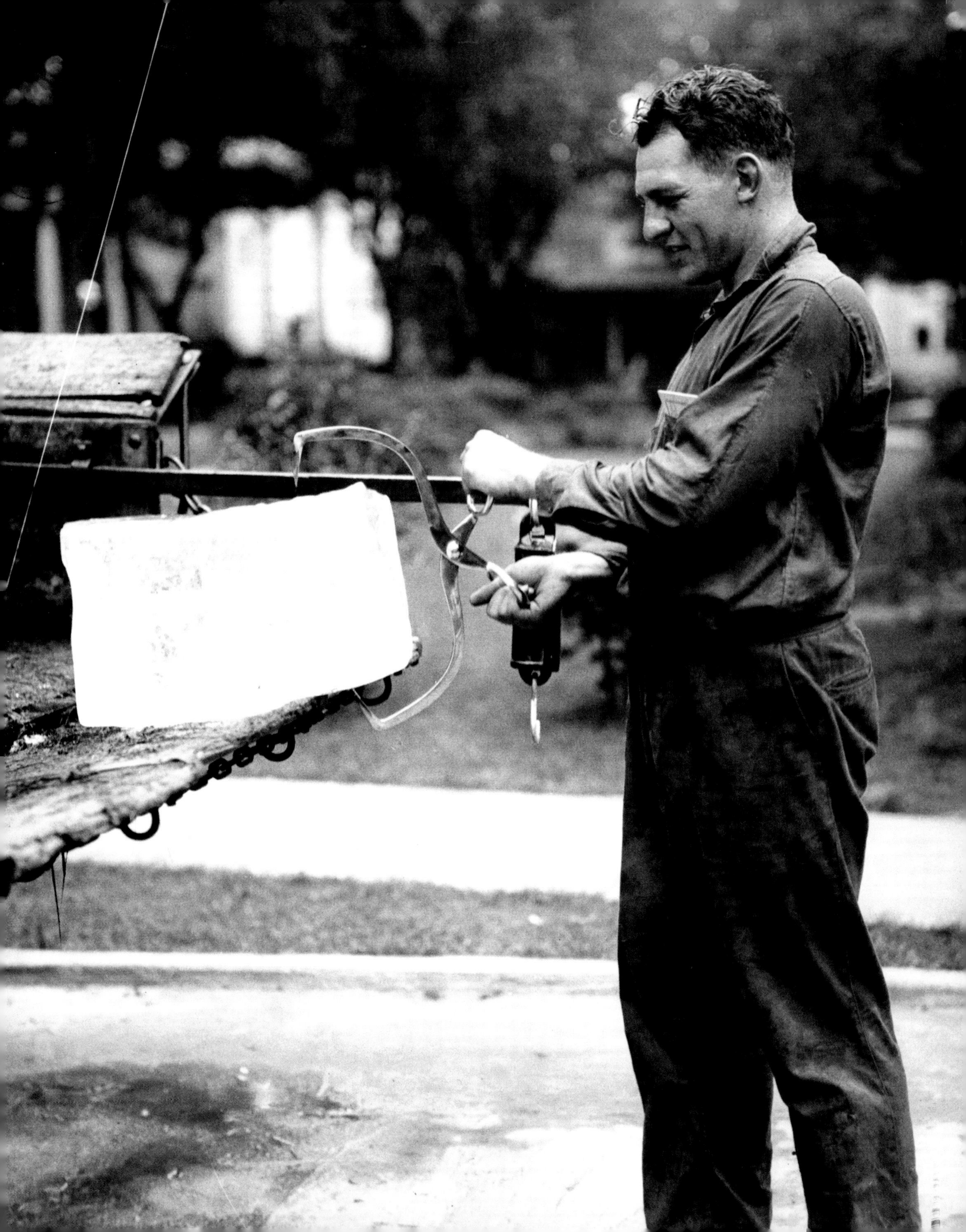

Red Grange

77 HALFBACK
1925, 1929–34

20

R ED GRANGE WAS RICH. He was famous. He was near the end of his career, a shell of his former self after a severe knee injury five years earlier.

Yet there he was, on Dec. 17, 1933, at Wrigley Field, sticking his uncovered nose in for what George Halas called the greatest defensive play he ever saw.

The Bears led the Giants 23-21 in an NFL championship game that still stands as one of the league's best. They took the last of the game's six lead changes on a trick pass from fullback Bronko Nagurski to Bill Hewitt, who lateraled to Bill Karr for a 19-yard touchdown with about a minute remaining.

On the game's last snap, the Giants looked to have struck gold. Quarterback Harry Newman heaved the ball to halfback Dale Burnett well beyond most of the Bears defense. Grange was the only Bear between Burnett and the end zone, and he spotted Giants center Mel Hein running just behind and to the side of Burnett.

In Grange's 1953 autobiography, "The Red Grange Story," he wrote: "I was the only one Burnett had to elude to cross the goal line with the game-winning touchdown. I knew Burnett would lateral to Hein as soon as I tackled him, so I grabbed him high, wrapping my arms around his, thus preventing him from getting the ball away. As I pulled Burnett to the ground, the gun went off ending the game."

The heads-up tackle gave the Bears their second consecutive NFL championship. In his 1979 autobiography, "Halas by Halas," which featured an entire chapter devoted to Grange titled "The Golden Lad," the Bears coach wrote: "Red knew if he made the usual tackle . . . we would lose the game. So Grange, the great Grange, made a new kind of tackle. He flung his arms around Burnett in a bear hug, clamping Burnett's arms to his side. It saved the game."

Eight years earlier, Grange joined the Bears as one of the pillars of American sport, equal to Babe Ruth and Jack Dempsey in name recognition and adulation. In the time between, in the 2019 biography "Red Grange: The Life and Legacy of the NFL's First Superstar," NFL Films historian Chris Willis writes: "Red Grange made the blueprint of what an NFL player could become: He left school early, signed with an agent, was paid the biggest salary in the history of the sport, made movies

Harold "Red" Grange, circa 1926, working on the ice wagon in Wheaton during a summer break from college.

in Hollywood, did endorsements, won two NFL championships and was elected to the Pro Football Hall of Fame."

Grange made his name in 1924 during an unprecedented junior year at the University of Illinois. As he captured the nation's attention with his touchdown runs, he earned the fawning words of the nation's most prominent sports writers. Grantland Rice nicknamed him "The Galloping Ghost." Damon Runyan wrote: "On the field he is equal to three football players and a horse."

On Oct. 18, 1924, against top-ranked Michigan at Memorial Stadium, Grange played perhaps the best game a football player ever has.

Michigan coach Fielding Yost didn't buy into the Grange hype, so he directed his kicker to boot the ball to him on the opening kickoff. Yost believed a crushing hit followed by a pile-on of Wolverines might take some pep out of Grange's step. Instead, Grange returned the opener 95 yards for a touchdown. He added scoring runs of 67, 56 and 45 yards by the end of the first quarter. He sat out the second quarter, then ran for a 12-yard touchdown in the third and passed for a score in the fourth.

Official stats credited Grange with 15 carries for 202 yards, three kickoff returns for 126 yards and 6-for-8 passing for 64 yards. In all, he contributed six touchdowns in the 39-14 win, and his legend grew exponentially.

Halas, a former Illini player, paid close attention to the ruckus in Champaign. The NFL was struggling to reach a mass audience, and the Bears barely made it from year to year by taking out loans.

Papa Bear wasn't the only one interested in Grange. Charles Pyle, owner of Champaign's Virginia Theatre, called Grange to a meeting after a movie one afternoon.

"How would you like to make $100,000?" Pyle asked. At the time, the average American made about $4,000 a year.

In Richard Whittingham's 1991 book, "What Bears They Were," Grange remembered the meeting.

"I thought he was crazy," Grange said. "But naturally I said I would—who wouldn't?"

Pyle, who went by his initials C.C., leading writers to nickname him "Cold Cash" or "Cash and Carry," explained his plan. Grange would join a pro team and tour the United States with it after Illinois' 1925 season ended. They would go to cites that had pro teams and play against them, then visit places with no pro football such as Florida and California.

He said the Bears would be an ideal match, and that he would work to get together with Halas to make it happen. If it did, Pyle would take care of all Grange's financial matters.

Pyle and Halas met in supposed secrecy, but word got out, and throughout Grange's senior season at Illinois the press wondered when he would turn pro. Grange stayed with the Illini through their season, which ended with a 14-9 win at Ohio State on Nov. 21. After the game, Grange left the Illini's hotel by the fire escape, boarded a train to Chicago and officially joined the Bears.

Grange played his first game with the Bears only four days after his final game as a collegian, joining Halas and his crew for their annual Thanksgiving game against the Cardinals. Most Bears games drew about 5,000 fans at the time, but 36,000 packed Wrigley Field to get a glimpse of Grange.

They came away disappointed as the Bears and Cardinals tied 0-0. Paddy Driscoll, later Grange's teammate on the Bears, punted the ball away from Grange all game, drawing a chorus of boos, and Grange rushed for only 36 yards.

"I decided if one of us was going to look bad, it wasn't going to be me," Driscoll told the Tribune's David Condon 40 years later. "Punting to Grange is like grooving a pitch to Babe Ruth."

The Bears immediately embarked on a 19-game barnstorming tour, with the team splitting revenues 50-50 with Pyle and Grange. The Bears guaranteed Grange a $100,000 contract, just as Pyle had predicted. One game at the Polo Grounds in New York drew 70,000 fans. It was the largest crowd to see a pro football game to that point, and it helped the struggling Giants stay solvent.

When the Bears went to Washington, Illinois Sen. William McKinley set up a meeting for Grange and Halas with President Calvin Coolidge. When they entered the Oval Office, McKinley introduced his guests as members of the Chicago Bears. Coolidge shook their hands and said, "I've always liked animal acts."

The Bears and Grange trudged through the trip, with Grange obligated to play whether or not he was healthy. If he couldn't run, he played quarterback and handed off, to the annoyance of the crowd. At one point the Bears played eight games in two weeks, sometimes changing out of their uniforms on the train to the next city and putting their dirty threads back on for the next game without a chance to wash them.

In California, Pyle set up Grange as a movie star. Grange was no actor, but he made plenty of money filming "One Minute to Play" in 1926, "A Racing Romeo" in 1927 and "The Galloping Ghost" in 1931. Pyle also arranged for the production of Red Grange-endorsed candy bars, footballs, dolls, clothes, ginger ale and malted milk. To Pyle's chagrin, Grange turned down a tobacco endorsement because he didn't smoke.

By the end of the tour, it became clear that Pyle had undersold Grange's earning potential. The two split about $250,000 for their share of the gate receipts, and Grange made another $100,000 in endorsements.

"Red came to the Bears famous," Halas wrote. "Ten weeks later he was rich."

Grange's teammates were jealous of his money but could not complain, since their salaries went up as more money came in. They soon found Grange to be just like them in most respects.

Bears quarterback Joey Sternaman, in "What Bears They Were," remembers testing Grange's team spirit.

"I was the play caller, and I said to him, 'Are you interested in yourself, or are you interested in winning football games?' " Sternaman asked. "Red was honestly interested in winning football games, and, as I found out, was one of the finest team players around."

Sternaman, whose brother Dutch co-owned the team with Halas, was amazed at Grange's talent but thought he could be even more useful as a decoy. Time and again the quarterback would call a play that had Grange carrying out a fake that would fool the defense.

"Why, they'd just clobber him, and hell, I'd be bootlegging it around the other end," Sternaman said. "We used a lot of deception, and it worked well. Red took a beating, especially that first year, but he never complained."

After the tour, Pyle pushed for Halas and Dutch Sternaman to give Grange a one third share of the Bears. They refused, and Pyle started the American Football League with Grange becoming player/owner of the New York Yankees. The league folded after one year, but Pyle persuaded the NFL to take on the Yankees, with Grange the main selling point.

In 1927, Grange severely injured his knee in a game against the Bears when George Trafton landed on it. Pyle urged Grange to play hurt, Grange's injury got worse and worse, and he was unable to play at all in 1928 as the Yankees folded without him. He considered himself retired until Halas convinced him to give it one more shot with the Bears in 1929.

Halas wrote: "I figured he would no longer gallop for touchdowns, but I liked his intelligence, his determination and his desire. I thought he still had a great contribution to make to football. Too, there was still magic in the Grange name."

"I guess I was about 70 percent of the football player I'd been," Grange said.

After Grange's big play in the 1933 title game, he toughed out one more season before his knee gave out for good. He served as an assistant coach for the Bears for three seasons, then as radio play-by-play man for 14 while going into the real estate and insurance businesses. He died at 87 on Jan. 28, 1991, in Lake Wales, Fla.

Grange's transition from college to the pros still resonates as college players try to better their situation and compensation. In 1925, college coaches thought it was a travesty that Grange was negotiating a contract while still a collegian. Halas and Grange were upbraided by one of their heroes, Illinois coach Robert Zuppke.

"Football wasn't meant to be played for money," Zuppke told Grange.

Grange answered: "You get paid for coaching it. Why should it be wrong for me to get paid for playing it?" ■

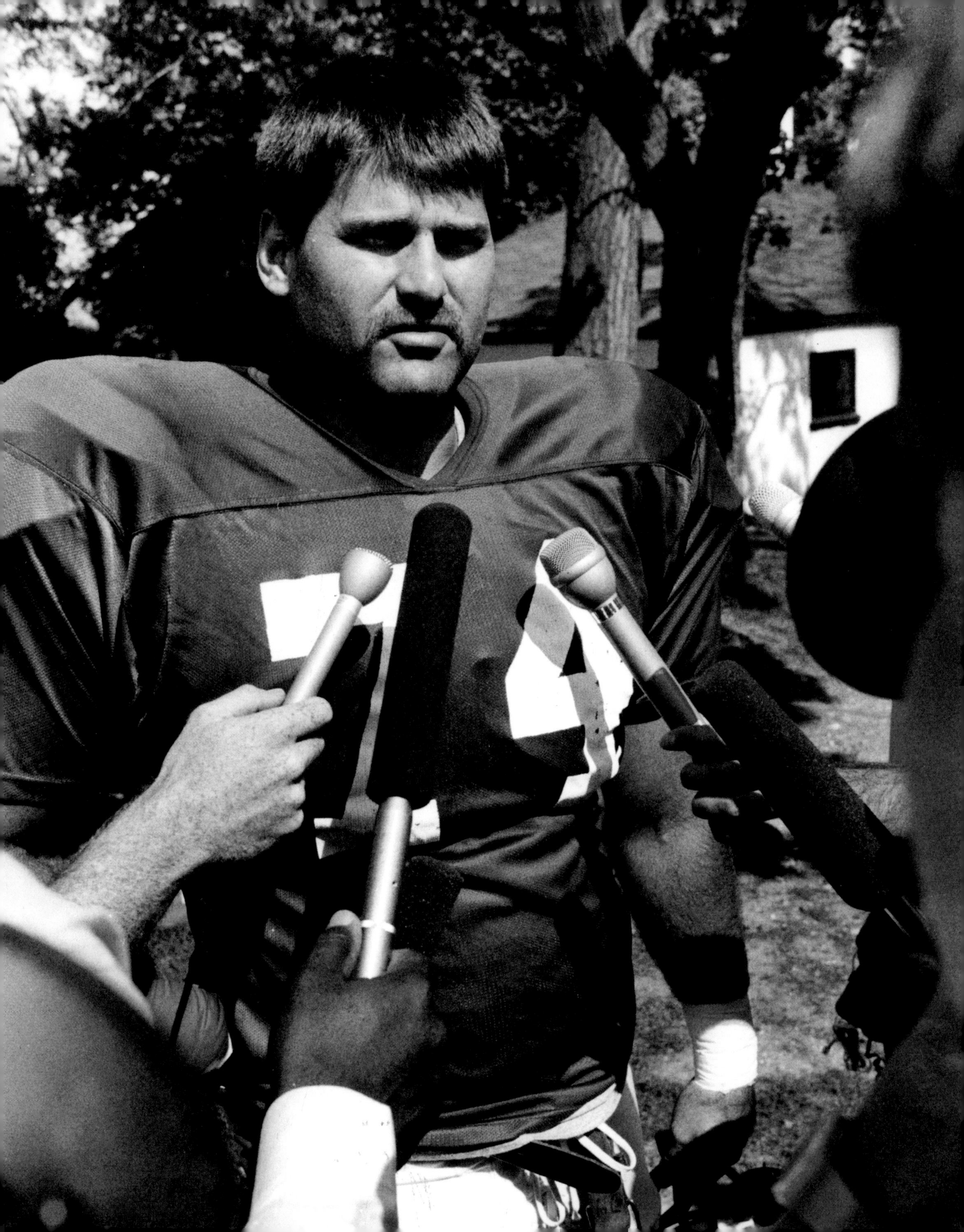

Jimbo Covert

74 OFFENSIVE TACKLE
1983–1990

THE BEARS OF THE 1980s had personalities of every kind, including some of the most rambunctious players in franchise history.

They could be kept in line by one man: 6-foot-4, 277-pound left tackle Jimbo Covert.

Steve McMichael was perhaps the rowdiest of the Bears' riled-up bunch. He wrote in the 2011 edition of "Amazing Tales from the Chicago Bears Sideline" that Covert could put anyone in his place quickly and emphatically.

"Jimbo's the reason I know anybody can get their ass whipped—I don't care how bad you think you are," McMichael wrote. "He was the only guy in a football practice I ever said 'Uncle' to."

During one scrimmage skirmish, Covert took exception to something someone said or did and assumed McMichael was the culprit. Covert came at "Mongo," who prepared for a fistfight. The high school wrestling champion from the steel-mill town of Conway, Pa., had another idea.

"That's where I learned about the hip toss," McMichael remembered. "He grabbed me, turned me, lifted me up and dropped me as he landed on top of me. He wasn't hitting me; he just pinned me there. Well, I couldn't move. Finally I said, 'Could you let me up?'"

Covert, who at his peak might have been the best offensive lineman in Bears history, brought a much-needed toughness to the offense after the Bears selected him No. 6 out of Pittsburgh in their bountiful 1983 draft. The team's defense was ready to compete at a championship level, but the offense was missing something that Covert had in abundance.

Bears coach Mike Ditka told the Tribune's Brad Biggs on April 17, 2015, "I needed a tough guy and I needed a leader. As good as our defense was, Covert didn't take any (crap) from anybody in practice. Our defense used to beat up on (the offense) in the first couple of years, but Covert stood up for us."

Covert helped the Bears offense develop into a tough unit in its own right. The key was an offensive line of, left to right, Covert, Mark Bortz, Jay Hilgenberg, Tom Thayer and Keith Van Horne that stayed intact for six seasons (1985-90). The Bears won Super Bowl XX after the 1985 season and the NFC Central Division in five of those six years.

Jim Covert (74) on Sept. 15, 1988, at Bears camp in Lake Forest.

As he did to McMichael and the Bears defense during practice, Covert quickly showed the rest of the league that the Bears offense could no longer get pushed around. In his third preseason game he got into a fight with Raiders defensive end Lyle Alzado, 11 years Covert's senior and one of the NFL's most feared players.

On Oct. 1, 1983, the Tribune's John Husar wrote: "Covert is proud of the way things worked out with that madman Alzado, even though it cost him $200 for being tossed from an exhibition game. The old firebrand had tried to intimidate the rookie by leading him around by the face mask. . . . Jimbo finally grabbed back and they started bruising their fists on pads and helmets. . . . The kid served notice on film that he wasn't going to be cranked around."

By his second season Covert was a team captain, and the Bears went 10-6 and lost in the NFC championship game. Covert never was one to advocate for himself, but he grew frustrated that no offensive lineman was named to the Pro Bowl despite the Bears leading the league in rushing for a second consecutive year.

"Walter Payton is the greatest running back who ever lived," Covert told the Tribune's Ed Sherman on Aug. 16, 1985. "Walter is so fantastic, people just assume he does it on his own, that the guys in front of him don't do anything. Well, that's not true. Walter may be great, but he needed some help."

The recognition came as everything clicked for the Bears in 1985. They led the league in rushing for the third of four straight seasons, and after the 46-10 win over the Patriots in Super Bowl XX, Covert and Hilgenberg went to their first Pro Bowls. Covert was named first-team All-Pro and would repeat both honors the next season as he entered the company of the game's best offensive linemen.

Covert's Pro Bowl appearances were the only ones by a Bears tackle between Kline Gilbert in 1957 and James "Big Cat" Williams in 2001. In 1994, the Tribune's Don Pierson and Fred Mitchell named Covert and George Connor the tackles on their all-time Bears team ahead of Hall of Famers Joe Stydahar and Ed Healey.

In 1990, the Pro Football Hall of Fame named Covert to its All-Decade team of the 1980s. Of the 22 players on the first team, all except Covert are enshrined in Canton, Ohio. Covert and Anthony Munoz were the first-team tackles, ahead of Joe Jacoby and Hall of Famer Gary Zimmerman.

When Bears linebacker Mike Singletary was inducted into the Hall of Fame in 1998, he called for the selection committee to recognize four teammates: Dan Hampton, Richard Dent, Hilgenberg and Covert.

Hampton was elected in 2002, Dent in 2011. During Dent's speech, he echoed Singletary's comments.

"I look forward to seeing you on this stage," Dent said to Covert.

McMichael wrote: "Jim Covert had the best technique at run blocking I've ever gone against. Most guys make the mistake of trying to get their head and body into you at the same time as their hands. That's compact. You can get around that. Jimbo led with his hands first to grab you. . . . His hands were on you before the body contact."

Pass blocking can be a passive endeavor, but Covert found a way to be intimidating while doing it. The Tribune's John Mullin wrote on Oct. 22, 2008, that "Dent said the best tackle he faced was teammate Jimbo Covert, who was a master at freezing a pass rush by firing out at the snap, then dropping quickly into his pass set."

As Covert told Sherman: "I'd say 75 to 80 percent of the game is technique, and 20 percent is strength. You can be the strongest guy in the world, but if you don't have good leverage, a guy weighing 200 pounds will be able to jack you up every time."

Covert learned from two of the game's best offensive line coaches. At Pitt, Joe Moore oversaw a procession of All-Americans that included Russ Grimm, Mark May, Covert and Bill Fralic. With the Bears, Covert met Dick Stanfel, a standout player in the 1950s and one of the NFL's blocking gurus.

When Covert retired in 1992, Stanfel said: "I have been coaching 29 years, and I was a player

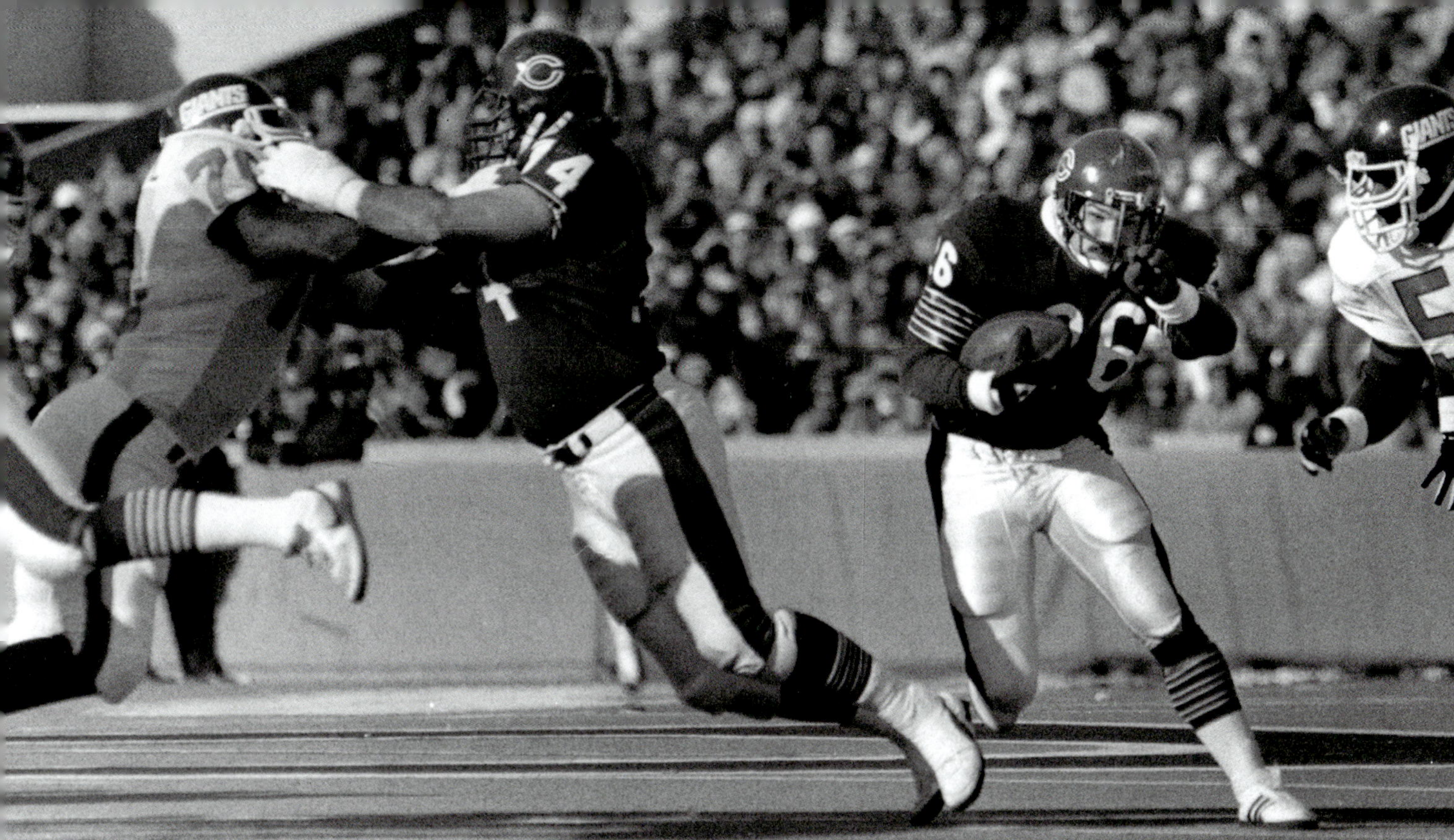

Jim Covert (74), center, during a game against the Giants in 1985.

eight years, and if I ever had to pick an All-Star team, my left tackle would be Jim Covert."

Durability was an asset for Covert at the beginning of his career. He started 63 of 64 games his first four seasons before, as Covert put it, "the monkey jumped on my back." He missed one game in 1985 because of back spasms, half the '87 season after breaking his shoulder, and in '88 he sprained his lower back in the first practice of training camp. He had microscopic disk surgery and missed half the season. He returned to play 15 games each in 1989 and '90 and kept up his strong play, but every day was a struggle.

He reinjured his back in training camp before the 1991 season, which he spent on injured reserve, and he retired in 1992, with his wife, Penny, having the final word.

"She was pretty strong on her point," Covert said. "She said she would kill me if I went back and played."

During his career Covert was one of the most charitable Bears, working with the United Way, March of Dimes, Boys Clubs of America and Christian Athletes. When he was voted offensive lineman of the year by the NFLPA in 1986, he donated the $25,000 prize to the Brian Piccolo Cancer Research Fund.

Ken Valdiserri, former Bears director of public relations, told the Tribune's Jim O'Donnell on Jan. 16, 1994: "I can remember many times when I needed a player to make some sort of charitable appearance. . . . I'd walk into the meeting room and explain what I needed. Invariably, one hand shot up to volunteer, and that was Jim Covert."

His work took on a larger meaning in 1987 when Covert's daughter, Jessica, was born with spina bifida. Since then he has been an advocate for people affected by the birth defect. He went into the medical industry and has served in many capacities.

Covert's story is one of success on and off the field. For those who watched the Bears in the 1980s, it's hard to believe the team ever will have a better left tackle.

When Covert retired, Ditka said: "This is not a happy day for me. I wish I had him lining up on the left side for about five more years. I don't think the Bears ever had anyone play left tackle as good as Jim." ■

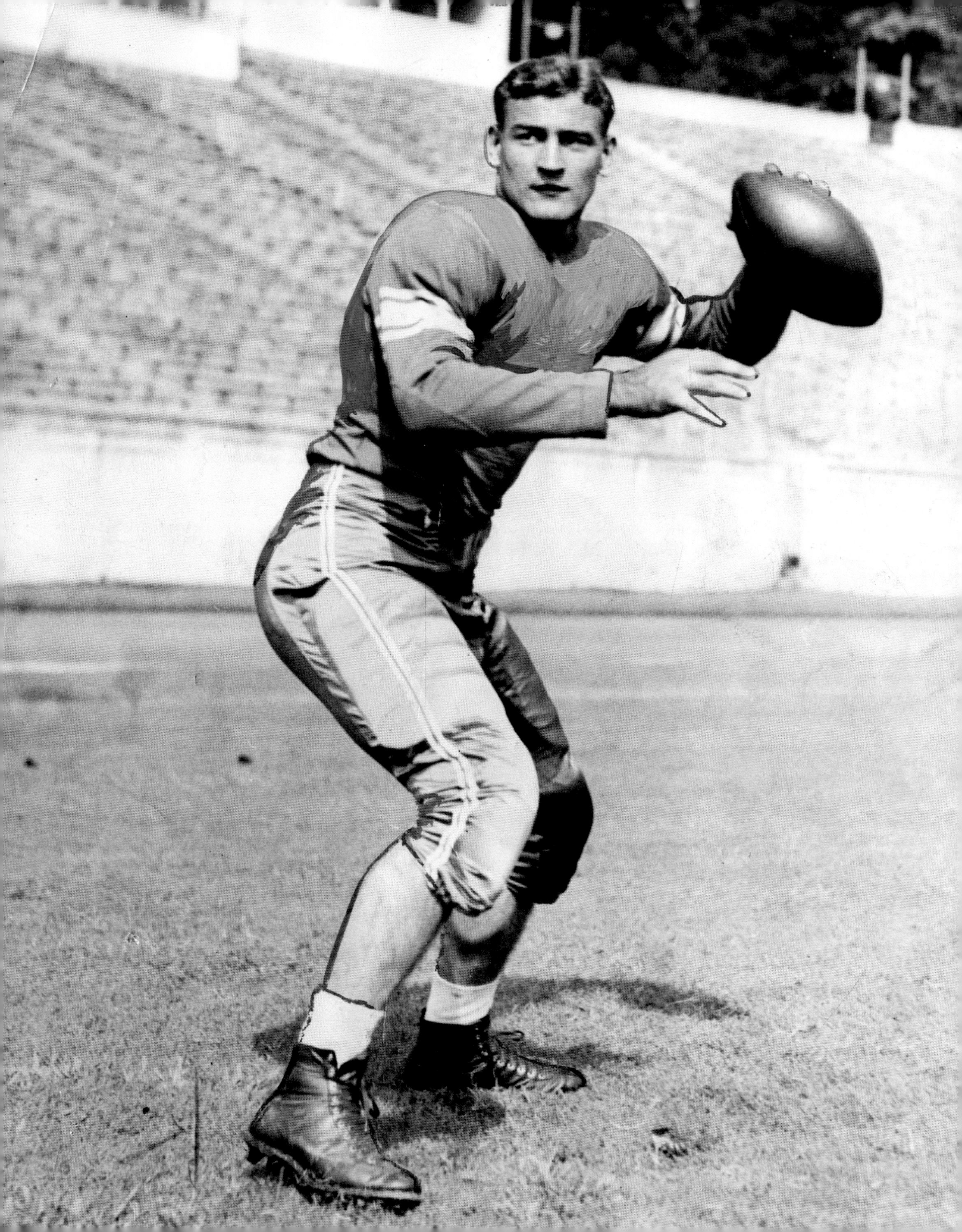

George McAfee

5 RUNNING BACK, DEFENSIVE BACK
1940–41, 1945–50

A s good as George McAfee was, he easily could have made an even bigger impact on the NFL.

The biggest impediment to that happening was his coach, George Halas. The Bears owner admitted as much, saying he didn't want to embarrass the league he had founded 20 years earlier.

The late Bill Gleason, a longtime sports writer for the Chicago American and Sun-Times, recalled a conversation he had with Halas to Jeff Davis, author of the 2005 book, "Papa Bear: The Life and Legacy of George Halas."

"I played McAfee a quarter and a half because if I played him more, he would have ruined the league," Halas told Gleason.

"And he meant that," Gleason said. "He was sincere about it. George Halas was not going to ruin the league. McAfee was that good."

McAfee earned the nickname "One Play" because he was a threat to score from anywhere on the field in any phase of the game. When he set an NFL record by scoring 12 touchdowns in 1941, his scores came on rushes, receptions, a kickoff return, a punt return, a fumble return and an interception return, and he added a touchdown pass, the third of his career, for good measure. His scoring plays included a 63-yard pass, a 70-yard run, a 39-yard reception, a 97-yard kickoff return and a 74-yard punt return. He even scored from zero yards when he intercepted a pass in the Rams end zone.

Forty years later, Walter Payton's teammates admitted to taking their eyes off their assignments to see what move the record-setting running back would make next. Sid Luckman, quarterback of the Bears' four championship teams in the 1940s, said he did the same with McAfee to the Tribune's Edward Prell on Oct. 29, 1941.

"The toughest part of the game for me," Luckman said, "is to carry out my assignments after giving the ball to George. You know, the quarterback has to make a fake on all plays unless he is willing to contribute $10 to the team's treasury. But even so, I always manage to at least get a quick look out of the corner of my eye at George as he gets underway."

McAfee came to the Bears as part of Halas' finest stretch of player acquisitions in his six-decade personnel career. From 1939 to '42, Halas added so much talent that many of his backups

George McAfee (5), circa 1940.

were All-Pro caliber. The 1940 draft was perhaps his best. In one of his most astute moves, Halas traded four veteran linemen who soon would be out of the league—Les McDonald, Dick Bassi, Milt Trost and Russ Thompson—for McAfee, the Eagles' pick at No. 2 overall.

McAfee was a Duke star who ran the 100-yard dash in 9.7 seconds and hit .390 for the Blue Devils baseball team. With the No. 7 pick in the same round, Halas selected Bulldog Turner, a center from Hardin-Simmons.

Turner and McAfee were elected to the Pro Football Hall of Fame together in 1966. They were named to the 1940s All-Decade team, and the Bears retired their numbers: McAfee's 5 and Turner's 66. Turner—an all-around terror as a center, linebacker, special teams player and emergency fullback—was as big a fan of McAfee's as Luckman was.

In Gary D'Amato and Cliff Christl's "Mudbaths and Bloodbaths: The Inside Story of the Bears-Packers Rivalry," Turner said: "I've made this statement several times. I think he's the greatest all-around football player I ever saw. He was like a ghost out there. You couldn't get a hold of him."

McAfee's 12.8 yards per punt return still is an NFL career record. He ranks seventh in Bears history with 25 interceptions, and his 234 points rank 19th. He totaled 3,044 yards from scrimmage and 5,313 all-purpose yards while scoring 39 touchdowns, passing for three others and serving as an occasional punter in his eight seasons with the Bears.

He impressed right away as a rookie. In his first exhibition game he returned a punt 75 yards for a touchdown with seconds remaining to beat the Brooklyn Dodgers. One of his first regular-season touches resulted in a 93-yard kickoff return for a touchdown against the Packers, and he added a 9-yard rushing score in a 31-10 win in Green Bay. In the Bears' 73-0 win against the Redskins in the NFL championship game, McAfee scored one of the team's 11 touchdowns on a 34-yard interception return.

In 1941, McAfee became one of the game's best players as the Bears had one of their greatest seasons. He was named first-team All-Pro while sharing snaps with fellow right halfback Hugh Gallarneau. The two backs and Packers receiver Don Hutson raced for the NFL touchdown record of 11, with McAfee and Hutson finishing with 12 and Gallarneau 11 as the Bears averaged 36 points per game while outscoring their opponents 396-147 in the regular season.

In two playoff wins that season, the Western Division tiebreaker against the Packers and the NFL title game against the Giants, McAfee carried 28 times for 200 yards, an average of 7.1 per carry, and caught four passes for 69 yards, 17.3 per reception.

McAfee volunteered for the Navy after the season, and he missed almost four seasons before returning toward the end of 1945. He resumed his fine play in the final two games of the season for a Bears team that had been 1-7 without most of its stars. McAfee rushed five times for 105 yards and two touchdowns and caught a 65-yard Luckman pass for a score in a win against the Steelers, then scored a 1-yard rushing touchdown in a 28-20 win against the Cardinals at Comiskey Park to close the season.

Halas responded by opening his wallet, signing McAfee to an unprecedented three-year contract after three teams from the upstart All-American Football Conference tried to sign him. In 1946, McAfee missed most of the season with a left knee injury. He never was the same but still was effective as a decoy, and his fake on Luckman's "Bingo Keep It" touchdown run was one of the key plays in the 1946 NFL championship game win against the Giants.

Red Grange said McAfee was unlike any running back he had ever seen.

"In my book there's never been a better broken-field runner," Grange told Prell on Dec. 12, 1948. "When you see him in slow-motion movies, his maneuvers are incredible. He jumps every which way and every muscle seems to be going full blast, like the guy is on fire.

"I remember a Bear film which shows George feinting around a tackler by hopping three times on his left foot. Then, without a loss of balance or speed, he came down on his right foot and was gone."

McAfee, the 10th of 12 children who grew

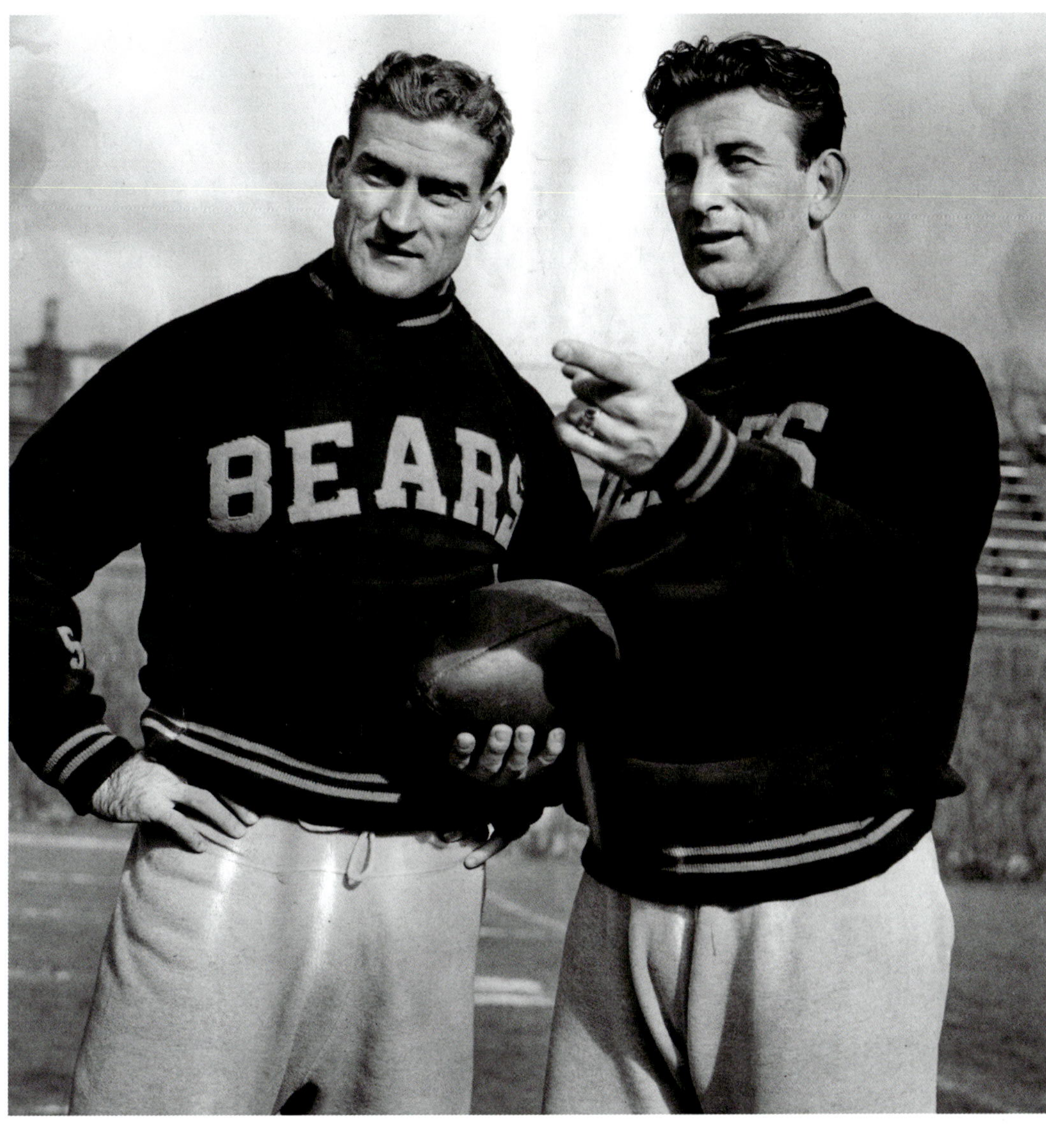

George McAfee (5), left, and Hugh Gallarneau (8) on Nov. 29, 1946, at Wrigley Field.

up on the Ohio River in Corbin, Ky., and Ironton, Ohio, retired after the 1950 season. He worked as an NFL referee for a short time, then started an oil business with his brother Wes, who played eight NFL games for the Eagles in 1941. With his wife, Jeanne, McAfee moved back to Durham, N.C., to raise his family, and he became a fixture at Duke sporting events.

When Gale Sayers became a rookie sensation for the Bears in 1965, Halas gave the running back and kick returner some of the kindest words he could.

"The highest compliment you can pay any ball carrier," Halas said, "is just compare him with George McAfee."

McAfee suffered from dementia in his later years and died at 90 on March 4, 2009, in an assisted-living facility in Atlanta. He had wandered into a janitor's room and drank from a bottle of industrial-strength dishwashing liquid. Its chemicals severely burned his lips, esophagus and lungs. The state of Georgia found Emeritus Senior Living negligent in his death, and his family settled with the company after suing it. ■

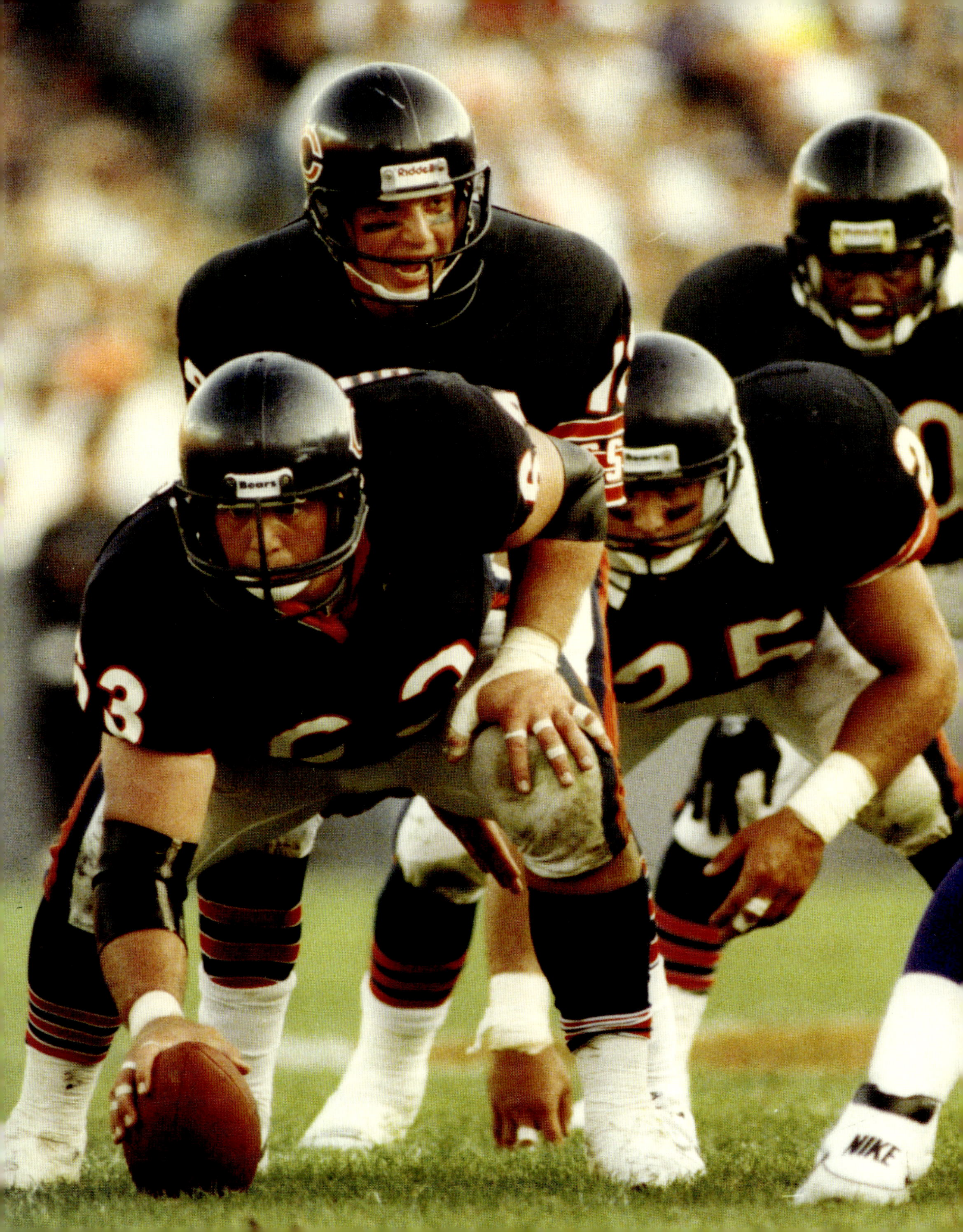

Jay Hilgenberg

63 CENTER
1981–91

O N MONDAY NIGHT, Oct. 19, 1981, the Bears were in the process of taking a beating that resulted in a 48-17 loss to the Lions on national TV.

The defeat dropped the Bears to 1-6. On the sideline, rookie center Jay Hilgenberg, mired in a backup role, shook his head and turned to teammate Revie Sorey.

"Revie, if we're the worst team in the league, and I can't even play for us, that means I must be the worst player in the league," Hilgenberg recalled to the Tribune's Bob Verdi on Dec. 14, 1987. "Revie just laughed."

Verdi wrote: "Hilgenberg can laugh now, too, because experience times hard work plus All-Pro status have brought him a Super Bowl ring."

Hilgenberg was in the middle of the best offensive line in modern Bears history, the one that helped pave the way to the Super Bowl XX championship after the 1985 season. From left to right, Jimbo Covert, Mark Bortz, Hilgenberg, Tom Thayer and Keith Van Horne started together for six seasons from 1985 to 1990. In Hilgenberg's nine years as starting center, the Bears led the NFL in rushing four times, finished second once and third another time.

The 6-foot-3, 259-pound Hilgenberg earned more accolades than his talented linemates combined. He was voted to the Pro Bowl seven times; Bortz and Covert earned two such honors apiece. In an era in which the Dolphins' Dwight Stephenson held a virtual lock on first-team All-Pro honors, Hilgenberg was voted the league's first-team center twice and second-team twice. His seven Pro Bowls are tied for fifth all-time among centers behind Jim Otto's 12, Jim Ringo's 10, Mike Webster's nine and Kevin Mawae's eight.

Hilgenberg often seemed annoyed at the attention and his teammates' lack of it. On Dec. 21, 1991, after he claimed his seventh straight Pro Bowl appearance, the Tribune's Paul Sullivan wrote: "Hilgenberg would much rather take a long ride on his motorcycle than have to sit and accept accolades on another Pro Bowl selection. The day the announcement was made, he shied away from reporters in the Bears' locker room."

"It's nice," Hilgenberg said. "But there's a lot of guys who should've gone that didn't go—like

Jay Hilgenberg (63) on Sept. 17, 1989, during a game against the Vikings at Soldier Field.

Tom Thayer or Keith Van Horne. Anybody on our line could've gone. I'm just a representative of our offensive line. We've had a good season."

The self-proclaimed worst player in the league turned himself into one of the game's best linemen. On Dec. 31, 1988, he proved just how good he had become during the Bears' 20-12 playoff win against the Eagles in what would become known as the Fog Bowl.

Eagles coach Buddy Ryan, the former Bears defensive coordinator, had a trick for his old team when he unexpectedly lined up All-Pro defensive end Reggie White at nose tackle to try to put Hilgenberg on the defensive. With the other Bears linemen busy blocking Eagles standouts Jerome Brown, Clyde Simmons and Seth Joyner, it was decided Hilgenberg would have to take on White mostly by himself.

The Bears rolled up 164 rushing yards, White had one sack, and the Bears moved on.

"I wasn't happy with the way we were going to block him," Hilgenberg told the Tribune's Bob Sakamoto and Fred Mitchell after the game. "He's their best lineman, and I wanted some help. . . . I guess the coaches put out a challenge to me. So, who won?"

"You did," Van Horne, seated next to him, said. "Take a compliment, will you?"

Hilgenberg turned to humor to again downplay his accomplishment.

"How did I handle White?" he asked. "Well, I got one of those stun guns that jolts you with a shock of electricity from a security guy and carried it onto the field during the fog."

Hilgenberg went undrafted out of Iowa in 1981 and made the Bears as a long snapper. His path to greatness was difficult but far from unprecedented for a center. Otto, acknowledged as the greatest of all time at the position, wasn't drafted. Neither were Pro Football Hall of Famers Jim Langer or Mick Tingelhoff, six-time Pro Bowl selections Jeff Saturday and Doug Smith, five-timer Bart Oates or three-time picks Kent Hull and Shaun O'Hara.

"I think I had an advantage in not being drafted," Hilgenberg told the Tribune's Ed Sherman on Jan. 13, 1986. "I wanted to prove I could make it. A lot of teams think you need a certain size, speed, weight. . . . All this game takes is to play with your heart."

Hilgenberg moved into the starting lineup in the middle of the 1983 season after Dan Neal hurt his back, and the job was his for the next nine seasons. Before then, Hilgenberg learned the ropes in practice against Bears defensive tackles Dan Hampton, Jim Osborne and Steve McMichael.

"The week of practice I'd have at Lake Forest a lot of times was harder than the games," Hilgenberg told the Tribune's Steve Rosenbloom on Nov. 7, 2005. To Don Pierson on July 30, 2002, Hilgenberg said of Hampton: "Once he beat you, he'd try to coach you. He wasn't being a smart aleck, just a good team player."

McMichael, in John Mullin's 2003 book, "Tales from the Chicago Bears Sidelines," said the young Hilgenberg "didn't know his way around how to play center in pro football. Me and Dan Hampton eventually taught him, though."

The Bears tough defensive tackles' methods produced quick results.

Hampton said to Mullin: "What Hilgy was so good at was letting you go the way you wanted, getting you off balance and then dumping you. He hardly ever was on the ground."

In 1981, Bears punter Bob Parson set an NFL record with 114 punts. All of Hilgenberg's long snaps were on target.

"My dad taught me how to snap in eighth or ninth grade," Hilgenberg said. "He said football teams always need players who can make the long snap."

Hilgenberg's teacher was a good one. Jerry Hilgenberg was an All-America center at Iowa. Jerry's brother Wally played in four Super Bowls as a Vikings linebacker. At Iowa, Jay was preceded at center by brother John, and he was followed by another brother, Joel, who played 10 NFL seasons at the position with the Saints.

"We're probably the only family that plays catch not facing each other," Jay Hilgenberg told Pierson in a Nov. 24, 1983, feature. CBS color commentator John Madden repeated the line often about Jay and Joel during the Bears' many appearances in the network's marquee game.

"I guess it's the genes," Hilgenberg told the Tribune's John Husar on Oct. 7, 1980. "We're like a good line of dogs. My mom and dad, they make good football players."

Jerry and JoAnn Hilgenberg's house was a snapping sanctuary. At one point the family would watch Joel in junior high games on Thursdays, Jay in high school on Fridays, Jim in college on Saturdays and Wally on Sundays, gathering around the TV in total concentration.

"It was like a ritual," Hilgenberg told Husar. "We were pretty intense. . . . No one ever talked except to discuss the different defenses and what the next play might be."

The Bears traded Hilgenberg to the Browns before the 1992 season for a fourth-round draft pick after the team and player could not agree on contract terms. He played one season in Cleveland and then served as Joel's backup for a year in New Orleans.

After 12 brutal seasons in the NFL trenches, Hilgenberg was training for one more, but he had a heart attack while playing pingpong with quarterback Mike Tomczak on April 8, 1994. It forced Hilgenberg's retirement at 35 and spurred him to lose so much weight he became hard to recognize.

Hilgenberg is a co-owner of the Club at Strawberry Creek, a golf course in Kenosha. If the Bears host a charity event, especially involving golf, Hilgenberg is almost sure to be there.

In 2008, the Hilgenberg tradition in Iowa City reached a third generation when Jay's daughter, Mara, joined the Hawkeyes' volleyball team.

"She's got a little bit of her dad in her," former Iowa coach Sharon Dingman, now the coach at the University of Chicago, told the Cedar Rapids Gazette on Aug. 19, 2009. "A little feistiness, a little sass . . . that 'Hit 'em in the mouth' kind of attitude."

Dingman's description matched what Jay heard from his Uncle Wally the one time he asked him for advice.

"Remember, first play of the game, no matter what it is," Wally told Jay, "you just hit the guy in the face as hard as you can." ■

> **I wanted to prove I could make it. A lot of teams think you need a certain size, speed, weight. . . . All this game takes is to play with your heart.**
>
> —JAY HILGENBERG

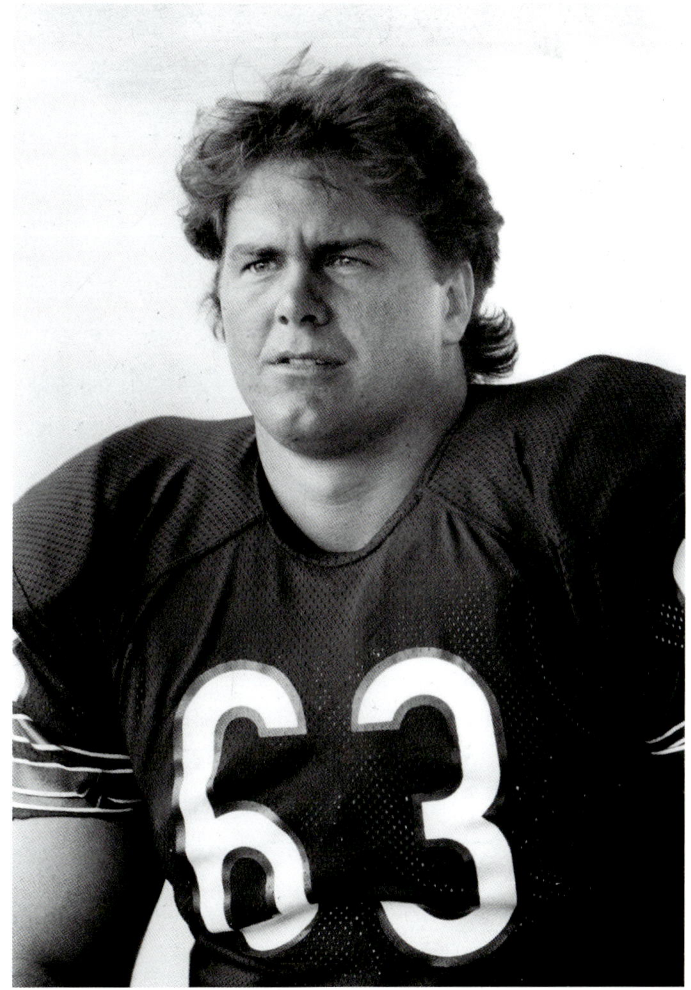

Jay Hilgenberg (63) on Dec. 23, 1991, during a game against the 49ers.

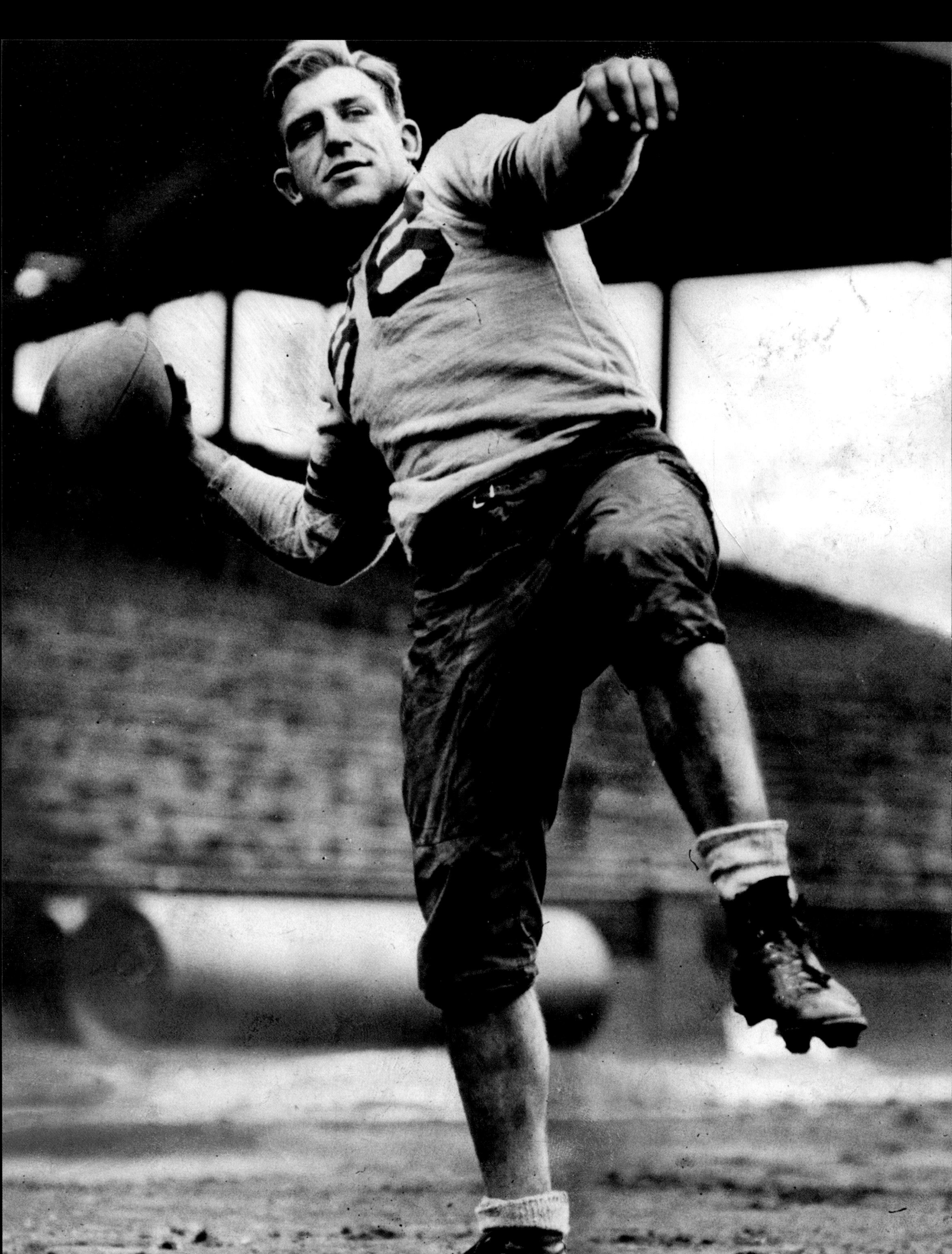

24

Bill Hewitt

56 END
1932–36

B ILL HEWITT TOOK A handoff from Bears quarterback Carl Brumbaugh and streaked to the right side of the field on an end around.

As seemingly the entire Packers team closed in on him, Hewitt slowed down and raised the ball behind his ear. He let it fly to fellow end Luke Johnsos, who was all by himself at the other end of Green Bay's City Stadium in the 1933 season opener.

"I shut my eyes and threw it as far as I could," Hewitt said, according to Jeff Davis' 2005 biography, "Papa Bear: The Life and Legacy of George Halas."

Johnsos hauled in the pass for a 46-yard touchdown. It was one of three huge plays by Hewitt—along with a blocked field goal and a blocked punt he returned for a touchdown—that led the Bears to a stunning 14-7 win against the Packers. It was one of seven wins the Bears snatched away from their opponents by seven points or fewer on their way to the 1933 championship.

Wilfrid Smith wrote in the Oct. 24, 1933, Tribune about the miracle Bears and their knack for winning close games late.

"We wait until the last minute so that when

we get ahead, the other team doesn't have time to catch up," Hewitt told Smith. "Someday the Bears will play the fourth quarter first and we'll run up an all-time scoring record."

Hewitt's pass to Johnsos exemplified how he thought about new ways to affect the game. He threw three touchdown passes in 1933 on the end-around pass, which he and Johnsos came up with during practice. When he was ready to make the play, Hewitt would tell only Brumbaugh and the receiver (Johnsos twice and end Bill Karr once) so that the Bears linemen would not block differently or watch the play develop.

Hewitt also implemented the hook-and-lateral play, in which he would catch a pass and pitch it to a receiver running to his side. The Bears used the play—with Hewitt catching a surprise pass from fullback Bronko Nagurski and pitching it to Karr for a 19-yard touchdown—for the last of six lead changes in their 23-21 win over the Giants in the 1933 championship game at Wrigley Field.

The Bears took a 16-14 lead near the end of the third quarter when Hewitt caught an 8-yard touchdown pass from Nagurski, who

Many consider Bill Hewitt (56) as the best two-way player of his era.

faked a run and threw a jump pass to Hewitt in the end zone.

Hewitt was known as an innovator on offense, and he was easy to identify as one of the last NFL players to play without a helmet. He also might have been the best defensive player in the league. He was the first player to try to time the snap count, and he often was in the opponent's backfield before the linemen were out of their three-point stances. Opposing fans nicknamed him "The Offside Kid" because they could not believe he was playing within the rules.

His Pro Football Hall of Fame bio reads: "Hewitt became the first player to make the masses take their eyes off the football just to watch him stymie the opponent. Because he had a jet-propulsion start at the snap of the ball . . . they couldn't fathom anyone reacting so quickly without being offside."

Gary D'Amato and Cliff Christl, former Milwaukee Journal Sentinel reporters, wrote in their 1997 book, "Mudbaths and Bloodbaths: The Inside Story of the Bears-Packers Rivalry," that "sophisticated statistics were not kept by the league then, but Hewitt is officially credited with throwing ball carriers for at least 300 yards in total losses during the (1933) season."

Hewitt, who studied pre-law at Michigan, offered a lawyerly response to his critics, telling the Milwaukee Journal that "I just anticipate when the ball is going to be snapped and charge in at the same time. Anyway, what is the head linesman for? It's up to him to call offside if he thinks I can."

While his performance in the 1933 opener was his best, Hewitt had many other great games against the Packers and became something of a legend in Green Bay for his performances in the rivalry. After one such game, the Green Bay Press-Gazette wrote: "Hewitt was a team by himself on the left side of the Bear line. The Packers would send two men and often three at him, trying to clear the way for a ball carrier. But Hewitt would smash through all of them to break up the play.

"When the Packers got into scoring territory the demon end would turn on even more steam and stop plays on the opposite side of the field."

Hewitt was at his best in 1933 and '34 while playing beside defensive tackle Link Lyman, who pioneered the use of pre-snap shifting. Hewitt was one of the first defensive players to freelance, and he did so with Lyman's assurance that he could handle both men's assignments if Hewitt found himself out of position.

Smith, in an eight-part Tribune series about Hewitt in 1933, wrote: "Sometimes Hewitt will leave his position to make a tackle in territory for which he is not responsible. You don't know where he'll be, but you can bet he'll be where the ball is."

Hewitt said his plan was simple: "Don't let anyone kid you. I just follow the ball."

In Hewitt's five seasons with the Bears he started 61 of his 63 games while the team went 45-10-9 (.773), won the 1932 and '33 championships and finished as runners-up in '34.

He scored 16 touchdowns with the Bears, including seven in 1936 to rank second in the NFL. In 1934 he led the league with five receiving touchdowns out of his 11 overall receptions. He was named first-team All-Pro in 1933, '34 and '36 and second-team in 1932.

After the 1936 season Hewitt retired, wishing to leave the game before his skills declined. He was coaxed back to the league by Eagles owner Bert Bell's offer of $200 per game, and he played four more seasons with them. In 1937 he became the first player to be voted first-team All-Pro for a second franchise. Hewitt was elected to the Pro Football Hall of Fame in 1971.

On Jan. 14, 1947, the Bay City, Mich., native died at 37 after his car skidded off a wet road and hit a culvert. In 1949, Halas decided to retire the uniform numbers of the most important players in team history. He chose three: Red Grange's 77, Bronko Nagurski's 3 and Hewitt's 56.

After Hewitt's death, Halas told the Tribune's Edward Prell: "Other teams might knock Bill down, but he would get up and wind up making the tackle 20 yards down the field. He had a flaming spirit."

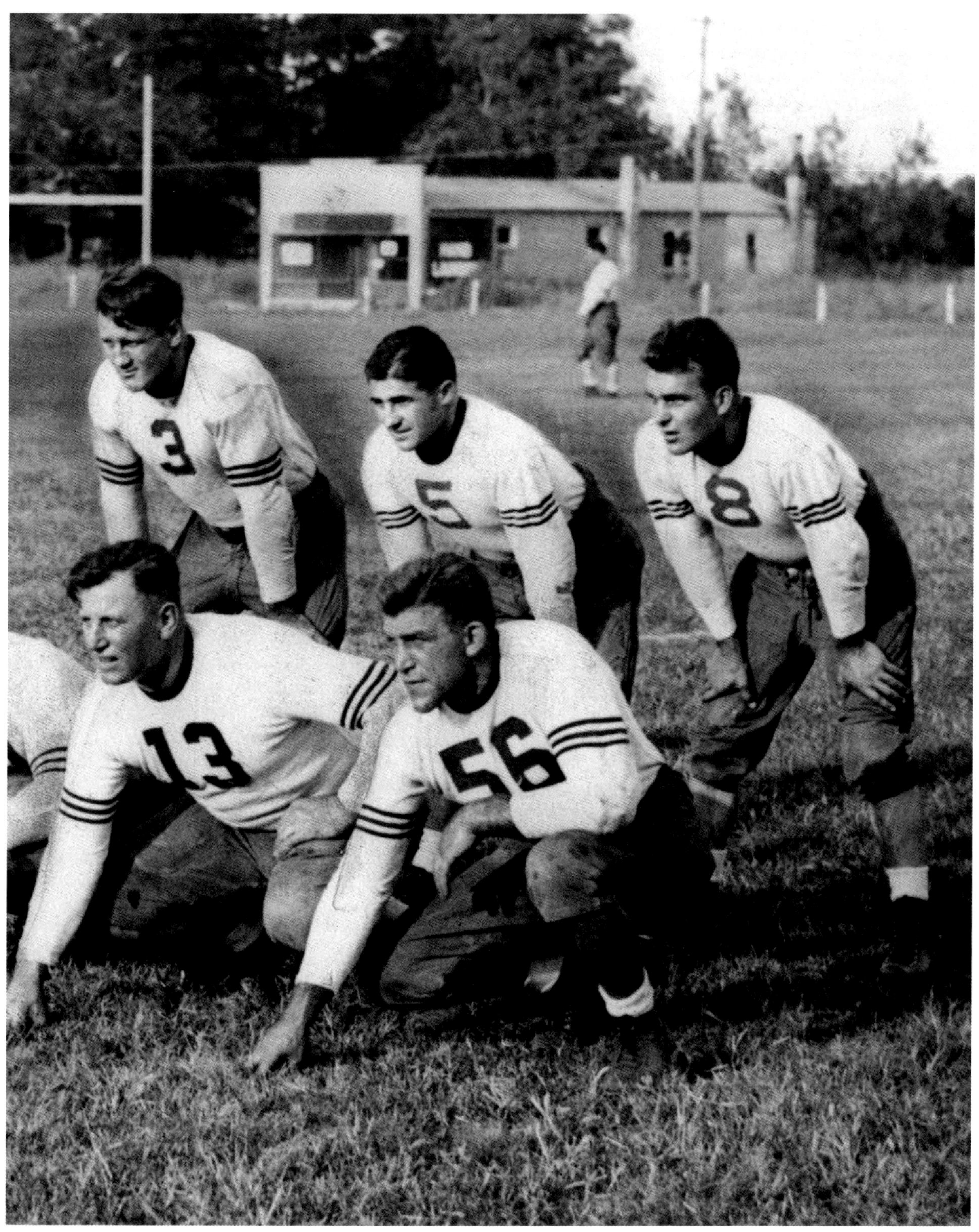

Teammates line up for a photo during practice in 1933. Shown kneeling, from left, are Link Lyman (13) and Bill Hewitt (56). In the back, from left, are Bronko Nagurski (3) George Corbett (5) and Carl Brumbaugh (8).

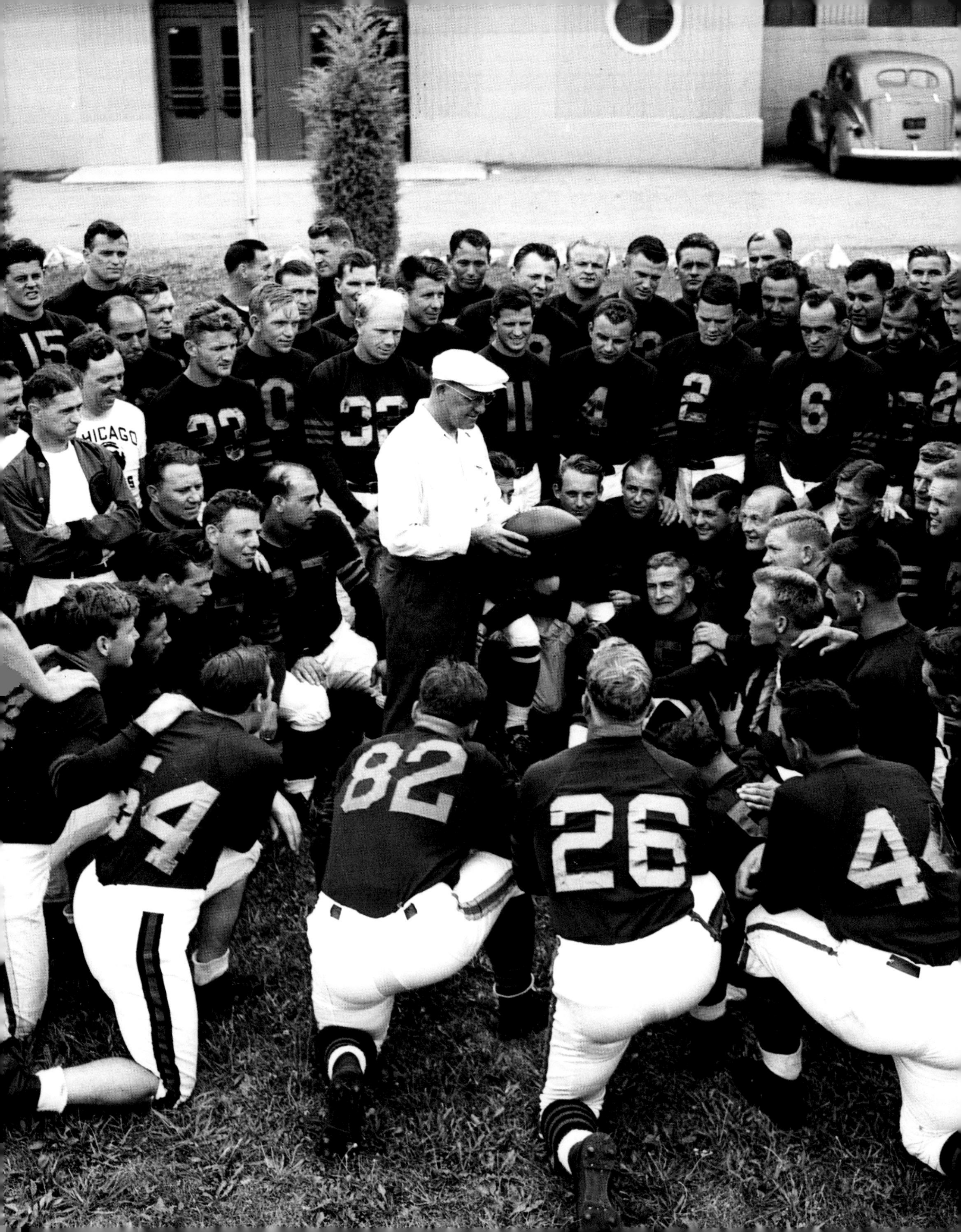

25

George Halas

7 END, HEAD COACH
1920–29, 1933–42, 1946–67

G EORGE HALAS WAS 25 when he created the National Football League. He was 70 when he won his final Coach of the Year award.

What he did between those landmarks in 1920 and 1965 is well-documented. Of the 100 players on the Tribune's list of the best Bears players ever, 75 played with or for Halas during his years with the Bears—64 seasons as owner, 40 as coach, nine as a player. Their stories are his story, as are the tales of every player who has put on an NFL uniform in the history of the team.

Halas' journey from the last of eight children, four of whom survived infancy, of Bohemian immigrants in Chicago's Pilsen neighborhood to his role as father of the NFL almost defies belief. In so many ways, the Chicago Bears almost never happened.

Early days

"Papa Bear" grew up in the modest home of Frank and Barbara Halas, who stressed the importance of religion, education, frugality and athletics. He would play all day with older brothers Frank Jr. and Walter and the other kids in the neighborhood. They included children of immigrants from Bohemia, Italy, Poland and Ireland. They cheerfully greeted each other with the ethnic slurs of the day, giving Halas a gateway to the profanity he used so profusely throughout his life.

Halas' father was a reporter for a Bohemian-language newspaper, then a successful tailor. According to several of his customers, Barbara sewed the city's best buttonholes.

In his 1979 autobiography, "Halas by Halas," George wrote: " 'Halas buttonholes' became part of the family's everyday speech. 'Halas buttonholes' taught me that a person must pay attention to the smallest details, and joy comes with any task well done."

His parents gave Halas 50 cents weekly allowance and demanded that he save most of it for a college education.

"I became frugal," Halas wrote. "Later it was sometimes said that I threw dollars around as though they were manhole covers. That is correct. It is precisely what I did do. By being careful with money, I have been able to accomplish things I consider important."

He attended Peter Cooper School, St. Vitus Church and the Pilsen Sokol, a social club that included a banquet hall, library and swimming

Coach George Halas, in white, gives the team a pep talk in 1946.

pool. One day Halas decided to teach himself to swim. In violation of club rules, he dived into the pool when no lifeguard was present. He sank to the bottom and nearly drowned before somehow pulling himself to the top of the side wall.

"I developed instant respect for rules and saw that behind each rule is a good reason," Halas wrote.

At Crane Technical High School on the Near West Side, Halas excelled at basketball, track and field and especially indoor baseball, but he had to play on the lightweight football team. He entered high school weighing 110 pounds and graduated at 120, sparking an obsession with weight that would last his entire life. Throughout adulthood, the 6-foot Halas would weigh himself every day and smile when the scale read 182 each time.

His Crane team won the city's indoor baseball title with Halas as its ace pitcher. During a game against Harrison, a female heckler let him and catcher Jack Hamm have it.

"Hamm and Eggs! Hamm and Eggs!" she shouted. "Hamm can't catch and Eggs can't pitch!"

Halas wrote: "I had to admit she was pretty. Certainly she was spirited. I made it my business to find out who she was."

She was Wilhelmina Bushing, and she eventually became Halas' wife, Min.

Off to college

George Halas followed his brother Walter to the University of Illinois, but between high school and college he worked for a year at Western Electric in Cicero. His most pressing concern was gaining weight. By the end of the year he weighed 140 pounds, a 20-pound improvement but still far too light to impress the Illini football coaches when he arrived in Champaign in August 1914.

He didn't make much of a mark as a freshman football player, then joined Walter on the baseball team in the spring.

Between his freshman and sophomore years, Halas planned to attend a Western Electric company picnic at Indiana Dunes. He showed up late on July 24, 1915, for the ride on the SS Eastland, and when he arrived he was shocked to see the ship had capsized in the Chicago River. The disaster killed 844 people.

He finally gained weight that summer and came back to Champaign as a 178-pound sophomore. He entered the starting lineup for renowned Illini coach Robert Zuppke, then joined the basketball and baseball teams. His basketball coach was Ralph Jones, who would succeed Halas as Bears coach in 1930 and install the T formation offense.

The three teams piled up Big Ten titles. One was won when Halas made a shot from nearly halfcourt to beat Wisconsin in basketball. Baseball probably was his best sport, as he spent much of his time injured in football.

During one practice, Zuppke called out Halas for loafing. Halas, who had been suffering from a leg injury but was keeping it to himself, exploded. He screamed at his coach and punctuated his rant by throwing his helmet in Zuppke's direction.

"My temper is always near the surface," Halas wrote. "That afternoon it went up like an explosion."

Halas' leg turned out to be broken, and he missed the rest of the season. While sidelined, he closely studied Zuppke's coaching and motivational methods.

In the Navy

In January 1918, with one semester left at Illinois, Halas enlisted in the Navy for World War I. He was sent to Naval Station Great Lakes near Waukegan. Illinois waived the six credits he needed to graduate and awarded him his degree in engineering.

Halas asked to become a submarine chaser in the English Channel and Atlantic Ocean. Instead, the Navy assigned him to its sports program.

There he joined star athletes such as Paddy Driscoll, Charlie Bachman, Jimmy Conzelman and Hugh Blacklock. The Great Lakes football team and other military outfits like it were allowed to compete against college teams. Great Lakes defeated Illinois, Iowa, Navy, Purdue and Rutgers and as the best team east of the Mississippi River was invited to play in the Rose Bowl against the Mare Island Marines from California.

Halas played the game of his life on Jan. 1, 1919. Great Lakes won 17-0. Halas was named the game's MVP after catching a 10-yard touchdown pass and returning an interception 77 yards to the Marines' 3-yard line. For the rest of his life he regretted not gaining those final 3 yards.

"After I took up coaching," Halas wrote, "I told the carriers that when they reach the 3-yard line, they should dive across the goal. Anyone who can't dive 3 yards should play Parcheesi."

Living his dream

With his service time over and college degree earned, Halas made good on a promise he had made at Illinois, where a Yankees scout had asked him to come to Florida and try out for the team. Halas was a huge Cubs fan growing up and dreamed of becoming the next Frank Chance.

During spring training in 1919, Halas injured his hip sliding into third base on a triple against Dodgers pitcher Rube Marquard. He made the team but played sparingly, getting two hits in 22 at-bats in 12 games, including four starts in right field.

Like many rookies, he was easily goaded. His teammates pressured him to tease Tigers legend Ty Cobb as he batted. Halas, who idolized Cobb, went along.

"I shouted nonsense at him, using some gutter terms," Halas wrote. "He dropped his bat and strode to the dugout."

"Punk, I'll see you after the game," Cobb said. "Don't forget, punk."

"I will look for you," Halas said.

Halas took a long shower, hoping Cobb would forget their meeting. Instead, they walked out of their facing clubhouse doors at the same time. Halas put up his dukes. Cobb extended his hand.

"I like your spirit, kid," Cobb said, "but don't overdo it if you don't have to."

The two became good friends. Cobb advised Halas to always stay positive and not waste time with negative energy.

"I should have changed my ways," Halas wrote, "but no, it was not the last time I made a chump of myself."

Halas played one game in his hometown, against the White Sox on June 5. In his only at-bat, he struck out on three pitches against Eddie Cicotte, who later that year would participate in the throwing of the World Series. After the game, Yankees manager Miller Huggins sent Halas to the minor leagues, and he never returned to the majors.

The Yankees wanted him to try again the next season. Halas figured if he couldn't beat out Sammy Vick for playing time in right field, he didn't have much of a chance against the team's new acquisition, Babe Ruth, so he declined.

'An exciting opportunity'

Halas, still yearning to compete, joined a semi-pro football team in Hammond that paid $100 per game. When Halas arrived he found Driscoll, Conzelman and Blacklock already there.

In 1920, Halas received a call from George Chamberlain of the A.E. Staley Company in Decatur. Mr. Staley wanted to build a company football team that could compete with not only other industrial teams around the Midwest but the semipro teams as well. Staley sought to improve company morale while spreading the name of his starch company. It had started a baseball team a few years earlier and had success.

Chamberlain asked Halas if he wanted to play on the baseball team and coach the football team. Halas listed his demands. Chamberlain agreed to let Halas recruit the players, who would receive full-time jobs at the plant, a share of profits from the games and two hours of daily practice on company time. On March 28, 1920, Halas took the train to Decatur.

"I was elated," Halas said. "I saw the offer as an exciting opportunity but did not suspect the tremendous future Mr. Staley was opening for me."

In August, Halas traveled to look for players. He brought aboard Ralph Scott of Wisconsin, Guy Chamberlin of Nebraska and Great Lakes teammates Blacklock and Conzelman.

He had hoped to sign Driscoll, but the former Evanston and Northwestern star already had agreed to become a coach and player for the Racine Cardinals, named at the time for their home street in Chicago.

Three players from Illinois—Burt Ingwersen, Ross Petty and Dutch Sternaman—joined the team, as did three more—Jerry Jones, Emmett Keefe and the great center George Trafton—from Notre Dame. Pard Pearce signed up from Pennsylvania.

Halas found his final six men in Decatur. Three—Kile MacWherter, Randy Young and Roy Adkins—played at Millikin University. Three others—Jack Mintun, Walter Veach and future big-league baseball player and manager Chuck Dressen—already worked at the plant.

Halas drilled his new team with the plays he learned from Zuppke at Illinois.

To that point, professional football was completely unorganized. Teams called or wrote each other to set up a game, advertised it quickly, then collected what they could from the small crowds that showed up.

Halas wrote to Ralph Hay, owner of the organized Canton Bulldogs, expressing his belief that a league needed to be formed. Hay replied that he agreed and had discussed the idea with Stan Cofall of the Massillon Tigers. Soon, owners from the teams in Akron, Cleveland and Dayton were on board.

The men elected Hay temporary chairman, and he called a meeting among representatives of 12 teams at his automobile dealership in Canton, Ohio, on Sept. 17, 1920.

Chairs were scarce in Hay's showroom, with four cars—two Hupmobiles and two Jordans—taking up most of the space. With Halas sitting on the running board of a Hupmobile, the meeting lasted two hours. It produced the American Professional Football Association.

The birth of the Bears

Halas was one of his team's better players but not a star like Trafton or Chamberlin. While his best game was the 1919 Rose Bowl, Halas' best play came in 1923, when he recovered a fumble by Jim Thorpe of the Oorang Indians, then outraced the superstar 98 yards for a touchdown. The play stood as the NFL's longest until 1972—even longer than his record of 324 coaching wins that Don Shula passed in 1993.

Halas never made an official All-Pro team, but the Pro Football Hall of Fame—which made Halas a charter member in 1963 and has an address of 2121 George Halas Drive in Canton—named him to its 1920s All-Decade team as a player.

Before play began in the APFA's first season, Halas bragged to the other owners about how talented his team was, and he was right. In their first two games, wearing the blue and orange of Halas' beloved Illini, the Staleys defeated the Moline Tractors 20-0 and the Kewanee Walworths 25-7. They scored three more shutout wins to start 5-0 before a 0-0 tie against the Rock Island Independents. Four more wins followed before their first meeting with the Cardinals. Driscoll's late extra point after a fumble return gave the Staleys their first loss, 7-6.

Halas was thrilled after the loss. It was a sellout, with 5,400 fans packing Normal Park on the South Side. The teams scheduled a rematch for the next week at Wrigley Field, which the Bears won 10-0. In the de facto championship game, the Staleys tied the Akron Pros 0-0. Both teams declared themselves champions, but the Pros are recognized as such with an 8-0-3 record that topped the Staleys' 10-1-2 mark. In their first season, the Staleys outscored their opponents 164-21.

Back at the plant, Staley noticed how much more money the games in Chicago, particularly the one played at Wrigley Field, made than the games the Staleys played in Decatur.

For the next season, Ohio State stars Chic Harley, Pete Stinchcomb and Tarzan Taylor came aboard on the condition that Halas cut in Harley's brother, Bill, on the money side of the operation.

Meanwhile, Staley could tell Halas was more interested in football than starch. He told Halas he could move the team to Chicago but that he would have to keep the Staley name for one more year. He also gave Halas $5,000 to cover expenses until the team turned profitable.

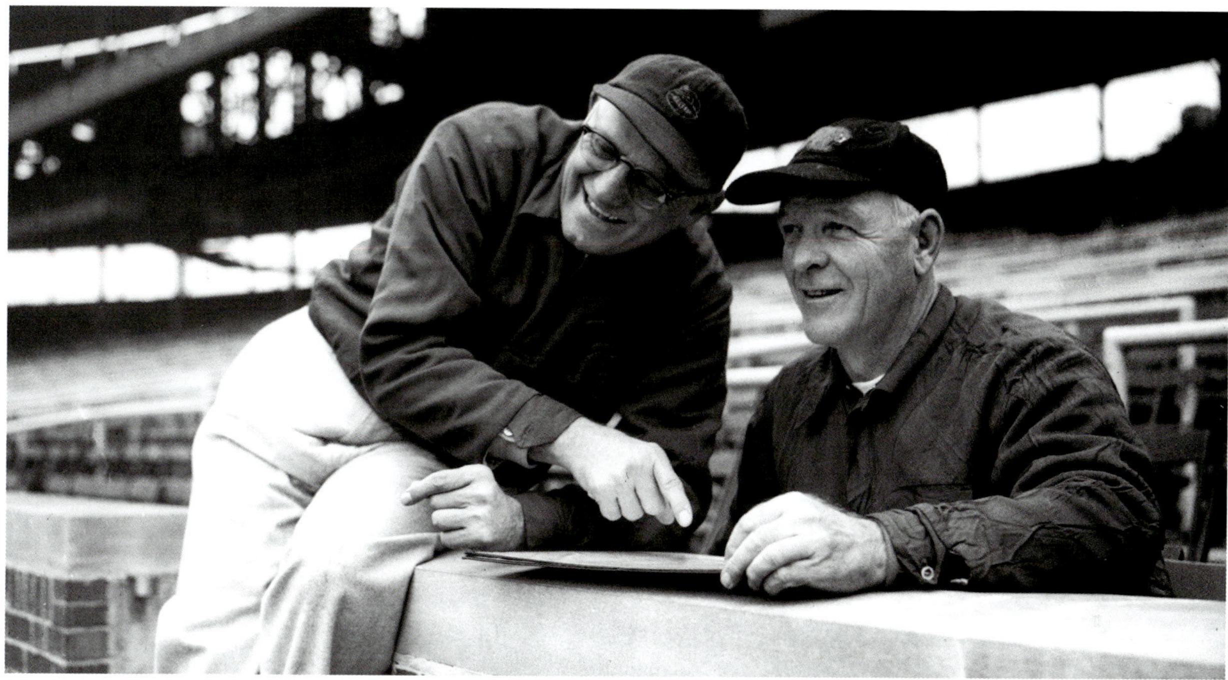

Coach George Halas, left, and former player and line coach Heartly "Hunk" Anderson in 1951 at Wrigley Field.

"Professional teams need a big-city base," Staley said. "Chicago is a good sports city. Look at the way the baseball games in Chicago draw profitable crowds."

Halas thought: "Five thousand dollars! Out of the goodness of his heart! A team of my own! Chicago! I could not believe such good fortune had come upon me. I was elated."

Halas wanted to use Wrigley Field, so he called William Veeck, president of the Cubs, and said he'd like to use the stadium for games and practices. Veeck liked the idea of money coming into the venue after baseball season and agreed to let the Staleys call the park home in return for 15% of the revenue from tickets and concessions.

Only one player, lifelong Decatur resident Mintun, kept working at the Staley plant, where he would become night superintendent after his seven-year pro career. Halas and the rest of his team headed to Chicago for good.

Halas found himself overwhelmed with the responsibilities of being the Staleys' owner, coach and right end. He took on Sternaman as a 50-50 partner.

The 1921 Staleys were excellent again, outscoring opponents 128-53. Their only loss came 7-6 to the Buffalo All-Americans on Thanksgiving, and they tied Driscoll and the Cardinals 0-0 on the season's final day. With a 9-1-1 record, the Chicago Staleys were undisputed AFPA champions.

In 1922, Halas married Min and was free of any duty to Staley. Halas proposed a name change for the league to the National Football League, since in baseball the leagues were a level higher than the associations. He planned to rename the team the Chicago Bears in honor of the Cubs, his favorite team and landlord.

"I noted football players are bigger than baseball players," Halas wrote. "So, if baseball players are Cubs, then certainly football players must be Bears!"

When Halas went to the AFPA board to make the transfer in ownership and name change official, he was hit with a surprise. Bill Harley, who had delivered the three Ohio State players to the Staleys the year before, demanded one-third ownership of the team. Halas deferred to the league's leadership.

The board voted in favor of Halas and Sternaman. The Chicago Bears were born. ■

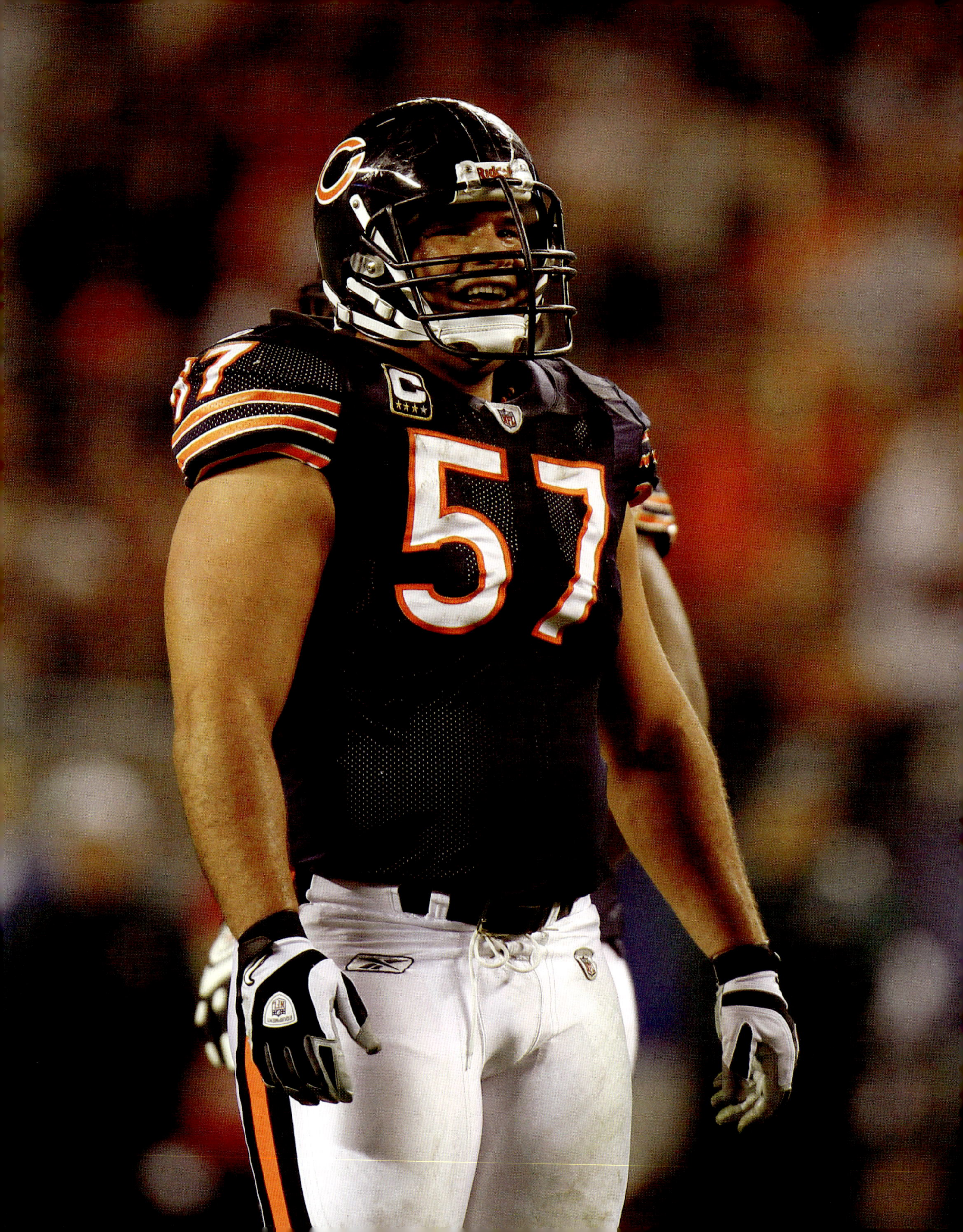

Olin Kreutz

26

WHEN TOMMIE HARRIS walked into Halas Hall for the first time, the first voice he heard was the most forceful one in the building.

"NFL, watch out for 97! NFL, watch out for 97!"

Harris, the Bears' first-round pick in 2004, had switched to No. 91 from his Oklahoma number by then, but Olin Kreutz was a stickler for accuracy. And any Bear who issued a boastful statement, as Harris did on ESPN after the Bears drafted him, would surely hear it recited back in a mocking manner by Kreutz, the team's stalwart center from Honolulu.

"He watches every show, reads every paper," Harris told the Tribune's Dan Pompei on Sept. 10, 2009. "He'll find out anything you said in the media. He calls you out. If you're going to talk about it with him around, you better be about it."

The defensive tackle was annoyed at first by Kreutz, but over time he understood the lesson and grew to admire his teammate's demanding leadership and outstanding play.

"He is an example of a perfect football player," Harris said five years after their first meeting.

Kreutz's style wasn't for everyone, and he made his share of enemies in his own locker room. As a rookie, he ended an argument with Moses Moreno about who was responsible for their bungled snap exchanges by shoving the quarterback to the ground. He fought with offensive tackle Fred Miller at an FBI gun range, taking a blow from a 10-pound weight before breaking his teammate's jaw.

In 2013, Hunter Hillenmeyer told Laurence Holmes and Matt Spiegel of WSCR-AM 670 that he "hated coming into work because of Olin" in 2004, when Hillenmeyer filled in at middle linebacker for an injured Brian Urlacher. "He was a jerk. He was riding me because I was . . . trying to fill in for a superstar."

Still, Hillenmeyer acknowledged: "I would go to the grave acknowledging that he thought that everything he was doing was in the best interest of the team."

Even the Bears' few superstars got the Kreutz treatment.

"He tested me right away," Urlacher, only

Olin Kreutz (57) on Nov. 22, 2009, during a game against the Philadelphia Eagles at Soldier Field.

125

a year younger than Kreutz, told Pompei. "He does it to everybody. At first you don't know how to take him. . . . I try not to mess with him too much. He knows too many moves where he can snap your arm in two."

When Kreutz felt he was the best man for a job, he decided it would become his responsibility. In one of his first years with the Bears, his more experienced linemates took turns making incorrect protection calls during practice.

Bob Wylie, the Bears' offensive line coach from 1999 to 2003, remembered Kreutz saying: "That's it—you guys are screwing up. Nobody makes any of the calls but me now. I got the whole thing."

"He took it over and did it for the next four years I was there," Wylie said.

Of the numerous things that upset Kreutz, nothing made him madder than a teammate missing a blocking assignment.

"If you're confused, then put in more freaking work, period," he told the Tribune's Vaughn McClure on Oct. 21, 2010. "If you can't handle it, you can't play in the NFL."

Kreutz took his team-building practices on the road too. As airport security tightened and lines increased after Sept. 11, 2001, he installed a rule that each offensive lineman would wait until the last one made it through, then walk as a unit to their flight.

He also claimed the sometimes-unpleasant task of media spokesman for the line. After the unit's worst game of his career, when the Giants sacked Jay Cutler nine times in the first half of a 17-3 loss on Sunday night, Oct. 3, 2010, Kreutz took the heat.

"To rectify the problem," he told McClure, "we have to (expletive) block people."

Right or wrong, Kreutz felt he was doing what he could to help the Bears become a better team. His play certainly did. In his 13 seasons with the Bears, he was named to the Pro Bowl six times with a first-team All-Pro selection in 2006 and a second-team nod in '05.

He was a backup in 1998, started all 16 games in '99, then missed nine games in 2000 after spraining his right MCL. Over the next 10 years he played and started 159 of 160 games. Kreutz's

191 games as a Bear rank second to long snapper Patrick Mannelly's 245. Kreutz's 183 starts are one behind all-time Bears leader Walter Payton.

Bears offensive line coach Harry Hiestand told the Tribune's Melissa Isaacson on Jan. 8, 2006: "There's nobody better at what he does, nobody. The guy is special, and I'm blessed to be around him every day."

It would have been ludicrous for a lesser player to try to lead the way Kreutz did. Because he was so good, he could.

"Kreutz can challenge any teammate because there isn't much to challenge him about," Pompei wrote. "Kreutz rarely makes a mistake. The key to his leadership is he does everything the right way."

Those who could handle Kreutz gave him their absolute loyalty. When backup Terrence Metcalf became the starting right guard in 2005, he said: "I just don't want to let Olin down. You know what I mean?"

In 2011 Kreutz finished his career playing four games with the Saints before retiring. One was a 30-13 win against the Bears on Sept. 18 at the Superdome. Kreutz found himself unable to stop trying to teach his former teammates.

Bears defensive tackle Anthony Adams told the Tribune's Brad Biggs: "He was still telling us, 'Hey, man, you're kind of heavy on your stance, you're doing this, you're doing that.' It's like playing against your dad or something."

In 1998 the Bears blundered by drafting running back Curtis Enis with the fifth pick but added much-needed toughness in Rounds 2 and 3 with safety Tony Parrish and Kreutz, teammates at Washington.

Kreutz saw plenty of good and bad times under coaches Dave Wannstedt, Dick Jauron and Lovie Smith, with most of the highs provided by Smith's defenses. Even during the playoff seasons of 2001, '05 and '10 and the Super Bowl year of 2006, the offenses were merely adequate. A typical season ended with the Bears represented in the Pro Bowl by linebackers Urlacher and Lance Briggs, perhaps another defensive or special teams player and Kreutz.

In his 13 seasons with the Bears, Kreutz played next to 12 left guards (from Todd Perry

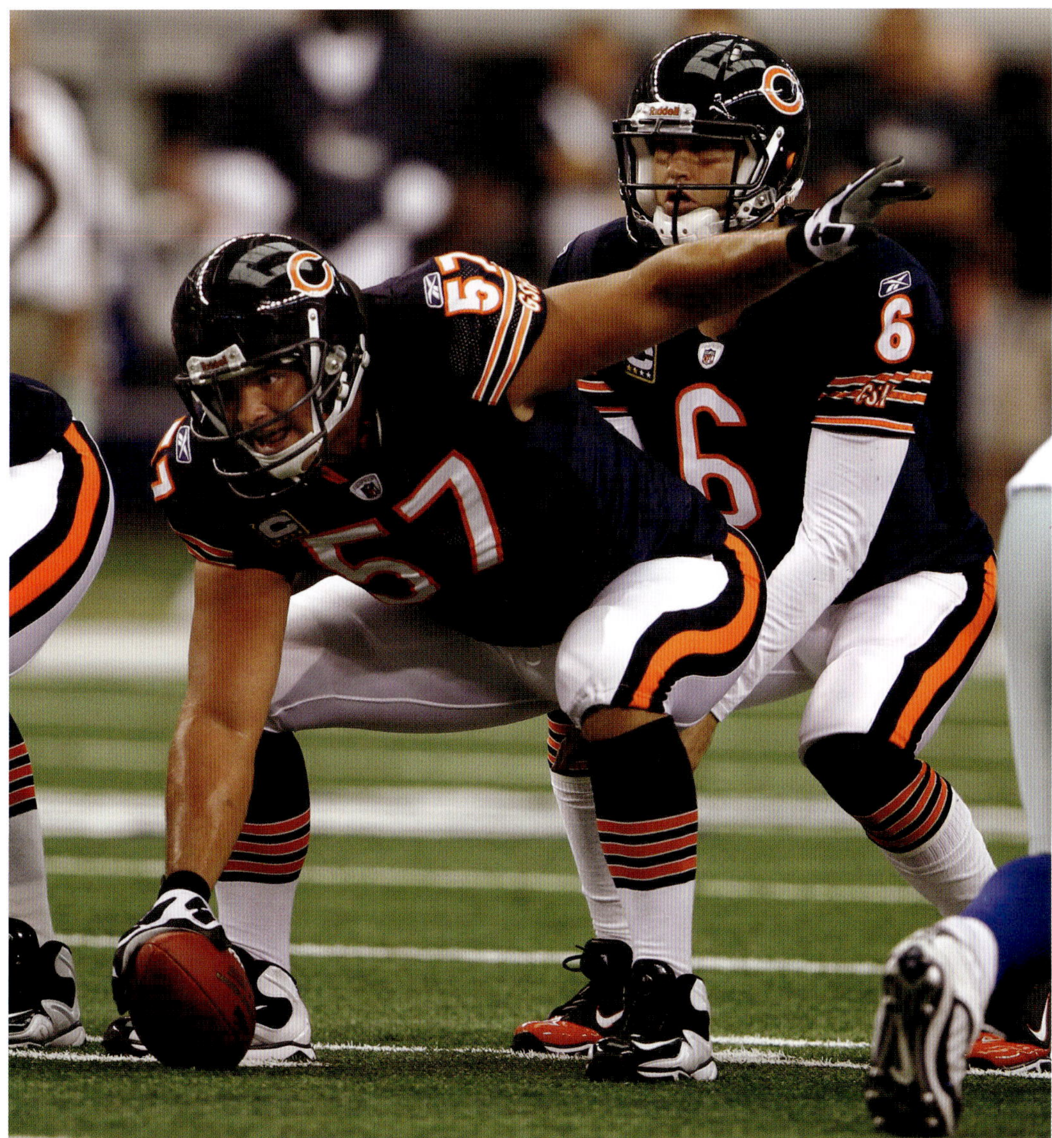

Olin Kreutz (57) and Jay Cutler (6) prepare to make a snap Sept. 19, 2010, during a game against the Dallas Cowboys.

to Chris Williams) and snapped to 18 quarterbacks (from Erik Kramer to Cutler). Through it all, he remained one of the NFL's best centers.

In the 2000-09 decade, only Kevin Mawae's seven Pro Bowl appearances topped the six of Kreutz and Matt Birk.

"I followed Olin's career closely," Mawae told McClure on Sept. 18, 2011. "Our games are a little different. He's a stronger player, where I was a technician. He has been one of the best centers in the game through the years . . . second to me."

Among Bears centers, only Jay Hilgenberg, with seven from 1985 to '91, made more Pro Bowls than Kreutz. Like Mawae—who was inducted into the Pro Football Hall of Fame in 2019—Hilgenberg admired everything about Kreutz's game.

"He's a great athlete," Hilgenberg told Isaacson. "He can move, he has great arm strength and he shows up every game.

"And I can't stress his leadership abilities strongly enough." ◼

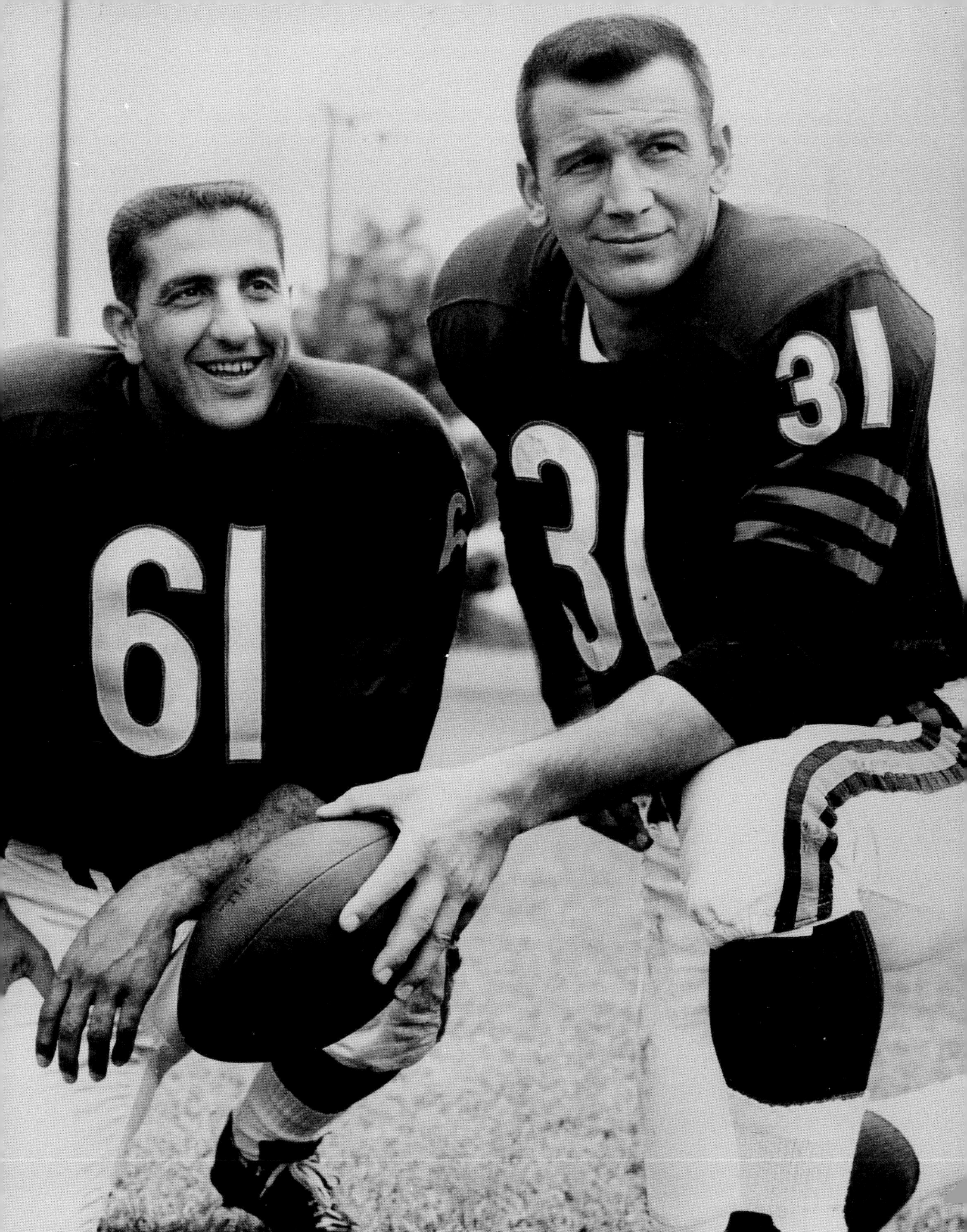

Joe Fortunato

27

31 LINEBACKER
1955–66

J OE FORTUNATO played about as well as anyone not in the Pro Football Hall of Fame.

Over the years, many players, coaches, writers and fans made his case, but the former Bears linebacker never thought it was a big deal.

His second wife, Catherine, would bring up the subject at her husband's autograph signings or when he met with an old teammate or coach, the Tribune's Lew Freedman wrote while catching up with Fortunato at his Natchez, Miss., home on July 27, 2006. Occasionally she wrote letters to people she thought could help his cause.

"Oh, Catherine," Big Joe would sigh.

She had a point, though. Of the 14 defensive players named to the Hall of Fame's All-Decade team of the 1950s, all but Fortunato have a bronze bust in Canton, Ohio. The 6-foot-1, 225-pound outside linebacker, a seventh-round future pick in 1952, was named to five Pro Bowls and earned first-team All-Pro honors three times and second-team once. The Bears had eight winning seasons in his 12 years, won the NFL championship in 1963 and finished as runners-up in 1956.

During his career, Fortunato played in 155 of 156 possible games, starting 153. His 22 fumble recoveries were an NFL record when he retired until Dick Butkus, his roommate for his final two seasons, broke it.

After Fortunato's death at 87 in 2017, former Mississippi State teammate Bobby Collins told Mississippi Today's Rick Cleveland that "if you didn't know Joe and you just sat down to talk to him, you'd never suspect he was this great football star, feared by his opponents. He was just a friendly, generous guy. He'd rather talk about you than himself."

Fortunato is a major part of the Bears' unmatched history at linebacker. The team's middle-linebacker heritage of Bill George, Butkus, Mike Singletary and Brian Urlacher is acknowledged as the NFL's best. The outside linebackers also are hard to top with George Connor, Fortunato, Larry Morris, Doug Buffone, Otis Wilson, Wilber Marshall and Lance Briggs.

Since Connor's first Pro Bowl appearance in 1950, Bears linebackers have been named to the game 56 times in 69 years. Three droughts—in 1973-82, 1993-99 and 2012-17—coincided with some of the team's toughest times. Khalil

Bill George
(61), left, and
Joe Fortunato
(31) on Aug.
3, 1960, in
Rensselaer, Ind.

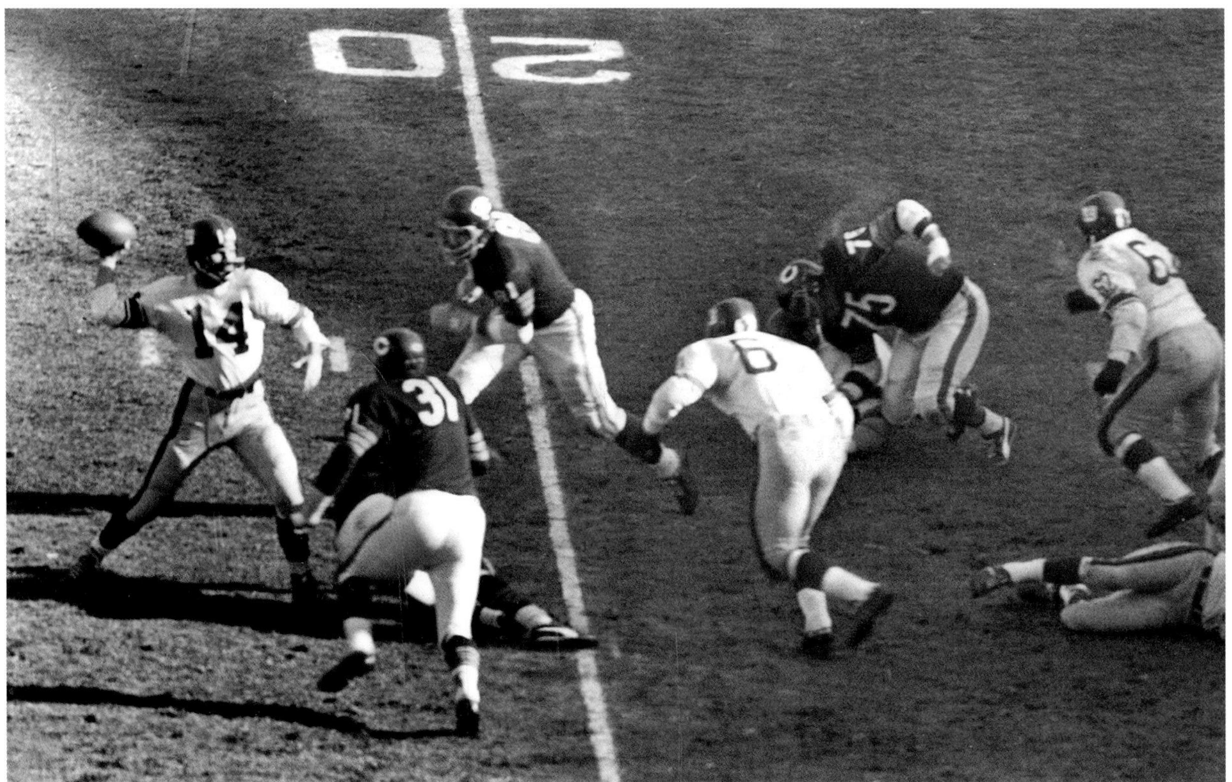

Joe Fortunato (31) draws a bead on Y.A. Tittle (14) of the New York Giants on Dec. 29, 1963.

Mack, a new kind of outside linebacker, made it in 2018, and inside linebacker Roquan Smith appears primed to join him in the near future, signifying good times likely are ahead.

Fortunato, George and Morris probably are the Bears' best linebacker threesome, with Fortunato and George members of the 1950s All-Decade team and Morris making it in the 1960s. They were starters together for six seasons, compared with three for the Bears' other great trio of Marshall, Singletary and Wilson. The group was at its best in 1963 under the guidance of defensive coordinator George Allen, who took over for Clark Shaughnessy during the 1962 season.

Allen and coach George Halas named Fortunato captain and signal-caller for a defense that led the NFL in scoring, total, rushing and passing defense as well as turnovers. Allen turned Fortunato and Morris loose on "red-dog" blitzes to force quarterbacks into quick throws. Those situations often led to interceptions, and the Bears led the league with 36 in '63.

"There's a great thrill to getting through there and breaking up the play before it gets started," Fortunato told the Tribune's George Strickler on Nov. 8, 1959.

Allen and the veteran Fortunato taught young defensive end Ed O'Bradovich how to anticipate screen passes. It paid off in the 1963 title game against the Giants. In the third quarter, O'Bradovich intercepted a Y.A. Tittle screen, leading to the winning touchdown in the Bears' 14-10 victory.

Halas told Cooper Rollow in the Tribune's game story: "It was just what we were looking for. It worked perfectly. We had a blitz on, and the red-dogger was Fortunato. Joe went in. O'Bradovich came over and protected Fortunato's position and he came up with the pass. It was a big one."

In the wild locker room, as the Bears celebrated their first championship in 17 years,

That danged Fortunato never makes a mistake, and moreover, he never hits you easy. He hurts more when he picks you off coming through the line than any linebacker in a league where there's a score of great linebackers.

Fortunato stood on a chair, delivered a short speech on Allen's importance to the team and tossed the defensive coordinator the game ball.

A knee injury ended Fortunato's career shortly before the 1967 season. He stayed on as an assistant coach, leading the linebackers in Halas' last season as head coach and becoming defensive coordinator under new coach Jim Dooley in 1968.

Fortunato believed linebacker to be the most difficult defensive position. He watched Bears games his entire life and loved watching the outside linebackers, particularly Marshall and Wilson in the 1980s, play the same way he did. In 2014, the Tribune's Don Pierson named Fortunato the sixth-best linebacker in team history.

"A linebacker has to know so many things," Fortunato told the Tribune's Robert Markus on Sept. 15, 1967. "He has to defend against the run and the pass. He has to coordinate with the front four and with the deep backs. He has to sometimes cover a halfback, and it's pretty tough to cover a 9.5 (100-yard dash runner) when you're a 10.6 or 11.6 runner yourself."

He said the key to success was limiting and eventually eliminating mistakes. Most games, he figured, were lost by miscues rather than won by exceptional play.

As an unnamed opponent told Strickler: "That danged Fortunato never makes a mistake, and moreover, he never hits you easy. He hurts more when he picks you off coming through the line than any linebacker in a league where there's a score of great linebackers. But don't use my name. I don't mind giving Fortunato credit; I just don't want the rest of these so-and-sos trying to convince me they can hurt more than Joe."

Fortunato grew up working in the steel mills of Mingo Junction, Ohio. He attended Virginia Military Institute for one year, then followed coach Slick Morton to Mississippi State. There, he met his first wife, Noonie, and moved to her family's hometown of Natchez. During his days with the Bears, he opened a book and toy store there and in offseasons helped tend to his mother-in-law's Hereford cows.

He left the Bears after one year as defensive coordinator and moved to Mississippi full time. He owned and operated Big Joe Oil Company, which explored for and drilled wells. He became known for his charity work in Mingo Junction, where a highway was named after him, and Natchez, where he started the Joe Fortunato Celebrity Golf Classic to raise funds for education in Mississippi.

Fortunato made a great number of friends in both places, but as Collins said, he usually was more interested in hearing their stories than in telling his.

As Strickler wrote in 1959: "Joe Fortunato of the Chicago Bears goes quietly through life wondering if anyone else is having so much fun." ■

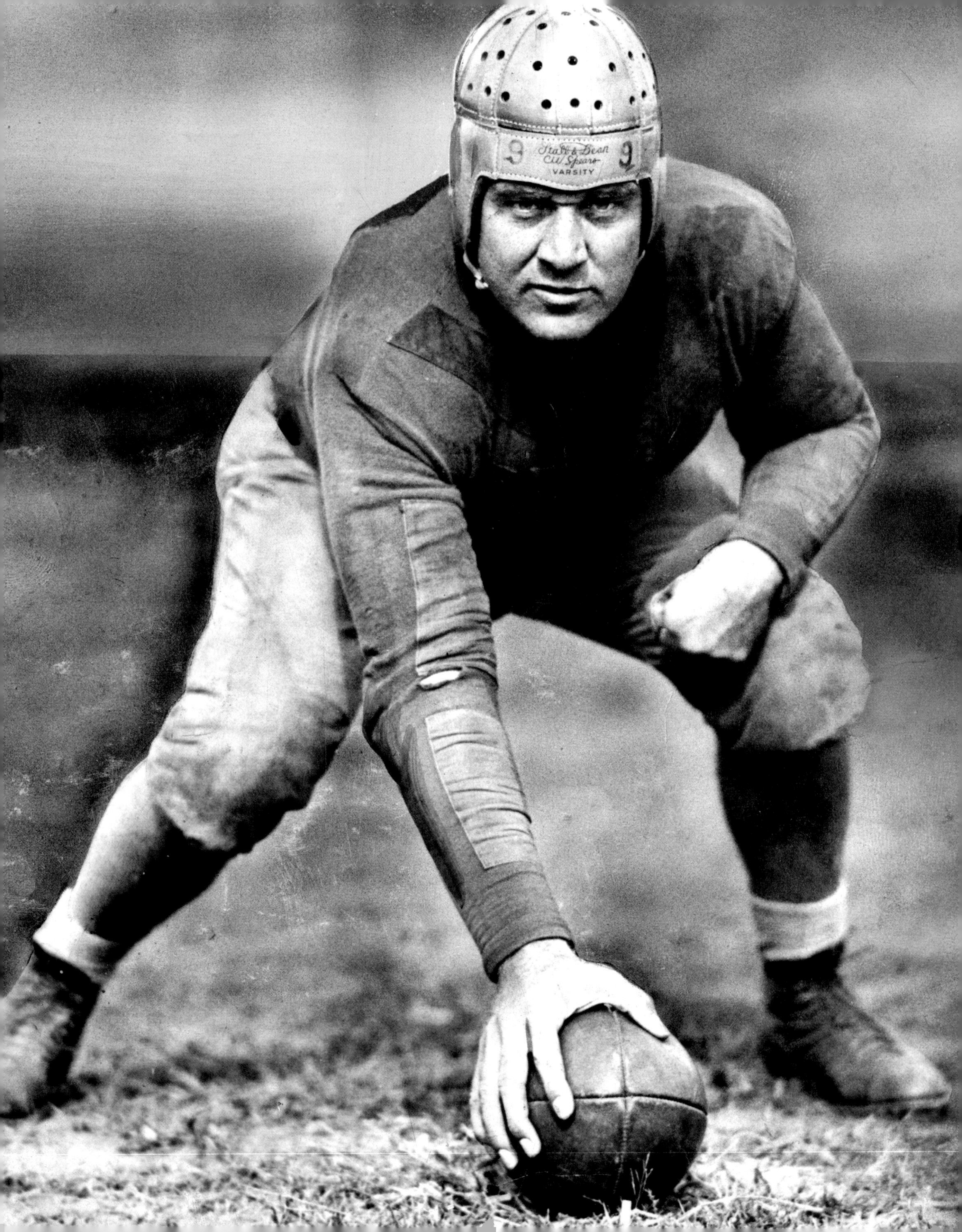
9   Stall & Dean
All Spero
VARSITY   9

28

George Trafton

IN THE FIRST YEAR of the National Football League, then known as the American Professional Football Association, George Trafton set a standard for performance in a rivalry series that has yet to be matched.

The Decatur Staleys and Rock Island Independents clashed in two of the roughest games of 1920. In the first one, Trafton sent four Independents off the field with injuries as the Quad Cities crowd booed. The worst fate befell halfback Fred Chicken, who broke his leg when Trafton tackled him into a fence post near the field.

Three weeks later, the teams met again in Rock Island. Gamblers—who had started to turn their attention toward pro football after the Black Sox scandal of the previous year made baseball a risky play for a short time—had lost money on the previous meeting and were looking to bounce back.

Bears owner, coach and right end George Halas sequestered his team across the Mississippi River in Davenport, Iowa, hoping to keep his players from unsavory interests. They soon learned, however, that the smart money was on a parlay involving the Independents winning and knocking out Trafton in the first quarter. The only information they could gather about the player who was to deliver the hit was that he went by "Mr. Chicken."

Almost every Bear honored Halas' directive never to bet for or against the Bears, but Trafton couldn't resist this one. He emptied his pockets betting on his team and himself and prepared for battle.

"Mr. Chicken" turned out to be not Fred Chicken but 6-foot-2, 200-pound lineman Harry Gunderson, who like the 6-2, 230-pound Trafton played offensive and defensive center. Lined up across from one another on every play, the two went at each other with gusto. Gunderson's quickness gave Trafton fits, and late in the first quarter he tackled a Staleys back behind the line of scrimmage. Trafton reacted by falling knees-first with all his weight on Gunderson's head.

Gunderson was knocked out and suffered a 6-inch gash that would require about 90 stitches. The rest of the game resembled a mob scene, with fans throwing rocks and bottles at Trafton. When it ended in a 0-0 tie, Bears trainer Andy Lotshaw put a gray sweatshirt

George Trafton (13) was one of the greats of the NFL's early days.

"

over Trafton's jersey to hide his number and told him to run as fast as he could out of the stadium. Halas surreptitiously stuffed an envelope containing the Staleys' share of the gate receipts in Trafton's trousers.

Fans blocked Trafton's path to the taxicabs outside the arena, so he took off sprinting down the road toward the bridge to Iowa, angry mob in tow. He was saved when a curious motorist asked what the fuss was about. Trafton replied that he was late to catch a train across the river, and the driver delivered him to the Davenport depot.

When Trafton caught up with his teammates at the train station, Halas asked for his envelope, which reports say held between $3,000 and $7,000. Trafton asked why in the world his coach left the money with him.

In his 1979 autobiography, "Halas by Halas," the Bears founder remembered his rationale: "I knew that if trouble came, I'd be running only for the money. Trafton would be running for his life."

Trafton became one of the greats of the NFL's early days. The Staleys moved to Chicago in 1921 and won the AFPA championship. In 1922 the Staleys became the Bears and the AFPA became, at Halas' suggestion, the National Football League. In 1932, Trafton's last season at age 36, the Bears won their second championship.

The center was named first-team All-Pro twice and second-team three times in his 12 seasons. He was elected to the Pro Football Hall of Fame in its second class in 1964, and it named him to its All-Decade team of the 1920s.

On offense, Trafton became the first center to snap the ball with one hand. On defense, he was the first center to drop back to defend against passes.

"Trafton would hand the ball with the laces in exactly the position (the quarterback) wanted them," Halas wrote. "When throwing back for punts, field goals or conversions, he could spiral the ball just enough to make it end up in the kicker's or holder's hands with the laces in the right position. It saved perhaps a half-second, but that was long enough to reduce the danger of a blocked kick."

Before joining Halas, Trafton honed his skills for two other all-time great coaches. He was a star for the early powerhouses at Oak Park High School under future University of Illinois coach Robert Zuppke, then he played for Knute Rockne at Notre Dame.

His time in South Bend ended early. When Rockne discovered that Trafton also was playing for the professional Hammond Pros under an alias, he kicked Trafton not only off the team but out of school. Halas, who was recruiting mostly former Illinois, Northwestern and Notre Dame players for his new factory team at Decatur's A.E. Staley starch plant, took advantage.

Trafton came on board and he was Halas' starting center for most of the next 13 years. In that time the NFL grew from a ragged consortium that included teams such as the Moline Tractors, Tonawanda Lumberjacks, Muncie Flyers, Kewanee Walworths and Wheeling Stogies to a big-time outfit that boasted teams in Chicago, New York, Washington and Boston.

Trafton remained notorious off the field. He became, like many athletes of the time, willingly or not, enmeshed with the mobsters, gangsters and gamblers who overran pro sports as well as much of society during the Roaring '20s. In his 2004 Bronko Nagurski biography, "Monster of the Midway," Jim Dent devoted a chapter to Trafton's extracurricular activities.

One group of gangsters held unlicensed celebrity boxing matches at the White City Amusement Park. In 1929, Trafton was challenged by Art Shires, a 6-foot-1, 195-pound White Sox first baseman. The two duked it out for a round, with the larger Trafton holding the edge, then danced and wheezed for the remainder of the fight.

Trafton—who had obeyed Halas' orders to play in a game against the Giants the day before, then became confused as different sets of firearm-toting mobsters instructed him to win and lose the match—was declared the winner. Dent wrote: "Al Capone stood and cheered as if Trafton had won the heavyweight championship of the world. Two days later, 'Machine Gun' McGurn would slide into the bar and deposit a thousand-dollar bill in Trafton's suit pocket.

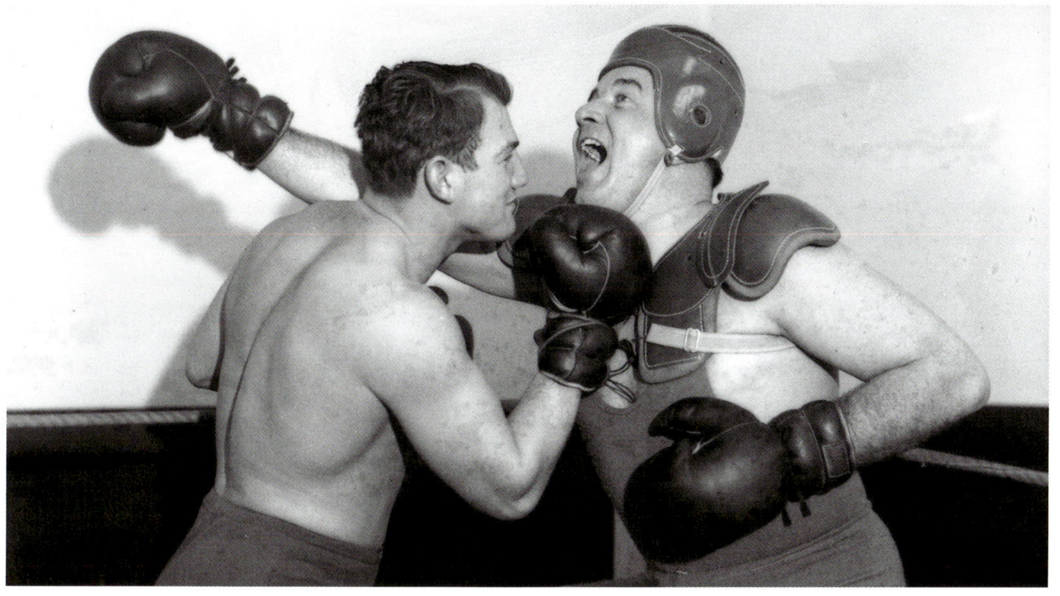

Boxers King Levinsky, left, and George Trafton, shown in 1932. Trafton had two stints with the Chicago Bears.

Big George didn't notice. He was too busy recounting the greatest fight ever to a bar filled with adoring fans."

A year later, Trafton met future heavyweight world champion Primo Carnera in a sanctioned bout in Kansas City, Mo., another mob stranglehold. Trafton went down three times in the fight's first 30 seconds, was banned for life by Missouri's boxing commission and years later said he was told at gunpoint to lose as quickly as he could.

Dent, who also wrote "The Junction Boys," continued: "At another time, maybe 30 or 40 years down the road . . . Trafton would have been a media darling. He might have been the Joe Namath of centers. But Trafton wasn't just talk. He had the game to back it up. . . . Halas once said, 'George's the toughest, meanest, most ornery critter alive.'"

Halas valued his friendship with Trafton even more in 1931, when the Bears founder put into action his plan to buy out co-owner Dutch Sternaman. Halas raised money from people who would become minority stakeholders in the franchise, including former Bears lineman Jim McMillen, former Crane Tech High School friend Ralph Brizzolara and Chicago Cardinals owner Charles Bidwill.

The biggest contributor, at $20,000, was Trafton's mother, whose name appears to have been lost to time. Years later, when she suggested her son should replace Halas as coach, Halas bought her out for $40,000.

In his 2005 biography, "Papa Bear: The Life and Legacy of George Halas," Jeff Davis wrote: "Mrs. Trafton not only saved the Bears for Halas but also just may have saved the National Football League. Had Halas failed, it is distinctly possible that the league would have crumbled."

After he retired in 1933, Trafton coached the Bears as an assistant and operated a boxing gym on Randolph Street. He moved to the Packers in 1944 and the Cleveland Rams in '45, then followed the Rams the next year when they moved to Los Angeles. In 1951 he became head coach for the first time with the CFL's Winnipeg Blue Bombers, a team that included future Bears coach Neill Armstrong. Even though the Blue Bombers won the Grey Cup in 1953, they fired Trafton, and he returned to Los Angeles to embark on a real estate career.

Trafton, one of professional football's original larger-than-life characters, died at 74 in 1971 in LA after complications from hip surgery.

One reporter from his playing days wrote that "Trafton was strongly disliked in every city in the NFL except Green Bay and Rock Island. In those places, he was hated." ■

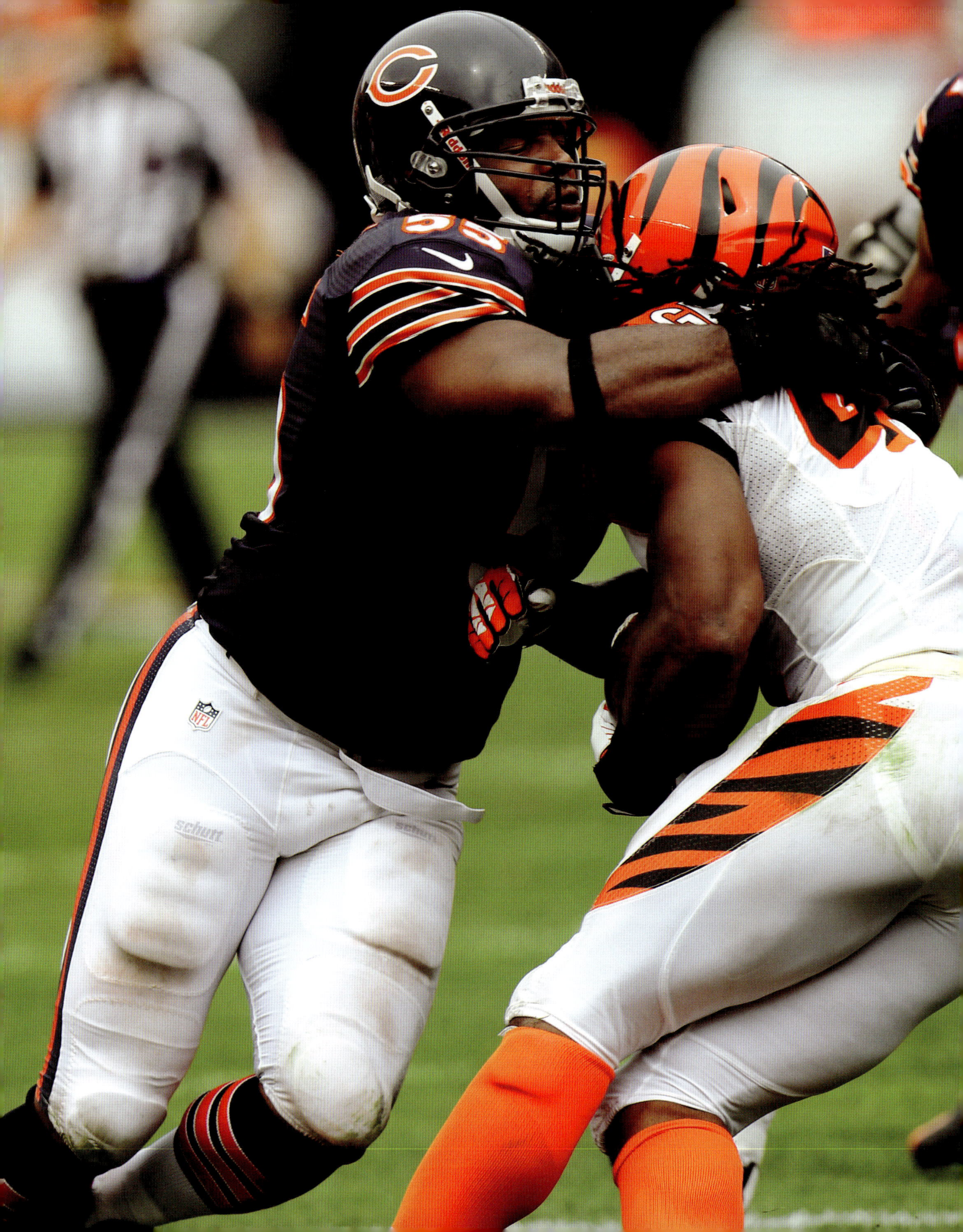

29

Lance Briggs

55 LINEBACKER

2003–14

WHETHER IT WAS fighting a fullback head-on in the hole, tailing a tight end or tailback in pass coverage, blasting between blockers to make a tackle for a loss or chasing down someone with sprinter's speed, Lance Briggs excelled at almost every aspect of defensive football.

Briggs was one of the best players on Bears defenses that typically were among the NFL's best. He didn't possess the otherworldly athleticism of fellow linebacker Brian Urlacher or the nose for the ball of cornerback Charles Tillman, but his excellent play at weak-side linebacker was one of the main reasons coach Lovie Smith's Cover-2 defense worked so well in Chicago.

"I've never been around anyone like him," Urlacher told the Tribune's Dan Wiederer on Nov. 9, 2014. "He knows what gaps to run through. He knows where to fit. If he takes a chance, it's always the right one.

"I didn't always know where Lance was going to be. But I knew he was going to be where the ball was."

Briggs, Urlacher and Tillman were mainstays as the Bears regained their fearsome defensive reputation under Smith after years of struggles on that side of the ball. The Bears spent 11 consecutive years outside the top 10 in yards allowed under coaches Dave Wannstedt and Dick Jauron; under Smith the Bears finished in the top 10 four times and in the top five three times.

The three Bears played together for 10 years, from when Tillman and Briggs were drafted in 2003 until Urlacher's retirement after the 2012 season. Briggs and Tillman played with each other for 12 years. Along the way they became each other's biggest fans as one would make plays that made the other two shake their heads in amazement.

Urlacher and Tillman could only laugh during a Monday night game against the Eagles in 2011 when Briggs streaked across the field and chased down scrambling quarterback Michael Vick.

"I was looking for a crosser behind me," Urlacher told the Tribune's Vaughn McClure on Nov. 11, 2011. "Then I was like, 'Oh, man. That was a nice play. Who was it?'"

Added Tillman: "I didn't know he was that fast. It just goes to show the kind of range and

Lance Briggs (55) tackles the Cincinnati Bengals' BenJarvus Green-Ellis (42) on Sept. 8, 2013, at Soldier Field.

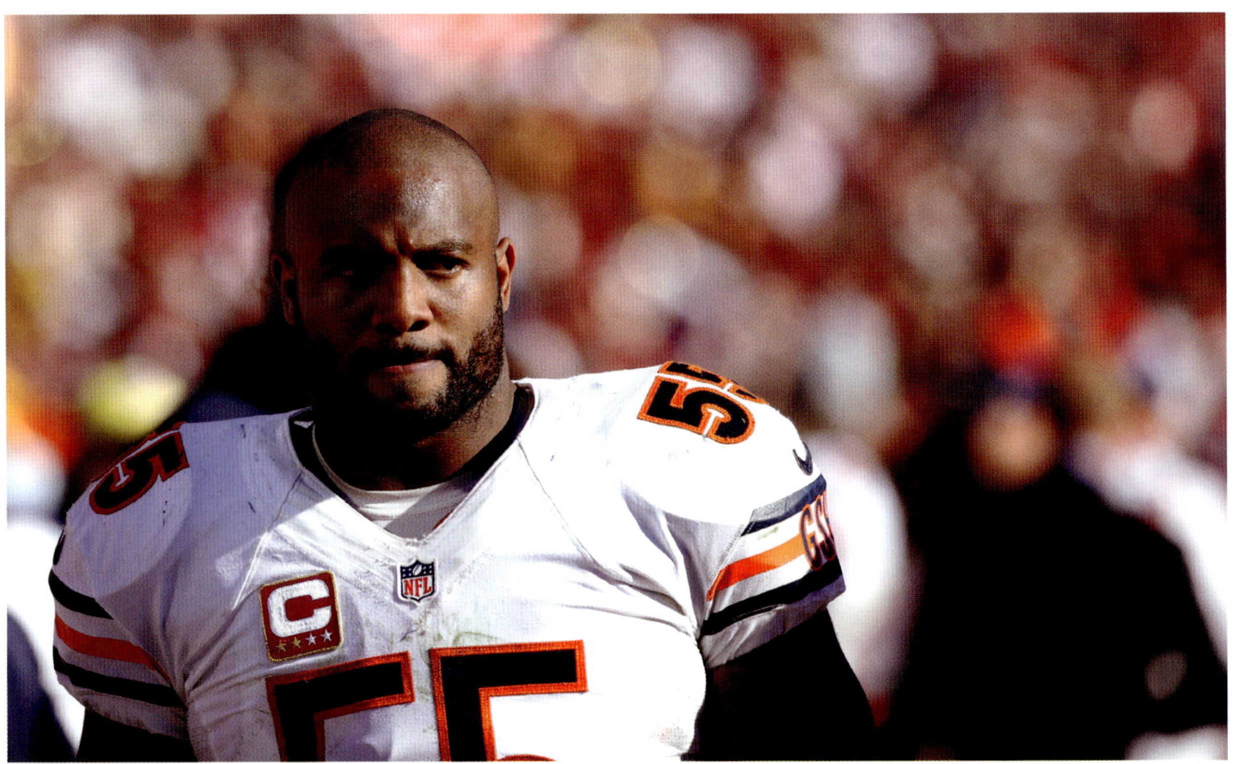

the kind of player he is. He's playing at a higher level. . . . I'm glad I don't play offense because I would hate to be hit by that guy."

Briggs also had moments against Bears tormentors Brett Favre and Aaron Rodgers, quarterbacks who led the Packers to nearly 30 years of dominance in the rivalry. Briggs' first interception, which he brought back 45 yards for a touchdown, came against Favre in 2003. Two years later his pick-six against Favre during a Christmas night win helped the Bears clinch their first NFC North title with a 24-17 win.

While the Bears' loss to the Packers in the 2010 NFC championship game was a crushing defeat, it also was one of the finest moments for Briggs and Urlacher. Rodgers was playing the best football of his exemplary career. The week before, he was 31 of 36 for 366 yards, three touchdowns, no interceptions and a 136.8 passer rating in a 48-21 rout of the Falcons. In Super Bowl XLV, Rodgers was 24 of 39 for 304 yards, three TDs, no picks and a 111.5 rating in a 31-25 win over the Steelers.

Rodgers looked to be on his way to a similar day at Soldier Field, leading the Packers to easy touchdown drives on two of their first four possessions. Briggs intercepted him before halftime, Urlacher picked him off in the second half and they led a defensive charge that kept the Bears in the game and the Packers out of the end zone before the eventual 21-14 loss. Rodgers finished 17 of 30 with 244 yards, no touchdowns, the two picks by the linebackers and a 55.4 rating.

"Urlacher and Briggs nearly willed their team to Dallas," McClure wrote on Jan. 24, 2011. The Tribune's Dan Pompei rated the Bears linebackers a 9 out of 10 on his postgame report card, writing: "Urlacher and Briggs made big plays, the kind of plays that usually turn games."

Briggs rarely was mentioned without Urlacher, much as Bears outside linebackers Joe Fortunato, Larry Morris, Doug Buffone, Otis Wilson and Wilber Marshall played in the shadows of middle linebackers Bill George, Dick Butkus and Mike Singletary.

Briggs never had more than three sacks in a season and finished with 15 in 12 years, but his peers and those covering the league understood his impact. Briggs was named to seven Pro Bowls, tied for seventh in team history with Jay Hilgenberg and Stan Jones. The only Bears with more were Singletary (10), Walter Payton (nine) and Doug Atkins, George, Butkus and Urlacher (eight each).

In 2005, Urlacher and Briggs were first-team All-Pro selections. Singletary and Marshall in 1986 were the only other Bears linebackers to earn the honor in the same season.

Mike McCarthy, coach of the Packers from 2006 to '18, called Briggs "one of the best or (possibly) the best linebacker I've seen in my time in the league."

Briggs was upset he lasted until the third round of the 2003 draft out of Arizona. He wasted no time making his mark in camp as a rookie. After a preseason loss to the Broncos, the Tribune's David Haugh wrote that "Briggs has emerged as the Bears' most active defensive player."

"I'm not surprised by this," Briggs told Haugh. "I'm not surprised by my ability to play the game. . . . I've been doing this all my life, and this is exactly what I'm supposed to be doing."

Briggs and Tillman, a second-round pick, entered the starting lineup the same day, Oct. 5, 2003, against the Raiders. The Bears had started 0-3 but won that game 24-21. They finished 7-9 in the first season at renovated Soldier Field, though, leading to Jauron's firing.

Tillman and Briggs played catch before most games for the next 11 years. In that time they helped Bears defenses to overall rankings of second in 2005, fifth in '06, ninth in '10 and fifth in '12.

Briggs was disciplined on the field but sometimes found himself in sticky situations off it. In 2007 he crashed his Lamborghini Murcielago on the Edens Expressway, left the scene, reported his car stolen and was sentenced to 120 hours of community service. In 2008, Loyola student Brittini Tribbett sued Briggs for child support and claimed he impregnated two other women while she was pregnant with his child.

He and agent Drew Rosenhaus constantly were in contact with general manager Jerry Angelo about Briggs' contract. In 2007, Briggs declared he had played his final snap with the Bears. In 2010, he demanded a raise and then a trade. Angelo, who preferred to avoid placing the franchise tag on any of his players, did it for the only time in his career with Briggs in '07. In 2010, Angelo basically ignored Briggs' requests.

Over Labor Day weekend in 2014, Briggs requested and received a personal day to attend the opening of his barbecue restaurant, the Double Nickel Smokehouse, in Elk Grove, Calif. Marc Trestman's awkward handling of the situation was the first misstep in his disastrous second and final season as Bears coach.

On the field, though, Briggs always was all business. The Bears credited him with 1,564 tackles in addition to his 16 interceptions, 16 forced fumbles, seven fumble recoveries and six defensive touchdowns. His 170 starts as a Bear rank fifth behind Payton's 184, Olin Kreutz's 183, Urlacher's 180 and Singletary's 172.

"He's a goofball," Bears defensive coordinator Ron Rivera told the Tribune's K.C. Johnson on Jan. 1, 2006. "Look at the way he dresses in his uniform. He's sloppy. He really is. But he's also a throwback because he plays hard-nosed, physical football. He enjoys himself and has a good time, but he takes his craft seriously. When it comes time to play, he shows up."

After missing four games in his first 10 years, Briggs sat out seven games in 2013 with a broken shoulder and eight in 2014 with broken ribs and a pulled groin. The Bears finished 30th in yards allowed both seasons.

Briggs has appeared on a Bears postgame show on NBC Sports Chicago, and his Briggs 4 Kidz Foundation is committed to helping at-risk youths.

In 2018, Urlacher was inducted to the Pro Football Hall of Fame in Canton, Ohio. Rodgers believes one day Briggs will join him there.

"He's had a Hall of Fame career," Rodgers said on a conference call with Bears beat reporters in 2014. "He does it all. He's been playing at a high level for a long time. . . . He plays snap to whistle extremely hard, but he does his job and brings it every single time he's out there." ■

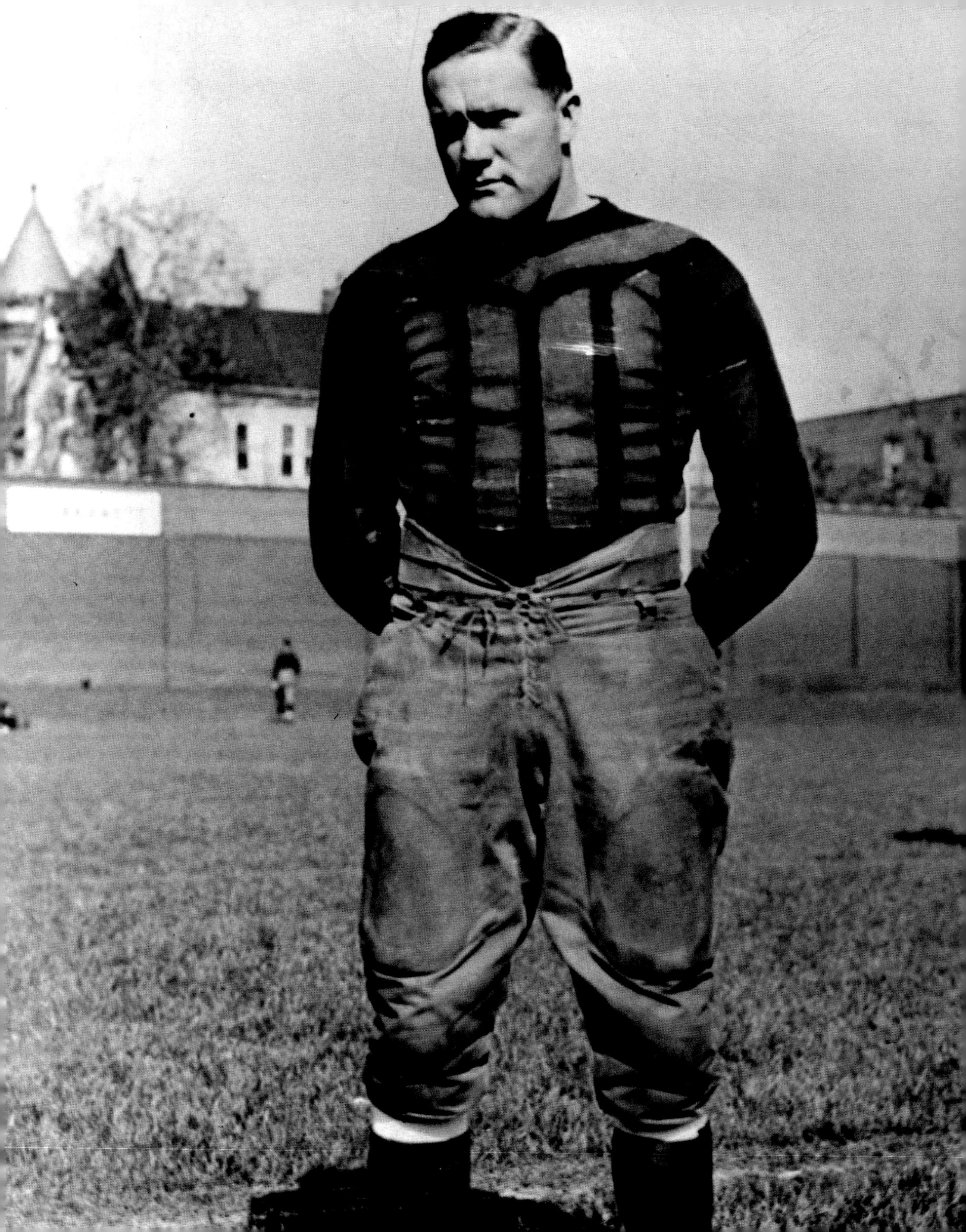

Ed Healey

30

16 TACKLE
1922-27

ED HEALEY DIED AT 83 on Dec. 19, 1978, at a South Bend, Ind., nursing home. About 90 miles west, the Bears were on their way to a 14-0 win against the Packers at Soldier Field.

When Bears owner George Halas heard in the press box of his friend's passing, he instructed public-address announcer Chet Coppock to make an announcement.

"We regretfully must inform you that Ed Healey, the greatest offensive tackle in Bears history, passed away today at his home in South Bend, Indiana," Coppock intoned, according to Jeff Davis' 2005 biography, "Papa Bear: The Life and Legacy of George Halas."

Halas and Healey met 57 years earlier. Halas played right end for the team he also owned and coached, and Healey was a powerful left tackle for the Rock Island Independents. On Oct. 10, 1921, the Bears—still known as the Staleys in their first year in Chicago—defeated the Independents 14-10 in a hard-fought game. No combatants went at it harder than Halas and Healey.

The 6-foot-1, 207-pound Healey was so dominant that the 6-foot, 182-pound Halas had to bend the rules to compete with him.

"The field was a quagmire and Healey was too much to handle with a legal block," Halas wrote in the Tribune on Jan. 27, 1967. "So I devised an unorthodox maneuver which involved a quick grab at Healey's ankles."

Bears halfback Dutch Sternaman kept making big gains with Halas holding Healey, so quarterback Joey Sternaman, Dutch's brother, kept calling the play. Healey got more and more upset until he reared back and tried to slug Halas.

"I was still down on my hands and knees when a sixth sense warned me to duck," Halas wrote. "It's lucky I did. Just as I jerked my head back, Healey's right fist whistled past my chin and buried itself in the mud, up to the wrist."

Both players appealed to a referee to eject the other. The official told them to play on.

Halas wrote: "When play resumed, I, as coach with the welfare of my right end at heart, ordered our quarterback to stop calling the off-tackle play. I also decided Healey was the kind of player I wanted on the Bears."

The Independents were a struggling franchise that, like many teams in the early days of the NFL, would not make it to the 1930s. Their

Ed Healy (16) was all-league five times during his career.

"

owner, Walter Flanigan, owed Halas $100. Halas offered to cancel the debt if Healey could join the Bears in the middle of the 1922 season. The teams agreed, and the first player sale in NFL history was in the books.

While Halas eventually would gain a miserly reputation, in the 1920s he was considered one of the league's most lavish spenders. He signed Red Grange from the University of Illinois in 1925 and Paddy Driscoll from the Chicago Cardinals in 1926 to the sport's biggest deals to date. When he arrived from the Quad Cities, Healey could not believe the Bears' luxurious accommodations.

"At Rock Island," he said, "we had no showers and seldom a trainer. At Wrigley Field, we had a nice warm place to dress and nice warm showers."

One of Healey's duties with the Independents was to break bad news to his teammates, who Flanigan figured would take it better from someone much bigger than most of them. During a game in 1921, "Big Ed" was sent onto the field to tell tackle Frank Coughlin he was fired as the team's coach and to inform Jimmy Conzelman he was the new coach. It is believed to be the only in-game coaching change in NFL history.

Healey became an even better player with the Bears. In 1922, Halas came up with the idea for an All-Pro team to honor the league's best players. He named 11 first-teamers and 11 second-teamers. Healey made Halas' first team along with fellow Bears Pete Stinchcomb, a halfback, and Hugh Blacklock, a right tackle. Second-teamers included Dutch Sternaman, Halas' co-owner of the Bears, and Packers halfback Curly Lambeau.

The next year several publications followed suit, and Healey was a consensus first-team All-Pro for the next four seasons. Halas named him to the Bears' all-time team in 1941. In 1964, Healey was elected to the Pro Football Hall of Fame's second class, and the Hall of Fame named him to the 1920s All-Decade team.

The Bears had winning records in each of Healey's six seasons with the team. In that time they never won the NFL championship by finishing first in the standings in the days before a title game decided the champ, but they finished in second place four times.

In 1923, Walter Camp, who selected the college All-America teams of the era, watched Healey dominate the Cardinals and wondered how he missed him when Healey played at Dartmouth.

"Who's that magnificent tackle?" Camp asked Halas, according to Halas' writings. "He's the best I ever saw."

Halas continued: "Camp overlooked Healey simply because Healey was an undistinguished 190-pound end at Dartmouth. Ed didn't mature until he filled out to 220 pounds in pro ball and shifted to tackle."

Halas called Healey, blessed with uncommon speed for a lineman, the most versatile tackle in history. Healey's two most memorable plays involved chasing down ball carriers from behind.

During the Bears' 19-game, 66-day barnstorming tour after they signed Grange, Healey ran down Los Angeles All-Stars running back George Wilson and hurdled some teammates to make a touchdown-saving tackle. With 60,000 fans in attendance to see Grange, Healey called the play his greatest thrill as a professional.

The other tackle came against a teammate, Joey Sternaman remembered in Richard Whittingham's 1991 book, "What Bears They Were." Against the Columbus Tigers, Bears defensive back Oscar Knop intercepted a pass, got turned around and started racing toward his own end zone.

"The entire Tiger team just stood there and watched as he started running the wrong way," Sternaman said. "Most of them were laughing, I think. I took off after him, yelling, but I guess he couldn't hear me.

"Ed Healey was after him too, and he made a lunging tackle that stopped Knop just before he got to the goal. If it weren't for Ed Healey, Knop would have had the distinction of being the first pro to score some points for the other team."

Healey grew up the only boy among six children in a logging family in Indian Orchard, Mass., gaining strength by working with the company's

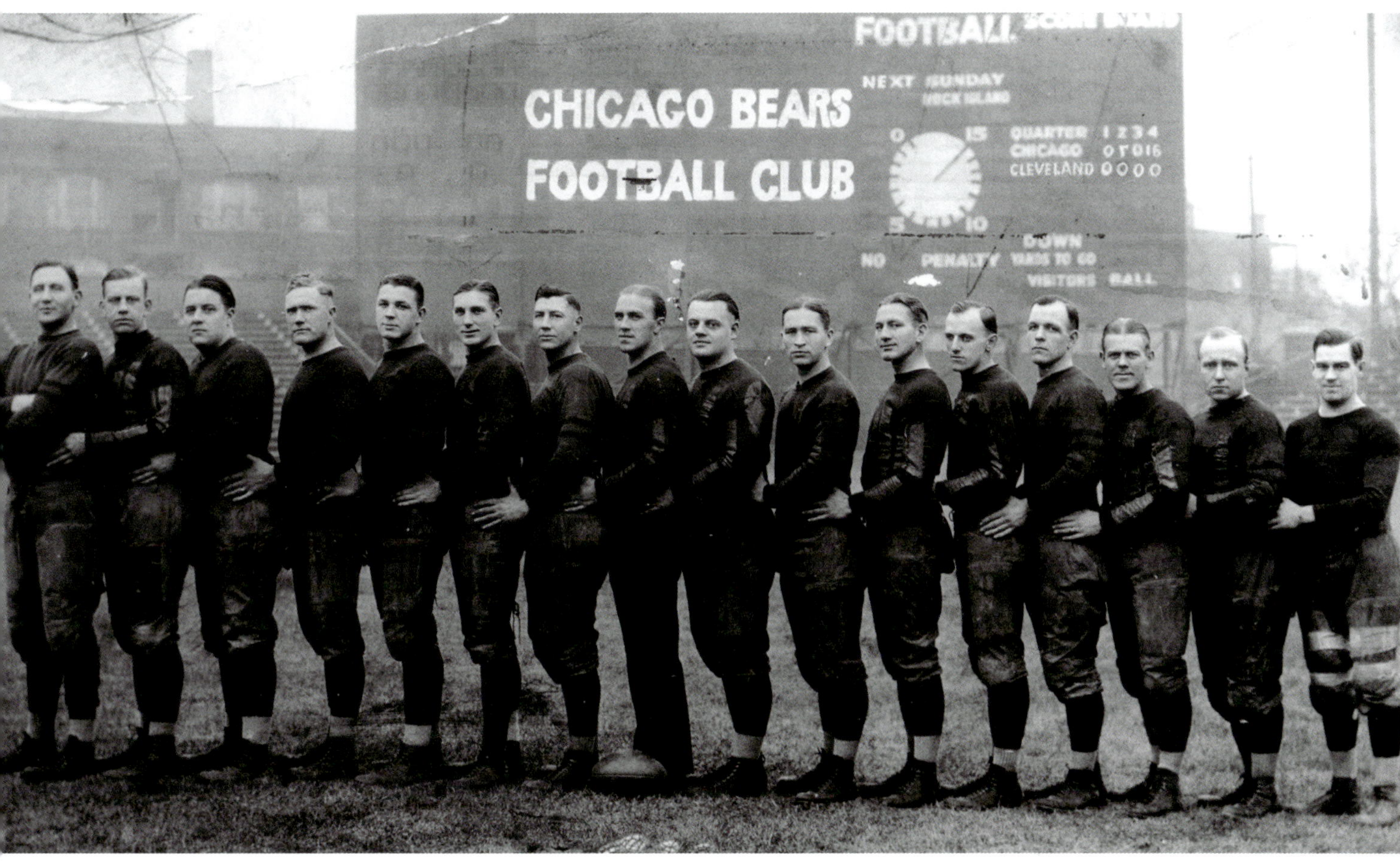

The Chicago Bears team of 1924. From left are: Ralph Scott, Oscar Knop, George Trafton, Ed Healey, Jim McMillen, Vern Miller, Hugh Blacklock, Frank Hanny, Joe LeFleur, Ralph Lanum, Roy White, George Halas, Hunk Anderson, Larry Walquist, Ed Sternaman and Joe Sternaman.

men from a young age. He took advantage of his Ivy League education and enjoyed showing off his way with words.

In Halas' 1979 autobiography, "Halas by Halas," Healey remembered the ups and downs of the 1925 barnstorming tour.

"It was a tiring season, long and arduous and rugged on the manhood," Healey said. "There were a lot of things to laugh at. Propinquity lends enchantment into anybody's life, you might say."

In 1926, Healey landed a $10,000 offer to play and coach for C.C. Pyle's New York Yankees of the new American Football League. Halas gave Healey a raise to stay with the Bears instead of joining "Cold Cash" Pyle, as Grange did.

Healey accepted and said he preferred to stay with Halas anyway since "if Pyle was clever enough to have been married and divorced three or four times, he was the kind of guy I didn't want any part of."

After his career Healey became a successful salesman and later sales manager for France Stone Company in South Bend. He became dismayed when football developed a two-platoon system, at one point lamenting that the modern "sissies" of the 1940s and '50s didn't have to play both ways.

"Football linemen of today hardly earn their money," Healey told the Tribune's Harry Warren on Dec. 5, 1949. "In the old days we used to go on the field prepared for 60 minutes of work, and nothing short of a broken leg, arm or ankle could get us out of there." ■

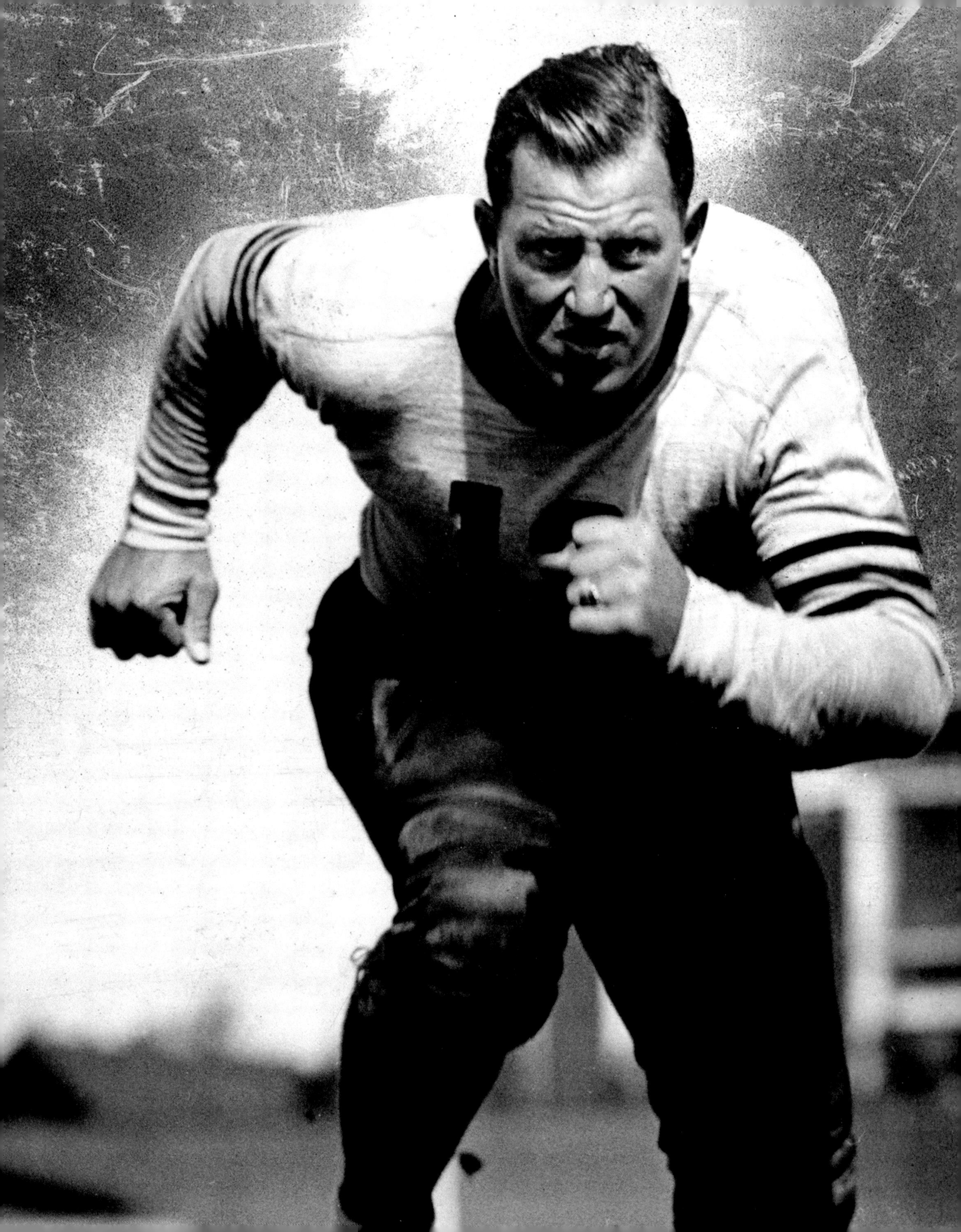

Link Lyman

31

2, 11, 12, 14 TACKLE
1926-28, 1930-31, 1933-34

EVEN THOUGH LINK LYMAN played 90 years ago, his style of play wouldn't be out of place in the 21st century.

On offense, the 6-foot-2, 233-pound Lyman was a fit, athletic left tackle with a combination of strength and athleticism that made him nearly impossible to get around. On defense, he pioneered the use of shifting, slanting and stunting that all defensive tackles perform today.

Lyman was one of the league's best linemen when he joined the Bears and had won three consecutive championships as a two-way star for the Canton and Cleveland Bulldogs in the early days of the NFL.

Bears owner and coach George Halas received permission from Commissioner Joe Carr to add players from other teams for the team's postseason barnstorming tour after it signed Red Grange from the University of Illinois in 1925. Lyman came on board from the Bulldogs, and Halas never let him go.

Lyman won everywhere he played. He was an early star at Nebraska, where the 1922 yearbook stated that "Lyman was, without a doubt, our fastest lineman. Roy is a big man, weighing 200 pounds, and could get down under punts almost as quickly as the ends." The Bulldogs won titles in 1922, '23 and '24, and the Bears had winning records in all seven of his seasons in Chicago.

He seemed to get better as he aged, earning first-team All-Pro honors in 1930 at 32 and 1934 at 36, and the Bears became one of the league's best teams in the early 1930s. They appeared in the NFL's first three championship games, winning the impromptu tiebreaker against the Portsmouth Spartans in 1932 at Chicago Stadium and the first scheduled title game over the Giants in 1933 at Wrigley Field before falling to the Giants at the frozen Polo Grounds in 1934, Lyman's final season.

Lyman's Pro Football Hall of Fame bio reads: "Whether it was luck or a result of his outstanding play, Lyman experienced just one losing season during his 16 years of . . . college and professional football. A contributor to the end, Bears coach George Halas insisted Lyman was stronger and tougher during his last two seasons than when he first joined the team eight years earlier."

He played until age 36, perhaps staying fresh because of a late start. Lyman grew up in

Link Lyman (12) was elected to the Hall of Fame in 1966.

145

western Nebraska and Kansas and did not play high school football.

"You see, I was born in a small town called Table Rock, Nebraska, and we only had about six or seven boys in the whole school, so I couldn't play in high school. I did know a little about the game, but it wasn't until I reached the University of Nebraska in 1917 that I was able to actually play in a real game," Lyman said in Chris Willis' 2005 book, "Old Leather: An Oral History of Early Pro Football in Ohio, 1920-35."

"From the first day, I just loved the game, and we had some pretty good teams too. My senior year, we only lost one game, to Notre Dame, and we outscored our opponents 283 points to 17. That was a fun year."

Lyman joined the Bears the same time Grange did, and both retired after the 1934 season. They spent five years as teammates and became close friends. When Grange left for the New York Yankees of the American Football League in 1926, Lyman wore Grange's No. 77 for the next three seasons. When Grange returned to the Bears in 1930, Lyman switched, and when they were teammates, Lyman wore Nos. 2, 11, 12 and 14.

The Bears played the 1934 championship game in honor of Lyman and Grange, who were playing for the final time.

Halas wrote in the Tribune on July 15, 1935: "In the clubhouse before the contest, I asked Red Grange and Link Lyman, who were to play the last games of their careers, to say a word or two. Both of these hoary veterans spoke feelingly. Lyman, the gigantic, even shed a tear or two."

Another Hall of Famer, Bill Hewitt, played next to Lyman at offensive and defensive end. Hewitt was one of the first players to try to anticipate offensive snap counts, and he often freelanced on defense. Lyman encouraged him to do so because he was sure he could handle both men's assignments if Hewitt were to find himself out of position.

When the defending champion Bears played the College All-Stars in a 1934 exhibition, All-Stars coach Dick Hanley of Northwestern paid particular attention to Lyman.

"The marvel of the squad to my mind is Link Lyman," Hanley wrote in a preview story for the Tribune on Aug. 6, 1934. "Here is an athlete who finished his college football career at the University of Nebraska 12 years ago. Yet, I would believe George Halas would nominate this fellow as one of the most important cogs in the Bears' march to the championship. He is big, tremendously so; active, fast, smart and strong. I am inclined to agree with Halas."

At the time, it was popular to ponder whether the best college teams could compete against professionals. Grange, in a 1932 essay in the Saturday Evening Post, argued that the notion was ridiculous. He pointed to Lyman as an example of why professionals were so much better than collegians.

"Link Lyman weighs 240 pounds including the towels. Very little of that poundage is blubber," Grange wrote. "Picture a fast, trimly built athlete, some lightweight prize fighter you've seen in action. Then magnify him proportionately until he weighs 240 pounds; that's Lyman."

In 1941, Halas picked an all-time Bears team covering the first 20 years of the franchise for the Tribune. Lyman was his left tackle.

"The best description of Link was that he was an enormous man who always was in the thick of things," Edward Prell wrote.

Halas added: "For all 'round tackle play, no one, in my judgment, ever held the edge over Link. He was also a great line leader."

Lyman took two years off from the Bears, in 1929 and 1932. He left first to play semipro ball in Texas and later to tend to his cattle ranch in Nebraska. When he reported to camp,

Picture a fast, trimly built athlete, some lightweight prize fighter you've seen in action. Then magnify him proportionately until he weighs 240 pounds; that's Lyman.

—TEAMMATE RED GRANGE

he usually brought a cooler filled with steaks to share with his teammates.

The rough-and-tumble cowboy also entertained friends with his unexpected talent, a powerful singing voice.

An uncredited "In the Wake of the News" Tribune column from Nov. 20, 1934, said that after a game in New York, Lyman "stole the show at the night club which the Chicagoans attended before leaving for home last night. Requested to sing, Lyman went to the annunciator and poured forth a baritone which brought encores until he was out of breath and knocked the mike over in a playful tackle."

After his retirement from the Bears, Lyman went into coaching, first as an assistant at Nebraska and then Creighton. He transitioned into the insurance industry in the 1950s and became a manager in San Antonio and an executive in Los Angeles.

He was so fond of his time in Canton that he lobbied for the Pro Football Hall of Fame to be based there. It was, and Lyman was elected to the Hall in 1964 in the second class with fellow Bears greats Ed Healey and George Trafton. Grange, Halas and Bronko Nagurski went in the year before; Paddy Driscoll, Danny Fortmann and Sid Luckman were enshrined the year after.

While all players played both ways in Lyman's era, few were equally regarded on offense and defense as he was. If one were to make an all-time Bears starting 11 of players from the two-way era who were equally effective on both sides of the ball, it might look like this: Lyman, Grange, Hewitt, Nagurski, Fortmann, Healey, Bulldog Turner, George Connor, Joe Stydahar, George Musso and George McAfee.

In 2014, the Tribune's Don Pierson ranked Lyman the Bears' sixth-best defensive lineman of all time behind Doug Atkins, Dan Hampton, Richard Dent, Steve McMichael and Ed Sprinkle. Lyman died in an automobile crash at 74 in 1972.

In his 2008 book, "Chicago Bears: The Complete Illustrated History," Lew Freedman wrote: "He was an advance model of the modern lineman—big, strong, with quick feet. . . . Being athletic as well as large at a time when 200-pound linemen were common made him virtually unstoppable. Wherever Lyman went, his teams won championships." ■

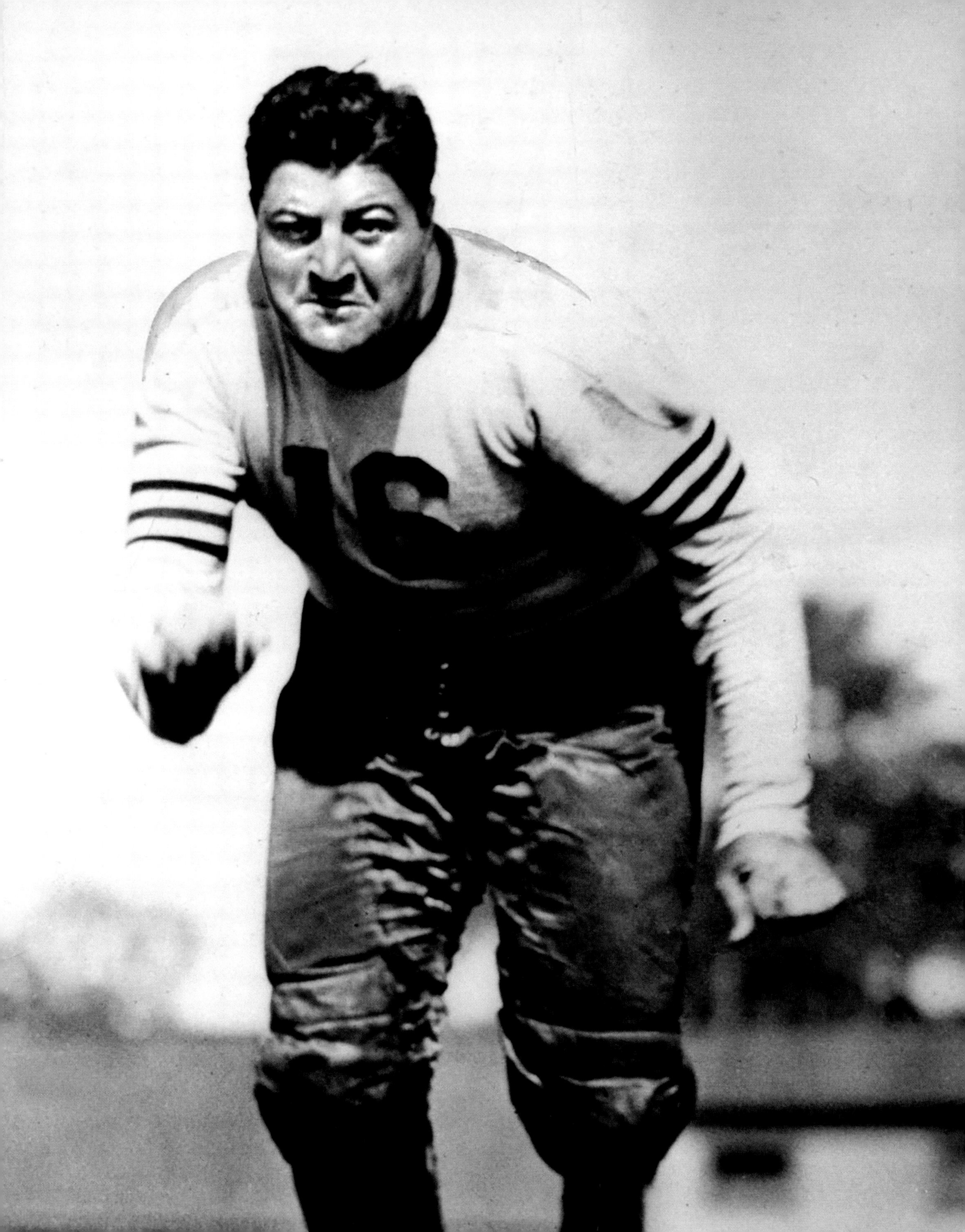

32

George Musso

16 LINEMAN
1933–44

INCREDIBLE BLOCKER. Impenetrable run-stuffer. Biggest man on some of the NFL's baddest teams.

Calorie counter?

George Musso, a two-way lineman who was huge for his time at 6-foot-2, 262 pounds, helped the Bears win four championships and reach three more title games in his 12 seasons from 1933 to '44. He kept himself in playing shape long after his lighter teammates fell off, with one of his secrets to longevity a book he kept in his pocket that listed the caloric content of each food item at the supermarket.

"Because he watched his food habits he prolonged his career," Bears owner and coach George Halas told the Tribune's Edward Prell on Nov. 16, 1951. "I've used Musso as an example to instill in others the will to keep their poundage down."

"Moose" bridged the gap between the great Bears teams of the 1930s and the Monsters of the Midway of the '40s. He was the only player from the 1933 title team active for the 1940s championships, and he's one of six Bears to win four titles. Musso was roommates with fullback Bronko Nagurski when his career started; in his later years he roomed with quarterback Sid Luckman. The Bears set the NFL record with 18 consecutive wins in 1933-34 and matched it in 1941-42. No team won more games in a row until the Patriots' 21 in 2003-04.

Besides Musso's healthy meal plan, his versatility helped him hang on as long as he did. He started out at right tackle on a formidable side of the line between guard Joe Kopcha and end Bill Karr. In 1937 he shifted to right guard and soon was part of an all-Hall of Fame middle of the line with left guard Danny Fortmann and center Bulldog Turner. Musso became the first NFL player to be named All-Pro at two positions; he was a second-team tackle in 1935 and a first-team guard in '37.

Switching one spot over on the line didn't seem like much work after he was a four-sport star at Collinsville High School near St. Louis and Millikin University in the Bears' birthplace of Decatur. In addition to football, Musso excelled at basketball, baseball and track and field. He was Illinois' high school champion in the javelin throw in 1929.

Despite his size, Musso was one of the game's best pulling guards. He led the way to

George Musso (16) was elected to the Hall of Fame in 1982.

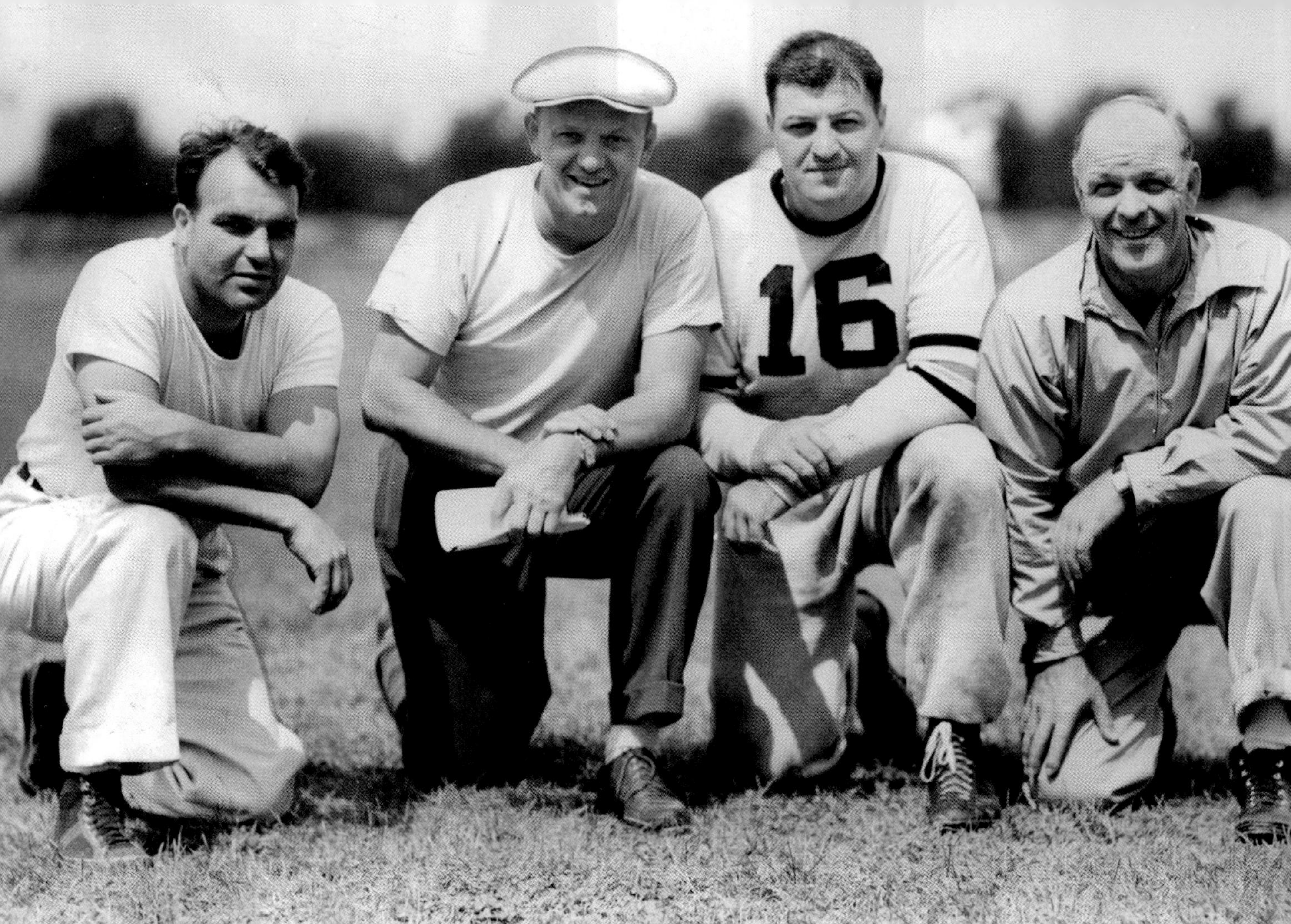

Carl Brumbaugh, quarterback coach, from left, George Halas, team owner and head coach, George Musso (16), team captain, and Heartly "Hunk" Anderson, line coach, circa 1940.

the left on the second play from scrimmage in the 1940 championship game, providing Bill Osmanski's first hole in his 68-yard touchdown run that began the 73-0 rout of the Redskins.

In Halas' 1979 autobiography, "Halas by Halas," Musso described his blocking style.

"If you got a knee in the ribs while blocking, that hurt," Musso said. "But if you blocked properly you didn't get hurt. You came up to your target until you were close enough to shake hands with him. Then you threw your body against him. You didn't go at him with a shoulder because if the target moved 10 inches, you missed him."

It's good for any organization when its largest member has the best sense of humor, and no one kept the Bears laughing more than Musso. He usually pointed the punchline at himself, on or off the field.

Clark Hinkle, the Packers' powerful fullback, once barreled past a prone Musso and met Nagurski head-on. Nagurski's hit sent Hinkle flying backward 5 yards. Somehow, Hinkle landed on his feet and was able to get past Musso again.

"It had to be some kind of record," Musso told Prell on Sept. 22, 1943. "While I was lying there, Hinkle went past me three times!"

One offseason, Musso tried horseback riding as a way to stay in shape.

"I thought (it) would be good as a general conditioner," he told Prell on Aug. 13, 1942, "never happening to think what it might do to the horse. The first one broke down with a

The players wouldn't have anyone else (as team captain). Halas let him give the pep talk before the big games.

—TEAMMATE RED GRANGE

bowed tendon. I tried another one and he just folded up, from general exhaustion, I guess."

Musso's attributes added up to make a perfect team captain, and he served that role for the Bears for his final eight seasons.

Red Grange told The Associated Press on Aug. 7, 1982: "The players wouldn't have anyone else. Halas let him give the pep talk before the big games."

Halas made all his players—team captains, All-Pros and undrafted rookies alike—compete for their positions every season. In 1941, Musso was the oldest player on the team at 31 and lost his starting spot at right guard to Ray Bray.

"Because you played last season or made All-Star or something didn't mean you would play the next year," Musso said in Halas' autobiography. "Halas had his own measuring sticks."

Musso worked his way back into the lineup in 1943. He no longer was the team's oldest player, as Halas had convinced the 35-year-old Nagurski to give it one more go after five years as a full-time professional wrestler. Halas entrusted Musso to get his old friend back into game shape.

The duo helped the Bears win the 1943 title, and Musso retired after the 1944 season. He returned to southern Illinois, where he became the sheriff of Madison County for eight years and county treasurer for 12. In 1960 he was elected president of the Illinois Sheriffs Association.

Musso garnered some national interest in the 1980s after two of his former opponents became presidents of the United States. At Millikin, Musso lined up across from Ronald Reagan of Eureka College. When the defending champion Bears played the College All-Stars in a 1934 exhibition, Musso faced off against Michigan's Gerald Ford.

In 1999, NFL Films' Chris Willis asked for Musso's scouting report on the future leaders of the free world.

Said Musso: "(Reagan) weighed about 165 pounds. . . . He was supposed to be handling me, of course, he couldn't do it. . . . He was quick, a good ballplayer, but . . . I could push him whatever way I wanted to push him.

"(Ford) was pretty rugged. He was pretty tough . . . a good ballplayer."

Musso died at 90 on Sept. 5, 2000, in Edwardsville, Ill. When he was 72, he was inducted into the Pro Football Hall of Fame, 38 years after his last game, in a class with Doug Atkins, Sam Huff and Merlin Olsen. When Musso got the news, he thought it was a prank and called Canton, Ohio, to confirm his selection.

"I didn't believe it," he told the AP. "I really didn't believe it." ■

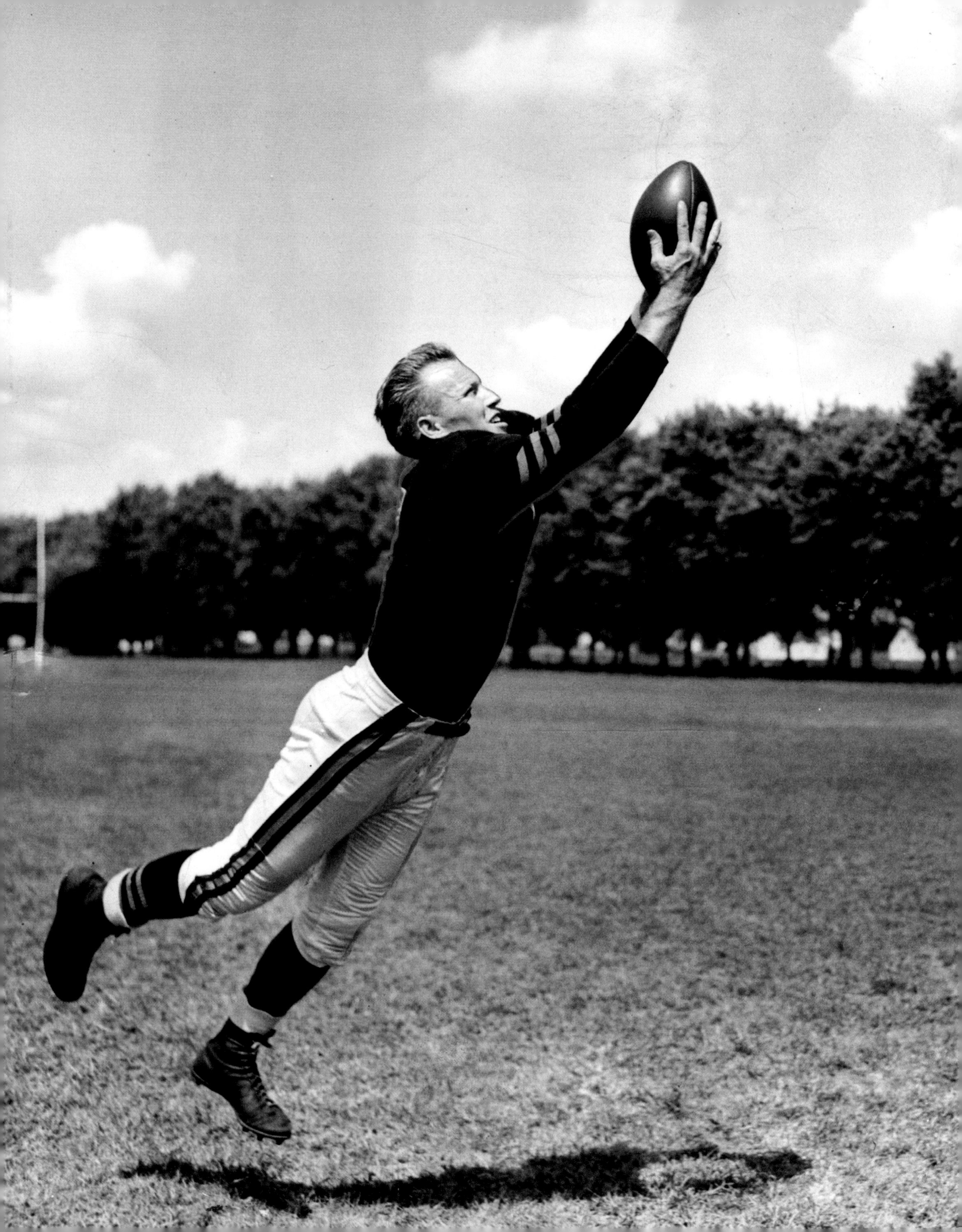

33

Ed Sprinkle

A QUARTER-CENTURY BEFORE "The Longest Yard" was released in theaters, one of its funniest scenes played out in an NFL game.

Ed Sprinkle, the almost unblockable Bears defensive end named "The Meanest Man in the NFL" by Collier's magazine in 1950, was giving the Chicago Cardinals all they could handle, so they tried a different approach.

Quarterback Paul Christman goaded Sprinkle by saying, "We're going to get you."

Sprinkle replied in typically feisty fashion: "I'm wearing No. 7, and I'm playing right end and I'll be here all day. You know where to find me."

On the next play, the Cardinals offensive line let Sprinkle through without touching him. Christman aimed the ball at Sprinkle's . . . bare face and fired.

"Fortunately it didn't hit me because he could throw pretty damn hard," Sprinkle remembered in Richard Whittingham's 1991 book, "What Bears They Were."

The play was not typical but it was indicative of how Sprinkle's tenacity affected other teams. They always were on the lookout for No. 7. They had to be as Sprinkle loved to hit anyone in his path as hard as he could.

"Did you ever hear football being referred to as anything but a contact sport?" he said. "The guys are taking shots at you, and I was geared that way. I loved contact. I liked to mix it up. I believed in hitting somebody."

Sprinkle was undersized even for his time at 6-foot-1, 206 pounds, but nobody played harder. Nobody played closer to the edge of the rules either. In the days before face masks, he was known on defense for "The Hook," a clothesline maneuver in which he would tackle ball carriers high with their uncovered faces in the crook of his elbow.

On offense, Sprinkle played end. He loved to split out wide on a running play, sprint inside toward the action and destroy an unsuspecting linebacker with a vicious crackback block.

"I'd come back across the field and hit a guy from the blind side," Sprinkle said. "He'd have his eyes on the ball carrier . . . and I'd just clobber him. I was devastating on that block. They wouldn't let me do it too much because I hit too many guys too hard."

When his most trusted moves didn't work, Sprinkle got creative. During one game against the mighty Browns, he was having all sorts of

Ed Sprinkle
(7), circa 1949.

"

Ed Sprinkle, pound for pound, was the roughest, hardest-playing football player I ever ran into.

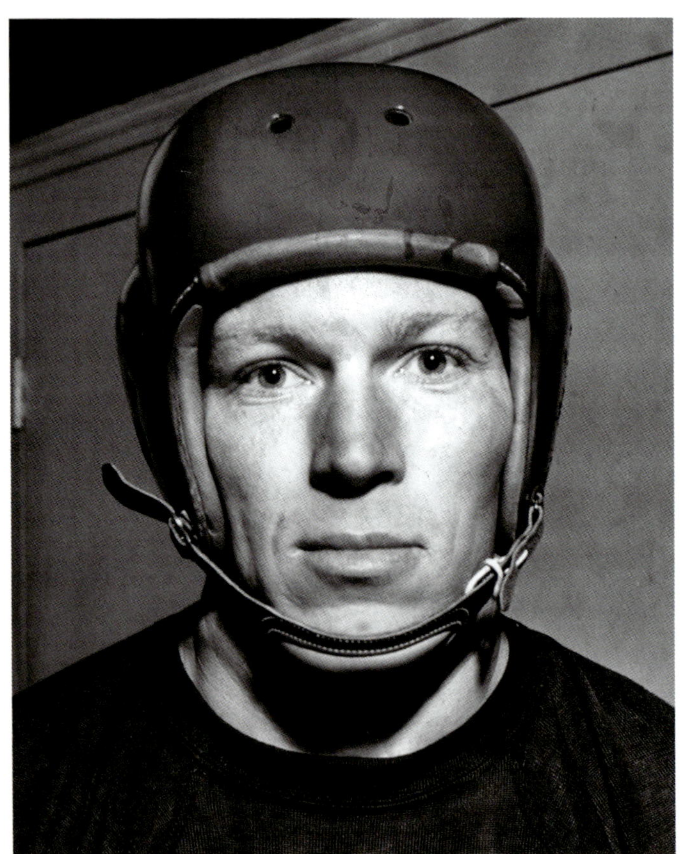

Ed Sprinkle (7), circa 1950.

problems getting around wide-bodied guard and future Bears coach Abe Gibron to get at All-Pro quarterback Otto Graham.

"So finally I just jumped over him," Sprinkle told Whittingham. "It surprised the hell out of him to see me going over the top of him. I got to Graham and sacked him. I was ecstatic. . . . They really set their whole offense to protect Graham, and that was maybe the only time I ever got to him for a sack."

Sprinkle met other quarterbacks much more frequently.

"I wish they had recorded sacks in those days," he said. "I used to get to the quarterback a lot. . . . Two guys I especially loved to chase down were Bob Waterfield and Norm Van Brocklin. They were both Rams then, and I know they remembered me long after they got out of football."

While Sprinkle made enemies across the league, he saved his hatred for the Packers. He terrorized them while making big plays every time he participated in the rivalry, which was at its nastiest during Sprinkle's 12-year career from 1944 to '55. The Bears went 17-6-1 against the Packers in that time, and Sprinkle became one of the all-time most hated Bears among Packers fans.

In 1946, Sprinkle returned a fumble 30 yards for a touchdown in a 10-7 win. In 1948, he caught two touchdown passes in a 45-7 rout and another in a 7-6 win. In 1950, his blocked punt led to the winning touchdown in a 28-14 victory. In 1952, he blocked a tying field-goal attempt in a 24-14 win.

In their 1997 book, "Mudbaths and Bloodbaths: The Inside Story of the Bears-Packers Rivalry," former Milwaukee Journal Sentinel reporters Gary D'Amato and Chris Christl recounted the havoc Sprinkle played on the Packers.

"No question, Sprinkle had some great games against the Packers," they wrote. "In fact, he may have made more big plays in the rivalry than any other lineman."

The authors asked five Packers of the era about Sprinkle. All answered with awe.

"I would say Ed Sprinkle, pound for pound, was the roughest, hardest-playing football player I ever ran into," said running back Don Perkins, who played for the Bears in 1944, the Packers in 1946 and both teams in '45. "He was not dirty, but he played hard. If you were going to get hit by Ed, you were going to get hit."

Opponents couldn't wait to get a crack at Sprinkle. He constantly was targeted, but not many got the better of him. Longtime rival Charley Trippi of the Cardinals was one who did.

The Hall of Fame halfback punctuated a rare win over the Bears in 1951 by decking Sprinkle with one punch. After he was ejected and informed he would be fined, Trippi said: "It was worth it."

Sprinkle came to the Bears on Bulldog Turner's recommendation in 1944. Turner was a few years ahead of Sprinkle at tiny Hardin-Simmons College in Abilene, Texas. The All-Pro center and linebacker thought Sprinkle, who played football, basketball and baseball at the school, was pro caliber and advised him to try out.

The Bears found room for Sprinkle right away, and coach George Halas even gave him his old number. After Sprinkle retired, Halas called him the best pass rusher he ever had seen.

"He and I got along real fine," Sprinkle said of the Bears founder in Jeff Davis' 2005 biography, "Papa Bear: The Life and Legacy of George Halas."

Davis wrote: "They did because Sprinkle played the game just the way the coach loved it. Hard, all-out and nasty."

When Sprinkle joined the Bears, they were a skeleton crew with so many players in the military for World War II. By 1946, everybody was back and the team was a juggernaut.

With Sprinkle giving the team an edge it lacked while winning titles in 1940 and '41, the 1946 team went 8-2-1 to win the Western Division and defeated the Giants 24-14 at the Polo Grounds for the NFL championship. During the title game, Sprinkle broke the noses of Giants quarterback Frank Filchock and running back Frank Reagan, and he separated running back George Franck's shoulder.

On offense, Sprinkle was used mostly for blocking. In his 12 years, he caught seven touchdown passes from five quarterbacks. One was All-Pro Johnny Lujack; three others—Sid Luckman, George Blanda and third-stringer Bobby Layne—became Pro Football Hall of Famers.

Sprinkle was inducted into the Hall of Fame in 2020. In a 2016 piece, longtime Dallas Morning News columnist Rick Gosselin compared him to Deacon Jones, Lawrence Taylor and Reggie White.

Sprinkle retired at 33 when he became one of the few Bears to call Halas' bluff during contract negotiations. The two proud men could not bridge the difference between the coach's offer of $14,800 and the player's request of $15,000.

In 2014, the Tribune's Don Pierson ranked Sprinkle the fifth-best defensive lineman in Bears history behind Doug Atkins, Dan Hampton, Richard Dent and Steve McMichael. Sprinkle's four Pro Bowl appearances match Hampton, Dent and Fred Williams for second among Bears defensive linemen to Atkins' eight.

During his career, Sprinkle worked as an engineer for Inland Steel and coached youth football. In retirement he became owner and operator of the Gridiron Tile flooring company in the Mount Greenwood neighborhood. The native of Bradshaw, Texas, died of natural causes at 90 on July 28, 2014, in Palos Heights. He was the last living member of the 1946 NFL champions.

Sprinkle roomed that season and seven others with Turner, who made a fine mentor as one of the smartest players in the league. Turner knew what every player on the field should be doing on every play, and he knew the type of attitude it took to succeed in professional football.

"Bulldog influenced me more than anybody," Sprinkle told Whittingham. "'Let the other team fear you,' he would say. 'Walk tall. Walk proud.' And when we went out onto the field, that's the attitude I had.

"I never feared an individual on a football field." ◼

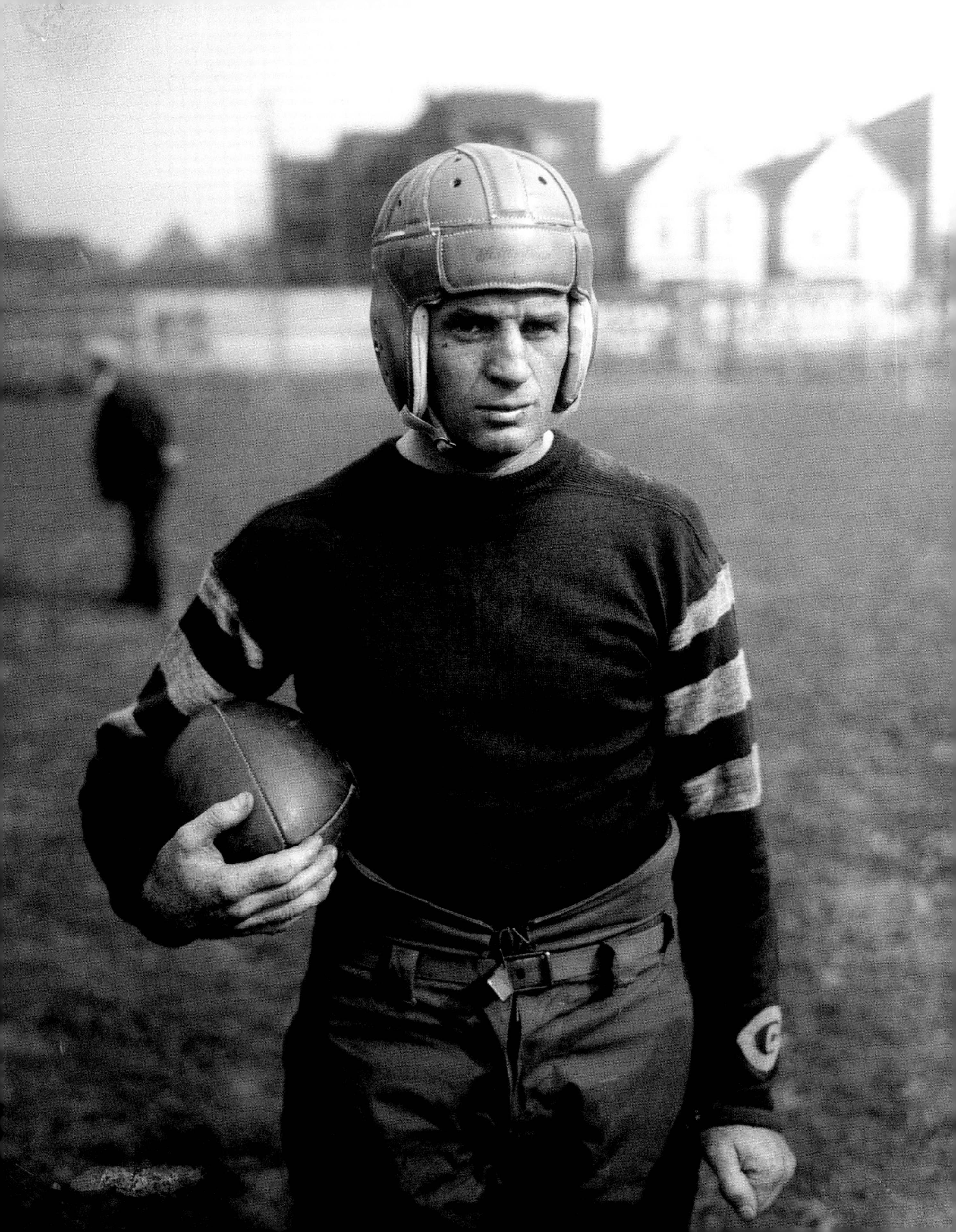

34

Paddy Driscoll

1, 2, 20, 26 RUNNING BACK,
QUARTERBACK, ASSISTANT COACH,
HEAD COACH, VICE PRESIDENT,
DIRECTOR OF PLANNING AND RESEARCH
1926–29, 1941–55, 1956–57,
1958–62, 1963–68

GEORGE HALAS SPENT much of his time as a young man admiring one football player.

When he was a student at Crane High School on the West Side, Halas likely read press clippings about Evanston star Paddy Driscoll. While Halas was an oft-injured player at the University of Illinois, Driscoll was an All-American at Northwestern. When Halas joined the U.S. Navy during World War I, he and Driscoll joined forces on the all-star squad that represented the Great Lakes Naval Training Station in Lake Bluff.

In the early days of the Bears franchise, with Halas serving as founder, owner, coach and right end, he watched time and again as Driscoll's all-around skill led the less talented Chicago Cardinals to upset victories in the crosstown rivalry. In the teams' first meeting Nov. 28, 1920, when the Bears still were the Decatur Staleys, Driscoll kicked the deciding extra point in a 7-6 win and kept the Bears in poor field position all afternoon with his precision punts.

"How I wished I could get him on my team!" Halas remembered thinking in his 1979 autobiography, "Halas by Halas."

In 1922, the 5-foot-8, 160-pound Driscoll, who switched between halfback and quarterback—then mostly a blocking position—led the Cardinals to 6-0 and 9-0 wins in their meetings with the Bears, scoring 12 of the games' 15 points on four field goals.

In 1925, Halas signed the one star who outshined Driscoll, adding Red Grange shortly after the final game of his legendary career at Illinois. When Grange debuted against the Cardinals in front of a packed house of 39,000 fans at Cubs Park, Driscoll neutralized the Galloping Ghost.

Each time Grange went back to receive a punt, the crowd rose and howled with anticipation. Almost every time, Driscoll delivered an unreturnable punt. The game ended in a scoreless tie. According to the Tribune's David Condon 40 years later, Driscoll punted 23 times and Grange returned three for little or no gain.

"I decided if one of us was going to look bad, it wasn't going to be me," Driscoll said. "Punting to Grange is like grooving a pitch to Babe Ruth."

The Cardinals went on to win the NFL championship. Driscoll scored 67 of their 229

John "Paddy"
Driscoll (2),
circa 1929.

points with four rushing touchdowns, 11 field goals and 10 extra points.

Halas seethed as another team stepped into the Chicago spotlight. To make matters worse, Grange left after his successful barnstorming tour with the Bears to help form the American Football League and join the upstart outfit's New York Yankees. Joey Sternaman, a former Bears quarterback and brother of Bears co-owner Dutch Sternaman, became the owner of the new league's Chicago Bulls.

Fate smiled on the Bears, however, when it became clear the Cardinals and owner Chris O'Brien would not be able to afford their new lease at White Sox Park without shedding assets. The bidding began between the Bears and Bulls for the Cardinals' most valuable property.

"Joey Sternaman offered Paddy a raise, and a big one, to join the Bulls," Halas wrote in his autobiography. "Alarm bells rang in my head. If they got Paddy, the Bulls might be a better club than the Bears. I could never let the Bears be second-best in Chicago."

Halas offered O'Brien $3,500 for his star's contract and Driscoll a raise to $10,000. Both accepted.

The move paid immediate dividends for the Bears. The difference Driscoll made was clear in his first game against the Cardinals on Oct. 17, 1926. He scored every point in the Bears' 16-0 win with three drop-kick field goals, a 5-yard rushing touchdown and the extra point.

"Paddy and the Bears proved to be a class above Paddy and the Cardinals," Halas wrote. "He was magnificent."

Indeed, the teams that had become equals with Driscoll playing for the Cardinals went in different directions after he switched sides. With Driscoll in 1920-25, the Cardinals were 4-4-2 against the Bears; when he played for the Bears in 1926-29, the South Siders went 2-5-2.

After their 1925 championship and Driscoll's departure, the Cardinals had one winning season (1935) in the next 20 years despite the presence of star players such as Ernie Nevers, Ollie Matson, Charley Trippi and Dick "Night Train" Lane. For the most part, the Bidwill family of owners made the tightfisted Halas look like Santa Claus. Well into the 1950s, the Cardinals were the last team in the NFL to still travel exclusively by train.

The Cardinals won their second and final title in 1947 and finished as runners-up the next year before reclaiming their usual spot at or near the bottom of the standings. They left for St. Louis in 1960.

Many games between Chicago's two teams devolved into all-out brawls. One such fight happened in the early days, with the Bears' Halas and Joey Sternaman taking on Driscoll.

The Cardinals' Pat Summerall got into a fistfight with Bears end Harlon Hill during a 1956 fracas. He remembered in Jeff Davis' 2005 biography, "Papa Bear: The Life and Legacy of George Halas," that life as a Cardinal "was not a happy existence."

"We always played second fiddle," Summerall, said. "The Bears and Wrigley Field got all the attention. The White Sox and us fought for a bigger piece of the pie."

Driscoll finished his career with 402 points: 244 for the Cardinals, 158 for the Bears. He scored 31 touchdowns and drop-kicked 63 extra points and 51 field goals. He ran for 17 touchdowns, caught one, returned a fumble for another and passed for 16 more.

He was named first-team All-Pro six times, served as a player/coach for the Cardinals for three seasons and in 1965 was elected to the Pro Football Hall of Fame's third class.

"Driscoll was a marked man in every game," the Tribune's Walter Eckersall wrote on Nov. 10, 1925. "He was among the first to use the pivot in dodging, and he ran with his knees kicking nearly as high as his chest. He was very quick to take an opening and shot through it with the speed of a sprinter.

"Unlike some good ball carriers, Driscoll was an excellent blocker. If he did not carry the oval, he helped to pave the way for a teammate."

Before he turned pro, Driscoll helped the naval base team he played for with Halas perform so well against college teams of the day that it earned a berth in the 1919 Rose Bowl, which it won 17-0 over the Mare Island Marines

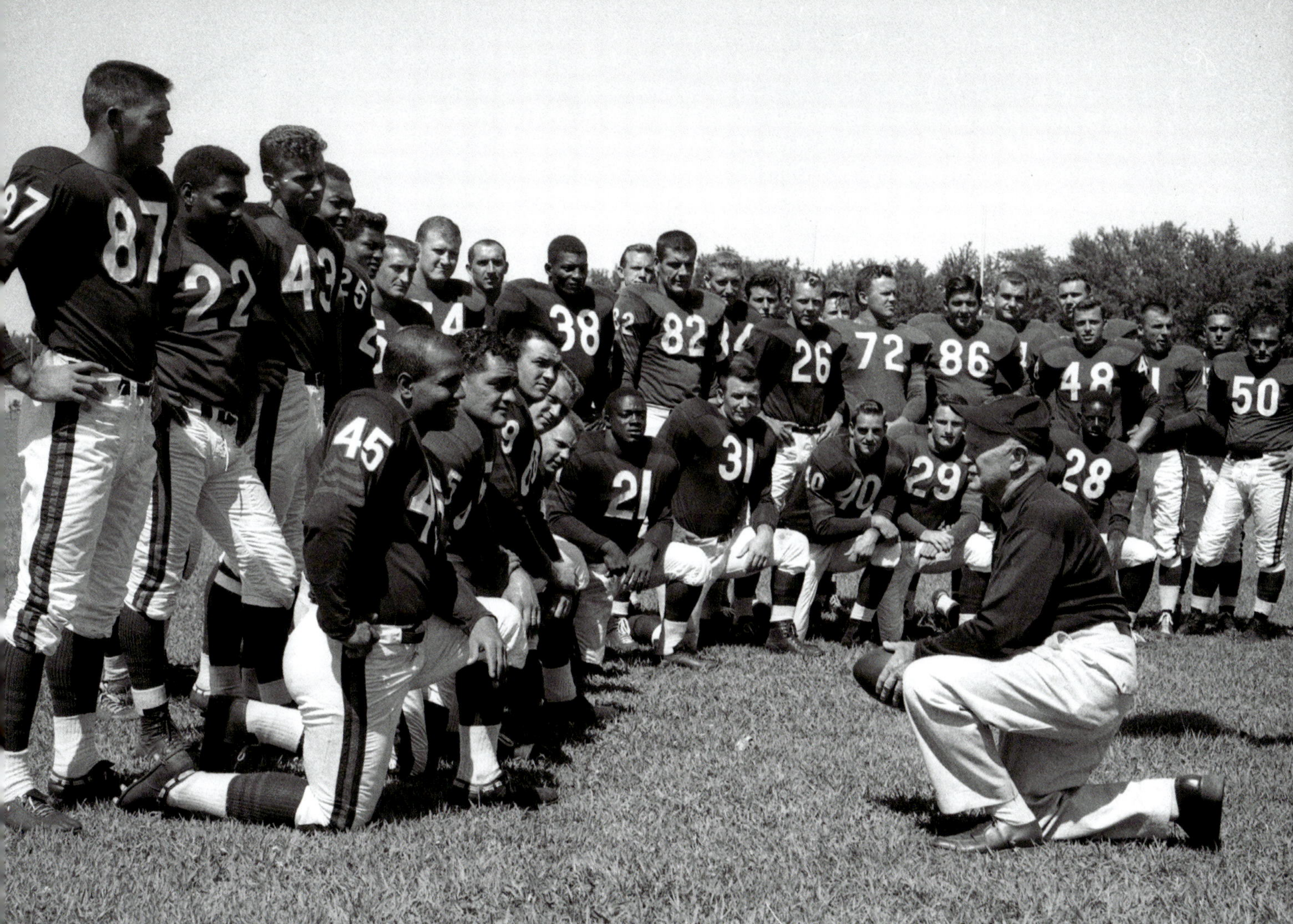

Coach Paddy Driscoll with the 1957 team.

of California. Like Halas, he had a cup of coffee in major league baseball; Driscoll played 17 games for the Cubs in 1917, Halas 12 for the Yankees in 1919. In 1920, Halas broke league rules by paying Driscoll $300 to play an unofficial playoff game for the Staleys after Driscoll's Cardinals were eliminated.

After he retired from playing following the 1929 season, Driscoll went straight into coaching. He was the athletic director and football and basketball coach at St. Mel High School until 1937, when he left to coach football at Marquette. He rejoined Halas as an assistant in 1941 and stayed with the Bears through their championship season of 1963.

In 1956, Halas stepped down as head coach and named Driscoll his replacement. The Bears were NFL runners-up with the league's best offense in '56 and went 5-7 in '57 before Halas reinstalled himself as coach.

"I felt I owed him the satisfaction of being head coach before he ended his career," Halas wrote. "I told Paddy, privately, the job would be his for two years and then I would return."

Hill said in "Papa Bear" that Halas "didn't really step down anyhow. He was behind the scenes. He was at camp, and he was calling the shots."

Driscoll spent the last years of his life living with his son John in Park Ridge. Visitors marveled at how difficult it was to get him to talk about himself or his athletic exploits. He died in 1968 at 73.

"Now he's gone," Halas told the Tribune on June 29, 1968. "It's a terrible shock. He was the greatest athlete I ever knew." ■

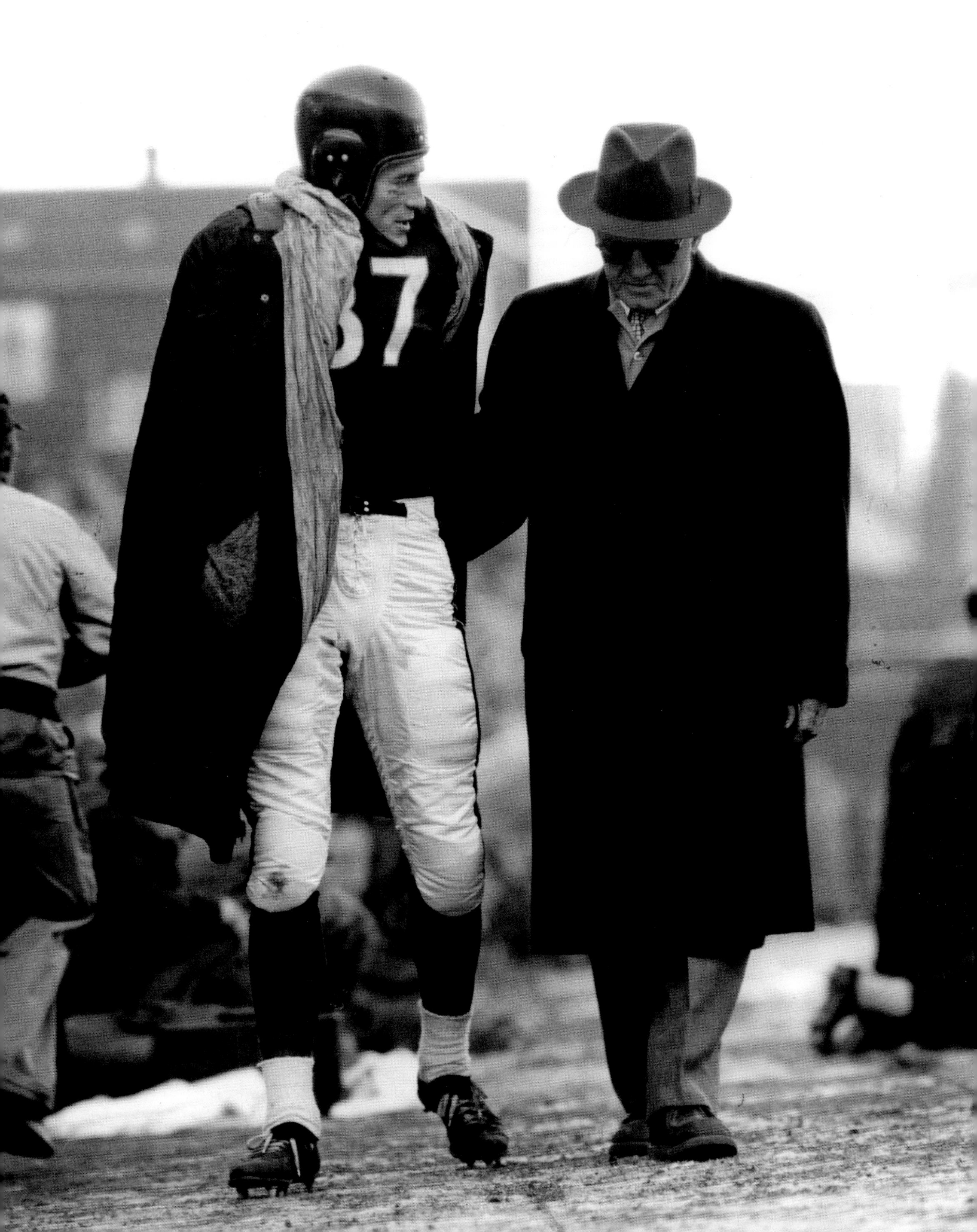

35

Harlon Hill

87, 82 END
1954–61

O F ALL THE great players in the Bears' storied history, three have been named the NFL most valuable player.

Walter Payton won the award in 1976 from the Sporting News, 1977 by consensus and 1985 from the Bert Bell Award committee and the DC Touchdown Club.

Sid Luckman won the Joe F. Carr Trophy in 1943.

And Harlon Hill won the Jim Thorpe Award in 1955.

For three years, Hill was as good as any player in the NFL. In 1954, '55 and '56, he made 134 receptions for 3,041 yards and 32 touchdowns, averaging 22.7 yards per catch and 4.2 catches per touchdown. People started to compare him to Raymond Berry, the best receiver of the time, and Don Hutson, the best ever at the time.

"Raymond Berry and I talked about Hill," Bears teammate George Connor told Jeff Davis in his 2005 book, "Papa Bear: The Life and Legacy of George Halas." "He had more moves, more speed than Berry."

"Football fans are forever comparing Harlon Hill . . . with Don Hutson," the Tribune's Cooper Rollow wrote on Nov. 3, 1957. "For Hill enthusiasts, the comparison is a favorable one. Hill . . . is off to a faster start in his pro career than Hutson enjoyed. In his first three years, Hutson caught 93 passes. Hill's three-year total was 134.

"Bear officials are cautiously reserving judgment on whether Hill is better than Hutson. The next few years will tell, they say."

Injuries and alcohol abuse ended those comparisons. Hill's Hall of Fame potential was not realized, as the game broke his body and the bottle splintered his spirit before he pulled himself together for a successful second act after his playing days.

"Harlon Hill should have been a Hall of Famer, but you don't get in on four years," Connor told Davis.

Hill was one of Halas' greatest scouting finds in a career filled with them. Halas particularly enjoyed finding professional talent at small schools, as he did with Bulldog Turner and Ed Sprinkle from Hardin-Simmons, George Musso at Millikin, Joe Kopcha at Tennessee-Chattanooga and Willie Galimore at Florida A&M.

Harlon Hill (87) is greeted by coach George Halas on Dec. 11, 1955, as he trots to the sideline during a game against the Philadelphia Eagles at Wrigley Field.

Harlon Hill was the best piece of raw-boned talent I ever saw walk into training camp. I swear he had three speeds.

—BEARS TEAMMATE GEORGE CONNOR

Bears defensive coordinator Clark Shaughnessy was scouting the 1954 Blue-Gray Game in Montgomery, Ala., when he overheard two coaches from Jacksonville State claim that the best player in Alabama, better than anyone at their school, or Auburn or the Crimson Tide for that matter, wasn't playing in the game. Instead, he could be found at Florence State Teachers College.

Shaughnessy repeated the claim to Halas, who requested film on Hill from the tiny school, which is now called the University of North Alabama.

In his 1979 autobiography, "Halas by Halas," the coach wrote: "Clark investigated Hill's performance. . . . I signed Hill. He had an uncanny knack for pulling down impossible passes."

The Bears waited until the 15th round to draft Hill, correctly betting he would be available after the big-school stars were picked.

"Sure, we gambled and won," Bears line coach Phil Handler told the Tribune's David Condon on Sept. 25, 1955. "I was over my nervous stomach within a few months."

Not long after Hill arrived for camp at St. Joseph College in Rensselaer, Ind., it became clear he was one of the team's best players. One by one, his new teammates challenged him to footraces in the parking lots; one by one they were humbled by the 6-foot-3, 199-pound marvel.

"Harlon Hill was the best piece of raw-boned talent I ever saw walk into training camp," Connor told Davis. "I swear he had three speeds."

Halas told Condon: "Harlon was a surefire regular from almost the first day of camp. I don't think our staff was ever more impressed by a rookie."

Unlike most of Halas' contentious contract negotiations, he had no problem getting Hill to sign his first pro papers.

"I really didn't know what George Halas or anybody else in the pros was like," Hill told Davis. "You know, coming from the sticks of Alabama. No TV back then. . . . The first year wasn't any negotiating at all. I was happy to sign anything."

Hill was by all accounts the NFL's best rookie in 1954, when he caught 45 passes for 1,124 yards and a league-best 12 touchdowns. In 1955 he had 42 catches for 789 yards while leading the NFL again with nine touchdown receptions and winning the Newspaper Enterprise Association's Jim Thorpe Award as MVP.

In 1956, Hill was the best player on perhaps the best offense in Bears history, with 47 receptions for 1,128 yards and 11 touchdowns. Teammate Rick Casares led the NFL with 1,126 rushing yards, and Ed Brown did the same with a 83.1 passer rating.

"Harlon was ahead of his time, running deep patterns," guard Stan Jones told Davis. "Without too many moves, he could run right past people."

Hill's practice habits were legendary; the team's most talented player also was one of its hardest workers. He gained his work ethic growing up in the cotton and corn fields of Killen, Ala. He amazed teammates with his ability to run all day without tiring. Well into his career he showed up to training camp a week early, when rookies were required to report.

"It's always the great players who work a little harder, who have that great desire to give just a little more," Halas told the Tribune on July 22, 1955. "Hill is that type. And it's because of that desire that he should become one of the great stars in Bears history."

In the 1956 NFL championship game, a 47-7 loss to the Giants, Hill hurt his back after he was tackled on the frozen turf at Yankee Stadium. He lost some of his speed and never was the same. In 1957 he suffered a season-ending separated shoulder, and the next year he tore one of his Achilles tendons.

He kept coming back to play but was a shell of his former self. He hastened his decline by self-medicating with alcohol. In his last six seasons he surpassed 500 receiving yards only once. Halas hired detectives to monitor Hill's nighttime habits and soon amassed a large folder filled with accounts of his drunken incidents and brawls all over Chicago.

Even defensive end Doug Atkins, whose love of the nightlife was legendary, began to keep his distance.

"I tried to stay away from him when he was drinking," Atkins told Davis. "Harlon just couldn't control it."

Halas moved Hill to defense in 1961 and traded him and Brown to the Steelers in '62. Hill played seven games apiece with the Steelers and Lions that season, his last in the NFL.

Hill struggled in retirement until he moved back to his hometown to become a teacher. He earned his master's degree in 1969, and five years later he decided to quit drinking.

"Smartest thing I ever did," he told Davis.

His career flourished, and he became principal at Brooks High School in 1980. When he retired in 1992, Hill was president of the state's principals association.

Hill wrote a book, "Victory After the Game," in 1977 with Ronnie Thomas. Since 1986, the Harlon Hill Trophy has honored the best player in Division II football.

Hill retired to a quiet life in Killen, where in his later years his family took care of him as he battled various ailments. He died on March 21, 2013, at 80. ■

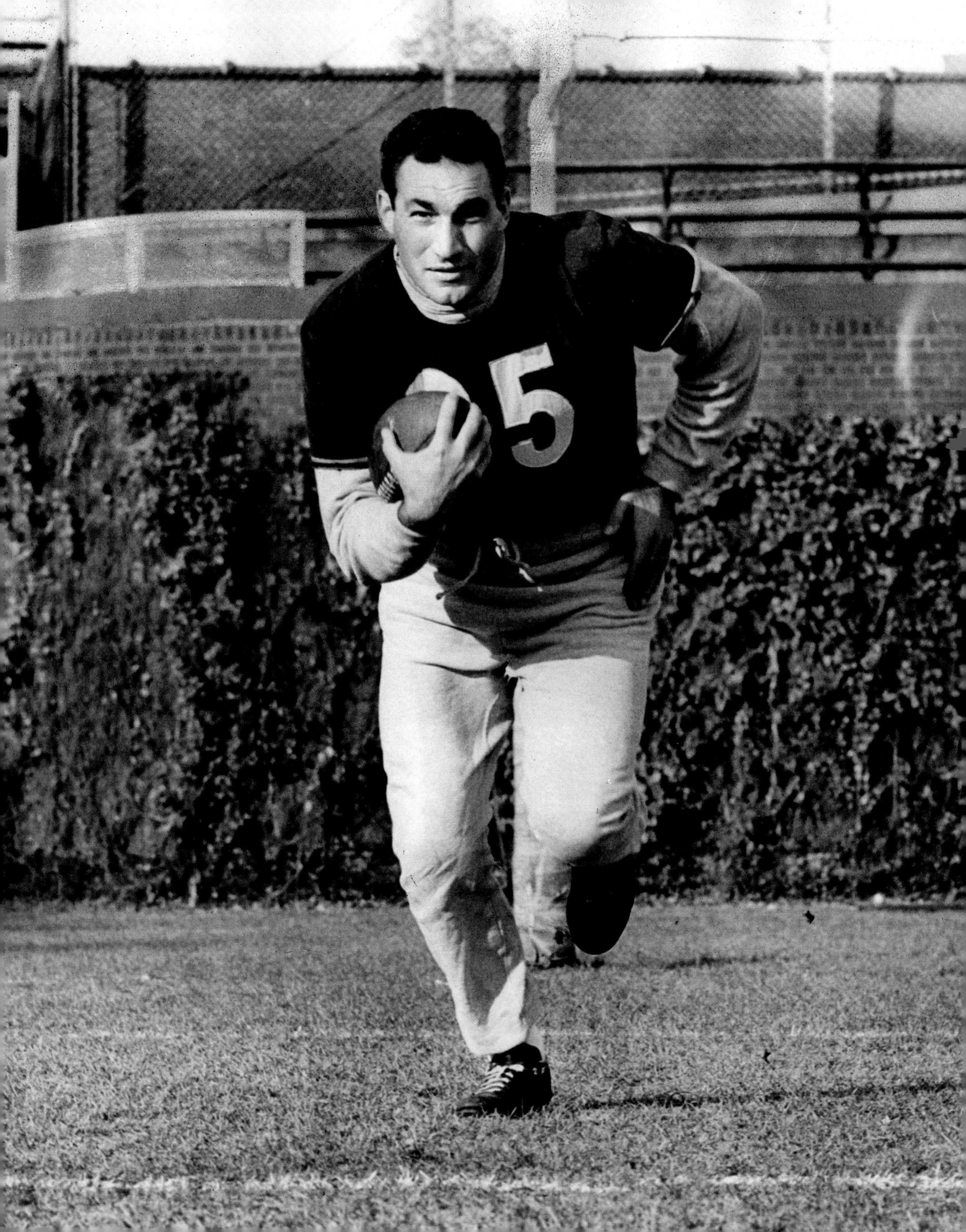

Rick Casares

36

35 FULLBACK
1955–64

RICK CASARES RAN FOR 49 touchdowns in his 10 seasons with the Bears. No one who saw it will forget his first.

With the 0-3 Bears facing the mighty Baltimore Colts on Oct. 16, 1955, at Wrigley Field, coach George Halas sent in the 6-foot-2, 226-pound Casares to give starting fullback Chick Jagade a breather in the second quarter.

Casares switched places with halfback Bobby Watkins before the snap after Watkins complained of dizziness from the previous play. Quarterback George Blanda called for a halfback toss and flipped the ball to where he thought Watkins would be. Instead, Casares grabbed the ball and took off to his left. End Bill McColl and center Larry Strickland threw key blocks, and Casares finished the 81-yard touchdown run with a vicious stiff-arm of fearsome Colts linebacker Bill Pellington.

The run inspired the Bears to a 38-10 rout of the Colts, who entered the game 3-0 and had defeated the Bears 23-17 in Week 1. Casares added a 2-yard scoring run to make it 31-3 in the third quarter, and he finished with 94 yards on nine carries after entering the game with 16 attempts for 85 yards.

It was the first of six straight wins for the Bears, who finished 8-4 after their poor start. The stretch included a 52-31 rout of the Packers led by Casares' 115 rushing yards.

The Bears finished second in the Western Division, a half-game behind the Rams. The next year, with Paddy Driscoll replacing Halas as coach for the first of two seasons, the Bears boasted the best offense in the league. They averaged 30.3 points and led the NFL in points, yards and rushing yards while ranking fourth in passing yards. Casares' 1,126 rushing yards led the league, as did Ed Brown's 83.1 passer rating. Harlon Hill caught 47 passes for 1,128 yards and 11 touchdowns.

The Bears won the Western Division with a 9-2-1 record but were routed in the NFL championship game 47-7. The Giants, with perhaps the greatest coordinator combination ever with Vince Lombardi leading the offense and Tom Landry the defense under coach Jim Lee Howell, focused their entire defensive plan on Casares. Landry used an extra lineman to tie up Bears blockers while instructing rookie middle linebacker Sam Huff to shadow Casares.

Casares managed 43 rushing yards and 41 receiving, but the rest of the Bears could not pick

Rick Casares (35), works out in a practice session Nov. 8, 1963, at Wrigley Field.

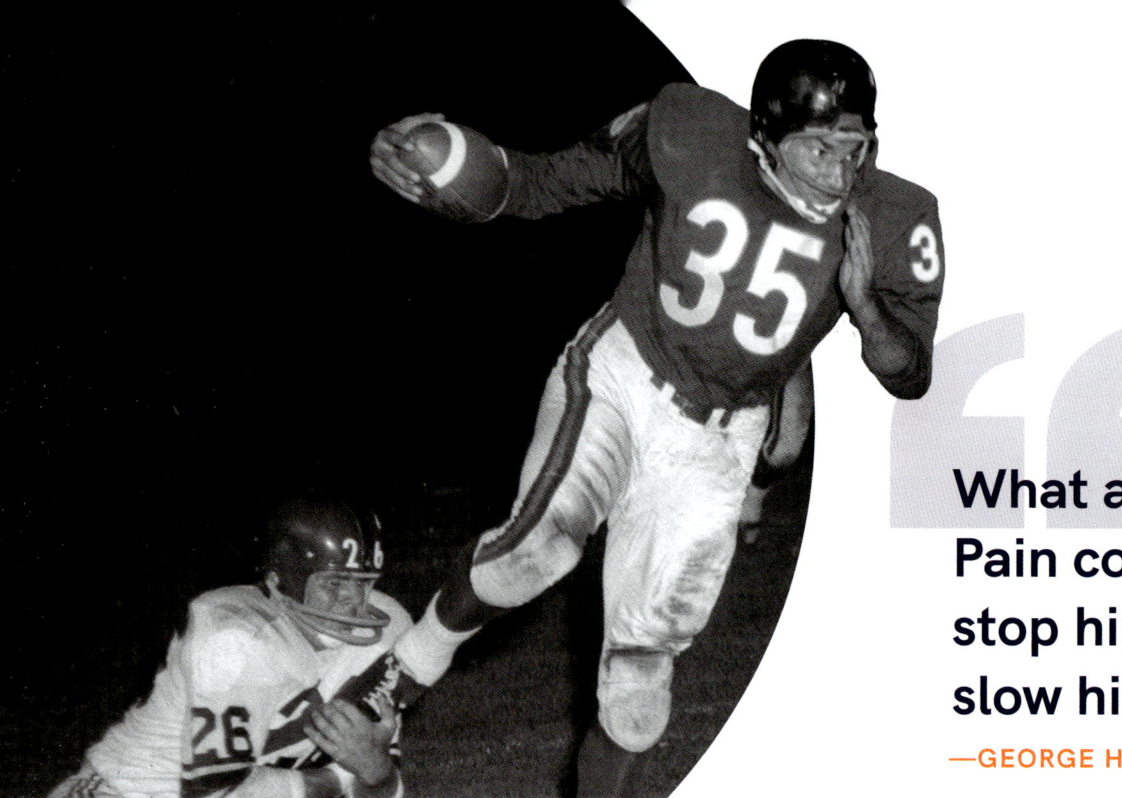

> ## "What a boy! Pain could not stop him, nor slow him down.
>
> —GEORGE HALAS

Rick Casares (35) yanks his leg away from the Giants' Don Sutherin (26) on Sept. 11, 1959, during the 14th annual Armed Forces game at Soldier Field.

up the slack, as quarterbacks Brown and Blanda and halfbacks J.C. Caroline and Bobby Watkins never got going.

The Bears and Casares thought the season could be the start of a long run of championship contention, but they did not make the postseason again until the 1963 title team.

Halas, who still called the shots while Driscoll coached, wasn't comfortable with Brown or Blanda and hoped Zeke Bratkowski would be the answer at quarterback. Casares questioned the move, and it was the start of a long-running feud between the owner and his star fullback.

"Halas screwed up our offense," Casares told Jeff Davis in his 2005 biography, "Papa Bear: The Life and Legacy of George Halas." "Ed Brown had led the league in passing, but Hallas didn't like Ed personally. So, we went from being favored to win the championship in '57 to finishing next to last. Halfway through the season, he was alternating the quarterbacks. It didn't work."

Casares is one of only five Bears—with Walter Payton, Gale Sayers, Bill Osmanski and Beattie Feathers—to lead the NFL in rushing. Casares' 5,657 rushing yards were a team record when he left Chicago and still ranks fourth in Bears history behind Payton, Matt Forte and Neal Anderson. Only Payton and Anderson rushed for more touchdowns than Casares' 49. Among Bears running backs, only Payton was named to more Pro Bowls than Casares' five.

"As far as the Bears are concerned," the Tribune's Cooper Rollow wrote on Sept. 9, 1958, "no other runner in football boasts Casares' combination of power, speed, maneuverability and stamina."

"Rick is our heavy-duty back, and I mean heavy-duty," Bears offensive coordinator Luke Johnsos told Rollow. "He's our bread-and-butter guy."

Still, Casares and Halas could not get along. As Davis recounted in his Halas biography, their interactions included:

— Casares making a mockery of Halas' weekly weigh-ins by showing up hungover in the hope that dehydration would lead to a lower weight.

— Halas denying permission to Sport magazine to single out Casares for a profile feature and the cover of its 1957 NFL preview issue, demanding the publication instead focus on the entire team.

— Casares grabbing a Coca-Cola from trainer Ed Rozy, who gave one to each player and coach at halftime of every game. Casares unwittingly took the bottle Rozy prepared special for Halas, and the fullback spit out his large swig immediately.

"That's not Coke! That's whiskey!" Casares said, blowing the secret of Halas' halftime anxiety reliever.

— Halas fining Casares for bringing a garment bag with a clothing change on a trip instead of the usual handbag with essentials, such as a toothbrush.

"What the hell is that?" Halas yelled.

"A change of clothes," Casares said.

"You're always thinking of (women)," Halas said. "You're up to no good. That's gonna cost you a hundred dollars!"

"What?" Casares asked.

"You're thinking about cabareting! We're gonna play a football game!" the coach said.

— Casares forgetting where to go on three straight plays against the Rams in 1960 the day after Halas installed a new goal-line set.

— The NFL investigating Casares for gambling. He was exonerated with the help of a lie detector test as the scandal saw stars Paul Hornung of the Packers and Alex Karras of the Lions suspended indefinitely in 1963.

— Halas remarking when Casares settled down with Polly, his wife for more than 40 years, that it was refreshing to see him with a classy woman instead of his usual "racetrack floozies."

— Casares allegedly training his Yorkshire terrier to defecate on Halas' doorstep each morning.

The worst offense in Halas' eyes came in 1962, when Ed Stone of the Chicago American asked Casares what he thought of Halas trading his friend Brown to the Steelers. Casares shared his opinion that Halas had derailed the team's once-great offense. The next day's headline read: "Casares rips Papa Bear." Halas promoted Joe Marconi to starting fullback.

Halas' first concern, however, was how a player performed, and Casares was one of his best. In the only description of the fullback in his 1979 autobiography, "Halas by Halas," the coach said: "What a boy! Pain could not stop him, nor slow him down."

Casares contributed to the 1963 championship team but missed the final five games of the season after Packers linebacker Ray Nitschke broke one of Casares' ankles on a tackle. Casares saw limited action with the Bears in 1964, then finished his career with the Redskins in 1965 and the AFL-expansion Dolphins in '66.

Casares grew up a special athlete in Tampa, Fla. After his father was shot and killed when Casares was 7, his mother sent him to live with an aunt and uncle in Paterson, N.J., where he became a Golden Gloves boxing champion. His mother forbade him to turn pro in boxing, though, so he returned to his home state and enrolled at the University of Florida. He was an All-SEC performer in two sports as an All-American in football and the Gators' leading scorer for two seasons in basketball.

After a year in the Army, Casares was offered contracts by the Bears and the Toronto Argonauts of the CFL. He chose the Bears, whose contract of $10,000 per year was half of the Argonauts' offer. Casares had hoped to impress Halas, saying, "I'm not about money."

Davis wrote: "Halas gave the young man a quizzical look over the top of his glasses. 'Most things are about money, kid. That's what we're doing here.'"

After his retirement from the Dolphins, Casares owned a bowling alley in Chicago, then returned to Tampa and worked in the construction and home improvement industries. He died of natural causes at 82 on Sept. 13, 2013, in Tampa. Former teammate Mike Ditka and rival Hornung eulogized him.

"He's who we all wanted to be," Ditka said.

Ditka remembered Casares in "The Chicago Bears Centennial Scrapbook" by former Tribune reporters Don Pierson and Dan Pompei.

"I idolized him," Ditka said. "He was a tough guy who didn't wear it outside. He did everything by example. He did nothing by word. . . . Nobody messed with Rick Casares." ■

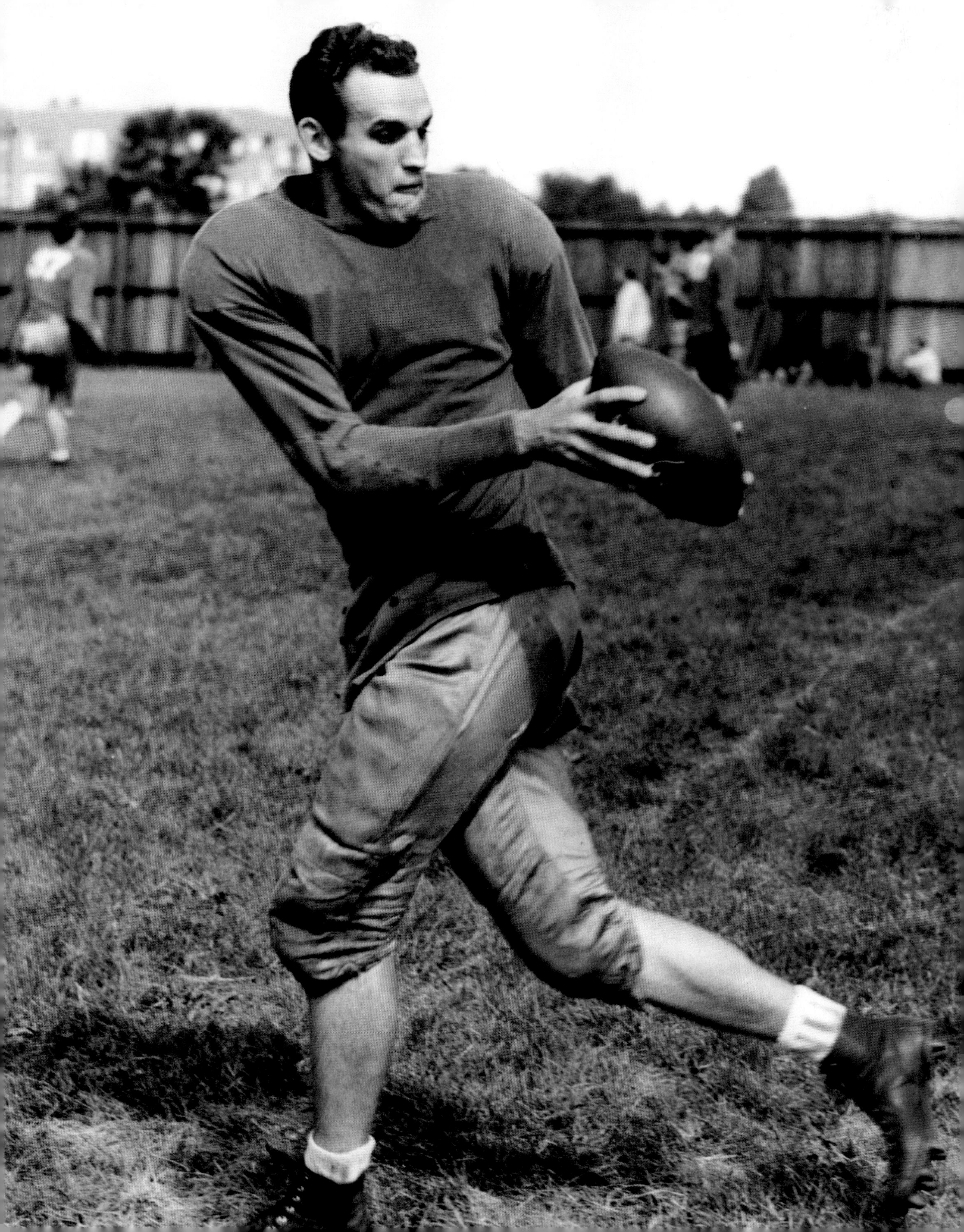

37

Ken Kavanaugh

51 END
1940–41, 1945–50

A FIRST BASEMAN FOR THE Kilgore Boomers was taking infield practice before an East Texas League game in 1940.

The tall 24-year-old was getting along just fine in his first professional season, batting .284 with five home runs and 17 doubles in 236 at-bats. A future with the St. Louis Cardinals was a possibility.

As he was fielding ground balls and scooping low throws out of the dirt, a clubhouse attendant approached him and told him he had a long-distance call.

Ken Kavanaugh picked up the clubhouse telephone.

"This is George Halas," the caller announced.

"Who are you?" Kavanaugh replied.

Halas had drafted Kavanaugh in the third round out of LSU, where he was an All-American end who led the nation in receiving in 1939. The 1940 draft stacked the Bears with talent that would help them dominate for the next decade. Ed Kolman, Hampton Pool, Lee Artoe and Harry Clarke were instant contributors, and first-rounder Bulldog Turner would become one of the NFL's best players.

Kavanaugh, Halas felt, was the missing link between the Bears and greatness. Quarterback Sid Luckman and the T formation with a man in motion were ready to render contemporary defenses obsolete; all they needed was a receiver to stretch the field. The 6-foot-3, 207-pound Kavanaugh was that player.

"You have to play in the (College) All-Star Game before I can sign you," Halas told Kavanaugh.

"I have to take infield," Kavanaugh said before hanging up.

The next day Kavanaugh received another phone call, from Tribune sports editor Arch Ward. Ward was a friend and confidant of Halas, but more relevant to the situation, he was the director of the College All-Star Game, which pitted the NFL champion against a team of star college graduates in preseasons from 1934-76.

Ward told Kavanaugh to report to Northwestern University for practice as soon as he could. Kavanaugh again hung up.

Kavanaugh enjoyed rare leverage for a player in contract negotiations against Halas, as Jeff Davis described as well as the conversations above in his 2005 biography of Halas,

Ken Kavanaugh (51), circa 1940.

169

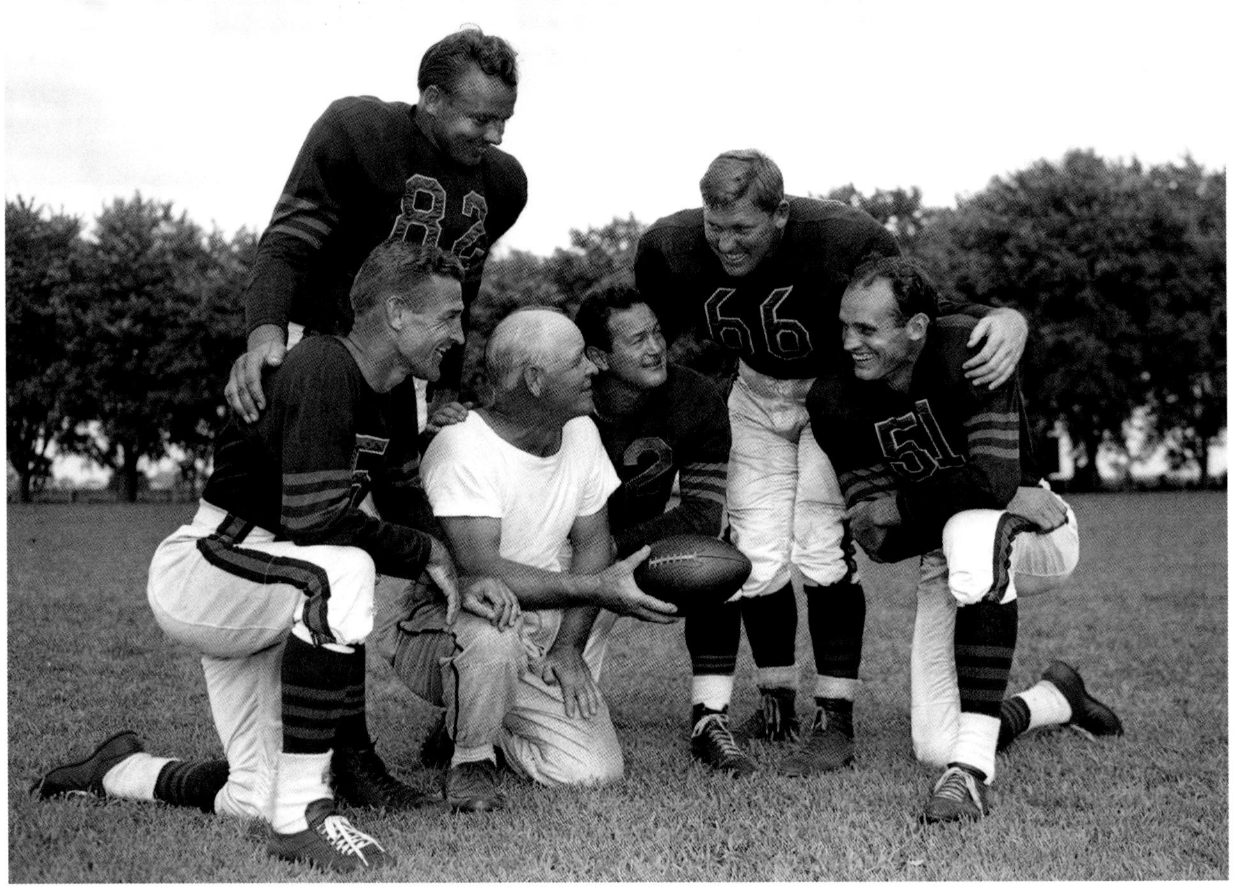

George McAfee (5), from left, Ray Bray (82), coach Hunk Anderson, Sid Luckman (42), Bulldog Turner (66) and Ken Kavanaugh (51) in 1949.

"Papa Bear: The Life and Legacy of George Halas." Cardinals executive Branch Rickey, knowing Kavanaugh was a commodity in two sports, signed him for a contract that paid him $300 per month.

Rickey allowed Kavanaugh to attend the All-Star game, which the Packers won 45-28. After competing against Don Hutson, the Packers' amazing receiver, Kavanaugh realized he wanted to become a football player and decided to sign with the Bears.

Halas initially offered $50 per game, then $100, then $150. Kavanaugh held out for $300. Halas relented and lamented, "You're getting paid better than anyone else in the league."

It turned out to be a steal for the Bears. Kavanaugh took the team to the next level with his uncanny ability to catch touchdown passes.

Sixty-nine years after his last game, Kavanaugh's 50 touchdown receptions are still the most in Bears history. His reception total was a modest 162 in eight seasons, but he averaged 3.2 receptions per touchdown. In 1947 he set a team record that still stands by catching a touchdown in seven consecutive games.

Even during seasons in which he wasn't a huge part of the offense, Kavanaugh made an impact in the end zone. He caught three touchdowns on 12 receptions in 1940, six on 11 in '41, five on 18 in '46 and six on 18 in '48.

"The average football end thinks he's open all the time," Bears assistant coach Luke Johnsos told the Tribune's Cooper Rollow on Dec. 26, 1963. "He's forever clamoring for the ball. Kavanaugh was just the opposite. Luckman would call his number on a pass play and,

(He) invariably came up with the big catch when you needed it most. . . . Virtually every third pass Kavanaugh caught was good for a touchdown!

—GEORGE HALAS

unless he knew he had the defensive man in his pocket, he'd say, 'Not yet, Sid.'

"Finally, Ken would say, 'I got this guy all set up now, Sid,' and when he said that, you knew he was touchdown-bound."

Later in life, Kavanaugh wished he would have called for the ball a bit more often.

"Luckman was a great player and smart," Kavanaugh told Davis in his Halas biography, "but he never threw the ball enough."

Kavanaugh helped the Bears win championships in 1940, 1941 and 1946. He scored touchdowns in all three wins, on receptions from Luckman in the 73-0 rout of the Redskins in 1940 and the 24-14 win against the Giants in 1946. In 1941 he put the finishing touches on a 37-9 title game win over the Giants with a 42-yard fumble return for a score.

He missed three seasons from 1942-44 while serving as a bomber pilot in Europe during World War II. He returned to the Bears right before the 1945 season and was a better player in his 30s than he was in his 20s. He led the NFL with 13 touchdown receptions in 1947—a team record Dick Gordon tied in 1970 and not matched since—and nine in 1949.

Kavanaugh's career total of 50 touchdown receptions was difficult to match well into the future. Wes Welker also ended up with 50 in his career, and Pro Football Hall of Famer Lynn Swann had 51. Kavanaugh's 48 touchdown receptions in the 1940s were second only to

Hutson's 63, and his 50 overall were second all time when he retired to Hutson's otherworldly 99, which still ranks 11th in NFL history.

In 1994 and 2005 the Tribune selected all-time Bears teams. In keeping with the franchise's strengths, three running backs and one receiver were named on offense. Both times, Kavanaugh was selected at receiver. He ranks 10th in team history with 3,626 receiving yards and 14th with 313 points, and the Hall of Fame named him to its 1940s All-Decade team.

When Kavanaugh retired as a player, the former baseball star moved forward with a life in football. He coached ends with the Bears in 1951, then at Boston College for two years and Villanova for one. In 1955 he found a home in New York with the Giants. He coached ends and receivers there until 1970, when he became a scout. After 45 years with the team he retired in 1999 to Sarasota, Fla., where he died at 90 in 2007 from complications from pneumonia.

In his 1979 autobiography, "Halas by Halas," the man who signed Kavanaugh still marveled about his ability to turn any catch into a score.

"Kavanaugh was a quick, resourceful operator who invariably came up with the big catch when you needed it most," Halas wrote. "These Kavanaugh specials were astonishingly productive. . . . Virtually every third pass Kavanaugh caught was good for a touchdown!" ■

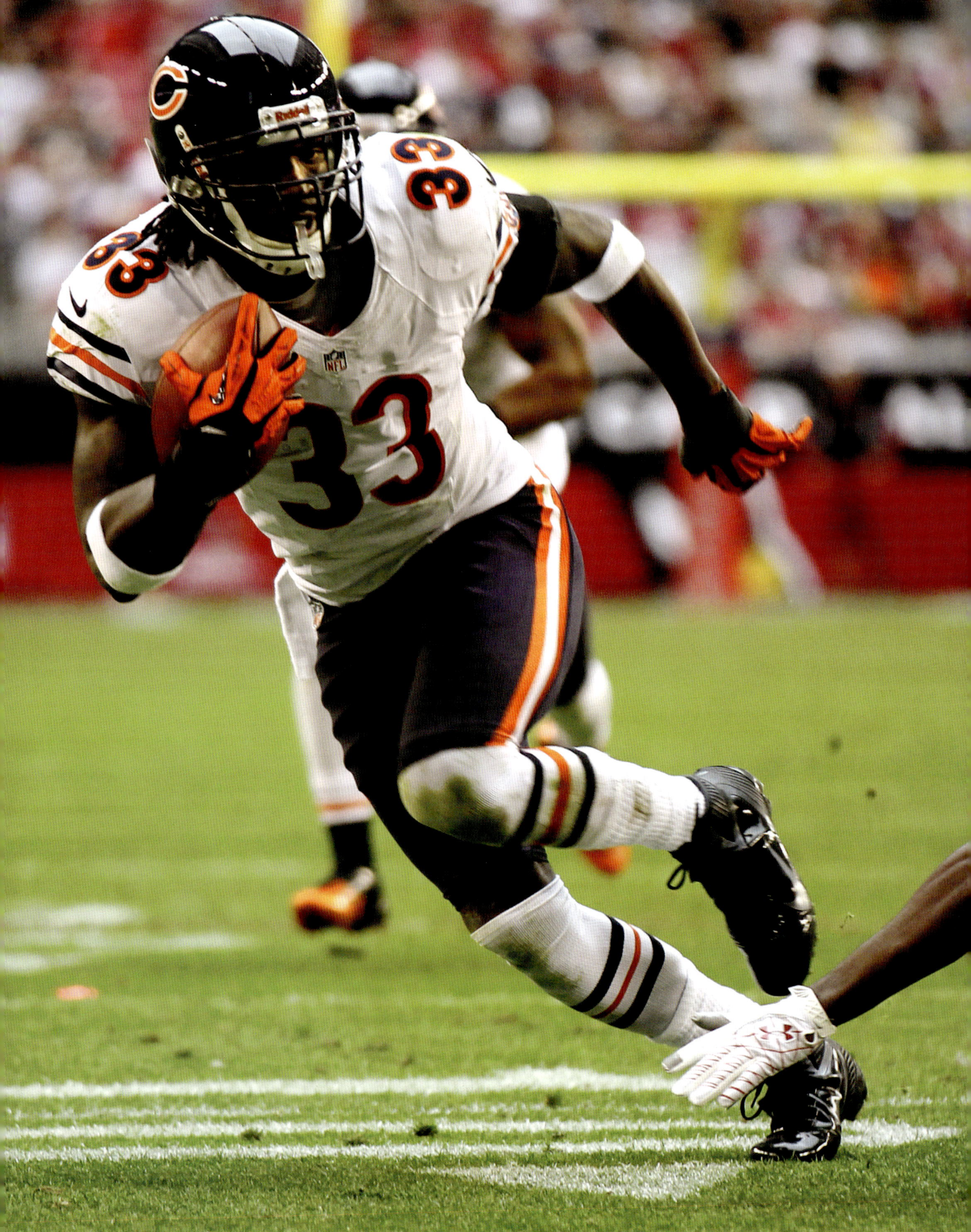

38

Charles Tillman

33 CORNERBACK
2003–14

IT'S DIFFICULT FOR a cornerback to dominate a game; when one is at his best, the ball rarely is thrown his way.

Charles Tillman found a unique way to do it. His "Peanut Punch" shifted many games' momentum and made him a hero among Bears fans.

While most fumbles are forced when a defensive player's helmet or shoulder pad pops the ball out of a carrier's hands or a pass rusher slaps it from an unsuspecting quarterback, Tillman used his fist to jab the seemingly secure ball from a back or receiver. The move was tricky; if he missed the ball and hit the player, it could result in an unsportsmanlike-conduct penalty or ejection. If he missed both, it could make for a blooper-reel missed tackle.

Tillman always seemed to strike his target, though. The Peanut Punch helped him cause 42 fumbles in his 12 years with the Bears, including 10 in 2012. He retired with 44 career forced fumbles, tied for sixth since the statistic became official in 1991. The top five are all defensive linemen; Brian Dawkins' 36 are the next most by a defensive back.

"I just had a knack for knowing when to shoot my punch," Tillman said at the Bears100 Celebration Weekend in June 2019. "And I got lucky. Forty-four times."

That knack never was more apparent than on Nov. 4, 2012, in Nashville, Tenn., where he forced four fumbles in a 51-20 win over the Titans. His punches separated the ball from wide receiver Kenny Britt, running back Chris Johnson and tight ends Craig Stevens and Jared Cook. Stevens' fumble rolled out of bounds; the Bears recovered the other three, two of which led to quick touchdowns.

"They didn't know how to hold on to the football," Tillman said at Bears100. "That's how it happened. They didn't hold on to it. I don't know, man. (Defensive backs coach) Gill Byrd used to always say, 'This ball is worth millions. Go get it!' So I said, 'Yeah. I'm going to get it.'"

"I'm telling you right now, he's getting Defensive Player of the Year," Bears linebacker Lance Briggs told the Tribune's Dan Pompei after that Titans game. "Hands down, there's no one playing better than him. . . . We're all seeing history being made. I've never seen anybody do what he's done and is able to do it so consistently."

Charles Tillman (33) returns an interception for a touchdown Dec. 23, 2012, against the Arizona Cardinals.

While Tillman's punching prowess was well-known for years in Chicago, it became a national story after the Titans game as the rollicking Bears improved to 7-1. The Tribune's Chris Kuc and Philip Hersh asked several boxers and mixed martial artists to grade Peanut's pugilism.

"He's got a good right hand," light heavyweight Andrzej Fonfara said. "He'd make a good boxer. If he punched somebody in the chin with that punch, he'd be knocking out guys."

The Bears finished 10-6 that season to miss the playoffs for the fifth time in six years, leading to the firing of coach Lovie Smith. For the previous nine years, Tillman was the perfect cornerback for Smith's Cover-2 defense.

At 6-foot-2, 210 pounds, Tillman was strong enough to defend the run and athletic and intelligent enough to excel at man-to-man or zone coverage. He also was a key special teams contributor for most of his career for Bears units that were consistently among the league's best.

Smith set a goal for his defense to lead the NFL in takeaways every year, and Tillman did his best to try to make it happen. In 2004, Smith's first season with the Bears and Tillman's second, the team ranked 16th in the NFL with 29 takeaways. In the next eight years, the Bears finished in the top 10 in the category seven times, in the top five four times and No. 1 with 44 forced turnovers in 2006 and 44 more in 2012.

Tillman caused more of those plays than any other Bear. In addition to his 42 forced fumbles, he had 36 interceptions—third in team history behind Gary Fencik's 38 and Richie Petitbon's 37—and 11 fumble recoveries. The sum of those three stats, 89, is far more than any other Bear, with Fencik's 63 the next most.

"I'm like everybody else," Smith told the Tribune's David Haugh after the Titans game. "I'm amazed too."

Tillman credited Rodney Southern, his coach at Belton High School in Texas, with giving him the idea to punch the ball. Southern visited for a game when Tillman played at Louisiana-Lafayette.

"He told me, 'You know, you could have forced a lot of balls out if you could just punch it,'" Tillman told Haugh. "Light bulb!"

"From that moment," Haugh wrote, "dark days loomed for receivers who dared to carry the ball loosely against the cornerback who committed his career to popping it loose."

The Bears selected Tillman in the second round with the 35th pick in the 2003 draft. With their two first-round picks, they took quarterback Rex Grossman and defensive end Michael Haynes. In Tillman in the second round and Briggs in the third, the Bears found two players who would start for mostly excellent defenses for the next 12 years.

General manager Jerry Angelo and coach Dick Jauron envisioned Tillman as a player who could contribute as a No. 3 cornerback behind Jerry Azumah and R.W. McQuarters as a rookie before finding a bigger role. Tillman forced his way into the starting lineup by the fourth game, moving ahead of Azumah on the depth chart.

An up-and-down rookie season followed, as Tillman struggled at first in coverage and drew some costly pass-interference penalties. The Bears stuck with him, though, and it became

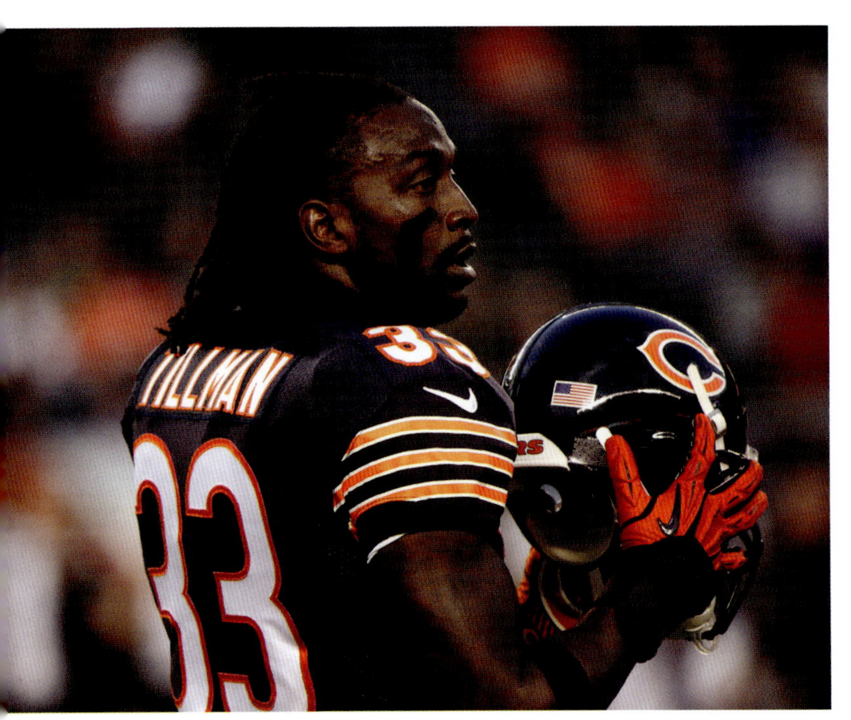

Charles Tillman (33) on Aug. 14, 2014, during a game against the Jacksonville Jaguars.

He's got a good right hand. He'd make a good boxer. If he punched somebody in the chin with that punch, he'd be knocking out guys.

—LIGHT HEAVYWEIGHT ANDRZEJ FONFARA

apparent he could become a special player with more experience.

In the 14th game of that 7-9 season that resulted in Jauron's firing, Tillman made perhaps the best play of his career. With the Bears leading 13-10 with a minute left against the Vikings, quarterback Daunte Culpepper lofted the ball toward 6-foot-4 superstar receiver Randy Moss in the end zone. Tillman leaped and reached over the head and shoulders of Moss and outfought him for the ball for a game-saving interception.

Defensive coordinator Greg Blache told the Tribune's Fred Mitchell on Dec. 15, 2003: "For a young kid to go up and take the ball away from Randy Moss with the game on the line, it was huge. It speaks a lot to his athletic ability but also to his confidence."

Later in his career, Tillman said he visualized making plays such as that interception and speaking them into existence.

"The tongue has the power of life or death," Tillman told Haugh. "Say it, speak it, believe it."

Tillman earned first-team All-Pro honors in 2012 and was voted into the Pro Bowl in 2011 and '12. Now 38, he is still visible in the Chicago area. In 2018 he earned his FBI agent badge after training at the organization's academy in Quantico, Va.

The Cornerstone Foundation, Tillman's charity organization, helps critically ill children in the Chicago area. Tillman founded the organization in 2005 but changed its focus from education to aiding ailing children after his daughter Tiana's life-saving heart transplant in 2009. He was named the Walter Payton Man of the Year by the NFL after the 2013 season.

"I've been around Charles my entire time here and he's done so many good things," Smith said when Tillman was named the winner of the Bears' Ed Block Courage Award on April 7, 2009. "On a personal note, he's gone through quite a bit. But you see the same Charles . . . the sun is shining every day in his life, and we're lucky to have him as part of our team." ■

Charles Tillman (33) celebrates his interception return for a touchdown Dec. 23, 2012, against the Arizona Cardinals.

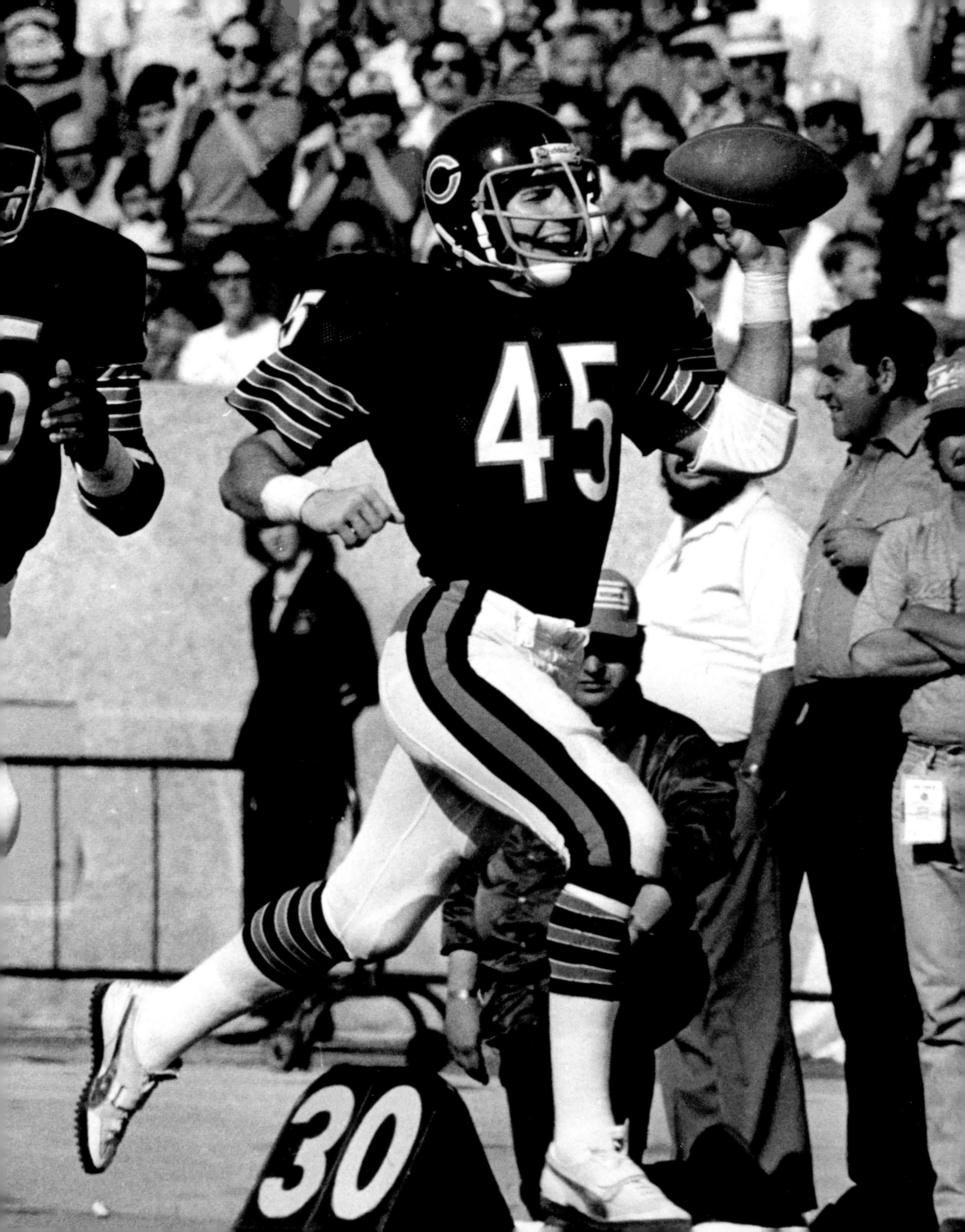

Gary Fencik

45 SAFETY
1976-87

GARY FENCIK NEVER SAW IT as an issue or even interesting, but he kept having to explain how his two sides coexisted.

On one hand, he was the epitome of the young, upwardly mobile city dweller of the 1980s. His face was fit for GQ; he was the magazine's cover model in September 1986. His hair always seemed perfectly coiffed; it was held in place by Consort mousse, which he endorsed. He had a series of strikingly beautiful girlfriends; one was Charlotte Kemp, Playboy's Miss December 1982.

He earned his bachelor's degree in history at Yale and his master's in business administration from Northwestern. His hobbies included reading a book per week, learning foreign languages, riding his 10-speed bike through Chicago's streets and running with the bulls in Pamplona.

Fencik was, as the headline of Sports Illustrated's profile of him in its Sept. 30, 1985, issue proclaimed, "The Pride of the Yuppies."

The 6-foot-1, 195-pound Bears safety also was one of the most violent players of his era. Fencik's thunderous hits on the Giants' Jimmy Robinson, the Buccaneers' Jimmie Giles and the Eagles' Wally Henry—as well as the time he kicked Packers tackle Karl Swanke—drew raves from fans, attention from the league office and a reputation among his peers.

In 1985, Fencik was voted "cheapest of the cheap-shot artists" in a Sports Illustrated poll of 200 players.

"Gary Fencik proved his point long ago," the Tribune's Don Pierson wrote on Dec. 22, 1985, "that he can abuse his brain and still use it."

The dichotomy fascinated a great number of football observers, and Fencik was asked about it often.

"I know, I know," Fencik told Sports Illustrated's Rick Telander. "Ivy League guy. Other interests. Football is a means, not an end. But I can't cavalierly say that it's just a game for me. I just can't. There is something in the performance that is as valid as anything. Plus, I want to win too much."

Fencik didn't do much of that early in his career. He grew up a fan of the Bears in Zion and Barrington and joined them in 1976, the final year of the team's 13-year playoff drought after the 1963 NFL championship.

His career, like his nature, could be split

Gary Fencik (45) is jubilant after intercepting a pass Sept. 20, 1981, in a game against Tampa Bay at Soldier Field.

into two halves: the gung-ho hard hitter of the 1970s who with fellow safety Doug Plank formed "The Hit Men," and the savvy, skillful leader of the great Bears teams of the '80s.

After his time as a record-setting receiver at Yale, the Dolphins drafted Fencik in the 10th round and converted him to safety. They cut him late in the preseason after he suffered a ruptured lung, and the Bears signed him to back up starting safeties Plank and Craig Clemons.

Fencik's first assignment after playing offense for so long was to figure out how to tackle NFL players.

"I had to learn," Fencik told the Tribune's Steve Rosenbloom on March 27, 2005. "Doug Plank was the tutor—for good or bad."

Fencik took Plank's lessons to heart and eventually applied them even more effectively. While Plank was hellbent on hitting any player who crossed his path, Fencik found a balance between going for the man and the ball. He holds the team record with 38 interceptions—one ahead of Richie Petitbon and two more than Charles Tillman—and the Bears credited Fencik with 12 forced fumbles and 10 recoveries in his 12-year career.

All the while, he was the one player whose huge hits could fire up Plank.

"Gary's hits were like electricity for me," Plank told Telander. "Gary hit (Robinson) so hard that the kid was lying there looking at both sides of the field at once."

When the Bears were losing, Fencik didn't go along to get along. His nicknames were "Bitch" (as in "and moan") and "Doom" (as in "and gloom") for constantly questioning the status quo and his ability to silence a table of laughing teammates with his nitpicking.

A change in attitude came in the middle of a preseason loss to the St. Louis Cardinals in 1983.

"I was angry, screaming and yelling at some players," Fencik told Pierson on Sept. 4, a few weeks later. "(Defensive tackle) Jim Osborne pulled me off on the sideline and said I couldn't do that anymore, that the younger players were looking to me as a leader.

"It sunk in. I can't change too much because I'm an emotional player, but if you cry wolf too often, it doesn't work. Everyone is trying really hard."

Winning also helped. In Fencik's first eight seasons, the Bears were 57-60; in his last four they went 50-13.

"One reason I'm quieter today," Fencik told the Tribune's Mike Kiley on Aug, 21, 1986, "is that there are not as many things wrong with the organization."

Fencik took to his new role as a leader. He moved from strong safety to free safety after Plank's retirement and mentored strong safeties Todd Bell and Dave Duerson as they became Pro Bowl players.

Duerson told the Tribune's Ed Sherman on Jan. 20, 1986, as the Bears prepared for Super Bowl XX: "It wasn't so much what he said to me. I learned so much from watching him. Gary plays with his body and mind. What he lacks in athletic ability he makes up for with intelligence. Gary plays intelligent on every play."

In many ways Fencik was a better player in his 30s than he was in his 20s. Although he made his two Pro Bowl appearances in 1980 and '81, many around the team felt he was just as deserving in '84 and '85, when Bell and Duerson made it, respectively.

"Fencik is having arguably his best season,"

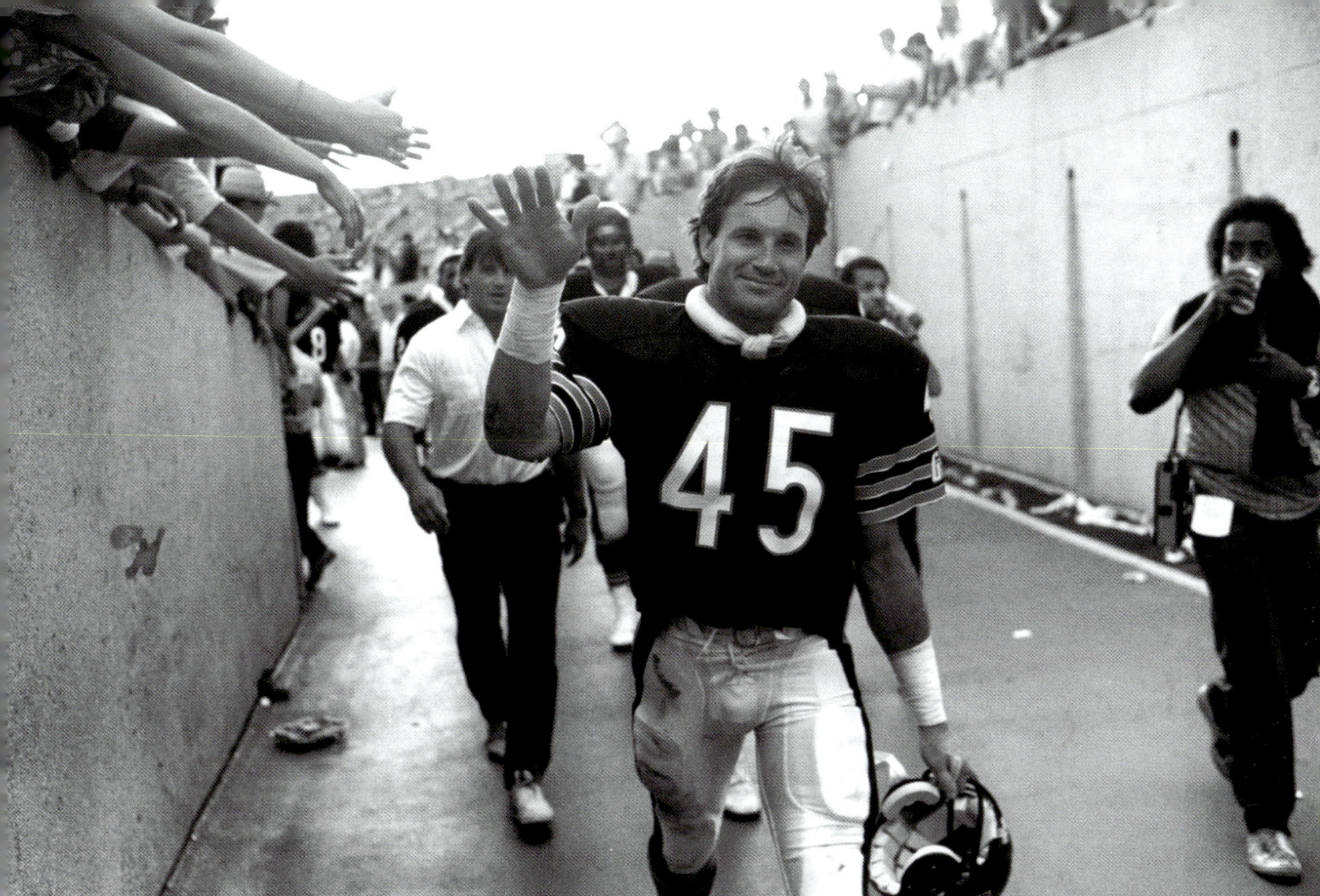

Pierson wrote on Dec. 22, 1985. "Like Walter Payton he refuses to fade away. In a near-perfect season for the Bears, it is somehow perfect symmetry that the oldest offensive starter and the oldest defensive starter very well could be the team's two most valuable players."

Fencik said the Super Bowl championship, earned with a 46-10 win over the Patriots, completed his career. Still, he felt compelled to put off full-time investment and mortgage banking for two more seasons with the Bears. He started again for the excellent 1986 defense, then played his final season as a backup as Bell and Duerson started together.

His last game also was Payton's, the crushing 21-17 loss to the eventual champion Redskins in the NFC divisional round. Fencik earned the start as the Bears tried to address their seasonlong inability to force turnovers.

In retirement, Fencik remained a presence analyzing the Bears on TV and radio while putting his MBA to use. Living with his wife, Sandy, in Chicago, he is an executive for Adams Street Partners, an investment firm, after stints at UBS Bank and Wells Fargo—places he presumably hasn't had many coworkers once nicknamed "The Hit Man."

Before Fencik's final game, Pierson wrote that Fencik's choice to delay his business career was an easy one when faced with the opportunity to compete against some of the world's best athletes.

"It's a high that Wall Street or Madison Avenue or the Ivy League or Hollywood cannot match," Pierson wrote in the Jan. 8, 1988, Tribune. "Not even being mayor of Chicago compares to the power experienced by a football player who has just intercepted a pass with millions of people watching, thousands cheering, 11 chasing." ■

Gary Fencik (45) leaves Soldier Field after a game in January 1988.

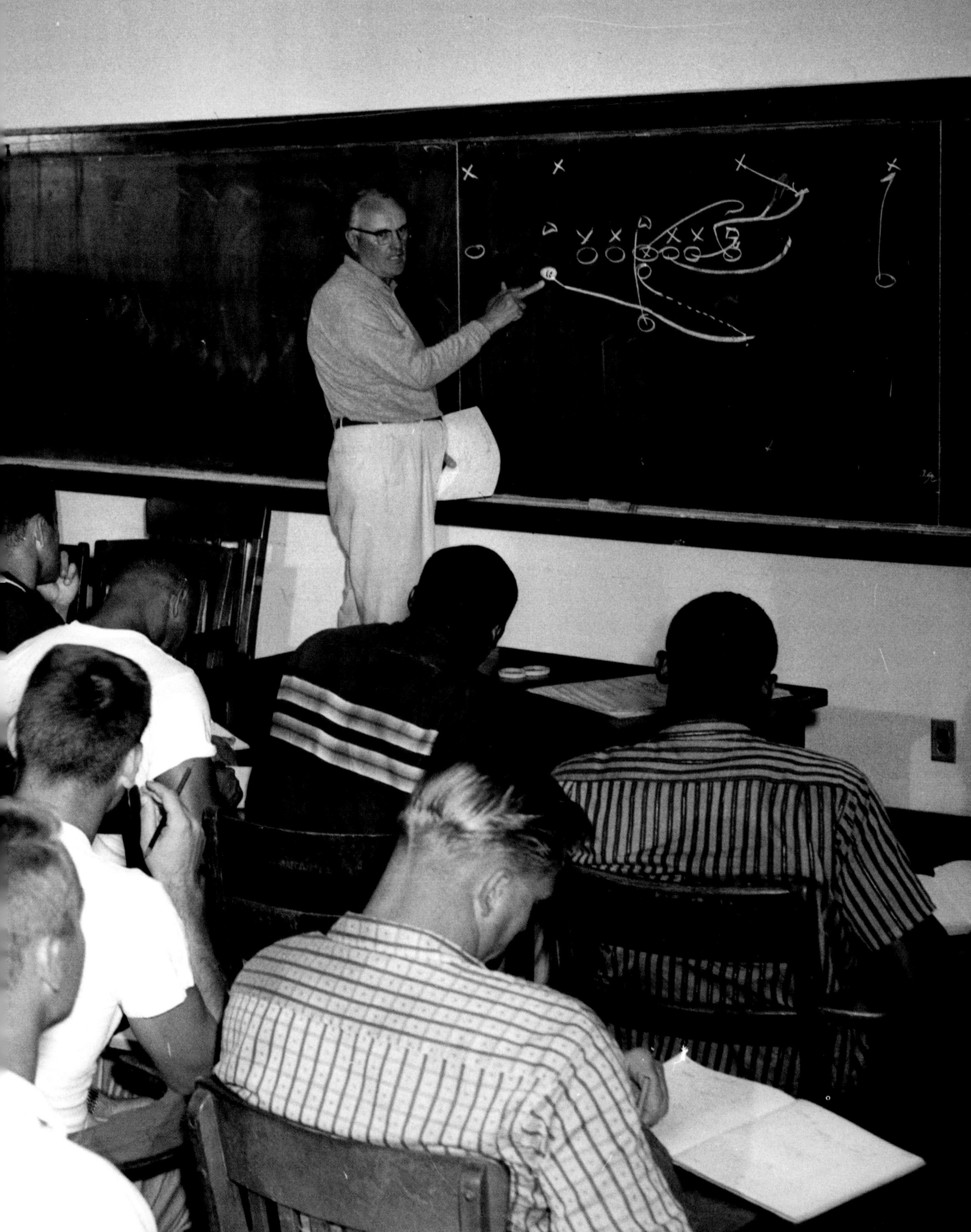

40

Luke Johnsos

24 END, ASSISTANT COACH, CO-HEAD COACH
1929-36, 1937-69

DURING HIS 40 YEARS with the Bears, Luke Johnsos' mind usually was a step or two ahead of his opponents. "The Professor" always looked for a mental edge, and more often than not he found it.

In 1932 against the Giants, Johnsos, a 6-foot-2, 195-pound end, scored the game's only touchdown when he pretended to tie his shoe near the sideline, caught a pass from Keith Molesworth uncovered and waltzed 29 yards into the end zone.

Bears coach George Halas claimed Johnsos once tricked former teammate Eggs Manske of the Eagles into lateraling him the ball.

"They had been very successful lateraling to each other," Halas wrote in "Halas by Halas," his 1979 autobiography. "In our next game (against him), Eggs took a pass and was well on his way to a touchdown.

"Luke was near but couldn't catch Eggs. He called out, 'Lateral, Eggs, lateral,' just as he had in the former days. Eggs didn't even look around. Luke's voice told him Luke was in the proper position, four steps to the side, two behind. Eggs tossed the ball. Luke caught it, stopped, turned around and ran."

Manske didn't play for the Bears until 1937, the year after Johnsos retired, but it's possible Halas remembered the play correctly with the wrong player.

Johnsos' mind was even more valuable as a Bears assistant coach. In 1940 he was the first coach to leave the sideline for the press box and its eye-in-the-sky view that helped diagnose formations and exploit weaknesses in them. Johnsos first used runners to take written information to Halas before the Bears installed telephones in the press box and on the sideline for quicker communication.

"He was the man up on the phone in the stadium, who can be tremendously important if you have confidence in him," Mike Ditka told the Tribune's Kenan Heise on Dec. 11, 1984. "He has to resist watching the ball carrier and follow the point of attack or look for patterns on defense."

Johnsos grew up in Logan Square, played football and baseball at Schurz High School, then played those sports plus basketball at Northwestern. He led the Big Ten with nine home runs in 12 games in 1928 and signed with the Reds, but his poor eyesight precluded a major league career.

Luke Johnsos, an offensive coach for the team in 1960, diagrams a play during training camp in Rensselaer, Ind.

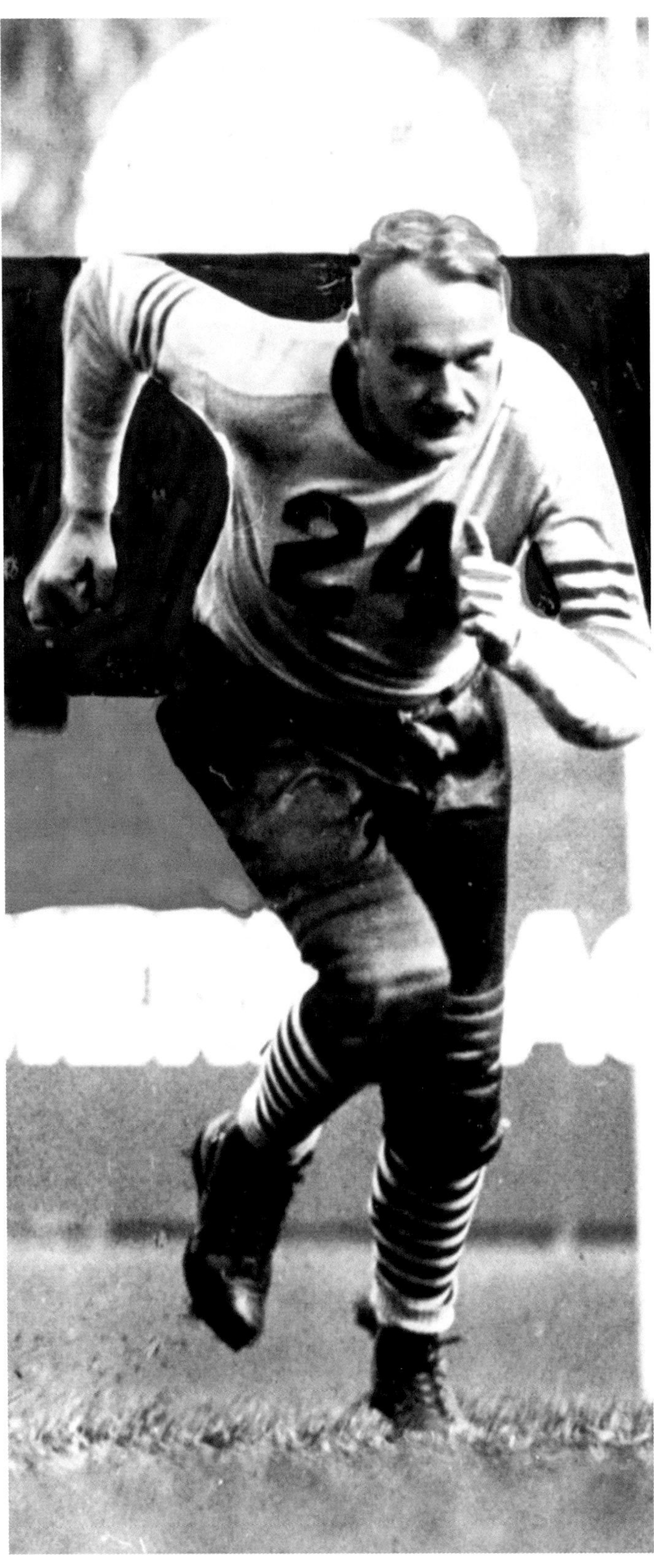

Instead, he caught on with the Bears as a throw-in with a more desired teammate. Halas offered Wildcats fullback Walt Holmer a $5,000-per-year contract, but Holmer said he wouldn't sign unless the Bears took Johnsos as well. Halas agreed, adding the end for $100 per game for the 1929 season.

"I was only bait for Holmer," Johnsos said in "Halas by Halas." "I thought it was kind of funny, but when we began playing, the humor departed. Holmer didn't make the (starting) team. I was out there getting the devil kicked out of me for a hundred bucks, and Holmer was getting his $5,000 sitting on the bench."

Johnsos more than held his own for the next eight years. He was named first-team All-Pro in 1930 and '31 and second-team in 1929 and '32. He helped the Bears win NFL championships in 1932, when he was second in the league with 19 receptions and 321 yards, and '33, when he caught an NFL-best three touchdowns.

In 1932 he scored four touchdowns: two receiving, one interception return and a blocked-punt return.

Johnsos totaled 22 touchdowns, 11 point-after kicks and one field goal for 146 career points. His field goal provided the winning points in a 9-6 victory over the Portsmouth Spartans in 1931. In his final year, 1936, he served as a player-coach, assisting Halas with the offense.

At 31, Johnsos was the third-oldest player in the NFL when he retired. Over the next three decades, his coaching career mirrored the Bears' ups and downs.

When Halas left to fight in World War II in the middle of the 1942 season, he named Johnsos and Hunk Anderson co-coaches in his absence.

"The division could have caused trouble but didn't," Johnsos said in Halas' book. "Neither of us told the other what to do. The team played both ways."

Johnsos coached the offense and Anderson the defense as the two-time defending champion Bears finished the 1942 regular season 11-0 but lost to the Giants 30-13 in the NFL

Luke Johnsos (25) in November 1935.

championship game. The Bears bounced back the next season to win their third NFL title in four years with a 41-21 win over the Redskins.

"Hunk and I felt pretty good," Johnsos said. "We had gone through that year without Halas. . . . Yet we achieved the championship."

Nineteen of the Bears' 28 players joined Halas serving overseas in 1944 as the war intensified. The Bears fell to 6-3-1 that season and 3-7 in 1945.

"We held tryouts at Cubs Park and signed up anybody who could run around the field twice," Johnsos said. "We had a very poor ballclub."

Halas returned to coach the 1946 team. As he wrote: "I found the Bears were quite different from the team I had left three years earlier. Luke Johnsos had kept me informed, somewhat. When we won, he sent a cable. When we lost, he wrote a letter. I think sometimes he put the letter in a bottle and dropped it into Lake Michigan."

With everybody back—including Halas and stars Sid Luckman, Bulldog Turner, George McAfee, Danny Fortmann and Bill Osmanski—the Bears rolled to their fourth championship of the decade.

In 1948, with former Bears great Red Grange, Johnsos hosted "The Bears Quarterback Club," a half-hour highlight show broadcast to TVs in the Chicago area. It did big ratings and was a precursor to televised games.

Things progressed smoothly for Johnsos until 1956, when Halas relinquished his coaching duties for the third time and was set to promote his successor from within.

Johnsos was slated to get the job, and the Chicago American got the scoop. Someone at the newspaper tipped Halas that they had the story. Halas, who favored the Tribune and often fed its writers breaking news, retaliated by telling the Tribune's Wilfrid Smith that assistant coach and former star halfback Paddy Driscoll, not Johnsos, would be the Bears' next coach.

Smith wrote that Driscoll was the "logical choice" to follow Halas. Johnsos seethed at the betrayal.

In his 2005 biography, "Papa Bear: The Life and Legacy of George Halas," Jeff Davis wrote: "Johnsos had proved his worth at all levels. He was a dedicated player for Halas from the time he joined the club in 1929 out of Northwestern and a loyal liege as an assistant from 1941 on. While the Old Man served with the Navy in the Pacific, Johnsos and Anderson guided the Bears to the 1943 title. He passed his tests with flying colors. Driscoll had much thinner coaching credentials."

In time, most came to believe that Johnsos himself fed the news of his hiring to the American.

"Halas had, in fact, likely told Johnsos the job was his, but he would have considered such a leak, especially to the 'wrong' paper, far worse than insubordination," Davis wrote. "To Halas, this was an act of betrayal."

Johnsos swallowed his pride and went along with the new setup, remaining an assistant until 1968. Driscoll coached the Bears for two years, including the 1956 NFL runner-up season, before Halas reinserted himself on the sideline.

In the 1963 championship game, Johnsos called a special play for Ditka at tight end that led to Bill Wade's winning quarterback sneak in the 14-10 win against the Giants.

Off the field, Johnsos owned a printing and packaging business with Charles Coppock, father of longtime Chicago sportcaster Chet Coppock. Johnsos died at 79 in Evanston in 1984.

Through all of his good and bad times with Halas, Johnsos never seriously considered leaving the Bears. He turned down at least one head coaching offer from the Cleveland Rams in 1945.

"I've always been a Bear and hope to spend my entire football career with George Halas," he told the Tribune. "He's good enough for my dough. Besides, this is my home, and I hold another position here. It is simple enough to solve: Two good jobs in Chicago are better than one in Cleveland."

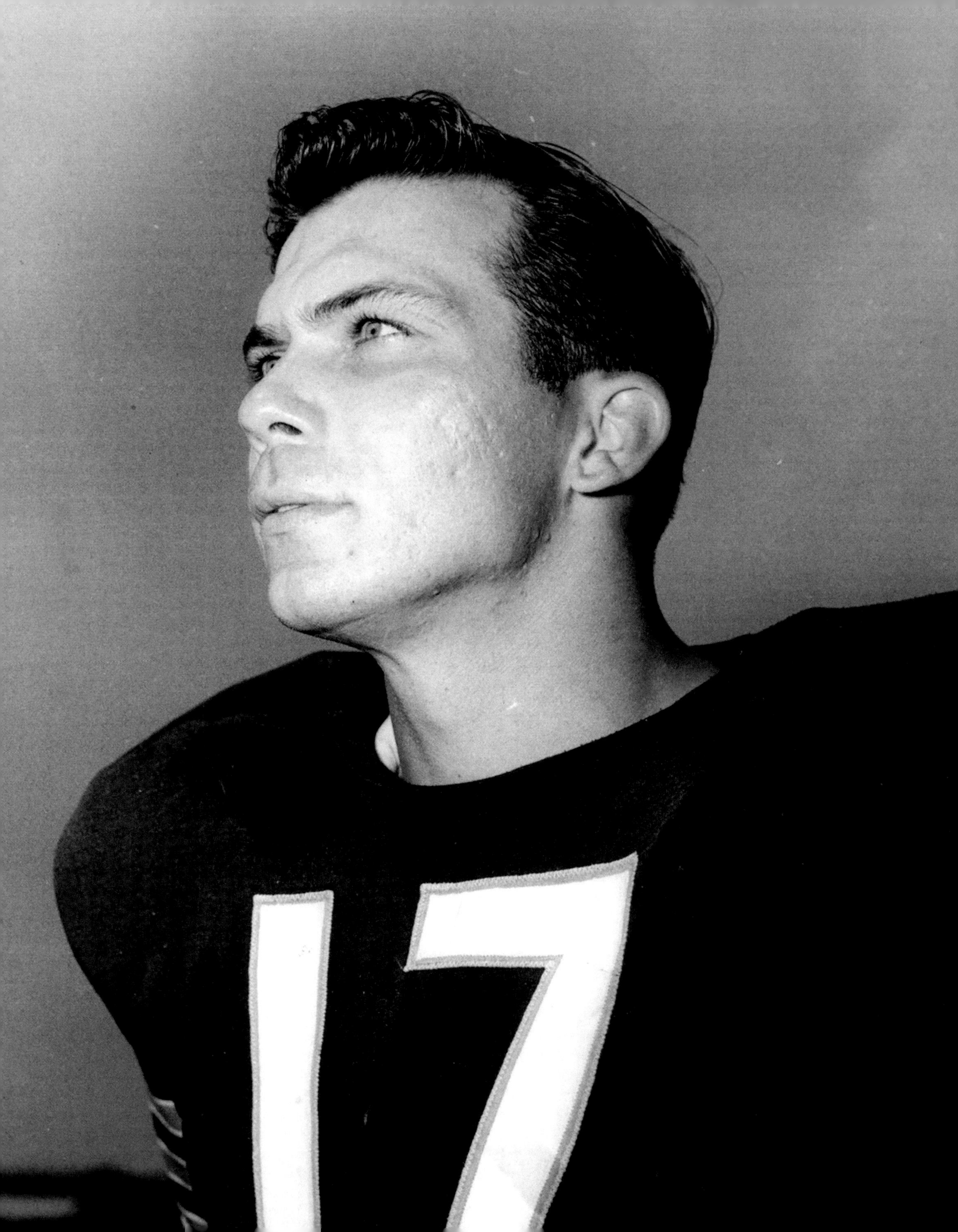

Richie Petitbon

41

17 SAFETY
1959-68

Richie Petitbon's easiest interception was his greatest.

The strong safety held the Bears record of 37 picks for 23 years until Gary Fencik passed it by one in 1986. Petitbon grabbed many of them using his 6-foot-3 height to reach over receivers or his sprinter's speed to maneuver around them.

On Dec. 29, 1963, all he had to do was wait for a falling wobbler. With two seconds left in the NFL championship game and the Bears nursing a four-point lead, Giants quarterback Y.A. Tittle reached back for a desperation heave to the end zone. The ball found its way to Petitbon, who cradled it in to clinch the 14-10 victory.

In his column in the next day's Tribune, David Condon wrote: "That catch was payday at the mill, Christmas at home, the kiss from the best gal, a double shot of 100 proof. This was the fuse that put the Bear fans into orbit."

The interception was the fifth of the day for Tittle by five Bears. Petitbon followed picks by Bennie McRae, Larry Morris, Dave Whitsell and Ed O'Bradovich as the Bears' dominant defense harassed the Hall of Fame quarterback into his worst day as a pro.

Giants receiver Del Shofner came into the title game with 64 receptions for 1,181 yards and nine touchdowns, and the Bears secondary shut him out. Frank Gifford had 42, 657 and seven during the season and three for 45 and a score against the Bears. Tittle passed for 36 touchdowns and 14 interceptions at a time when good quarterbacks broke even in the two categories. His ratio in the final was 1-5.

Coordinator Clark Shaughnessy molded the great defense, and his successor, George Allen, perfected it. Shaughnessy, an innovator on offense and defense, put in a system in which a basic defense was called, then a separate set of signals were relayed to Fred Williams for the line, Bill George for the linebackers and Petitbon for the backs. He also let his defensive backs play a combination of man-to-man and zone to confuse the offense.

Allen popularized the nickel defense, replacing a linebacker with an extra defensive back on passing downs.

"When it comes to football, Clark Shaughnessy is the only one I'd call a true genius," Petitbon told Warner Hessler of the Newport News (Va.) Daily Press on Aug. 29, 1993. "As

Richie Petitbon (17), circa 1963.

185

Few in NFL history knew defense like Richie Petitbon—knew how to play it, knew how to coach it.

—DALLAS MORNING NEWS COLUMNIST RICK GOSSELIN

with most geniuses, some of Clark's stuff was off the wall. . . . George took Clark's good stuff and threw out the bad."

One result was the Bears' best secondary ever. Petitbon, free safety Rosey Taylor and cornerbacks McRae and Whitsell all possessed speed, power and intelligence, and they worked tremendously in tandem. In the 1963 season they combined for 29 interceptions: Taylor with a league-high nine, Petitbon with eight and Whitsell and McRae with six apiece.

"We were doing a lot of things that nobody had done before," Petitbon told the Tribune's Dan Pompei on Sept. 1, 2013. "We caught the league napping on some things. The credit has to go to George Allen on that."

The Bears drafted Petitbon in the second round with the 21st pick in 1959, and he played every game for them in the next 10 years. He had been a star quarterback at Tulane, and even though Bears coach George Halas planned all along to use him as a defensive back, he let Petitbon play one series as a quarterback in a 1959 exhibition game.

His one pass was dropped by Lionel Taylor, and Halas cut Taylor and moved Petitbon permanently to defense. Taylor went on to become an All-Pro with the Broncos of the AFL, and Petitbon became one of the NFL's best safeties.

"Had the ball been caught, things might have been different," Petitbon told Hessler. "I feel I would have been a good quarterback. With a legitimate shot, I could have made it."

Petitbon, the son of a French immigrant, originally planned to become a dentist. He started studying for the profession while on a track-and-field scholarship to Loyola University in his hometown of New Orleans.

His hands proved too large to comfortably perform a dentist's delicate tasks, and track wasn't going well for him either as Loyola switched him from the 100- and 220-yard dashes to the grueling 440.

"After a few of those, I figured football couldn't be that tough," Petitbon told Hessler. "So I walked across the street to Tulane and asked if that football scholarship was still available. It was."

His speed served him well in his new sport. Petitbon's 37 interceptions came with a Bears-record 643 return yards. In 1962 he ran back six picks for 212 yards, including a team-record 101-yarder against the Rams on Dec. 9. In 1963 he gained 161 yards on eight interceptions.

Petitbon was named to the Pro Bowl after the 1962, '63, '66 and '67 seasons, tied with Dave Duerson for the most appearances by a Bears safety. Petitbon and Taylor were named the first-team All-Pro safeties in '63, and they're considered the best duo in team history ahead of Fencik and Doug Plank, Fencik and Todd Bell, Fencik and Duerson, Mark Carrier and Shaun Gayle and Mike Brown and Tony Parrish.

In 1985, 1994 and 2005, Tribune panels named Petitbon and Fencik the starting safeties on their all-time Bears teams.

Petitbon reunited with Allen twice after the Bears assistant left to become a head coach, first with the Rams in 1969-70 and then with the Redskins' "Over-the-Hill Gang" in 1971-72.

While his career as a player was outstanding, Petitbon was even better as an assistant coach. The Redskins' Jack Pardee hired him to coach his secondary in 1978, and in 1981 the team's new coach, Joe Gibbs, named

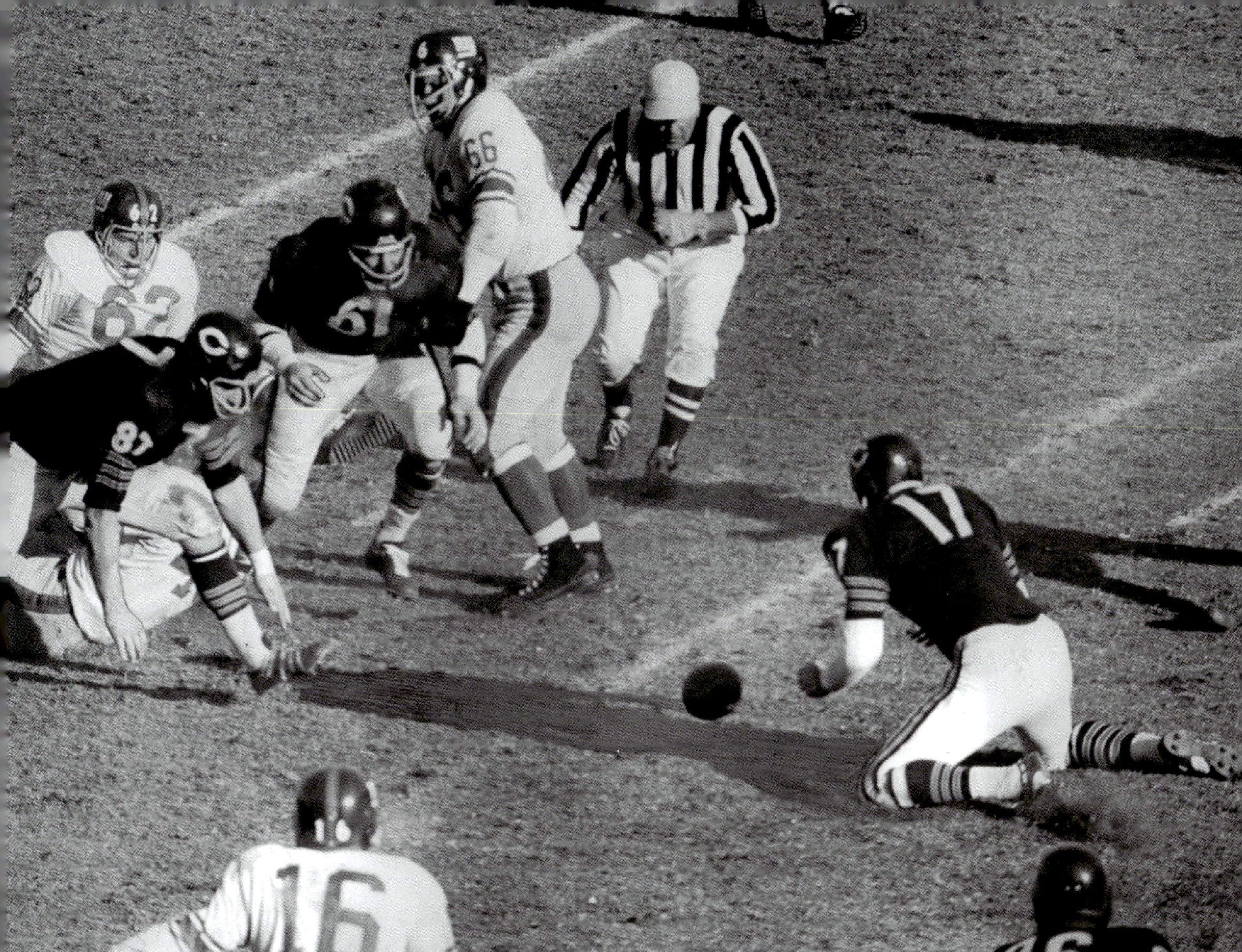

Petitbon his defensive coordinator. Gibbs ran the offense and Petitbon the defense for three Super Bowl champions, and Petitbon was added to the team's Ring of Honor in 2011.

"Few in NFL history knew defense like Richie Petitbon—knew how to play it, knew how to coach it," longtime Dallas Morning News columnist Rick Gosselin wrote in a Dec. 10, 2018, piece calling for Petitbon to be considered for the Pro Football Hall of Fame. "He was among the best at what he did as a player and among the best at what he did as a coach."

Nearly half of the league's teams at some point requested to interview Petitbon for head coaching positions, and he turned down all inquiries except two. His hometown Saints hired Jim Mora over Petitbon in 1986, and the Bears chose Dave Wannstedt in 1993.

Petitbon became a head coach after 16 years as an assistant when the Redskins named him Joe Gibbs' successor in 1993 after Gibbs retired to focus on his NASCAR team. Petitbon went 4-12 in his only season before the Redskins fired him. He never returned to coaching, and he is enjoying retirement.

For his Bears teammates, Petitbon's success on the sidelines was not a surprise.

"Richie had this funny way of talking, and I remember he was a smart player," defensive end Doug Atkins told Hessler. "You know, it seemed like he studied football a lot more than the rest of us." ■

Richie Petitbon (17) pounces on a fumble by Joe Morrison (40) of New York on Dec. 29, 1963, at Wrigley Field.

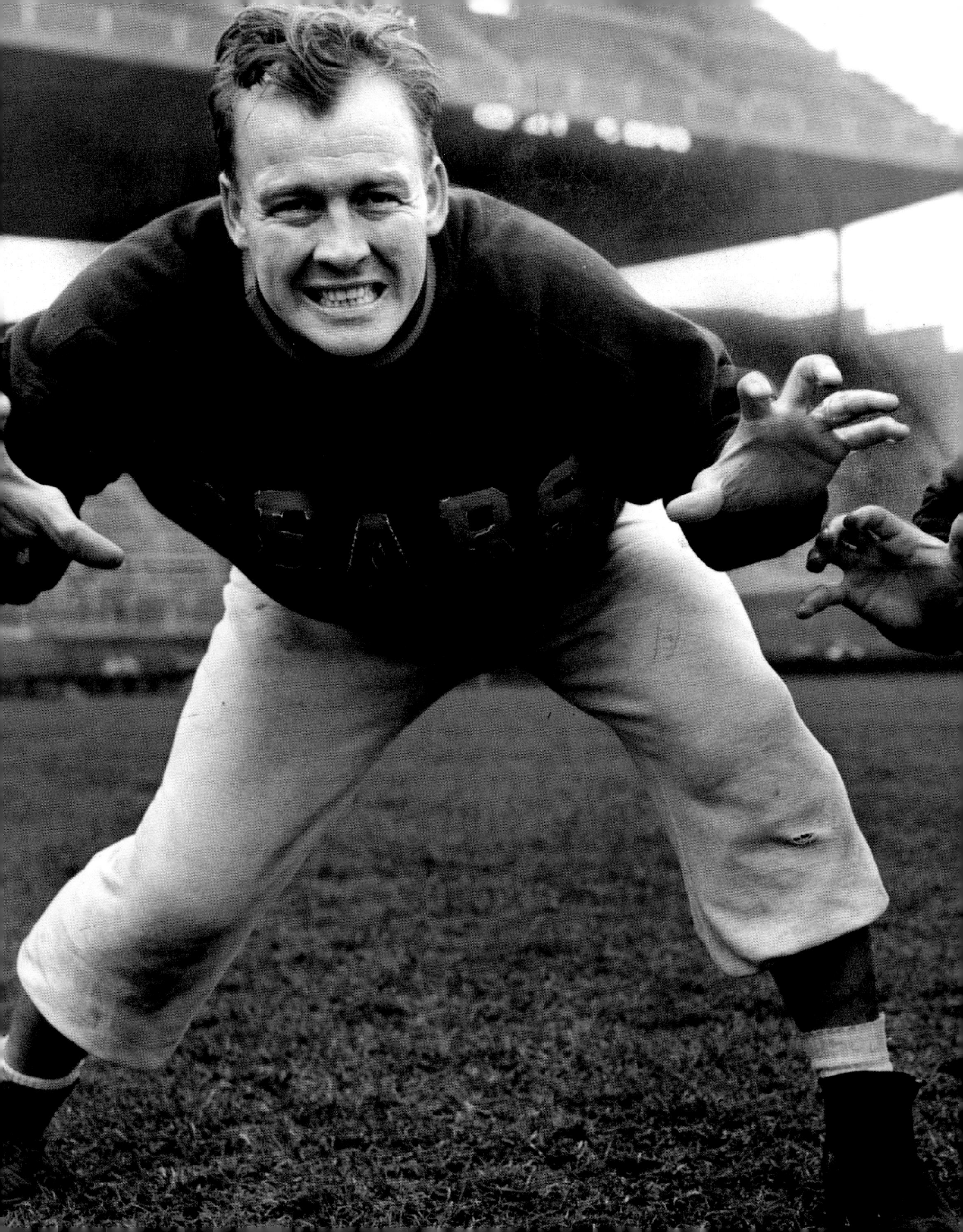

42

Ray Bray

BEARS ROSTERS OF THE 1940s were filled with the names of intimidating men, ones who earned the nickname "The Monsters of the Midway" while winning four NFL championships.

Bulldog Turner, Joe Stydahar, Danny Fortmann, George Musso, Bill Osmanski, George Wilson, Aldo Forte, Ed Kolman and Hampton Pool were among the Bears' toughest players.

Ray Bray, the right guard nicknamed "Muscles," was the one guy not to mess with.

George Connor was by all accounts the Bears' toughest player of the 1950s. His career overlapped with Bray's from 1948 to '51.

"Bray was the strongest man I ever saw," Connor told Jeff Davis in his 2005 book, "Papa Bear: The Life and Legacy of George Halas." "He could do 50 one-armed push-ups, switch hands and knock off 50 more with ease."

Solly Sherman, a backup quarterback from 1939-40, told the Tribune's Don Pierson on Dec. 9, 1990, that Bray "could pick up a car to change a tire."

Bray left an open invitation to the rest of the Bears. If one thought he was tougher than Bray, a wrestling match would determine whether he was right. Not many took the bait.

Ed Neal, acquired from the Packers in 1951, was one. Despite being two years younger and 40 pounds heavier than Bray, Neal's attempt went the same way all other comers' did.

Bray was even meaner to his opponents, particularly the Packers. Hal Van Every, a halfback in 1941-42, recalled in Gary D'Amato's and Cliff Christl's 1997 book, "Mudbaths and Bloodbaths: The Inside Story of the Bears-Packers Rivalry," that Bray "was the worst. He'd slug you in the face any time. He'd make a charge and he'd start out with his fist down low to the ground and he'd come up and hit you right in the face. . . . He'd level you. Ray Bray. I remember him above all of them."

Bray did not become a great player until he learned to curb his temper and his appetite. He regularly was ejected from games as a young player and struggled to pass coach George Halas' infamous weigh-ins. Musso helped his teammate learn to conquer both adversaries until he became a 6-foot, 237-pound slab of well-controlled muscle.

Ray Bray (82) was a defensive lineman on three NFL championship teams.

"Bray says that year-around exercise and avoidance of fatty foods are his secrets," the Tribune's Edward Prell wrote on Nov. 16, 1951.

"In the winter I play handball and in the summer it's tennis," Bray told Prell. "I eat a lot of meat. During the season I have a two-pound steak every day, with salad and vegetables. If I didn't watch myself during the offseason, I'd weigh at least 260 when football time came around."

The Bears selected Bray in the ninth round of the 1939 draft out of Western Michigan, eight rounds after taking Sid Luckman and Osmanski. Bray was a backup in 1939 and for the 1940 NFL champions, moved into the starting lineup for the 1941 champs and the great '42 runners-up, then served in the Navy in World War II for three years.

Bray returned a better player, starting 58 of 70 games from 1946 to '51 while being named second-team All-Pro in 1949 and '50 and to the Pro Bowl in 1950 and '51.

He was one of 17 Bears, including Halas, who returned from battle to lead the dominant Bears to the 1946 NFL title. Bray's most enduring moment came during the 24-14 win in the

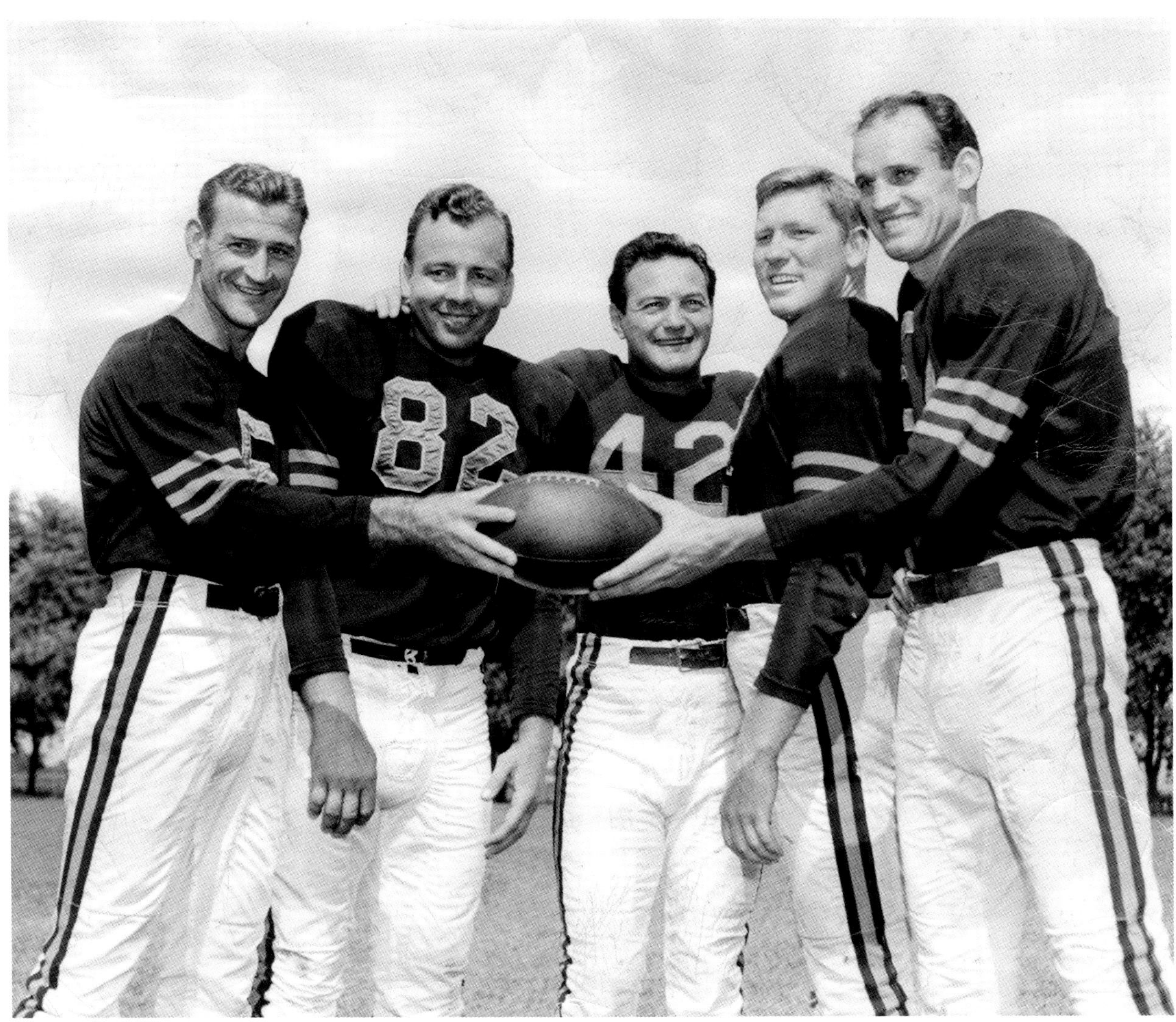

In 1949, five players remained from the 1940 championship squad: George McAfee (5), from left, Ray Bray (82), Sid Luckman (42), Bulldog Turner (66) and Ken Kavanaugh (51).

championship game against the Giants on Dec. 15 at the Polo Grounds.

The score was tied 14-14 early in the fourth quarter. Halas, aided by assistant coach Luke Johnsos in the stands above the action, called a new play, "Bingo Keep It," which called for Luckman to fake to halfback George McAfee and run a quarterback keeper in the other direction.

"The Giant line—which had been smashing Chicago running plays all afternoon—poured through and overwhelmed McAfee," William Fay wrote in the Tribune's game story. "Luckman kept the ball and whirled to the right without interference."

Fay continued on Aug. 7, 1947: "Bray knocked down two Giants. . . . When the Bears huddled in the end zone, Ray received more back pats than Sid."

"That's the one thing about the Bears," Chuck Drulis, the team's other guard, told Fay. "The backs always know where their last block came from. I can't remember a touchdown run when the carrier didn't give a thank-you slap on the pants of the blocker."

Drulis was one of three great guards Bray teamed with in tandem with center Turner in the middle of the Bears lines. He played with Hall of Famer Fortmann in 1941-42 and All-Pro Dick Barwegan in 1950.

Guard might be the most unheralded position on the field, but the Bears have had their share of great ones. Eleven players on the Tribune's list of the top 100 Bears played the position primarily.

Of those great players, Bray was one of the best. In 1986, a Tribune survey of its football writers named Bray and Fortmann the team's all-time starting guards. In 1994, Don Pierson and Fred Mitchell picked Bray and Stan Jones.

Bray ended his career with one season with the Packers in 1952 as coach Gene Ronzani, a former Bears halfback, populated his roster and staff with players the Bears had cut. Ronzani lasted only four seasons as coach in Green Bay, going 14-31-1 from 1950 to '53.

Toward the end of his career, Bray continually threatened to retire, but as he told Prell in 1951, "When a new season rolls around, I feel so good I decide to play one more year."

Bray finally did walk away at 35 after the 1952 season, his 11th in the NFL. He went on to a successful career selling Cadillacs. The native of Caspian, Mich., died at 76 in Mesa, Ariz., on Dec. 26, 1993. ■

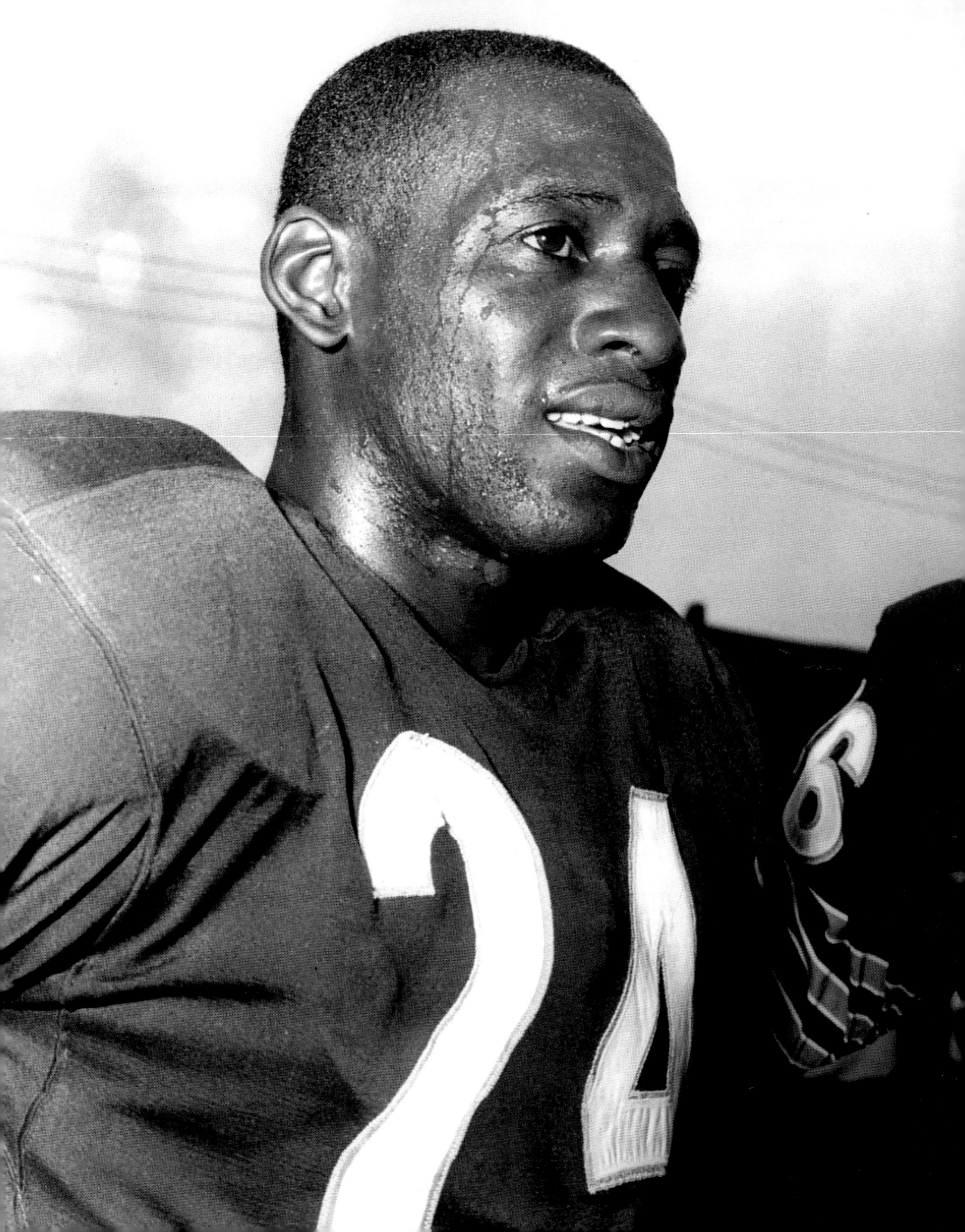

Rosey Taylor

24 SAFETY
1961–69

THE 1963 BEARS DEFENSE was one of the best in NFL history. Rosey Taylor was one of the biggest reasons why.

Taylor had a knack for big plays in his 12-year NFL career, and he was at his peak in '63. For a team that allowed the fewest points, total yards, passing yards and rushing yards in the league while forcing the most turnovers, Taylor had nine interceptions and three fumble recoveries.

The 12 takeaways are tied for a franchise season record 56 years later. Taylor's 23 interceptions in nine seasons with the Bears rank 10th in team history.

He wasn't done when he caught an interception, either. His 23 returns with the Bears went for 414 yards, an average of 18 yards per runback. He returned three picks for touchdowns and another fumble recovery for a score.

"(Bears defensive coordinator) George Allen taught me the most important thing there is for a defensive back to know in football," Taylor told the Tribune's Cooper Rollow on Nov. 1, 1964. "He pounded it into me that once that ball goes up in the air, it belongs to anybody who can get it."

Small even for a free safety of his time at 5-foot-11 and 186 pounds, Taylor usually was as fast as any player on the field and almost always had the highest vertical leap.

Rollow wrote: "Bear opponents have learned, to their dismay, that the odds somehow seem to favor Taylor in what often appears to be an even battle for the ball. Several reasons have been cited for this edge—competitive instinct, eyesight, reflexes—but the key may be Taylor's tremendous jumping ability."

"That's one of the big reasons I made the pros," Taylor told Edmund W. Lewis of Louisiana Weekly on Aug. 6, 2012. "When they saw me jump up and grab the crossbar on the goal post, it was over with."

After emerging from the rough Lower Ninth Ward of New Orleans, Taylor carried himself with a quiet confidence. Later in his career he felt that if he had been more boastful he would have received more recognition than his two Pro Bowl appearances, in 1963 and '68. He was named first-team All-Pro in '63 and second-team in '65.

"In 1963 . . . Larry Wilson of the Cardinals and Willie Wood of the Packers were getting

Rosey Taylor (24), circa 1963.

all the publicity as being the best free safeties in the game," Taylor explained to the Tribune's George Langford on Oct. 10, 1969. "A reporter asked me about it and I said: 'The fans need to stop and watch me. I'm doing a hell of a job.' Well, the story was blown out of proportion a little, but people did watch me and they saw. And the league office recognized me and I made every All-Pro team in the U.S.

"I haven't talked about myself since and I haven't made an All-Pro team since. Sure, I think I'm still the best. Have you ever seen anybody who didn't?"

Likewise, he feels the 1963 defense has not been properly recognized for its place in NFL history. That team allowed 10.3 points per game compared with the 1985 Bears' 12.4.

Taylor told the Tribune's Terry Bannon on Sept. 9, 2004: "The '63 team has been given so little credit, but we did so many things nobody's touched since. We led the league in interceptions with (36) in a 14-game season. If it was done nowadays, they'd be America's Team."

Those who studied Taylor's play knew how good he was. He was described by Tribune sports writers during his career as a "super safety," "the best in the league at his job," "the dandy little defensive back from New Orleans" and "pro football's slickest free safety."

Taylor attended Grambling State to play basketball but was cut from the team twice. He turned to Eddie Robinson's football team, caught on and played well enough to earn three varsity letters, but he never cracked the regular starting lineup.

The Bears discovered him when Allen traveled to Grambling, La., to try to sign defensive tackle Ernie Ladd, whom the Bears selected in the fourth round of the 1961 draft. Ladd would sign with the AFL's Chargers, but Robinson told Allen that Taylor was worth a look.

That Taylor was good enough to start for 11 years in the NFL was testament to how much talent Grambling had at the time. Taylor and Ladd were two of four future All-Pros on the 1960 SWAC champions with Pro Football Hall of Famers Buck Buchanan and Willie Brown. In 1971 Grambling had 43 former players in the NFL, more than any other college.

"It's generally accepted that on a given day several of Robinson's teams in the '60s could have beaten any school in the country," Sports Illustrated's Rick Telander wrote in the Sept. 1, 1983, issue.

"(We) would have beat the living hell out of the best—Michigan State, Ohio State and all these schools—if we could have played against them," Taylor told Lewis.

The Bears signed Taylor as an undrafted free agent and made him a backup cornerback to J.C. Caroline and Dave Whitsell in '61. Taylor never forgot his "Welcome to the NFL" moment.

"Tommy McDonald, then an Eagle star, was the receiver," Taylor told Rollow. "Not only did he fake me out of my socks and run past me like I was a Boy Scout, but when I recovered and jumped up to try to knock the ball down, I missed it and landed facedown. I bloodied my nose, got dirt in both eyes, and when I got up, everybody on the team was glaring at me."

The Bears shifted Taylor to free safety in his second year, and he stayed in the starting lineup the rest of his career. He made one of the biggest plays of the 1963 championship game, tackling the Giants' Hugh McElhenny after he had broken free on a kickoff return to save a touchdown in the 14-10 win.

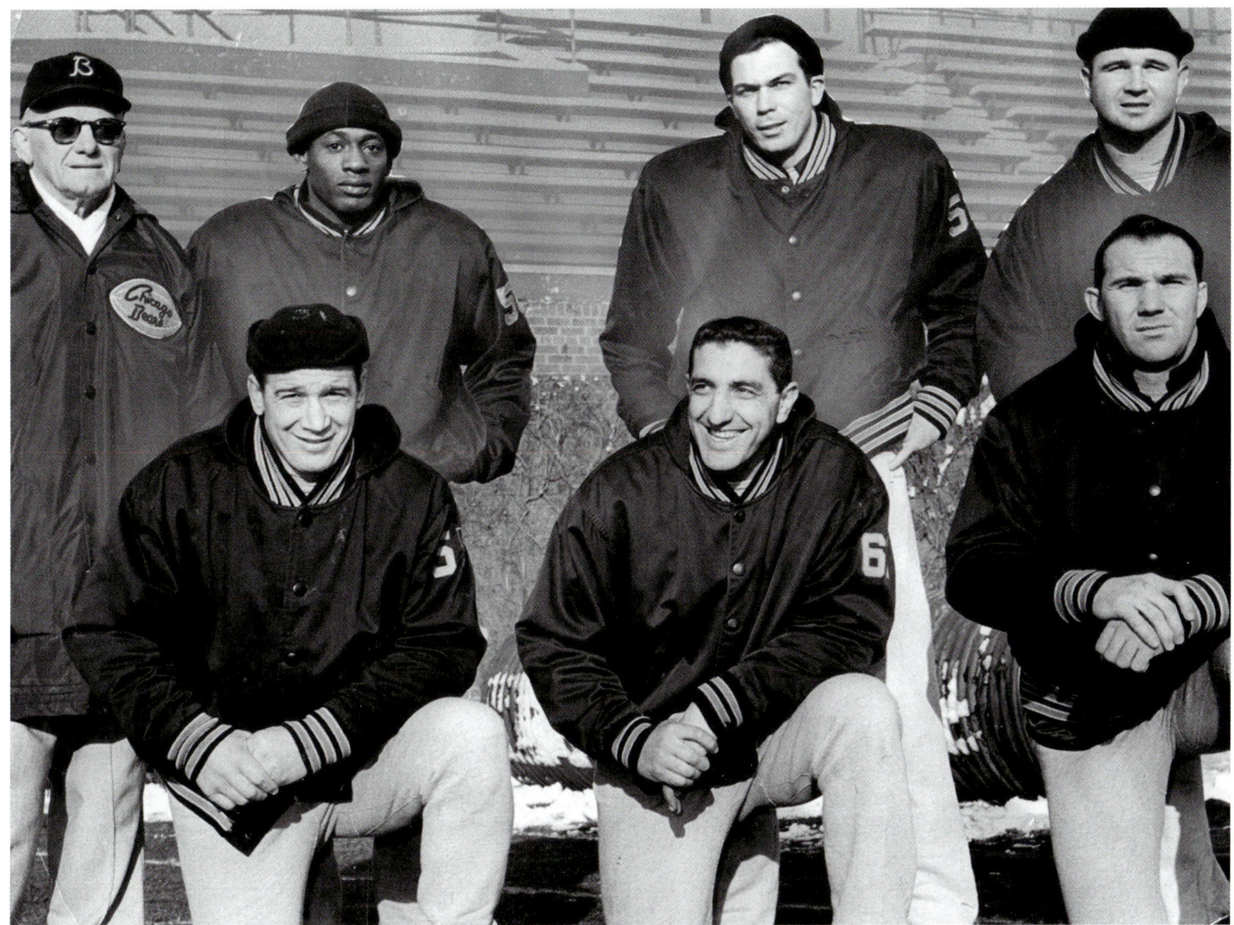

Coach George Halas stands proudly with six players who made the All-Pro team in 1963. Back row, from left, are Halas, Rosey Taylor (24), Richie Petitbon (17) and Mike Ditka (89). Front row, from left, are Joe Fortunato (31), Bill George (61) and Doug Atkins (81).

"It was my biggest thrill in football," Taylor told Rollow. "I had the last shot at him. I let him wiggle and shake his head, but finally he had to make a move, and then I got him low."

The Bears failed to turn their championship into a run of success, though, and steadily got worse as the decade progressed. They traded Taylor to the 49ers in the middle of the 1969 season for guard Howard Mudd.

Trading the 32-year-old Taylor for the 27-year-old Mudd seemed like a good idea. Mudd had been named to the Pro Bowl the previous three seasons, and the Bears badly needed offensive linemen. A serious knee injury limited Mudd to 18 games after the trade, though, while Taylor played 48 and remained an NFL starter through 1972.

His last season, at 35, was one of his best. Taylor started all 14 games for the 1972 Redskins, who went 11-3 and cruised through the NFC playoffs before losing Super Bowl VII 14-7 to the undefeated Dolphins. The season reunited Taylor with his old defensive coordinator, Allen, the Redskins' head coach.

During his career, Taylor spent his offseasons as a teacher and an insurance salesman. After his playing days he operated 17 businesses. Brian Taylor, one of the three children of Taylor and his wife, Claudia, played five games with the Bears in 1989 and three with the Bills in '91. Rosey Taylor died May 29, 2020. He was 82. ■

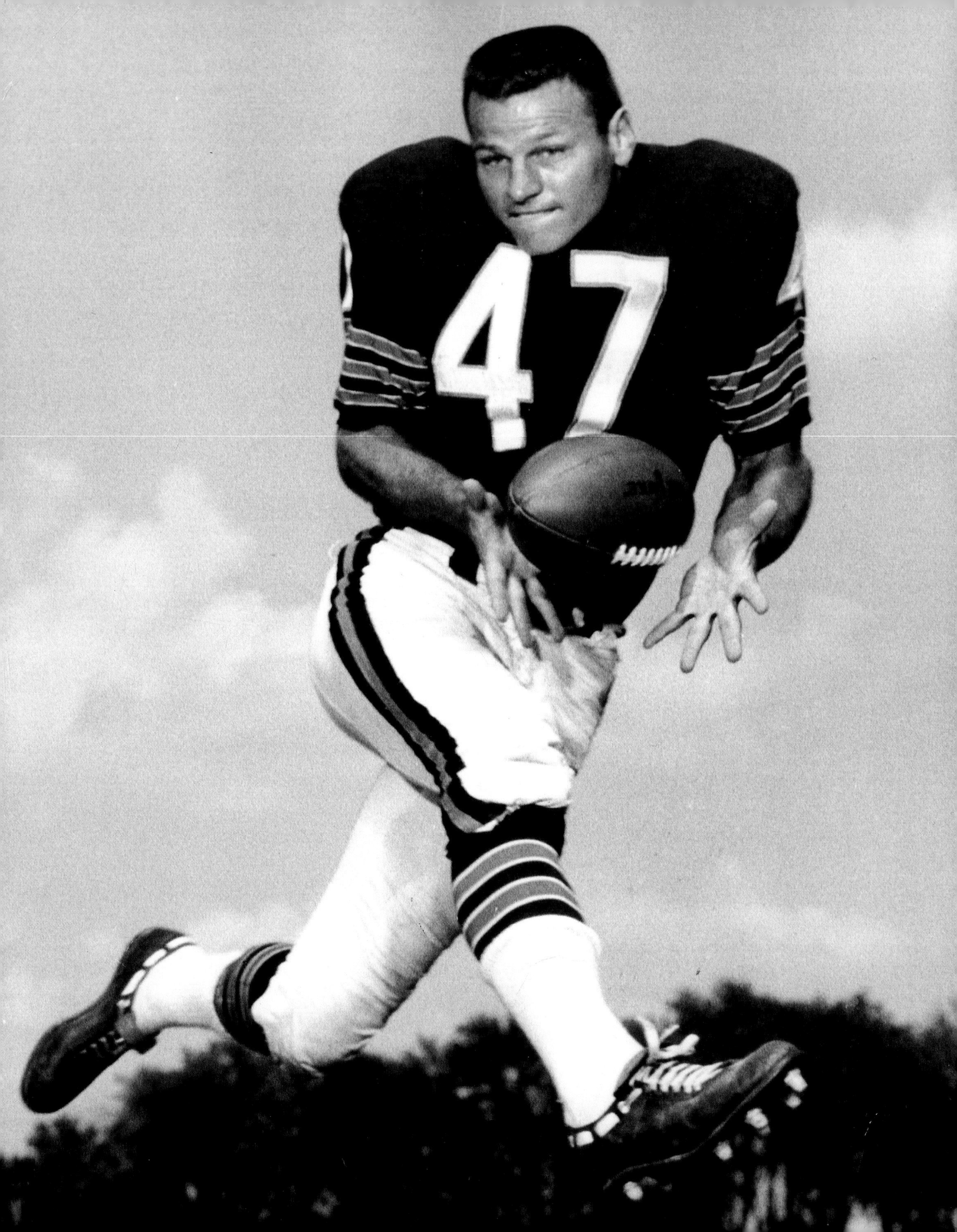

Johnny Morris

J OE DiMAGGIO HIT SAFELY in 56 consecutive games. Wayne Gretzky scored 2,857 points. Brett Favre started 321 consecutive games; Cal Ripken Jr. played in 2,632 straight. Cy Young earned 511 wins.

Johnny Morris' Bears record for career receiving yardage isn't mentioned among sports' unbreakable records. Perhaps it should be. After all, even though his total of 5,059 yards is the lowest of any of the 32 NFL teams' receiving records, he has held it for 54 years—the longest of any franchise leader, with only Don Maynard's 47 years as the Jets record holder (11,732 yards) close.

Bears receivers haven't had the combination of talent, opportunity and longevity needed to pass Morris, who played his last season in 1967. For an idea of what the Bears offense has looked like over the last 50 years, the only two players with more receptions than Morris' 356 are running backs Walter Payton (492) and Matt Forte (487).

Any receiver who has come close to Morris' mark left the Bears as he approached it. Curtis Conway signed with the Chargers as a free agent in 2000 after gaining 4,498 receiving yards with the Bears, 561 short of Morris. Marty Booker had 3,895 yards—1,164 shy—when the Bears traded him to the Dolphins for Adewale Ogunleye in 2004. Alshon Jeffery was 27 and only 510 yards behind Morris with 4,549 when he signed with the Eagles in 2017.

"Contrary to perception, Chicago Bears receiving records are not kept in manuscript form and filed away under 'Medieval Monsters of the Midway.' It's also untrue that they were last updated by a monk with a quill pen who was adept at calligraphy. But crack open those statistics and the dust flies."

The Tribune's Mike Kiley wrote that on Sept. 10, 1995.

Twenty-six years ago.

"We have been in the dark ages for years," Morris told Kiley. "Can you imagine, there have been cities who have seen modern passing games for years and, finally, Chicago may be one of them. I see light at the end of the tunnel."

Morris' short-lived excitement stemmed from Conway and Jeff Graham, who while playing with quarterback Erik Kramer became the first Bears teammates to crack the 1,000-yard receiving mark in the same season in 1995.

Johnny Morris (47), circa 1964.

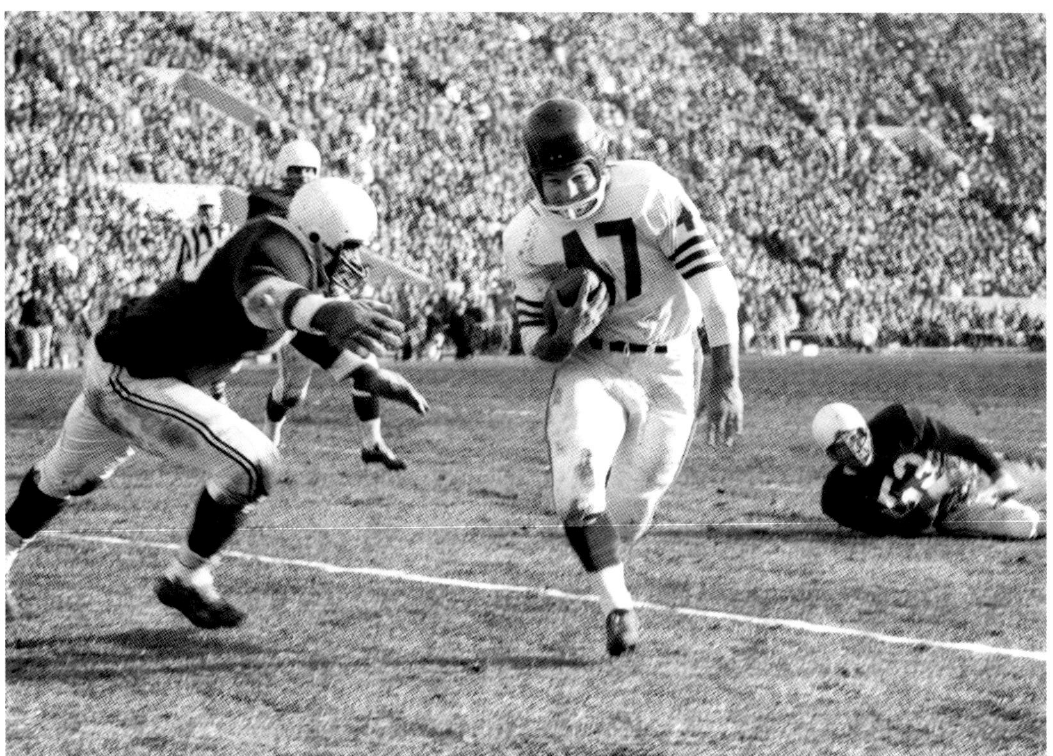

Johnny Morris (47) on Nov. 29, 1959, during a game against the Cardinals at Soldier Field.

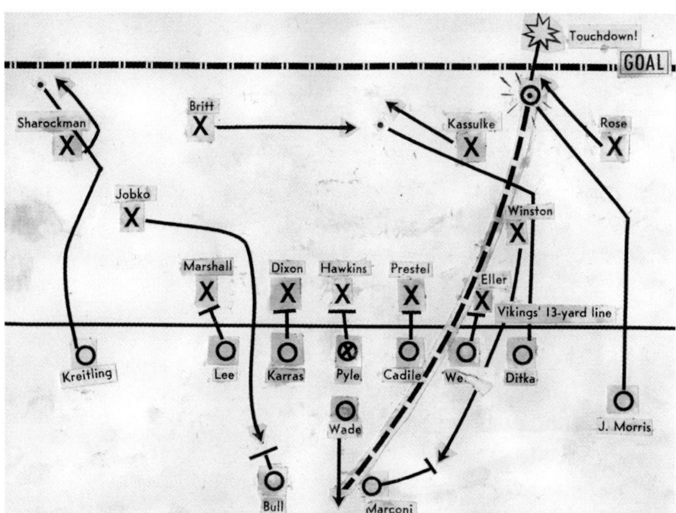

The play that put the Chicago Bears ahead 14-7 in the second quarter of a game against the Minnesota Vikings on Sept. 20, 1964: Bill Wade to Johnny Morris. This same play also scored the team's third touchdown (Wade to Morris) and then set up No. 4. All told, Morris caught 10 passes for 135 yards in the 34-28 victory.

The record turned out to be safe, though, as it will be for at least the next few years.

Fifty-four years after his last game, Morris still gets questions about his receiving record and what it says about his former team.

"It's shocking, actually," he said in June 2019 at the Bears100 Celebration Weekend. "There's a couple guys that would have broken it, but they were traded and moved on. It'll be broken one of these days. But when you throw 50 passes a game and probably run 20 times—back in our game, we ran 50 times and threw 20—that's why I'm amazed it hasn't been broken."

Morris held another long-standing record that held more leaguewide significance. During his landmark 1964 season, he led the NFL with 1,200 receiving yards and 10 touchdown catches, and his 93 receptions broke the record of 84 set by the Rams' Tom Fears in 1950. Morris' mark stood for 20 years until the Redskins' Art Monk caught 106 passes in 1984.

The Bears never expected anywhere close to that production from Morris when they drafted him in the 12th round out of UC Santa Barbara in 1958. The 5-foot-10, 180-pound halfback played mostly special teams at first and became an outstanding punt returner. He made the Pro Bowl as a returner in 1960, then switched to flanker, where he started for six seasons. Morris' easygoing personality, California good looks and TV-ready grin belied how tough he was as a player.

A knee injury sapped Morris' effectiveness for his final few seasons. When he failed to get to the corner on an end around, George Connor, Hall of Fame tackle and Bears color commentator, said on the game broadcast that it "looks like Morris has lost a couple of steps."

"It really bugged me when I heard about it," Morris told Tribune TV critic Gary Deeb on Aug. 5, 1975. "I was terribly upset. But what he said was true as hell. I guess that's what made me so mad."

The moment stuck with Morris, and he decided to approach things from Connor's perspective. Morris became one of the city's most popular TV broadcasters, starting out analyzing film during his final few years with the Bears before ascending to WBBM's sports anchor position.

"When I first started sportscasting, George Halas thought I was still a Chicago Bear," Morris told Deeb. "It was hard for him to accept me otherwise. And when I made constructive criticisms of the Bear operation, he kind of took it personally.

"I wish I could sit each athlete down and try to put things in proper perspective for him . . . 'cause I know exactly how these guys feel and I also know how a good sportscaster ought to perform."

Morris and Jeannie, his wife for 25 years before their amicable divorce, teamed up as anchor and features reporter as Jeannie helped pave a path for female journalists. Johnny Morris spent nearly his entire career at WBBM except for a six-year stretch at WMAQ. He returned to WBBM, along with Jeannie, in 1975, when news anchor Walter Jacobson recruited him to replace sports anchor Brent Musburger, who left Channel 2 for a job in New York.

Morris also served as a color commentator for NFL games on CBS, making sure his contract allowed for a certain number of Bears games. In the 1985 championship season, he and partner Tim Ryan broadcast seven of the Bears' 16 regular-season games.

Morris also hosted the "Mike Ditka Show" during the Bears coach's heyday. Some clips of the back and forth between the fiery Ditka and the laid-back Morris still are crowd-pleasers on Reddit and YouTube.

Morris was proud to excel at sportscasting on his terms. No dumb jock, he helped pioneer use of the telestrator on TV broadcasts.

"The former star flanker for the Chicago Bears is now probably the best of Chicago's television sports commentators," the Tribune's Robert Markus wrote in an Oct. 24, 1974, column. "(It's) a position of eminence no one would have predicted for the shy, faltering, boyish-looking young man who made his debut analyzing Bear film highlights during his last two playing seasons. Johnny has picked up a lot of polish since then."

Morris went into semi-retirement in 1992, then full retirement in '96, stepping away after covering the Bulls championship teams. He has stayed mostly out of public view since then, showing up for Bears alumni events and spending much of his time handicapping horses at Arlington International Racecourse, where he is recognized more for his three decades on TV than for his days as a player.

"Chicago is the best TV market in the country," Morris told the Tribune's Steve Nidetz on May 25, 1992. "People here are interested in city politics, they're interested in sports and they watch TV. . . . A sportscaster is a much bigger figure in Chicago than in Los Angeles or New York, where they have different kinds of celebrities.

"I always felt sports was the most important part of the broadcast because it's a family unifier. It creates a city esprit de corps. We're always fighting for time, but I felt sports is a big necessity in Chicago." ■

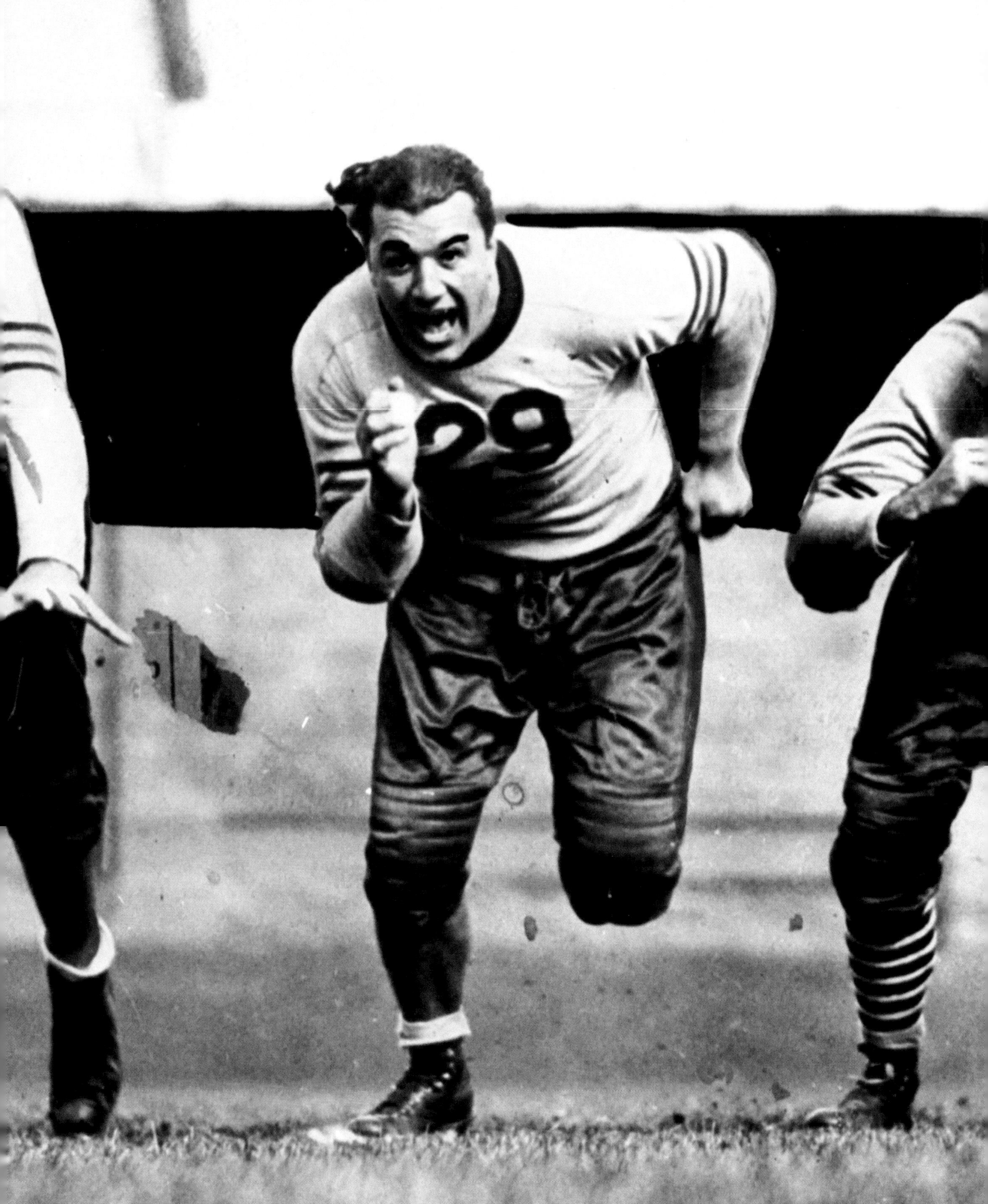

45

Joe Kopcha

29 GUARD, DEFENSIVE LINEMAN
1929, 1932–35

Thirty Bears have been inducted into the Pro Football Hall of Fame, the most of any NFL team.

They might also lead the league in all-time medical degrees. At least nine Bears players have become doctors during or after their playing careers.

George Halas, who ran the franchise for six decades after its inception in 1920, had a reputation for stinginess matched by few other figures in NFL history. His thrifty ways and shrewd negotiations with players are legendary, but members of the Chicago Bears Doctors Club told a different story.

Joe Kopcha was the charter member of the group. The 6-foot, 220-pound guard and defensive lineman joined the Bears from the Tennessee-Chattanooga in 1929, then left the team the next year to study medicine at Alabama. Two years later Kopcha rejoined the Bears and continued his studies at Rush Medical College.

He practiced football in the morning, attended classes in the afternoon and studied at night. Halas helped Kopcha pay for his education and excused him whenever he needed to miss practice.

"Coach Halas will always be No. 1 in my book," Kopcha told Jim Campbell of the Professional Football Researchers Association (PFRA) in 1985. "Not only did he tolerate my medical studies—he encouraged them. Never once did he think twice about time I'd miss from practice because of my studies. Also, in my day guards earned $90 a game. Halas gave me 110 because I advised the trainer on injuries."

After he was done with football, Kopcha set up practice as an obstetrician in Gary and delivered hundreds of babies during a long career. Other Bears Halas helped become doctors include surgeons John Morhardt, Danny Fortmann, Tony Ippolito and Bill McColl, physicians Jim Logan, Paul Podmajersky and Nick Sacrinty and dentist Bill Osmanski.

"If Halas could help out, he did," Kopcha told Leo R. Joint of the PFRA, also in 1985. "He helped a lot of guys. That was the 'other man.' The public, they thought he was a bastard."

Kopcha was a prep standout in northwest Indiana as the starting center on powerhouse basketball teams at Whiting High School, which did not have a football team. He was

Joe Kopcha (29) in November 1935.

recruited to Chattanooga by their football coach, former Notre Dame quarterback Frank Thomas. Kopcha won 10 varsity letters with the Moccasins while competing in football, basketball, baseball, track and swimming. He spent a year with the Bears, then enrolled in medical school and helped coach football at Alabama when Thomas became the Crimson Tide's head coach.

After two years in Tuscaloosa, Kopcha told Halas he wished to rejoin the Bears. Halas thought there was no way he would make the team after two years away from playing football but invited him to try out.

Kopcha not only made the team, he went straight into the starting lineup at left guard and became one of the NFL's best linemen on some of the Bears' best teams. He was named second-team All-Pro in 1932 and first-team the next three years.

The Bears won championships in 1932 and '33, then lost the title game in 1934 with their best team of the three. Kopcha and Beattie Feathers missed the loss to the Giants—the "Sneaker Game" in which the Giants wore basketball shoes on the frozen turf at the Polo Grounds—with injuries.

Years later, Halas remembered how determined Kopcha was to play. In a story he wrote for the Tribune on Feb. 9, 1967, Halas said there was a commotion on the train en route to Detroit for the final game of the regular season.

"I was summoned to the dining car by a steward who said one of our players was acting strangely," Halas wrote. "I found Kopcha in the gallery, brandishing a meat cleaver in his left hand and chipping away at the huge plaster cast encompassing his right hand.

" 'Just experimenting a little, Coach,' Joe explained. 'If I can cut this thing down a bit, maybe the trainer can slap a soft bandage around it, and I can play.'

"Kopcha didn't play. It was very important that the bone in his right hand heal properly because Joe was then an intern working toward a career in surgery. . . . I would not take a chance on ruining what since has developed into a distinguished medical career."

The hatchet job on his cast was far from the first time Kopcha altered his equipment. During his rookie year, a bewildered Paddy Driscoll found Kopcha punching holes in three pairs of leather shoulder pads with an awl and lacing parts of them together to make a more protective version. He also added extra padding to the inside and outside of his helmet, and his homemade shin guards helped him combat the leg-whipping that was widespread at the time.

He told Driscoll that his goal with the shin guards was to protect against osteomyelitis. The star halfback shook his head and walked away.

Kopcha's shoulder pad design caught on quickly. He later claimed a Spalding salesman saw his pads in the Bears locker room and borrowed liberally. Kopcha said he never thought about trying to patent the design and was glad more players were able to protect themselves better because of his innovation.

"Shoulder pads in those days were nothing more than epaulets—like a hotel doorman wears," Kopcha told Bob Braunwart and Bob Carroll of the PFRA in 1980. "I resurrected a set to actually fit my shoulders and protect my collarbone and the acromioclavicular joint.

"A lot of guys got hurt needlessly in the old days. I like to think that my ideas helped change some of that."

Years later he recalled that Driscoll was laid up at the Mayo Clinic with the exact condition Kopcha had hoped to avoid with his shin pads.

"Osteomyelitis," Kopcha told Braunwart and Carroll. "Paddy said, 'Years ago we had a medical student that used that word. I thought he was crapping me!'"

Kopcha requested a trade to the Lions in 1936 so he could finish his internship at Detroit's Harper Hospital. Halas reluctantly agreed and sold his contract. The next year Kopcha returned to his home in northwest Indiana to begin his second career.

> ## A lot of guys got hurt needlessly in the old days. I like to think that my ideas helped change some of that.

—JOE KOPCHA

"It will be tough to give it up," he told the Tribune's George Strickler on Dec. 5, 1935, "but linemen are not like old man river. They can't just go on rollin' along."

Kopcha became an early historian of his sport and was a charter member of the PFRA. He had a small printing press in his cellar and liked to amuse friends with personalized cards or pamphlets. One card had the words "Remember, you're not finished until you've done the paper work!" over a picture of an outhouse.

He printed a gold-embossed book for his friend and fellow football researcher, titled "Highlights in the Sex Life of Bob Carroll, Authentically Described and Accurately Illustrated." Classified as nonfiction, it contained all blank pages.

Kopcha died at 80 in Hobart, Ind., in 1986. During the last year of his life he gave many interviews as the 1985 Bears brought about an increased interest in the team's history.

"These fellas aren't playing any different than we did," Kopcha told Joint. "I'm thinking about all this and the Bear shuffle and all that stuff. Hell, we did a lot of goofy stuff back in our day."

Kopcha often was asked if he was jealous of the modern players' salaries.

"No," he told Joint. "Ninety dollars a game made it possible for me to get through medical school. . . . If I was making $90,000 like Richard Dent and a few of those others . . . there wouldn't be any incentive for me to go to school." ■

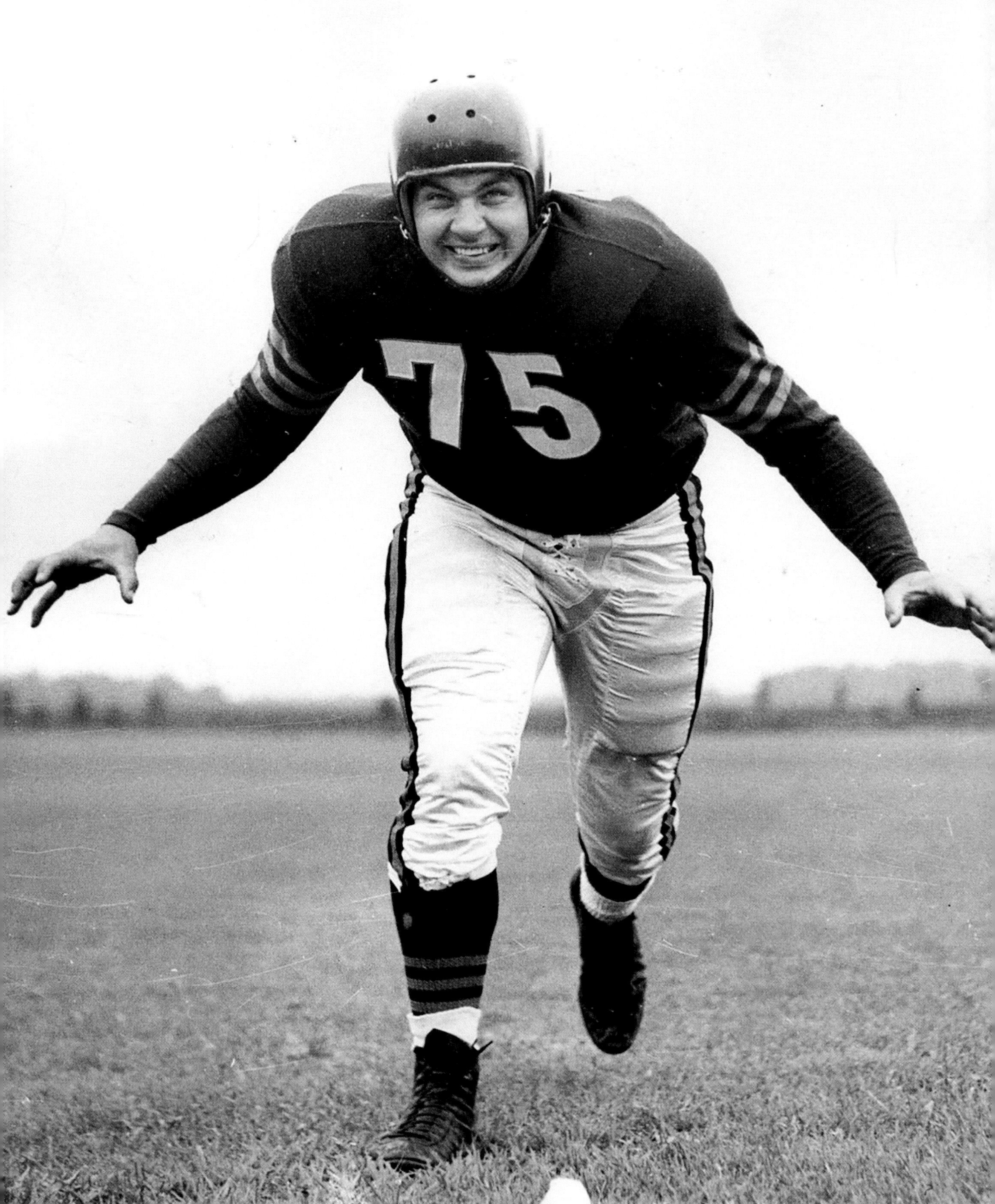

46

Fred Williams

75 DEFENSIVE TACKLE
1952–63

FRED WILLIAMS PLAYED in the shadow of Ed Sprinkle and Doug Atkins, two of the best defensive ends in Bears history.

Very little, though, overshadowed Williams' sense of humor. The 6-foot-4, 250-pound defensive tackle from Little Rock, Ark., had a quip for every situation, helping his teammates stay loose during good times and bad.

In 1959 he was asked if the Bears defensive line was the best in the NFL. "I don't know if we're the best, but we sure are the ugliest."

In 1985 he noticed that drugs were becoming a problem in sports. "We didn't have to worry about dope back in my day. We couldn't afford it. Halas saw to that."

At a reunion for the 1963 championship team in 1988, Williams said, "The whole dang team is going into the Hall of Fame. I know the only thing that kept me out is ability."

When the Bears signed first-round rookie defensive end Loyd Phillips of Arkansas in April 1967, the Tribune's Cooper Rollow rejoiced, hoping the Bears had found another Williams to fill his notebook.

"Once again, there's to be a hillbilly humorist on the Bears," Rollow wrote. "Not since Williams ended a 12-year career as a Chicago pro three autumns ago has the Bears' playing roster included the name of an Arkansan. The Bears have missed Williams' Ozarkian drawl, quick wit and direct approach to all situations."

Rollow's wish was not granted; Phillips never warmed up to Chicago's winters and lasted only three years in the NFL.

Williams joined the Bears as a fifth-round pick out of Arkansas in the 1952 draft. He was one of six future starters—with Jim Dooley, Bill McColl, Ed Brown, Joe Fortunato and Bill Bishop—the team added in the class. They helped form the core of the 1956 NFL runner-up, and Williams' final game with the Bears was the 14-10 win against the Giants in the 1963 championship game.

In his 12 seasons with the Bears, Williams was the rare lineman who was strong enough to play defensive tackle and quick enough to play end. Even though he was nicknamed "Fat Freddie" as a pro, he was an excellent athlete growing up, playing center on a state championship basketball team in high school and winning local titles in boxing and wrestling.

Fred Williams
(75) in 1955.

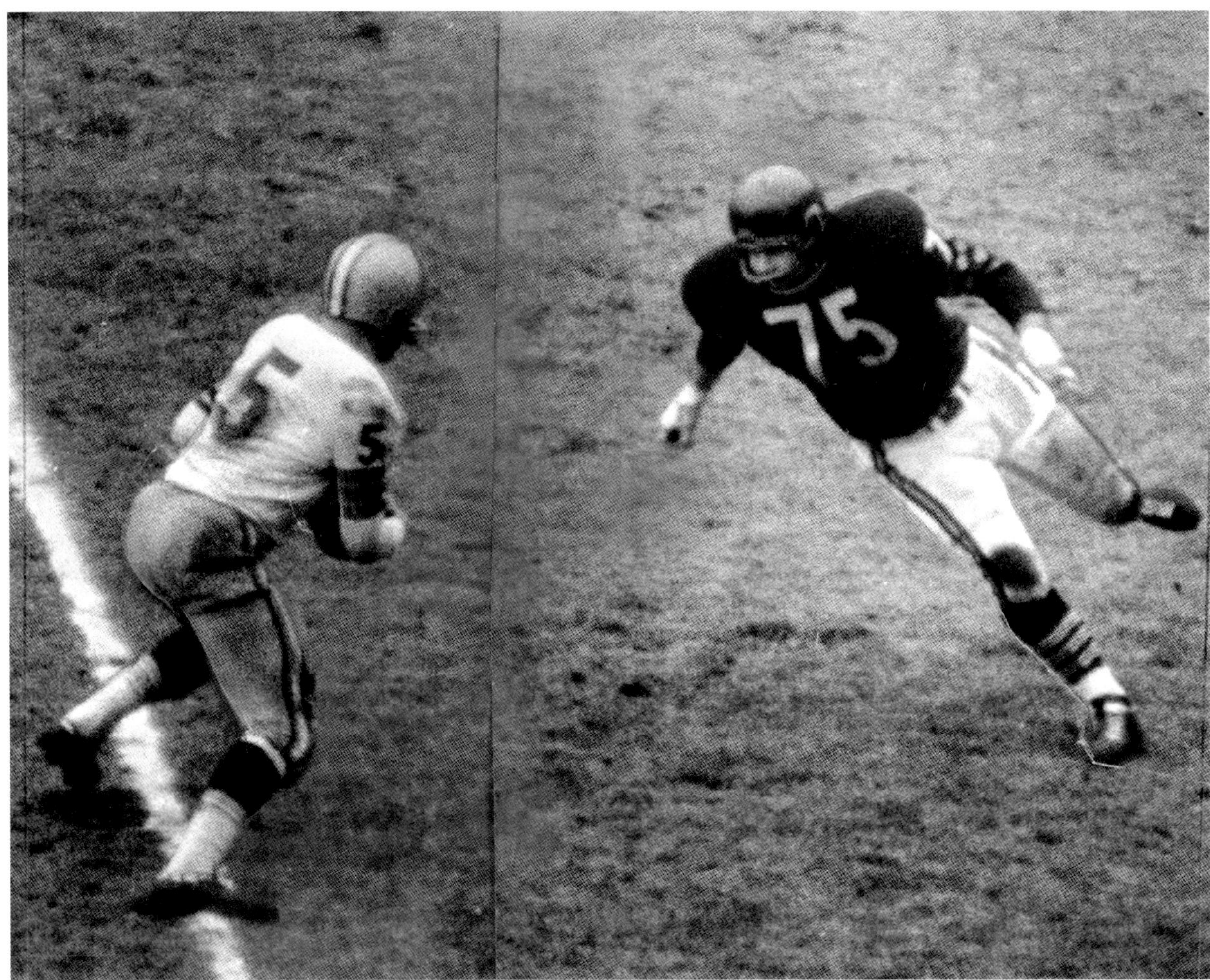

Fred Williams (75) goes after the Packers' Paul Hornung (5) on Dec. 5, 1960, at Wrigley Field.

Justin Smith, who played for the Bengals and 49ers from 2001-14, is a modern player similar to Williams. In 2011, Smith was voted All-Pro at both tackle and end. Williams was voted to four Pro Bowls—the same number as Bears defensive line greats Sprinkle, Dan Hampton and Richard Dent—but he never was named to an All-Pro team.

"Williams' versatility has prevented him from attaining recognition at any one position," Rollow wrote on July 2, 1961. "The wise-cracking Arkansan has, at various times, played both sides of the line at tackle and end, and even has performed as a linebacker."

Bears defensive coordinator Clark Shaughnessy declared "Williams is probably the most versatile lineman in the National Football League."

Williams was Sprinkle's teammate for his first four seasons in the league (1952-55) and Atkins' for nine years (1955-63). Atkins, an eight-time Pro Bowler, was known to take plays off, but Williams went all out all the time.

After Williams left a Dec. 7, 1958, game against the Chicago Cardinals with an injury, the Tribune's George Strickler wrote: "Fred's departure was the best break the Cardinals got all afternoon. He was their chief tormentor for two periods, brushing aside (the) protection and piling up plays like a beast berserk at a Sunday school picnic."

Williams and Atkins were tough to deal

with on Sundays and even harder to corral after hours. Bears coach George Halas assigned Williams the impossible task of keeping the wild, 6-foot-8 Atkins out of trouble; more often than not he joined in the high jinks.

The story of their martini-drinking contest has been passed down through generations of Bears. Over the years the details of the fuzzy night have been hard to pin down, but two facts have remained constant through all the tellings. Atkins and Williams each drank 21 martinis one night, and Williams woke up the next morning in his bathtub, unable to move. Williams' wife called the only person she knew who could lift her husband, and a few minutes later a tattered Atkins showed up to help his friend out of the tub.

Williams' teams in the 1950s and '60s were like many throughout Bears history, with great defenses and mediocre-or-worse offenses. Williams' humor turned harsh when pointed at his team's offensive players, even during the 1963 championship season.

"I don't know why we put up with that offense," Williams told the Los Angeles Times' Randy Harvey on Jan. 6, 1985. "They couldn't make a first down against a strong wind. We should have voted those offensive boys half-shares of the championship money.

"After the championship game, all these reporters stuck their microphones in (quarterback) Bill Wade's face. I don't know why they wanted to talk to him. He threw such bad passes, they couldn't even be intercepted."

Williams might have gotten off a few zingers while bickering with Bears offensive players; he fared much worse in his squabbles with Halas over money.

"I asked him once for a $5,000 raise," Williams told Harvey. "Halas offered $500. I said, 'I guess you'll just have to trade me.' Halas said, 'I've been trying, but nobody wants you.'

"Halas always got the last word," Williams continued. "Just when you thought you had him, he'd get a phone call. That would give him time to think. Turns out he had a button under his desk that he could push to make the phone ring."

Halas found a taker for Williams in 1964 and traded him and receiver Angelo Coia to the Redskins for their first-round pick in '65. In his first game against his old team, Williams sparked a brawl with a forearm to center Mike Pyle's head.

The draft pick the Bears received for Williams ended up No. 6, giving them three of the first six selections. They chose Dick Butkus third, Gale Sayers fourth and defensive lineman Steve DeLong, who ended up signing with the AFL's Chargers, sixth.

Williams boasted the Redskins got the better of the deal, saying, "They got Sayers and Butkus in 1965 and couldn't bat .500 with them, so I always figured Sayers and Butkus couldn't replace me."

After two years with the Redskins, Williams retired and became a liquor salesman in his hometown. He died on Oct. 11, 2000, at 71 after suffering a stroke.

In 2014 the Tribune's Don Pierson ranked Williams the Bears' seventh-best defensive lineman ever behind only Atkins, Hampton, Dent, Steve McMichael, Sprinkle and Link Lyman. ◼

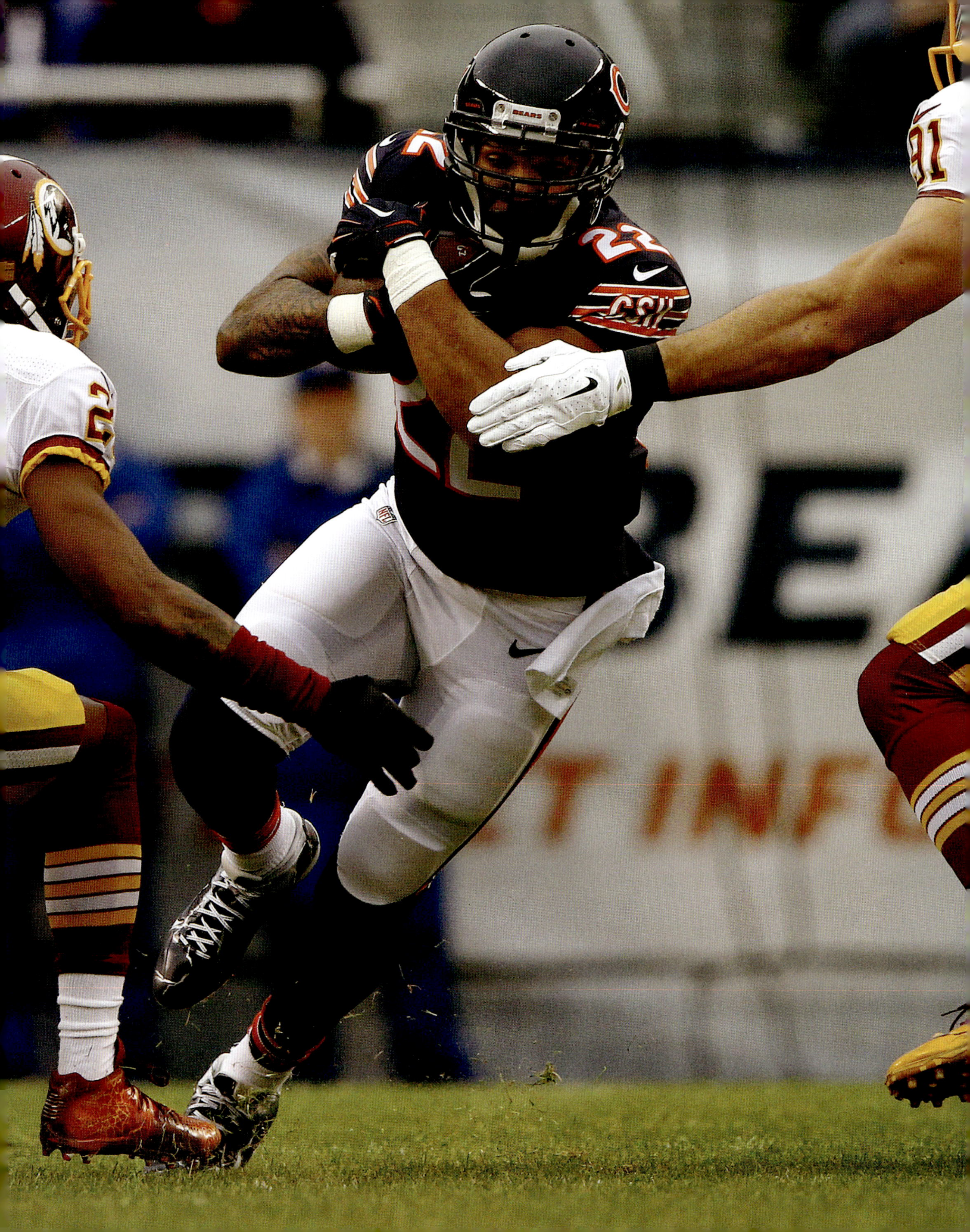

47

Matt Forte

22 RUNNING BACK
2008–15

Matt Forte took the handoff from Kyle Orton and veered to his right.

He followed a crushing block by guard Roberto Garza, made a move that left Colts safety Antoine Bethea grasping air, then outraced the other safety, Bob Sanders, to the end zone.

Forte's fourth carry of his first game showed that the Bears might not have to worry about the running back position for a while. It was part of one of the best Bears debuts ever: 123 yards on 23 carries as the first rookie to start at running back since Walter Payton, who carried eight times for zero yards in his first game in 1975.

After Neal Anderson retired in 1994, the Bears had placed their hopes in a new rookie running back about every three years. Rashaan Salaam in 1995, Curtis Enis in '98, Anthony Thomas in 2001 and Cedric Benson in '05 had varying amounts of success, and Thomas Jones had an excellent three-year run as the team's feature back from 2004 to '06. But Forte solidified the position long-term for the first time in a generation.

Forte set the tone for his great start when he arrived in a suit and tie for his first practice as teammates showed up in sweats or shorts.

"The way he has done everything since he showed up his first day at Halas Hall—just ready to go on a business trip—that's what we've gotten from him," coach Lovie Smith told the Tribune's Vaughn McClure on Aug. 26, 2011. "He has come to work every day; hasn't missed a beat, missed a practice."

His flashy first impression showed Forte's talent, but it did not exactly foreshadow what he would bring to the Bears. For the next eight years Forte's value showed in the small details, such as knowing how many yards to set up his pass route for a first down or choosing which blitzer to block to ensure his quarterback could get off a pass.

"He's such a smart player and so versatile," quarterback Jay Cutler told McClure. "This offense really can't run without him back there. . . . He's a threat all over the field. There are not many running backs in the league that can do what he does. . . . He's like another quarterback."

Forte was not the greatest goal-line back, nor did he possess the breakaway speed of

Matt Forte (22) looks to cut through Washington's defense Dec. 13, 2015, at Soldier Field.

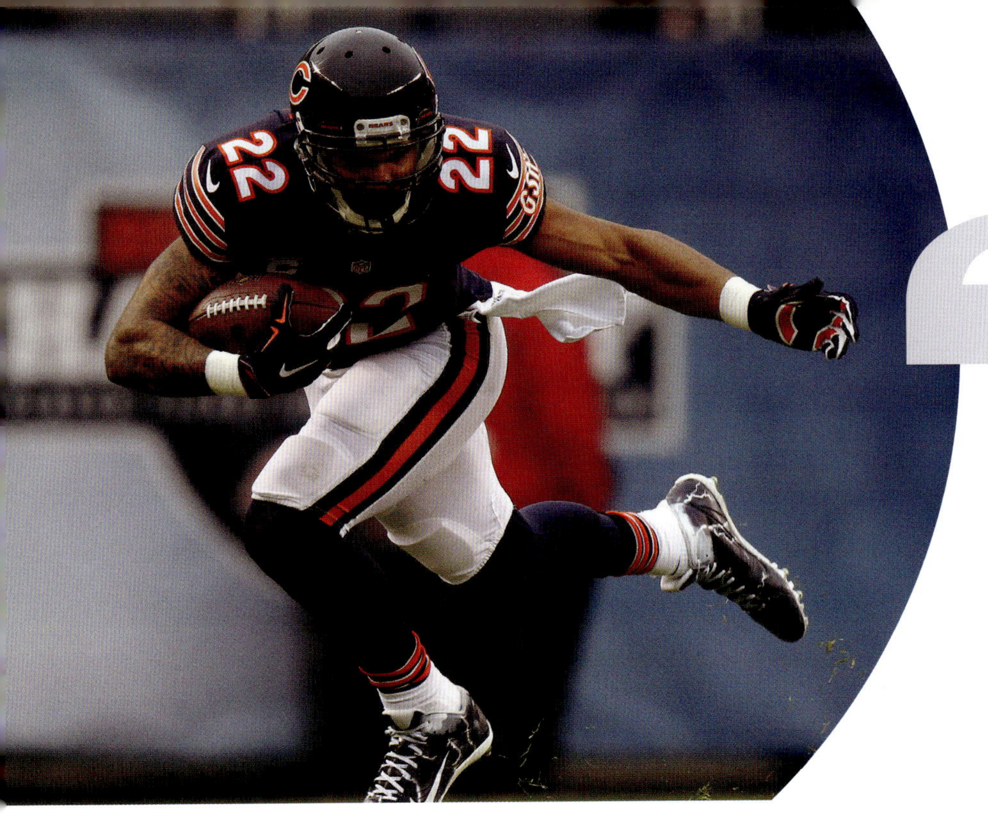

Matt Forte (22) dodges a tackle Dec. 13, 2015, in a game against Washington at Soldier Field.

a Chris Johnson or Adrian Peterson. But as a total running back, the 6-foot-1, 220-pound Forte compared favorably with most players of his era.

During his 10-year career, nobody gained more than his 14,468 yards from scrimmage, and he became the NFL's first player with 900 rushing yards and 400 receiving yards in each of his first four seasons.

In 2013 Forte set an NFL record for running backs with 102 receptions. A 2014 Sports Illustrated feature labeled him "more important to his team than any other back in the NFL."

Forte finished his Bears career with the best statistics of any running back other than Payton. He ranks second in team history with 8,602 rushing yards, 12,718 net yards, 487 receptions, 24 100-yard rushing games and five 1,000-yard rushing seasons. His 1,339 rushing yards in 2013, when he was named to his second Pro Bowl, are the most by a Bears running back besides Payton.

His savvy shows on the NFL's list of all-time two-point conversions, where Forte's six rank behind only Marshall Faulk's seven.

"I don't just want to be a player that played this game and was a good running back," Forte told the Tribune's David Haugh on Oct. 13, 2014. "When I leave the game, I want them to be able to say things about me that leaves a mark in the NFL for a long time."

The 2008 draft was a good one for running backs, and Forte—a second-round pick who attended Tulane, his only FBS scholarship offer—turned out to be the best of the 10 backs taken in the first three rounds.

His 9,796 rushing yards topped Johnson (9,651), Jamaal Charles (7,563), Jonathan Stewart (7,335), Ray Rice (6,180) and Darren McFadden (5,421). Forte's 75 touchdowns rank ahead of Jordy Nelson's 72 and the 64 of Johnson and Charles, and his 554 receptions trail only Pierre Garcon's 628, Nelson's 613 and DeSean Jackson's 589.

Pro Football Reference's approximate value metric ranks Forte as the fourth-best player from that draft after Matt Ryan, Calais Campbell and Joe Flacco.

"He walked in high-pedigree, high-IQ, strong-willed, driven to be a great player," former Bears general manager Jerry Angelo told Sports Illustrated's Tim Layden. "You wish every player you draft had Matt Forte's intangibles."

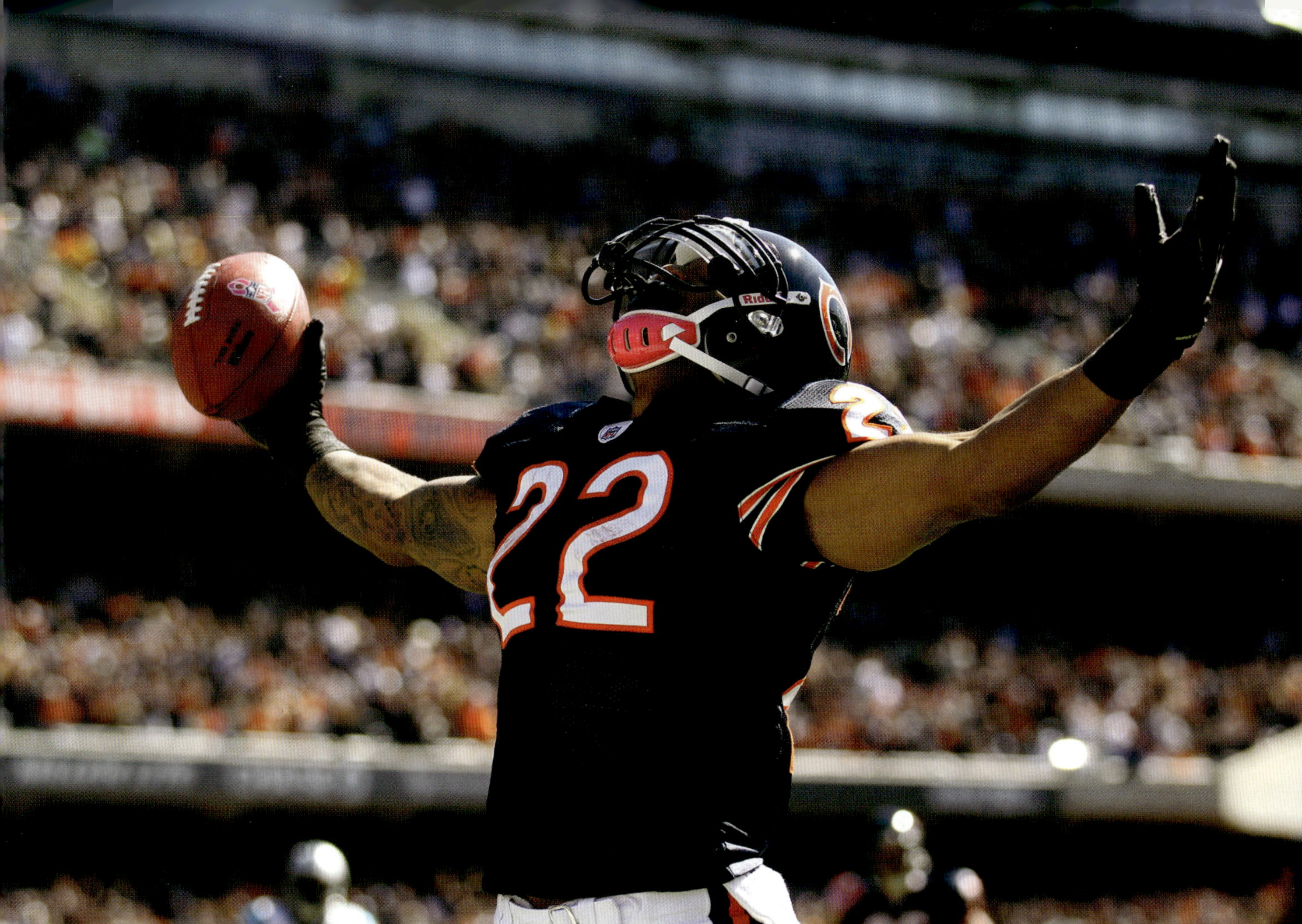

Forte's quiet leadership spoke volumes, even as the Bears offense added volatile personalities such as Cutler, wide receiver Brandon Marshall and tight end Martellus Bennett.

"When things get out of control in the locker room, he'll step up and whip somebody into shape," Culter told Layden. "B-Marsh is his favorite target for that. But any way you put it, he's one of the leaders on the team. And he works harder than anybody else."

Forte signed with the Jets as a free agent in 2016 and played two years in New York before retiring after the 2017 season. He returned to Chicago and added his name to the long list of former Bears with a Sunday postgame show; he appeared on NBC Sports Chicago with former teammates Lance Briggs and Alex Brown.

The native of Lake Charles, La., spends much of his time doing charity and social-justice work. He has worked to improve relations between police and citizens on Chicago's South Side. In 2018, Forte held a protest at the James R. Thompson Center to try to lessen the bail burden for people awaiting trial. The protest was part of Malcolm Jenkins' and Anquan Boldin's Players Coalition.

"They have a lot of different fronts that they are fighting against," Forte told the Tribune's Phil Thompson on Sept. 18, 2018. "We can as players kind of pick and choose whatever your passion is about. I'm all about helping anyone who has been wronged or injustice of any type." ■

Matt Forte (22) rushes for a touchdown Oct. 2, 2011, against the Carolina Panthers at Soldier Field.

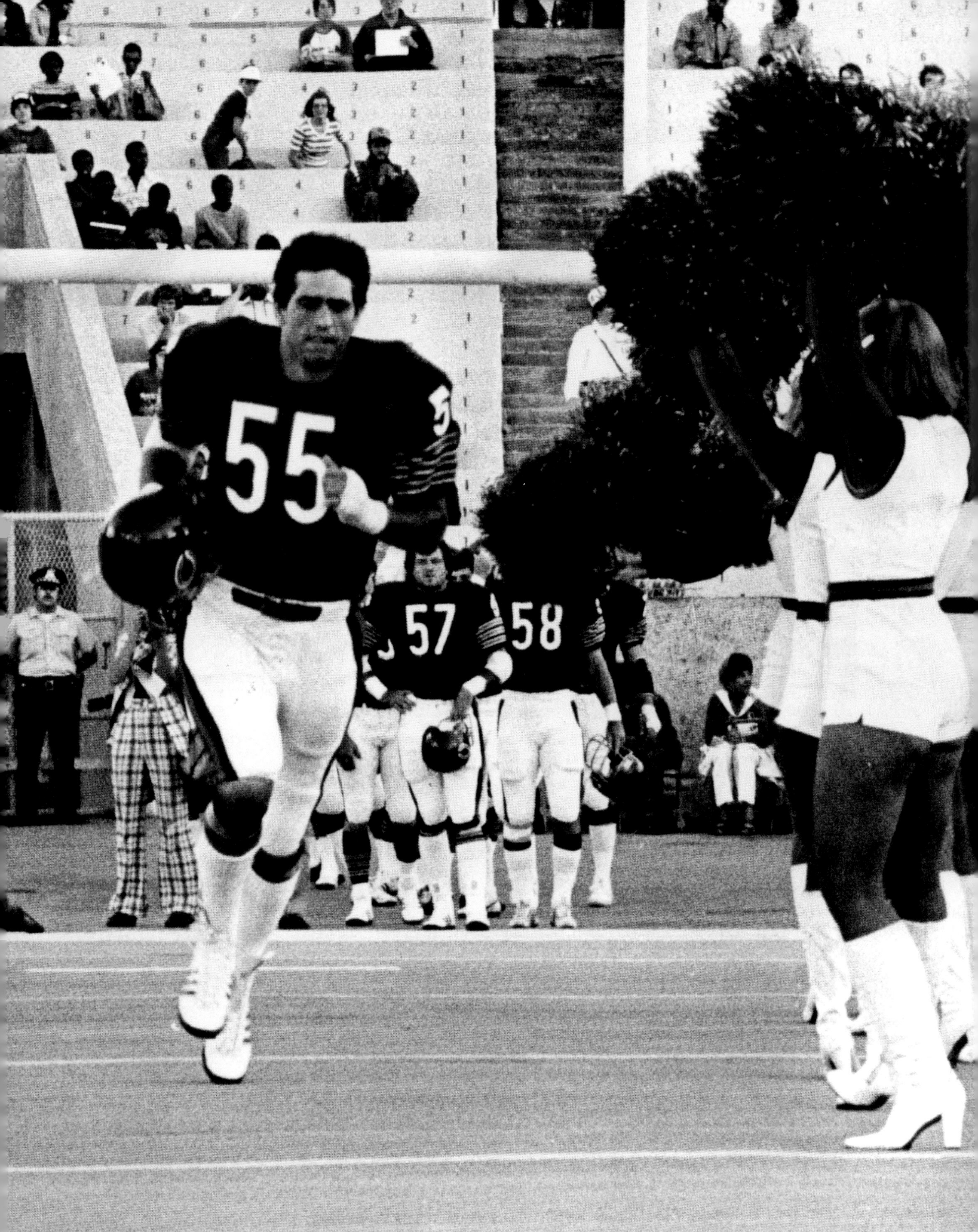

48

Doug Buffone

55 LINEBACKER
1966–79

T HE LOVE AFFAIR between Bears fans and Doug Buffone lasted nearly 50 years.

From the time he was drafted in the fourth round out of Louisville in 1966 to when he died of natural causes at 70 on April 20, 2015, perhaps no Bear connected with Chicago fans the way Buffone did. He played 14 years at linebacker for mostly terrible teams, then spent more than 30 on the radio analyzing teams that often were just as bad.

His attitude about football and life, though, made Buffone a legend in Chicago.

"Not only a great football player, a great person on the radio, but more than anything, just a great individual," WSCR-AM program director Mitch Rosen told the Tribune's Fred Mitchell and Peter Nickeas on April 21, 2015. "Somebody that everybody loved. When you met Doug Buffone, you fell in love with him."

Shortly after sports radio came to Chicago full time with The Score in 1992, Buffone became the voice of Bears fans. His co-hosts included Mike North, former Bears teammate Dan Jiggetts and former Bulls star Norm Van Lier, but his best work came on Bears postgame shows with Ed O'Bradovich.

Each Bears loss from 1992 to 2014 had a silver lining: listening to Buffone find creative ways to describe his disgust with what he just watched. His partnership with O'Bradovich—another beloved former Bear who didn't mince words—saw both men finding their groove as their blood pressure increased.

Sometimes Buffone's words were fiery: "I want somebody to get kicked in the ass!" or "These guys couldn't play dead!" Sometimes they came out jumbled: "You better have a damn good fullblack," or "It's gonna be the best . . . whatever . . . since sliced breast."

He could sum up the feelings of a fan base in one sentence: "I could have gone to Rush Street last night and found 24 players who could do better." "I'd rather spend a weekend in jail than watch this game again."

Bad Bears teams were "tomato cans" and "soft as a grape." Callers he disagreed with were advised to "stop yourself!"

We never found out why hitting a bull in the ass with a banjo would be a good thing, but thanks to Buffone we learned that Caleb Hanie not being able to do so was an indictment of his quarterback skills.

Doug Buffone (55) runs through the Chicago Bears' new cheerleader corps, the Honey Bears, on July 25, 1977.

Intentionally or not, Buffone was so funny he could make listeners laugh until they cried. His words always came from the heart, though.

"I don't mind you getting beat; I got my ass whipped many times," Buffone said in an impassioned rant after one loss. "But I tell you, I took somebody down with me. That's what I want to see! Not today. . . . You are a professional team! Act like one for God's sakes!"

The Tribune's David Haugh wrote on April 21, 2015: "If the late Ron Santo was beloved in the city for always putting a positive spin on the Cubs, Buffone built his popularity on the basis of brutal honesty analyzing his beloved Bears. . . . He harshly criticized the Bears because, beneath all the bluster, he deeply loved the franchise."

As Buffone told the Tribune's Ed Sherman on Oct. 30, 2014, during his last season as postgame host: "I didn't play the trombone for 14 years. I played football. Don't give me this Kumbaya stuff and 'We'll try again next week.' You're trying to tell me I don't know what's going on? Even a moron would know after 14 years."

Buffone was part of plenty of losses—116 of them in fact, against 80 victories in his 14 seasons. He was a Bear through some of their darkest days, including the franchise-worst 1-13 record in 1969.

He set a Bears record with 186 games played, a total that now ranks fifth behind Patrick Mannelly (245), Steve McMichael and Olin Kreutz (191 apiece) and Walter Payton (190). He still owns the team record—unlikely to be broken—by playing for five coaches: George Halas, Jim Dooley, Abe Gibron, Jack Pardee and Neill Armstrong.

Buffone's 24 interceptions are a Bears record for linebackers. His first three picks came against Bart Starr, Johnny Unitas and John Brodie; his final three came against Steve DeBerg, Dan Fouts and Steve Grogan. The Bears credit Buffone with 1,257 tackles—including more than 100 seven times—10 fumble recoveries, nine forced fumbles and 37 sacks.

While the Bears' middle linebacker tradition—Bill George to Dick Butkus to Mike Singletary to Brian Urlacher—is well-known, their left outside linebacker streak also was impressive. Joe Fortunato, Buffone and Otis Wilson manned the position for all but a few years from 1955 to '87.

The 6-foot-3 Buffone was not a great athlete but kept himself in great shape; he weighed in at 222 pounds as a rookie and in his final season. In 1977 he became the first Bear to return from a torn Achilles tendon. During rehab he trained so vigorously that trainer Fred Caito and weight coach Clyde Emrich made him take 10 days off in February.

In a Dec. 9, 1977, story by the Tribune's Don Pierson, Emrich recounted telling Buffone: "You're driving me crazy, you're driving Freddie crazy and you're driving yourself crazy. Now get the hell out."

That 1977 season saw the Bears return to the playoffs for the first time since the 1963 championship season. Buffone, a 12-year veteran, threw a wild party at his Bombay Bicycle Club on East Division Street. The celebration included dancing by the Honey Bears cheerleading squad and guard Revie Sorey controlling the tape deck. Sorey interrupted the disco hits of the day several times to play "Bear Down, Chicago Bears."

"Hell, I don't know what it cost," Buffone told the Tribune's John Husar on Dec. 20. "And I don't care. When you average it out over 12 years, it isn't that much."

Buffone's burgeoning career as a nightclub owner—he also ran Sweetwater and Hotspurs in Chicago, the Nickelbag in Schiller Park and Jubilation in Las Vegas—led many to wonder why the son of a coal miner from Yatesboro, Pa., kept coming back to the Bears as he reached his mid-30s.

In 1978 he relished the chance to set the team record by playing in his 162nd game, passing George.

"At first I took it lightly," he told Pierson on Oct. 13. "Then I got to thinking. All those names. Bronko Nagurski. Beattie Feathers."

Pierson pointed out that Feathers played only four seasons with the Bears.

"Yeah, but it's a great name."

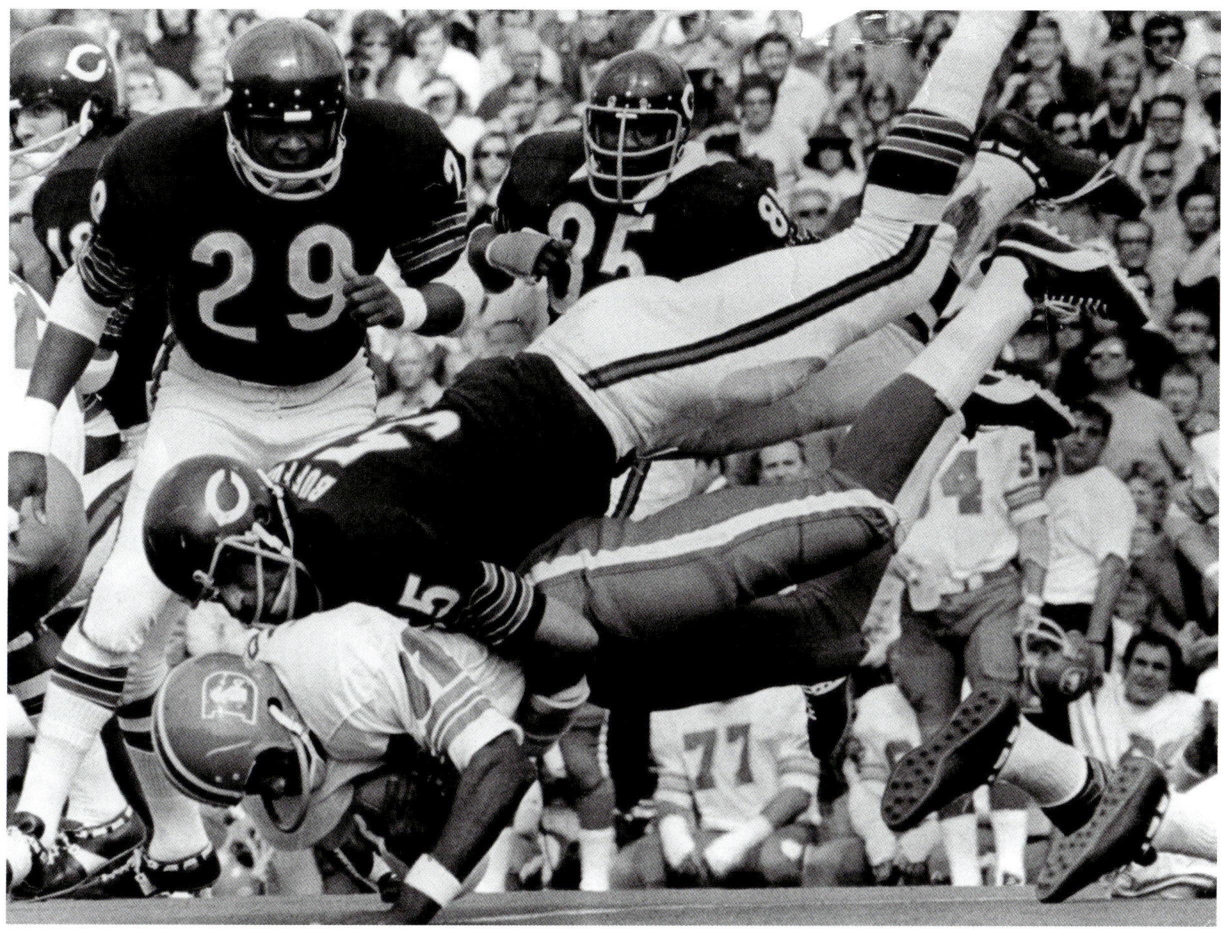

A flying tackle by Doug Buffone (55) holds Denver's Dwight Harrison to a short gain in the third quarter on Sept. 12, 1971.

Buffone always could find humor even in the bleakest moments. He recalled to Pierson on Dec. 15, 1979, an exhibition game 12 years earlier that the Bears lost 66-24 to the Chiefs. Buffone felt bad about the final score but worse for the white horse that ran laps around the field after each touchdown.

"I'll never forget that poor horse's tongue hanging out."

Ronnie Bull was a member of the 1963 championship team who later played four years with Buffone and couldn't help but be impressed by his attitude.

"Doug was always the kind of guy to have a big smile on his face," Bull told chicagobears.com after Buffone's death. "And that's the reason everybody liked him. Nobody had a bad word to say about Doug."

For his play and his personality, Bears fans adored Doug Buffone. He might have loved them even more.

"I always play for the fans," Buffone told the Tribune's Bill Jauss on Aug. 25, 1974. "I swear to God, they make me sky high. The year we were 1-13 we finished against Detroit in Wrigley Field, and they were cheering for us! I said, 'Doug, go all out for these people!'"

When Buffone came back for his final season in 1979, he was a battered 35-year-old with no starting position for the first time since he was a rookie. He just had to give it one more go.

"I happen to like to play this game," he told Pierson. "What the hell's wrong with that? The money's there and the money's fine, but maybe that isn't where it's all at. It's my life, my job, the thing I do best.

"I love it. What can I say?" ■

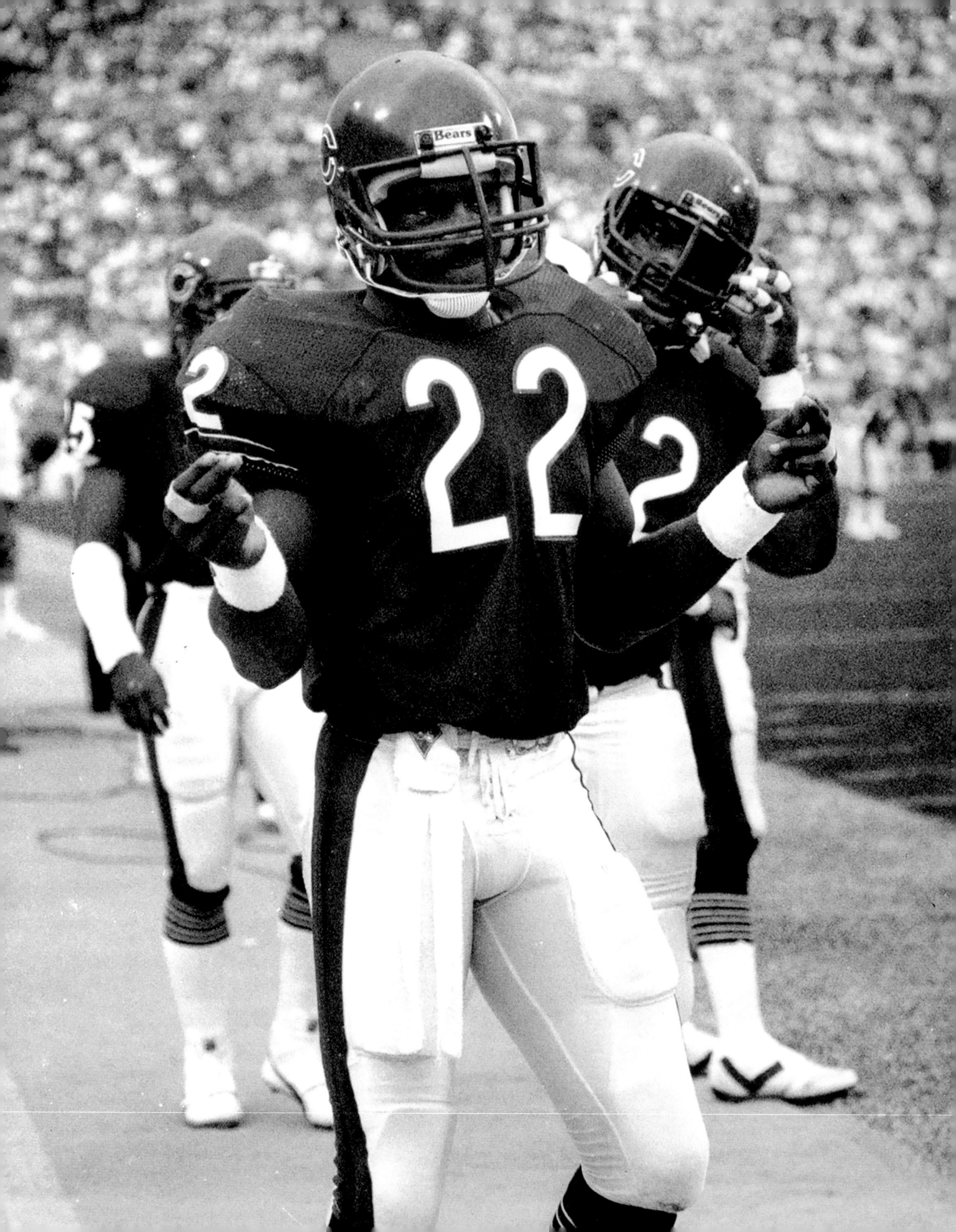

49

Dave Duerson

IT HAS BEEN 10 YEARS since Dave Duerson shot himself in the heart so that his brain could be sent to Boston University's Brain Lab and be tested for chronic traumatic encephalopathy.

At the time, there was some pushback among a portion of football fans, players and executives who said the sport's concussion and CTE problems were overblown. Duerson's suicide was a turning point that changed the debate from "Is there a problem?" to "What do we do about it?"

In the years since, the NFL settled a lawsuit by former players who suffered concussions for $765 million. Duerson's brain tested positive for CTE. Hall of Fame linebacker Junior Seau followed Duerson's lead by shooting himself in the heart; his brain also tested positive. The movie "Concussion," produced by Ridley Scott and starring Will Smith, was released in 2015; Duerson's family was upset by his portrayal in it.

Tregg Duerson, one of Dave's four children, has become an advocate for concussion awareness. He has campaigned for a bill that would ban tackle football for children younger than 12 in Illinois. The Dave Duerson Act to Prevent CTE was sponsored by state Rep. Carol Sente, a Vernon Hills Democrat. It passed through a House committee but was not called for a vote, with Sente citing a lack of realistic support for it to pass into law.

How football deals with the effects it has on the brains of its players will be a huge part of Duerson's legacy. It should not be forgotten, though, that during his playing days he was a terrific defensive back.

The Bears selected Duerson in the third round out of Notre Dame as part of their historic 1983 draft that netted seven players who would start for 1985's Super Bowl XX championship team. He served as a backup cornerback and safety for two years, a period when Buddy Ryan, the hard-nosed defensive coordinator, had little use for Duerson, the erudite and polished Golden Domer.

Duerson entered the starting lineup by necessity in 1985 when strong safety Todd Bell, one of Ryan's favorite players, held out for the entire season because of a contract dispute. Duerson rarely left the field after that, becoming one of the historically great defense's key

Dave Duerson (22) was voted to the Pro Bowl after each of his first four seasons as a starter.

217

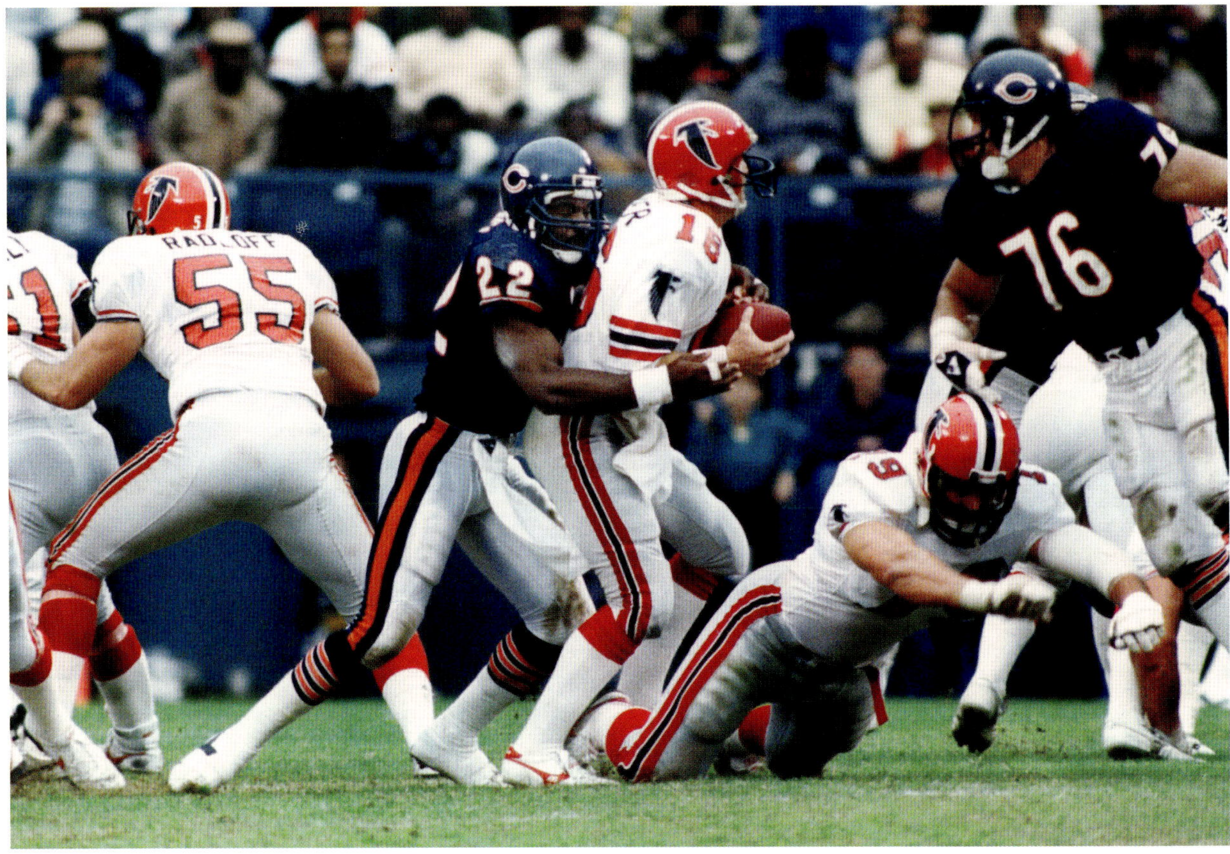

Two sacks and an interception by Dave Duerson (22) were part of a win against the Atlanta Falcons in November 1986.

players. He was voted to the Pro Bowl after each of his first four seasons as a starter.

"If anyone's playing better, I'd like to see him," coach Mike Ditka told the Tribune's Don Pierson on Oct. 6, 1986.

Added defensive tackle Steve McMichael: "He's the MVP of our defense as far as I'm concerned."

Duerson could play both safety positions with equal effectiveness. When Bell returned to form and the starting lineup in 1987, Duerson shifted to free safety and beat out Gary Fencik for the starting job. After Bell left to rejoin Ryan with the Eagles the next year, Duerson went back to strong safety with Shaun Gayle assuming free safety duties.

In contrast to Bell and Doug Plank, two of his predecessors at safety, Duerson was more of a ballhawk than a huge hitter, and he had five interceptions in 1985 and six in '86. He was an excellent blitzer, though, and in '86 he set an NFL record for a defensive back with seven sacks. The mark stood for 19 years until the Cardinals' Adrian Wilson had eight in 2005.

Duerson was an extremely proud man who remembered slights and held grudges. In 1986 the Bears played the Eagles and Ryan—their new head coach who had given Duerson no encouragement—in Week 2. Duerson had 11 tackles, a sack, an interception and a forced fumble on the opening kickoff of overtime that led to the winning points in the Bears' 13-10 victory.

In 1988, he forced a fumble with a jarring hit on Eric Dickerson after the Colts running back said Duerson wasn't a hard hitter. After the Bears cut him in 1990, Duerson caught on with the Giants. He told his coaches everything he knew about each Bear player during an hour-and-a-half meeting before a divisional-round playoff game between the teams. The Giants routed the Bears 31-3 on the way to winning Super Bowl XXV.

After the Eagles game, Duerson was happy. His coach, who had even more dust-ups with Ryan, was thrilled.

"Duerson got one," Ditka beamed to the Tribune's Ed Sherman. "I think he'd like to prove to some people with other teams that he's the great football player we know he is and some people never thought he was or would be."

The Bears cut Duerson and his $600,000 salary shortly before the 1990 season. Teammates such as Gayle and Wendell Davis criticized the move. For one of the only times in his career, Mike Singletary declined to speak to the media.

Duerson was just as impressive off the field. In college he interned for Indiana Sen. Richard Lugar in Washington. He was an alternate player rep behind Singletary during the players strike of 1987. His many charitable endeavors included DAMCO II, which worked to keep children away from drugs and alcohol. He was voted NFL Man of the Year in 1987. He is one of five Bears—with Walter Payton, Singletary, Jim Flanigan and Charles Tillman—to win the award, which now is named for Payton.

Duerson and Fencik were at times considered future political candidates, with Fencik mentioned as a possible mayor of Chicago. Duerson had even higher aspirations.

"He's a Chicagoan; I'm not," Duerson told Pierson. "But it would be wild to see Gary and I run on the same ticket. Presidential candidates."

Duerson could have fun too. He was able to play any brass instrument and was in a short-lived rock band called the Chicago Six with teammates Payton and Dan Hampton and Blackhawks Troy Murray, Curt Fraser and Gary Nylund.

After his retirement from the Phoenix Cardinals in 1993, Duerson ran a number of businesses, including the Fair Oaks sausage company. After a Bears career that included five playoff appearances in seven seasons, it seemed everything he touched turned into a success.

That all changed in his 40s, when his increasingly erratic behavior led to bankruptcy and divorce from his wife of 25 years, Alicia. Duerson had an inkling that something was wrong with him as he struggled to complete thoughts and simple tasks and complained of acute pain on the left side of his head.

As CTE started to become big news, Duerson decided to end his life. The native of Muncie, Ind., shot himself at age 50 on Feb. 17, 2011, in Sunny Isles Beach, Fla.

"It was shocking to me," former teammate Richard Dent, also a part of the 1983 draft class, told the Tribune's Dan Pompei on Feb. 27, 2011. "I felt pain. He had a house on a lake in Mundelein, and we all used to hang out there. Back then, I always thought he would be a politician. He was so strong-minded, always fighting for something better for the players and former players. Maybe at the age of 50, he just couldn't see the light at the end of the tunnel anymore." ∎

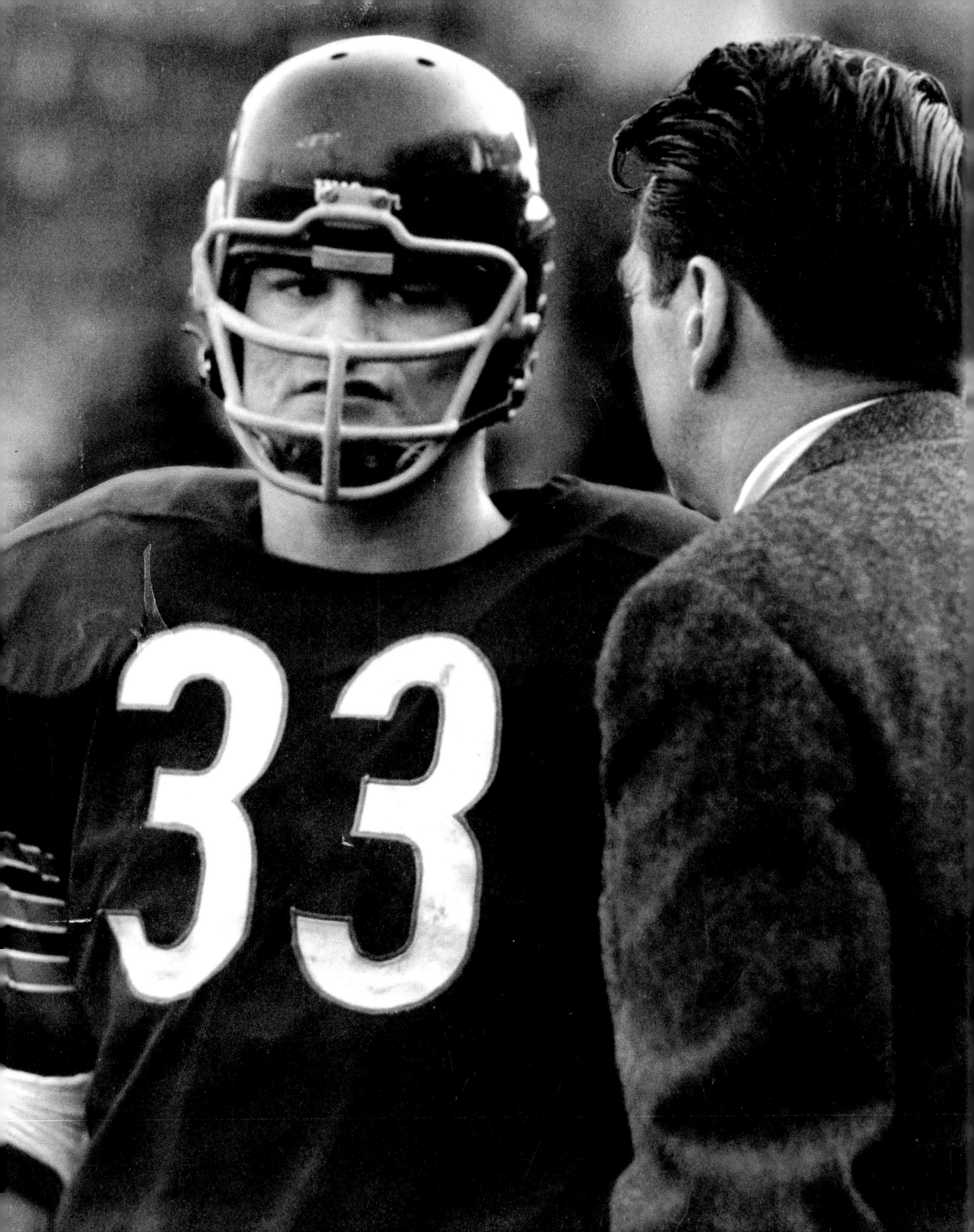

50

Larry Morris

33 LINEBACKER
1959–65

Larry Morris played his best game in his biggest game. The outside linebacker was named the MVP of the 1963 NFL championship game after the Bears' 14-10 victory against the Giants.

Morris was no one-game wonder, though. The Pro Football Hall of Fame named him to its 1960s All-Decade team, one of five linebackers on the squad. The other four—Dick Butkus, Ray Nitschke, Tommy Nobis and Dave Robinson—all are in the Hall of Fame.

For most of his seven years with the Bears, the 6-foot-2, 226-pound Morris was one-third of one of the best linebacker groups of all time. Bill George in the middle and Joe Fortunato and Morris on the outside generally were considered the best unit of their era.

In the Dec. 23, 1963, Tribune, Giants scout Em Tunnell said the Bears combination was "the greatest I've ever seen since I've been around the pros. Fortunato, George and Morris have size, mobility and experience."

Still, one game defined Morris' career. On a frozen afternoon at Wrigley Field, he terrorized Giants quarterback Y.A. Tittle all game long. In the first quarter, as Tittle connected with Frank Gifford for a touchdown pass that put the Giants ahead 7-0, Morris nailed the quarterback's left knee.

Later in the quarter the Giants were driving again. Morris intercepted Tittle and returned the ball 61 yards to the Giants' 5-yard line, leading to a tying quarterback sneak by Bill Wade and changing the momentum of the game.

Late in the second quarter Morris struck again, hitting Tittle as he passed on another blitz. Tittle heard a snap in his bad knee, struggled to get off the field and didn't play the final six minutes of the first half. The ultracompetitive Hall of Famer returned to play in the second half but was not the same, throwing four interceptions after halftime.

On the Giants' second-to-last drive, with the Bears clinging to a 14-10 lead, Morris blitzed and hit Tittle again, this time forcing a high pass that was intercepted by Bennie McRae in the end zone.

"Larry Morris, football's most underrated linebacker, strangled the Giants' vaunted attack and . . . harassed Tittle to distraction," George Strickler wrote in the Tribune's game story on Dec. 30, 1963.

Larry Morris (33) talks with coach George Allen on the sidelines on Nov. 9, 1964.

Morris was voted the game's MVP and received the Corvette that came with the honor. Before the game, Morris tried to go in on a plan with quarterback Bill Wade or tight end Mike Ditka to split the spoils if either of them were named MVP. The offensive players, much more likely to earn such an honor, scoffed. Instead, Morris went thirds with George and defensive tackle Fred Williams.

"It was worth about $3,000," Morris told the Tribune's Don Pierson on Sept. 14, 1977, "so I sent Bill a check for $1,000 and Fred a check for $1,000. Bill sent it back and said, 'No, it was just a joke.' I didn't hear from Fred until the next training camp. He said, 'I made a little investment for us down in Hot Springs on the horses and we didn't do so good.'"

Morris received a rarer prize than a sports car late in the game. Halas embraced him, and legend has it that a Bears assistant remarked that it was the first time he ever saw Halas hug someone.

As in the 1963 title game, Morris inflicted much of his career damage as a blitzer under the creative schemes of Bears defensive coordinators Clark Shaughnessy and George Allen. One of his favorite moves was to use 6-8 defensive end Doug Atkins as a screen, hiding behind him at the beginning of the play and springing through a hole when no one was paying him attention.

"Most opponents were unable to do much about this truck-and-trailer defensive act," the Tribune's championship preview story on Dec. 23, 1963, said. "Sometimes they both got through. It got wonderful results for the Bears."

Morris had the fortune of playing with Atkins on the field and the misfortune of being his road roommate. Atkins was one of the game's best players and one of its hardest-to-handle individuals, and Morris was given the impossible task of trying to keep him in line.

"I was Doug's roommate eight years, and it seemed like 15," Morris told the Tribune's Fred Mitchell on April 17, 1994. "My wife once said to Doug: 'I see you've stopped drinking. Is it the Lord?' Doug said: 'No, it's my liver.'"

The Bears acquired Morris in 1959 from the Redskins for a 1960 draft pick. Morris began his career with the Rams, who picked him seventh in the 1955 draft. They traded him to the Redskins in '58, but he did not report to Washington and missed the season with a knee injury.

In 1966 Morris forced a trade from the Bears. He had started a real estate business in Atlanta and said he would retire if the Bears did not send him to the expansion Falcons, and the Bears complied for two future draft picks.

The native of Decatur, Ga., was an All-American at Georgia Tech, helping the Yellow Jackets win the 1952 national championship. He played one year for the Falcons before retiring at 33.

Morris was a business success until things started falling apart quickly. Some erratic decisions and irrational behavior led to a downturn that kept going until he was indicted and sentenced to probation in a multimillion-dollar savings-and-loan scandal.

Morris' business problems ran parallel with his physical and mental decline. He suffered from debilitating injuries for his final 20 years and dementia for his final 10.

"He recognizes family, but he can't say my name or that I'm his wife," Kay Morris told the Tribune's David Haugh on April 15, 2007. "I call Larry my 2-year-old teenager."

Former teammates and opponents rallied around Morris' plight. Ditka and Packers Hall of Famer Jerry Kramer took the lead in fighting for better benefits for retired players.

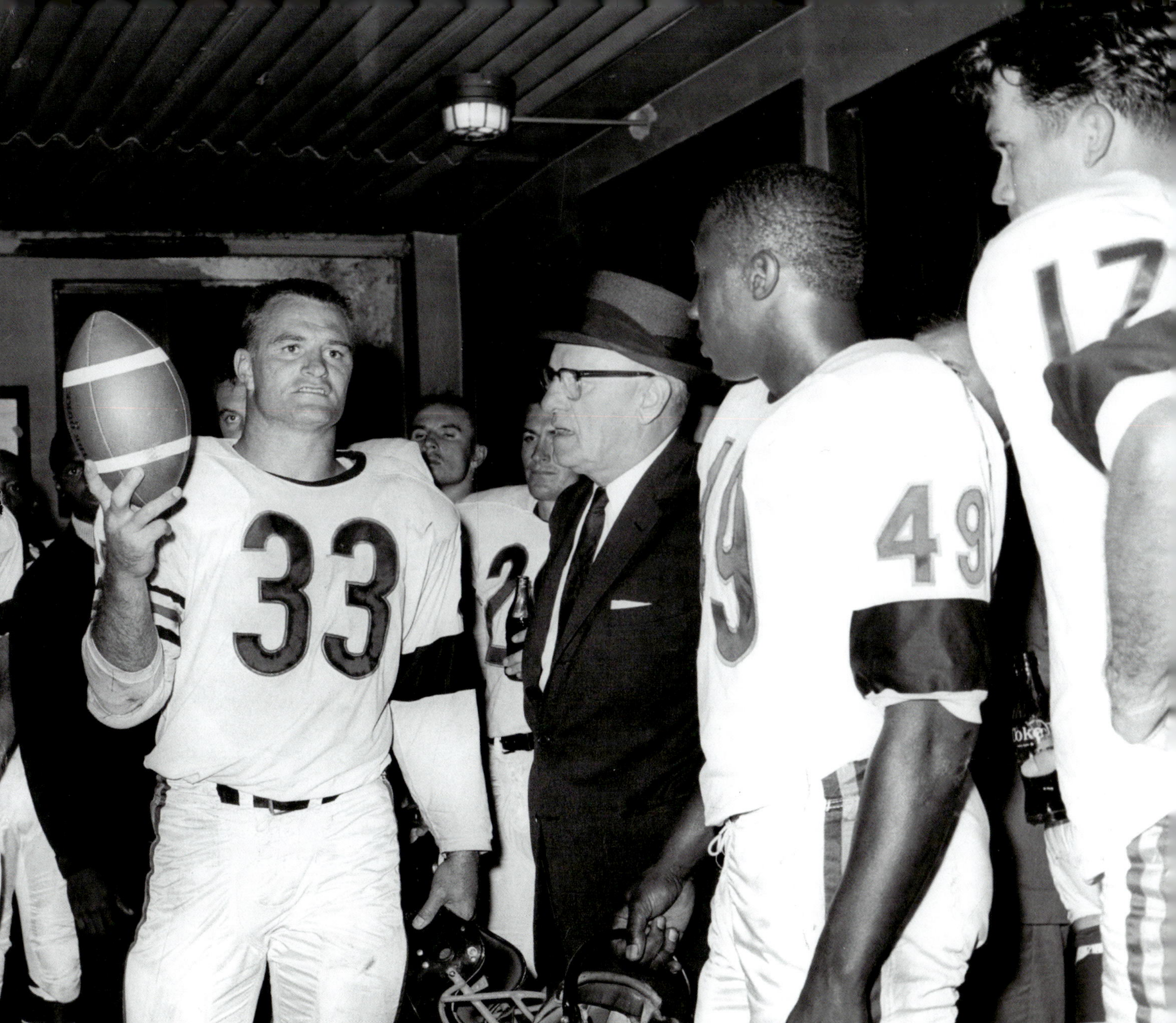

Larry Morris (33), in the team's dressing room Aug. 7, 1964, dedicates the game ball to teammates Willie Galimore and John Farrington, who were killed in a car crash. George Halas is at Morris' right.

Morris' case helped lead to the 88 Plan, named for former Colts great John Mackey. It allowed families of a former player as much as $55,000 to care for him at home or $88,000 for assisted living.

Morris died at 79 in Austell, Ga., on Dec. 19, 2012. Two years later, Pierson ranked "the Brahma Bull" the ninth-best linebacker in the team's rich history at the position.

"I felt good for him when he passed away," Kay Morris told the Tribune's Dan Pompei on Aug. 13, 2013. "I was happy for him to escape that body that wasn't working anymore. But it was harder than I thought it would be. It's been a tough 20 some years. We made it by the grace of God." ■

Photo Credits

All photos are Chicago Tribune historical photos, unless listed below.

Page ii: Phil Mascione, Chicago Tribune
Page: viii: Charles Cherney, Chicago Tribune
Page 3: Phil Mascione, Chicago Tribune
Page 4: Walter Neal, Chicago Tribune
Page 7: Michael Fryer, Chicago Tribune
Page 8: Steve Lasker, Chicago Today
Page 11: Steve Lasker, Chicago's American
Page 18: Chicago Herald-American
Page 20: Phil Mascione, Chicago Tribune
Page 23: Chicago American
Page 47: Louis DeDecker, Chicago Tribune
Page 50: Ed Wagner Jr., Chicago Tribune
Page 53: John Dziekan, Chicago Tribune
Page 54: Charles Cherney, Chicago Tribune
Page 56: Jim Prisching, Chicago Tribune
Page 59: Nuccio DiNuzzo, Chicago Tribune
Page 60: Charles Cherney, Chicago Tribune
Page 63: Ed Wagner, Chicago Tribune
Page 74: Ed Wagner Jr., Chicago Tribune
Page 90: Bob Langer, Chicago Tribune
Page 94: Chris Sweda, Chicago Tribune
Page 96: Nuccio DiNuzzo, Chicago Tribune
Page 98: Chicago Herald and Examiner

Page 102: Ovie Carter, Chicago Tribune
Page 105: Charles Cherney, Chicago Tribune
Page 109: Ed Feeney, Chicago Tribune
Page 110: Phil Greer, Chicago Tribune
Page 124: Nuccio DiNuzzo, Chicago Tribune
Page 127: Nuccio DiNuzzo, Chicago Tribune
Page 128: Ray Gora, Chicago Tribune
Page 136: Chris Sweda, Chicago Tribune
Page 138: Brian Cassella, Chicago Tribune
Page 166: Cliff Oliver, Chicago American
Page 172: Scott Strazzante, Chicago Tribune
Page 174: John J. Kim, Chicago Tribune
Page 175: Scott Strazzante, Chicago Tribune
Page 176: Ed Wagner Jr., Chicago Tribune
Page 179: Charles Cherney, Chicago Tribune
Page 180: Al Phillips, Chicago Tribune
Page 198, top: Steve Lasker, Chicago Tribune
Page 206: Tony Berardi Sr., Chicago Tribune
Page 208: Anthony Souffle, Chicago Tribune
Page 210: Anthony Souffle, Chicago Tribune
Page 211: Scott Strazzante, Chicago Tribune
Page 212: Ed Wagner Jr., Chicago Tribune
Page 215: Ed Wagner Jr., Chicago Tribune
Page 216: Bob Langer, Chicago Tribune
Page 218: Ed Wagner Jr., Chicago Tribune
Page 223: Ed Feeney, Chicago Tribune